Entrepreneurial Finar

"Vega and Lam have written a highly readable book, packed with information on the 'complex' subject of entrepreneurial finance. Great for students at any level as well as budding entrepreneurs, *Entrepreneurial Finance* discusses recent innovations in small business finance while providing students and starters of new businesses with real cases for 'hands-on' practice."

Lal Chugh,
University of Massachusetts Boston, USA

Entrepreneurial Finance: Concepts and Cases explores issues that are often overlooked in traditional finance textbooks—namely, how to handle the unique financial challenges faced by startups and small businesses.

The book is structured around seven modules or building blocks designed to be taught across a full semester with natural break points built into each chapter within the modules. The building blocks present macro-concepts, which are explored in greater detail in each of the chapters. A starting chapter provides guidance on the use of cases for students and a concluding chapter advises how to win business plan competitions. Each concept is illustrated by a short case, and followed by thoughtful questions to enhance learning. The cases, previously unpublished, are written by an international group of experienced case writers from the field of finance, and deal with real companies, real problems, and currently unfolding issues. A case teaching manual geared to finance in general, and short cases in particular, is provided for the instructor and includes specific tips, techniques, and activities for each case in the text.

Written for upper level undergraduate students of entrepreneurship, this highly accessible book breaks down complex concepts and includes hands-on cases and exercises, making learning a breeze!

Gina Vega owns Organizational Ergonomics, an academic consulting firm. She is professor of management (ret.) at the Bertolon School of Business at Salem State University, USA. She taught classes in entrepreneurship and small business management, organizational behavior, and corporate social responsibility. She is a prolific case writer, having won an Outstanding Case Teaching Award, as well as several Case Mentoring awards from the CASE Association. She is also the founding director of the Center for Entrepreneurial Activity.

Miranda S. Lam is professor and chair of the Accounting and Finance Department at the Bertolon School of Business at Salem State University, USA. She teaches entrepreneurial finance, investments, and financial institutions, where she emphasizes technology and experiential learning. She was executive editor of the *Journal of Business and Economic Studies* and has been a Chartered Financial Analyst for over a decade.

Entrepreneurial Finance
Concepts and Cases

Gina Vega and Miranda S. Lam

NEW YORK AND LONDON

First published 2016
by Routledge
711 Third Avenue, New York, NY 10017

and by Routledge
2 Park Square, Milton Park, Abingdon, Oxon OX14 4RN

Routledge is an imprint of the Taylor & Francis Group, an informa business

Library of Congress Cataloging in Publication Data
A catalog record for this book has been requested

ISBN: 978-1-138-01358-2 (hbk)
ISBN: 978-1-138-01360-5 (pbk)
ISBN: 978-1-315-79516-4 (ebk)

Typeset in Times New Roman
by Cenveo Publisher Services
Printed and bound by CPI Group (UK) Ltd, Croydon, CR0 4YY

Contents

Figures

Tables

Boxes

Cases

Case Contributors

Frederic Aiello is Associate Professor of Business at the University of Southern Maine (USM), a research associate with its Center for Business and Economic Research and a management consultant, focusing on the development of strategy and organizational capacity in entrepreneurial small businesses. He was a co-founder of the USM Business Plan Competition, Director of the USM Small Business Institute, a certified business counselor with the Maine Small Business Development Center, and a leader in the creation of the USM Center for Entrepreneurship and Small Business. He has taught managing organizational behavior and entrepreneurship at USM for 31 years.

Christine P. Andrews, DBA, is Associate Professor of Accounting at Salem State University in Massachusetts. Prior to teaching, she worked as a certified public accountant for 11 years in New York State. Her research focuses on financial reporting issues and environmental contingency reporting, as well as pedagogical issues. Her primary teaching areas are financial accounting, accounting information systems, and managerial accounting.

Richard H. Borgman is Professor of Finance at the University of Maine. Previously, he was a project manager for Dominion Bankshares Corporation and General Manager and Book Buyer for Printer's Ink Bookstores. He holds a Master's degree in English. Dr. Borgman has published in *Financial Decisions, Journal of Business and Economic Perspectives*, *Journal of Financial Education, Journal of Behavioral Finance, The CASE Journal, Journal of Business and Economic Studies, Commercial Lending Review, Credit and Financial Management Review*, and *Journal of Financial Services Marketing*, among others. He teaches courses in corporate finance, international finance, and financial institutions.

Sergio Canavati is a Ph.D. candidate in Economics and Entrepreneurship & Innovation at the University of Missouri-Kansas City. He holds Bachelor's and Master's degrees in Business Administration, and is a Master of Arts in Economics. Sergio has taught graduate and undergraduate strategy, economics, and entrepreneurship courses. An avid researcher, Sergio has published in entrepreneurship journals and presented in multiple management, entrepreneurship, and economic conferences. His research interests include entrepreneurial cognition, corporate entrepreneurship and financialization, family entrepreneurship, and product platforms.

Edward Desmarais, DBA, is Professor of Management at the Bertolon School of Business, Salem State University. He has four published cases and uses cases extensively in his teaching. His research interests include business strategy and strategy implementation. He has received awards for his teaching and writing.

Caroline Glackin holds the Edward L. Snyder Endowed Chair at Shepherd University, is the author of works on access to microloan capital, the potential for behavioral economics to inform an understanding of the borrowing process, and the role of savings as a proxy for credit history. She has co-authored research on entrepreneurial finance courses and the range of pedagogies employed in entrepreneurial finance education. Dr. Glackin has co-authored texts with Network for Teaching Entrepreneurship founder Steve Mariotti entitled *Entrepreneurship, 3e* and *Entrepreneurship and Small Business Management, 2e.*

Karen Hallows, Ph.D., is a lecturer in the finance department at the Robert H. Smith School of Business, University of Maryland. She currently teaches business finance in the undergraduate program. Her current research focuses on case writing in finance. Prior to joining the Smith School, Karen was director of the executive MBA program and finance faculty member at George Mason University (GMU) from 1998–2011. In 2009, she was awarded one of six GMU university-wide Teaching Excellence Awards. Karen has led many short-term study courses around the world and has conducted finance executive education seminars.

Bill Hamilton is Entrepreneur in Residence in the Hull College of Business and Assistant Professor of Neurology in the Medical College of Georgia at Georgia Regents University. He received a BA in History and Economics from Emory University and a Master's degree in Business Administration and Health Administration from Georgia State University. Bill is a founder of REACH Health, Inc., which provides a clinical interface for the treatment of acute stroke via a web-based telemedicine system. While at REACH, he filled many roles, including Executive Vice President, Interim President/CEO, Chief Operating Officer, and Key Account Manager.

David C Hess, MD, is Chairman, Professor, and Distinguished Presidential Chair in the Department of Neurology at the Georgia Regents University. He is Co-Director of the Brain and Behavior Discovery Institute at Georgia Health Sciences University. He is a graduate of the Johns Hopkins

University and the University of Maryland School of Medicine. Dr Hess is Board-certified in Internal Medicine, Neurology, and Vascular Neurology. He has been named one of America's Top Doctors and Best Doctors in America every year since 2000. He has over 150 peer-reviewed publications and has been involved in basic, pre-clinical, and clinical stroke research for almost 20 years.

Jaime Martínez has been a lecturer at the Monterrey Institute of Technology and Higher Education since 1993 and has collaborated with other universities in Mexico City. He holds a Master's degree in Business Planning and is a member of the North American Case Research Association. Jaime has been in charge of several coaching projects related to change management, knowledge management, and organizational development, contributing to the development of executive people in more than 50 organizations, including multinational companies in Mexico City. He is the author of more than eight case studies on leadership, change management, and project management.

Simon Medcalfe is Associate Professor of Finance and Director of Graduate Studies in the Hull College of Business at Georgia Regents University. He received his Ph.D. in business and economics from Lehigh University in Bethlehem, PA. He has published cases focusing on businesses in the sports and healthcare industries. Other published articles and research interests include the economics of religion and economics education.

Kirk Ramsay owns several businesses in Maine, including Bangor Window Shade and Drapery Company (co-owner) and Ramsay Guitars, a maker of hand-crafted guitars, as well as several apartment complexes. Whether working at his camp on the Penobscot River, accessible only by boat, or in any of his woods cottages scattered throughout Northern Maine, he is always accompanied by his two huskies, Wylie and Ike. He graduated with a degree in finance from the University of Maine.

Gina Vega, owns Organization Ergonomics, an academic consulting firm. She is Professor of Management (ret.) at the Bertolon School of Business, Salem State University and Founding Director of the Center for Entrepreneurial Activity. She is widely published in academic journals and has written four books. Professor Vega is a Fulbright Specialist (Russia 2010; UK 2012), past president of the CASE Association, a CASE Fellow, editor of *The CASE Journal* and past associate editor of the *Journal of Management Education.* She has received numerous awards for case teaching, case research, case writing, and mentoring of case writers. Her research interests include small business transitions, corporate social responsibility, and organizational structure.

John Voyer has advised many public and private concerns, has authored many journal and conference articles in his fields of strategy, organization theory, and system dynamics, and is a member of the editorial board of *Problems and Perspectives in Management.* He has held the title of Price Babson Fellow (2000) and Sam Walton Fellow (since 2003) and has taught the executive course in the Art and Practice of Leadership Development at the Harvard Kennedy School. He has served as Dean, Associate Dean and Director of the University of Southern Maine's School of Business, where he has taught for 27 years.

Susan White is a Distinguished Tyser Teaching Fellow at the University of Maryland, College Park. She teaches corporate finance for undergraduates and MBAs. She received her undergraduate degree from Brown University, her MBA from Binghamton University, and her Ph.D. in finance from the University of Texas, Austin. Susan's primary area of research is case studies, with cases and articles published in the *Business Case Journal, CASE Journal, Case Research Journal, Journal of Financial Education, Journal of Financial Research, International Journal of Financial Education*, a restructuring case book, and a personal finance collection.

Foreword

Entrepreneurial Finance: Concepts and Cases achieves the delicate balance between theory and practice that is much needed in the field. It bridges the chasm between repackaged corporate finance texts and individual entrepreneurial finance case studies. By pairing concepts and cases in a single volume, Gina Vega and Miranda Lam have created a potent resource. It uses accessible college-appropriate language and includes clear descriptions of concepts.

Gina Vega is widely recognized as an authority in the development and writing of teaching cases. She is editor of *The CASE Journal* and author of *The Case Workbook: A Self-Guided Workshop* as well as of numerous published teaching cases and academic articles. She has taught entrepreneurship and small business management for twenty years. Miranda Lam has been teaching entrepreneurial finance for over a decade and has been editor of *Journal of Business and Economic Studies* and authored numerous academic articles. She is a chartered financial analyst. Among the contributors to the book are experienced case teachers and writers who share interesting stories with provocative financial challenges for students to address.

Entrepreneurial Finance: Concepts and Cases goes beyond conventional coverage for added learning value. It includes the customary chapters on forms on business organization; financing a business; financial statements and analysis; cash and working capital management; forecasting cash flows; pro forma statements; capital budgeting and costs of capital; business valuation; and exit and harvest. However, it also discusses the effective analysis of cases and offers tips for success in business plan competitions, adding value for its readers.

The authors have created continuity and the opportunity to see how various components of entrepreneurial finance fit together through cases and examples. Coos Bay Organic Products, Inc. is the focal point for three case studies, so that students can see the evolution of the financial analysis and financing for a real company. Peace Blossom and Tasty Taco are fictionalized examples based on real companies and are used throughout the text to illustrate key concepts.

Instructors will enjoy the convenience of a comprehensive text with teaching cases: no supplemental materials are needed as all notes appear in an instructor's manual. Students will secure the value of purchasing a single text that delivers the instructional resources they need to succeed. It is a winning combination.

Caroline Glackin, Ph.D.

Preface

We came to write this book out of frustration. Our undergraduate non-finance students were struggling to learn the basics of finance for entrepreneurs because of the density with which most books on the subject were written. We thought carefully about this and concluded that it's just not that hard. If presented in a "need-to-know" way, the complexities of entrepreneurial finance could be made accessible to undergraduate business students, without "dumbing down" the content. Plus, we are both committed to teaching with cases and believe passionately that students' ability to apply concepts appropriately can be developed through the use of case examples.

As a finance professor and an entrepreneurship professor who have written together successfully in the past, we decided to test the market and determine the interest level among our peers nationally. We asked at conferences, we examined the existing books, and we spoke to as many colleagues as were willing to discuss our proposed project. The response was universally favorable, so two purists began the process of unpacking finance to its critical elements and soliciting new, unpublished, cases about real companies to illustrate these elements.

The result is this text, which is designed for handling the unique financial challenges often faced by startups and small businesses. It is written for the upper level undergraduate business major and focuses heavily on the basics.

Each main concept is illustrated by a short case (between 500 and 1,000 words), followed by thoughtful questions to enhance learning. These fresh, previously unpublished, cases have been written by an international group of experienced case writers from the field of finance and entrepreneurship and deal with real companies, real problems, and currently unfolding issues. The 11 chapters or building blocks of entrepreneurial finance are designed to be taught across a full semester. A starting chapter that provides guidance about the use of cases for students and a concluding chapter that delivers information about how to win business plan competitions round out the offering.

We hope you will find this text as useful as we found it enjoyable to write!

Gina Vega
Miranda Lam

Module 1

Getting Started with Cases

1 Case Preparation and Analysis for Students

What is education but a process by which a person begins to learn how to learn?
Peter Ustinov

Why Are You in this Class?

Perhaps you are concentrating on entrepreneurship or small business management. Perhaps you are a finance major who is taking this class as an elective. Maybe you are a business major who wants to learn a bit more about entrepreneurship and finance. Maybe the class was the only one open that fit into your schedule.

None of that matters. What does matter is your willingness to participate in your own learning, rather than wait for someone to *tell* you what to learn.

What to Expect from a Case-Based Class

If you are used to a traditional lecture format class, a case class will be a big change for you.

In a traditional class, you are the recipient of knowledge. The instructor is the giver of knowledge, and you receive her words of wisdom passively.

In a case class, you are the creator of knowledge and the discoverer of insights. The instructor is your guide and your facilitator, and she shares in the creation and discovery processes with you.

In a traditional class, the instructor works hard and you sit quietly. You can send in a tape recorder and listen to the lecture later. You can watch a video and play computer games. You can check your email. You can update your Facebook account.

In a case class, you both work hard and are very much present. You are alert the whole time, because you are responsible for your learning and the learning processes of your classmates. Case learning is social learning and requires active involvement.

Here's how it works:

- You read the assigned case ahead of class. You might consider trying the "three reads model" given in Appendix 1.1.
  - Take notes as to the individuals involved, the situations presented, and any connections you can make to theory or analogous characters or situations you have been exposed to before, either in classes or in your work or life experience.
  - Identify your assumptions and the information that is missing for you to make a thorough analysis.
  - List the problems and select one problem to focus on at a time. Most cases present multiple problems; your ability to identify a key problem will give your case analysis structure and meaning.
  - Do any preliminary analysis you can, such as financial comparisons and ratios, statistical analysis or other quantitative exploration. If your analysis is to be qualitative, determine the foundation of your analysis and articulate reasons for and against a strategy or position.
  - Write down as many possible recommendations as you can, then select one and commit to it.
- Go to class and get ready for an engaged discussion.
  - The instructor may start off with a précis of the case (or ask you to provide one) and then toss out some icebreaker questions—easy questions to get the conversation moving.
  - The instructor may continue to toss questions to the group or, depending on personal style, may ask questions or opinions directly of one individual.
  - The instructor will tease out a series of analyses, decision-making perspectives, and positions from the class members.
  - The class reaches a conclusion, recommendation, decision, or final analysis.
- You may be assigned to a team.
  - If you have been assigned to a case team before the classroom discussion, your preparation should take place with this team.
  - You can expect a lot of lively discussion during the preparation phase, and you will generally (but not always) come to an agreement before class.
  - The class discussion will be between team positions rather than individual positions and will proceed as before.

Hints for success in a case class

- Be prepared.
- Participate actively.

- Allow your emotions to become involved along with your critical analysis.
- Respect your peers' input.
- Try to understand the alternative perspectives put forth in the classroom.
- If in a team, be a "good" team member—no one likes a free rider.

Two Different Types of Case

There are two different kinds of case: decision-based cases and descriptive or illustrative cases (Table 1.1).

In either kind of case, your job will be clear to you, if not from the narrative, then from the questions that follow the case. Be sure to read and think about those questions, and use them as guidance in your analysis.

Preparing a Written Case Analysis

The cases in this book are short, designed specifically to help you focus primarily on the financial aspects of problems presented. You will, of course, find information in the cases that is not financial in nature. Pay attention to this information, as it is likely to be important in your analysis. However, it

Table 1.1 Types of Case

	Decision-based cases	*Descriptive or illustrative cases*
Description	Decision-based cases will require you to make a reasoned recommendation, supported by facts and theory, for the case protagonist to follow.	Descriptive or illustrative cases do not conclude with a call for a recommendation. Instead, they present a situation that has occurred and your job is to analyze the protagonist's actions.
Example	Your recommendation might be for the protagonist to seek alternative sources of funding rather than depending on friends and family. These might include a bank line of credit, loans, or angel investors. These three sources involve less emotional investment and more straightforward financial analysis to convince lenders.	You may determine that the protagonist should have taken a different set of action steps that might have led to a better outcome. Or you may decide that the actions taken were justified and provided the best outcomes under the existing circumstances. Or your recommendation might be to take advantage of a favorable economy to expand now rather than waiting until the company has accumulated more assets. Even though the protagonist tends to a conservative approach to expansion, it makes sense to exploit opportunities that present themselves. This may be a less secure position to take, but the potential rewards might be greater.

will not drive your analysis, which should be focused, instead, on the financial components presented in each case.

The analysis of a full-length case can be expected to take a significant period of time to complete. The analysis of a short case should be, by its nature, short. It will contain all (or most) of the elements described next, but the elements will be short and concise. It is likely that your analysis will include answers to (or take direction from) the questions at the end of the case.

Although it might sound easy to write a short case analysis, do not allow yourself to be tricked into thinking that such an analysis is a snap to put together. It requires discipline to write concisely and to explain complex concepts using simple, clear language. That will be your challenge throughout this course.

Written Analysis of a Short Decision-Based Finance Case

If you are preparing for a class discussion, the "three reads method" (Appendix 1.1) will suffice. However, if you have been assigned a written analysis of a decision-based case, it can be hard to know where to start. The following model can help you complete a clear and organized decision-based analysis. You can generally use tables, formulas, or matrices instead of narrative sentences if they will support your analysis better.

1. *Executive summary* Write this section last even though it appears first in the case analysis. The goal of the executive summary is to provide a *brief* overview of the main issues, the proposed recommendation, and the actions to follow. (2 or 3 sentences).
2. *Statement of the problem* Describe the core problem(s) of the case and the decision(s) to be made by the protagonist. Include the symptoms of the problem(s) and differentiate them from the problem(s) themselves. For example, the spots on your face are a symptom. The problem is that you have the measles (or acne, or an allergy to some skin product, or some other infection). This statement of the problem is a *diagnostic process*, and you need to build the rationale for your diagnosis into this section. (2 or 3 sentences).
3. *Causes* This section is an exploration and discussion of potential causes of the main case problem(s). Support your exploration by the application of relevant theories from this course or others. Be sure to use financial tools that will support your decision-making process and will illustrate your analysis. (2 or 3 sentences).
4. *Possible solutions or alternatives* Surface as many possible solutions or alternative actions as you can. You should not limit your possibilities to what you think is easy to accomplish or logical, but rather entertain a wide variety of options. You do not have to recommend all of these options, but you need to make your instructor aware that you have considered them. (2 or 3 sentences).

5. *Selection of criteria and analysis of alternatives* Select the criteria for determining the basic feasibility of the alternatives identified. These criteria will guide you in considering the pros and cons of each feasible alternative. Consider at least three alternatives in this section. Sometimes, a tabular format will keep this section organized and clear. You should be prepared to provide financial analysis in this section. (2 or 3 sentences or a small matrix).
6. *Recommendation* What do you recommend that the protagonist do? Support your recommendation with a rationale that is based on both facts and the appropriate theory for the problem (i.e., market analysis, financial statements analysis, the impact of organizational structure, supply chain management, or other disciplinary focus). (2 or 3 sentences).
7. *Implementation* Your instructor may state that no case analysis is complete without providing the action steps to implement the recommendation. What steps should the protagonist take in order to make your recommendation happen? Identify, to the greatest extent possible, the responsibilities, costs, timeline, and measurement of success of the final implementation.

Appendix 1.2 provides a sample written analysis of a short decision-based case.

Written Analysis of a Short Descriptive or Illustrative Finance Case

If you are preparing for a class discussion, the method already mentioned or the "three reads method" at the end of the chapter will suffice. However, if you have been assigned a written analysis of a descriptive or illustrative finance case, it can be hard to know where to start. The following model can help you complete a clear and organized analysis. You can generally use tables, formulas, or matrices instead of narrative sentences if they will support your analysis better.

1. *Executive summary* Write this section last even though it appears first in the case analysis. The goal of the executive summary is to provide a *brief* overview of the main issues, your analysis, and your conclusions. (2 or 3 sentences).
2. *The facts* This is not simply a list of case facts. You need to determine which facts are relevant and which are simply background information or environmental "noise". If you are analyzing a business ethics case, for example, it probably does not matter that the action takes place in the fall. However, in a finance case it may well matter that the action occurs at the end of a sales period, a fiscal year, or at some other critical period.
    Draw facts not only from the case narrative but, notably, from the exhibits, attachments, financial records, spreadsheets, and other sources

within the case. Be sure to peruse these figures carefully for possible errors, misinterpretations, and potential clues to case solutions. (bulleted list)

3. *Inferences to be drawn* Why did things happen as they did? What else might happen as a consequence? What are the implications of these actions in terms of attitudes and relationships? Financial decisions, especially in entrepreneurial environments, are rarely based solely on the numbers. Numbers are generally rational; people rarely are and their decisions reflect this. (2 or 3 sentences).

4. *Theory- and technique-based discussion of the case action* Apply relevant theory and financial analysis techniques to an explanation of actions and consequences, implications of actions and consequences, and the impact of various outcome criteria on the decisions that were made in the case. The true value of learning entrepreneurial finance lies in the use of actual data to guide future decisions and to draw sensible conclusions about potential outcomes. The financial analysis helps you look to the future as well as reflect on the past. (2 or 3 sentences).

5. *Options to the actions within the case* Compare the actions of the protagonist with the other courses of action that were open at the time. What might have been the logical outcomes of those actions? Determine a hierarchy of preferred actions based on the outcome criteria you established in part 4. This section may logically take a tabular format.

6. *Conclusion and reflection* This is your rationale for preferred action. If the protagonist has done the right thing according to your analysis, explain why. If the protagonist should have done something else, explain why. Reflect on your reasoning. In a descriptive or illustrative case, your reflection is often the most valuable section because it is from these reflections that future courses of action will derive. (2 or 3 sentences).

Appendix 1.3 provides a sample written analysis of a short descriptive case.

How Will Your Written Case Analysis Be Evaluated?

Because case evaluation can be highly subjective, many instructors will prepare a rubric for you to measure your own work against. You can find a basic rubric that outlines generic expectations and clarifies the standard you should be aiming for in Appendix 1.4. Each instructor's rubric is unique, but the generic rubric provides some guidelines for you to follow.

Appendix 1.5 is a self-grading rubric to help you check your own work for completeness before submission. This self-grader will help to keep you "honest."

Appendix 1.1 Preparing for a Case Discussion— The "Three Reads Model" for a Short Case

Reading and preparing a case for class discussion involves more than reading a blog, your email, a novel, or a chapter in a textbook. You can develop your case reading skills through the technique outlined here. This technique allows you to make the best possible contribution during the class case discussion. It requires you to read the case (even short cases) three times, twice briefly and once extensively. If you are working with a team, you will want to adapt this process to assure topical coverage.

First Read

- Find *six minutes* (yes, six minutes is enough for the short cases in this book) to sit down uninterrupted. Turn off your instant messaging and mute your cell phone so that you do not get distracted during this short reading period.
- Read the hook. This may be several paragraphs long in a full-length case, but is just one or two sentences in the cases in this book. The hook will introduce you to the case "problem." Jot down the problem in the margin.
- Read the first sentence (and *only* the first sentence) of each paragraph in the case. Write a keyword or two in the margin next to the paragraph.
- Read the *titles only* of any attachments and exhibits.
- Turn your instant messaging and cell phone back on and go about your business.

Second Read

- This is the big one – a two-page case will take you *at least 30 minutes*. Remember that if you have interruptions, this period must be extended.
- *Read the entire case*, slowly and carefully. Jot notes as you go along about the characters and their behavior, the situation and the action. Sometimes preparing a timeline of action makes it easier to follow and remember. Be sure to include any exhibits and attachments during this read.
- *Jot down your own response* to the situation and the characters, even if it's unsupported by theories or formal concepts. Make any connections you can to analogous situations you have experienced or read about. What are the differences or similarities to this situation? Remember, these notes that you are making are yours alone—no one else will be looking at them. It doesn't matter if they are messy, have lines drawn all over them, are put together in right brain or left brain style, just as long as they exist. They are meant to help you.
- *Make a list of the assumptions* you are making, the financial analysis you need to conduct, and the information you still need before you make

a recommendation. Something is always missing, or the case would be really boring. So, what is missing?

- *List the alternative solutions* to the case, their pros and cons, and then select one recommendation. You always have to commit to one recommendation and provide a rationale for it. This recommendation should be supported by theory, experience, quantitative analysis, or other rationale.
- *Prepare any case questions you have been assigned.* Be sure to check any spreadsheets for errors or misinterpretations.
- You should be tired at this point. Put the case away.

Third Read

- This last read takes place not too long before class. The point of it is to make sure that the case is fresh in your mind and that you are still comfortable with your recommendation.
- This read resembles the first read: read the beginning, the first sentence of each paragraph, etc. But this time, include both your marginal notes and the notes you have made during the second read. You will need these notes to participate actively in class. Remember that class participation means that you have to talk—it's OK to read aloud what you have written if you are uncomfortable talking off the cuff.
- The entire process has taken two hours or less, which is about two-thirds the amount of time you should anticipate using for class preparation for a 1½ hour class. If your class period is longer than this, your preparation should be commensurately more extensive.

Appendix 1.2 Sample Written Case Analysis for a Short Decision-Based Finance Case[1]

Executive Summary

Koehler Propane was a small, family-owned propane dealer with a very small heating oil division inherited through a prior acquisition. A local heating oil dealer was put up for sale and Koehler had to decide whether or not to purchase it and, if so, at what price and on what terms. The best strategy for Koehler is to offer a cash price of between $800,000 and $850,000.

Statement of the Problem

The propane and heating oil dealership industry was in the declining phase of its life cycle and was characterized by high fluctuations in revenue, owing to uncertainty in energy prices and weather, high fixed-assets requirement, and regulations by both federal and state agencies. Competition was high and business growth either involved intense price competition or acquisition of competing companies. Koehler and his son had to decide whether to buy the heating oil company or to close down their own small heating oil division altogether.

Causes

Some of Koehler's current equipment needed replacement if he were to remain in the heating oil business. Koehler had an advantage over competing bidders in a cash deal but not in a stock deal. The four valuation methods (discounted cash flow valuation and multiples valuation, multiples valuation, EBITDA multiple method, and percentage of annual sales + inventory method) range from $624,019 to $918,606, averaging $818,469. A reasonable cash price ranged from $800,000 to $850,000.

Possible Solutions or Alternatives

Koehler Propane had three alternatives:

- Close down the oil business: Closing down the heating oil business would eliminate a break-even or money-losing division and allow Koehler to stay focused on its core business of propane delivery but it would be contrary to their vision of developing Koehler into a large energy company.
- Purchase two new trucks to replace existing ones: Purchasing new trucks required capital investments into a potentially money-losing division. Given the low volume and the surcharge they had to pay due to lack of bulk storage, they were at a cost disadvantage, severely limiting their ability to compete on price.
- Acquire the heating oil company: This would advance Koehler toward a more diverse product line and increase the size of its business. It would provide Koehler bulk storage facilities and make them a major heating oil distributor in the vicinity. If Koehler failed to acquire the heating oil company, one of its competitors would gain entrance into its primary territory and Koehler would face increased competition in its propane business.

Selection of Criteria and Analysis of Alternatives

See Table 1.2.

Table 1.2 Selection of Criteria and Analysis of Alternatives

Criterion	Pro	Con
Growth	Koehler want to be industry leaders, larger customer base	Declining industry, high competition
Diversification	One of the main business goals	High risk, expensive
Capital investment	More dependable equipment	Potential dedication of needed cash to non-liquid assets

Recommendation

Both companies are located in the same town, and the two owners have past business relationships, therefore Koehler will have better knowledge of the oil company than competing bidders. Competing bidders may be unwilling to offer a cash deal, or they will likely offer a much lower cash price. Koehler has an advantage over competing bidders in a cash deal but not in a stock deal. Given the advantages of a cash deal to the oil company, the best strategy for Koehler is to offer a cash price.

Implementation

1. Agree on a valuation.
2. Structure the deal internally.
3. Negotiate with the seller for a mutually agreeable acquisition.

Appendix 1.3 Sample Written Case Analysis for a Short Descriptive or Illustrative Finance Case[2]

Executive summary

A school teacher has decided to open a taqueria in a small, historic New England city. The problem is whether or not he should launch his business at the time of the case in light of the many challenges facing him. He could not provide all the necessary information and was reluctant to listen to advice. He should not launch his business at this time.

The facts

The entrepreneur knew a little bit about a lot of things, but not enough about any one of the functional elements of his business to run it on his own. He had insufficient funds to last through a dry spell; he was being pushed to launch because the landlord of his desired location was in a hurry to get the lease signed. He did not have a full liquor license. Money was tight, loans were non-existent, and his debt to asset ratio did not approach the industry standard. It also looks like he needs to make a closer examination of his anticipated revenues.

Inferences to be drawn

The Howling Wolf is likely to create value for the customer, as there appears to be growing demand for this type of cuisine and there is little direct competition. However, the money-making potential of the restaurant is unclear, and the owner's ability to sustain operations with the proposed staff of family and friends is doubtful. A launch would be a high-risk, minimal-reward strategy.

Theory- and technique-based discussion of the case action

A SWOT analysis showed that the entrepreneur had some significant strengths and opportunities in terms of personal contacts and an opening in the restaurant market. His passion, product and service differentiation, and personal skills suggest that he can provide an appealing venue for locals to enjoy a unique culinary experience. Potential funders have not been found, the economy is weak (although beginning to rebound slightly), and money is scarce. Although the entrepreneur believes strongly in his restaurant, he has been unable to provide financials that support that belief for banks or other funders. Computing break-even revenue and cash burn rate show that break-even weekly revenue is 4.35 percent below the original estimate. Total monthly cash outflow excluding COGS is over $34k compared with a beginning cash balance of only $61k. If revenue is more than 23 percent below the original estimate, he will run out of cash in 6 months.

Options to the actions within the case

Decision criteria: Potential to make a good return. Likelihood of staying in business without a liquor license. Potential to survive on limited investment. Likelihood of family and friends to continue providing low-cost assistance.

The entrepreneur has to weigh the importance of each of the decision criteria before making his decision. There are two possible decisions:

- The entrepreneur could open based on the support that he had from his family and his experience with this type of cuisine and confidence that the tourist season would likely be able to cover the slow season.
- The entrepreneur could postpone opening until acquiring more funds, a liquor license, and business advisors.

Conclusion and Reflection

Based on these analyses, I would not recommend launching the business at this time. I think the entrepreneur should find an angel or other investor to provide the financial stability that will cover him through the tough times during the first year of operations. He should continue his efforts to obtain a full liquor license. He should plan to invest in advertising prior to his launch, and he should conduct a full-scale location analysis prior to signing his lease.

Appendix 1.4 Generic Grading Rubric: How Will My Written Case Analysis Be Evaluated?

Because evaluation can be highly subjective, many instructors will prepare a rubric for you to measure your own work against. This rubric outlines the instructor's expectations and clarifies the standard you should be aiming for.

Each instructor's rubric is unique, but the generic rubric outlined in Table 1.3 provides some guidelines for you to follow.

Appendix 1.5 Self-Grading Rubric

Use the rubric outlined in Table 1.4 to evaluate the quality of your own work before you hand it in.

Table 1.3 Case Analysis Evaluation

Suggested criteria	Poor, weak, needs improvement	Satisfactory, acceptable, good	Outstanding, exemplary, excellent
Thoroughness	One or more required sections are missing or treated perfunctorily	All required sections are addressed to a great extent	All required sections are addressed completely
	X points	X points	X points
Theoretical relevance	The analysis does not incorporate relevant theories	Addresses theories and course concepts appropriately	Addresses theories and concepts appropriately and insightfully
	X points	X points	X points
Quality of Analysis	Does not suggest careful thought or provide insights	Analysis suggests both effort and understanding of the material	Detailed analysis that offers careful and logical inferences
	X points	X points	X points
Conclusions or Implementation	Unsupported or missing arguments overlook salient issues	Supported arguments capture main issues	Supported arguments address both main issues and subtle or secondary problems
	X points	X points	X points
Writing quality	Careless writing, many grammar and spelling errors, poor organization	Clear writing, few grammar and spelling errors, organized presentation	Flawless writing, clear organization, correct grammar and spelling
	X points	X points	X points

Table 1.4 Self-Grading Rubric

	Something is wrong	*Everything is correct*	*Student comment here*
Presence of all required elements (refer to original assignment)	What is missing? Add it.	In the column to the right, list the items that appear in the Table of Contents.	
Issues	Some primary or secondary issues are missing.	All the primary and secondary issues have been dealt with and prioritized.	
Adequacy of discussion of consequences, depth of data analysis, application of theory	Weak in one or more of the listed areas.	Issues are fully developed, including alternatives; consequences are clearly spelled out; data analysis is comprehensive; theory is applied correctly	
Quality of expression	I have not run spell check or grammar check. I have not had someone else proofread my work.	My work has been proofread by someone else and all errors have been corrected.	
Would I be willing to turn in this report to my employer?	If no—fix it!	If yes, you're done. Hand it in.	
What grade would you give this project?	C or less	A or B	

Notes

1 This abbreviated analysis was prepared from Lam & Luther (2012).
2 This abbreviated analysis was prepared from Vega & Lam (2013).

Bibliography

Lam, M., & Luther, R. (2012). The Offer Price. *The CASE Journal*, 8(2).
Ustinov, P. (1977) *Dear Me*. London: Heinemann.
Vega, G., & Lam, M. (2013). Howling Wolf Taqueria: Feeding the Good Wolf. *Case Research Journal*, *34*(2).

Module 2
Getting Money and Getting Going

2   Forms of Business Ownership

Well begun is half done.

Aristotle

You have a great business idea and are ready to get started. The first decision you have to make as an owner is the form of business organization you want to have.

This chapter introduces the different legal forms of organization and important factors to consider when you select the most appropriate form for *your* specific business. These factors include:

- the cost of organization;
- reporting requirements;
- tax consequences;
- impacts on succession planning or future sale of the business.

Most of these factors, except federal income tax, are governed by state statutes and therefore vary, on occasion significantly, from state to state. Federal income taxes are determined by tax codes administered by the Internal Revenue Service (IRS) and are consistent nationwide. While many entrepreneurs are eager to get started with the business, it is always a good idea to consult a lawyer and an accountant to ensure your business is launched from a sound foundation.

The Three General Forms of Business Organization

The three general forms of business organization are sole proprietorship, partnership, and corporation. The limited liability company (LLC), a hybrid form with special tax treatments, will be discussed in a separate section. According to data from the Internal Revenue Service (1990–2008), sole proprietorship was the most popular form (Table 2.1), representing over 70 percent of businesses that filed returns, followed by corporations, at over

Table 2.1 Data on Forms of Business Organization

Year	As a percentage of total number of returns filed			As a percentage of total business receipts reported		
	Non-farm proprietorships (%)	Partnerships (%)	Corporations (%)	Non-farm proprietorships (%)	Partnerships (%)	Corporations (%)
1990	73.72	7.75	18.53	6.00	4.44	89.56
1991	74.06	7.39	18.55	5.84	4.41	89.75
1992	74.32	7.12	18.56	5.86	4.54	89.60
1993	74.47	6.90	18.63	5.74	4.75	89.51
1994	73.46	6.79	19.75	5.50	5.09	89.41
1995	73.06	7.03	19.90	5.16	5.46	89.37
1996	72.96	7.12	19.93	5.03	6.21	88.76
1997	72.64	7.44	19.92	4.82	7.18	88.00
1998	72.20	7.69	20.11	4.83	8.08	87.09
1999	71.89	7.92	20.19	4.66	8.79	86.55
2000	71.60	8.23	20.17	4.45	10.10	85.45
2001	71.62	8.33	20.06	4.44	11.22	84.34
2002	71.59	8.48	19.92	4.57	11.84	83.59
2003	71.71	8.64	19.65	4.44	11.93	83.63
2004	71.76	8.88	19.37	4.38	12.09	83.53
2005	71.79	9.24	18.96	4.22	12.82	82.96
2006	71.53	9.55	18.93	4.06	13.12	82.82
2007	72.06	9.65	18.29	3.99	13.68	82.33
2008	71.55	9.95	18.50	3.93	14.79	81.28

Source: http://www.irs.gov/uac/SOI-Tax-Stats-Integrated-Business-Data

18 percent. Partnerships remained the least popular of the three. However, the businesses that filed as corporations were significantly larger than the other forms, and corporations generated over 80 percent of total business receipts. Although partnerships represented slightly less than 10 percent of all returns filed, this form gained popularity steadily throughout the 1990s and 2000s, and generated about 14 percent of total business receipts. Sole proprietorships, though largest in number, garnered only 4 percent of total business receipts.

2.1 Size of Business Versus Number of Tax Returns

Since each business files one return with the IRS, the total number of returns filed represents the total number of businesses. Business receipts comprise total revenues generated. The fact that the corporate form of business files the fewest returns but represents the largest business receipts means that the average size of corporations is larger than the average size of sole proprietorships.

Sole Proprietorships

Sole proprietorship is the simplest form of business organization. It makes no legal distinction between the owner and the business. In general, a sole proprietorship is limited to one owner. The exception is a "Qualified Joint Venture," which is a business owned by a married couple. The only form required to start a sole proprietorship in most states is a "doing business as" (DBA) statement, and this is only required if the business has a different name from the owner.[1] If the business has the same name as the owner then no form is required. There is no annual reporting requirement and no annual fees are due to the state. All income from the business is passed through to the owner as personal income. Therefore, the owner of a sole proprietorship has to report all business-related revenues and costs on her personal tax returns at both the federal and state levels. In addition, the owner must file self-employment tax, Social Security and Medicare taxes, and Federal Unemployment (FUTA) tax.

Because there is no legal distinction between owner and business, the owner is personally liable for all business debts and liens. In other words, creditors can attempt to obtain payment from the personal property of a proprietor for debts related to the business. If the business is not a married-couple business, the liability of the other spouse and marital properties depends on the state of residence. For states that treat all marital properties as "community property," a spouse is responsible for debts incurred by the other spouse regardless of his involvement in the business.[2] Another disadvantage of sole proprietorship is that funding for the business is restricted to the personal wealth and borrowing capacity of the owner. In addition to restricting the sources of funds available to the business, the single-owner limit also makes succession planning and sale of the business difficult because the original owner must sell the entire business to the new owner and cannot retain any equity stake.

The advantage of reduced reporting requirements at the state level is greatest for simple, small businesses that do not require special licenses. Therefore, many businesses start as sole proprietorships and become corporations or partnerships as they grow, when the disadvantages quickly outweigh the advantages.

Qualified Joint Venture

The Small Business and Work Opportunity Tax Act of 2007 permits a married couple in a joint venture who are filing a joint return not to be treated as a partnership for federal tax purposes. If a married-couple business satisfies the requirements of a qualified joint venture, the couple can file a joint personal income tax return and operate the business as a sole proprietorship.

The qualifying requirements are that:

1.   The only members of the joint venture are a married couple.
2.   Both spouses participate materially in the business.
3.   Both spouses elect to be treated as a married-couple business and not a partnership.

Partnerships

2.2 Limited Liabilities

With limited liabilities, the personal properties of owners are separated from the properties of the business. If the business fails or is sued in a lawsuit, losses to the owners are limited to their investments in the business. Unfortunately for small business owners, banks often require them to co-sign loans for the company. When owners co-sign a loan, their personal properties can be at jeopardy, up to the amount of the loan.

There are two types of partnership, *General Partnership* and *Limited Partnership*. In a general partnership, all partners participate actively in the operation of the business. In a limited partnership, one or more *general partners* operate the business, and one or more *limited partners* do not actively participate in the business. The limited partners enjoy limited liability in that their losses are limited to their investments in the partnership and their personal wealth is protected from business creditors. The tax provisions for limited partnerships can be very complicated. They are explained fully in tax accounting texts (e.g. Anderson et al. 2014). This section focuses on general partnership and the general partners in a limited partnership because small business owners and entrepreneurs are most likely to be active general partners in the business.

2.3 Partnership Agreement

A partnership agreement is a written document detailing specific rights, responsibilities, obligations, and benefits of all partners in the business. It is a legally binding contract. A well-written partnership agreement will include as many scenarios as possible. If a situation occurs that is not specified in the partnership agreement, the Revised Uniform Partnership Act and state laws will apply. This can lead to significant delays and legal fees. Therefore, it is well worth the time and effort to be as detailed as possible when drafting a partnership agreement.

A partnership is a business venture owned by two or more entities. The terms of a partnership, including transfer of ownership and distribution of gains and losses, are described in a partnership agreement. In many states, the partnership agreement can be as informal as a verbal acknowledgement, or it can be a formal legal document. Even when there is no mandate from the state, it is always a good idea to have all business agreements set out in writing and signed by all partners. A clearly written partnership agreement can reduce potential friction among partners farther down the road and make transfer of ownership and succession planning a lot easier.

Even though statutes on partnerships vary by state, the Revised Uniform Partnership Act (RUPA), issued in 1994, provided useful guidance on the important elements to include in a partnership agreement. Specifically, it recommended that the following issues be clearly addressed in the agreement of a general partnership:

- Amount of capital contributed by each person; if more capital is needed at a later date, who contributes it; and any limitations to someone's maximum contribution. If labor or assets are contributed in place of money, the value attributed to these contributions is included.
- Distribution of profits and losses among the partners. The proportion of distribution does not need to be based on contribution.

- Voting rights of each partner. Unless explicitly stated, RUPA gives each partner equal voting rights, regardless of the amount of capital contributed.
- Responsibilities of each partner.
- Distribution of assets upon dissolution of the business. The proportion of distribution upon dissolution does not need to be based on contribution or on distribution of profits and losses.
- Succession and exit plan. If one partner decides to retire or leave the business, the partnership ends. If all the partners agree to terminate the partnership, they can sell the entire business to another owner. However, it is best to have a plan in place that allows the other partners to carry on the business if they choose. Some options for such a plan include the right of first refusal or right of first offer. In the case of the right of first refusal, the departing partner allows the remaining partners to buy out the share of the business at the same price as a *bona fide* external offer. In the case of the right of first offer, the departing partner offers to sell his share of the business to the other partners before offering it externally. A succession provision will allow a partner to pass on her share to a designated heir without invoking the right of first refusal or first offer. The agreement may also contain a provision for an arbitrator or mediator.

Some states require partnerships to file an annual report, whereas others do not. However, most states require partnerships to pay an annual fee. Partners are not considered employees of the business and are responsible for self-employment taxes if they are applicable.[3] The Internal Revenue Service (IRS) requires partnerships to file an annual return of income, regardless of state requirements. This form is in addition to the personal income tax return that each partner must file individually.

In a general partnership, there is no legal distinction between the partners and the business. As with sole proprietorships, all profits and losses are passed through to the owners and distributed according to the partnership agreement. Partners include the distributed profits or losses in their personal income tax returns. This pass-through feature means that partners must include business profits as personal income whether or not the partnership actually disperses cash payouts to partners. The advantage of this is that the partnership itself does not have to pay any income tax. Also, pass-through losses can be used to reduce taxable incomes by the partners.

The main disadvantage of a general partnership is unlimited liability. Each partner is jointly and individually liable for the partnership's obligations, which include business debts and liabilities resulting from the wrongdoing of other partners or employees of the business. Hence, the personal wealth of each partner is subject to potential claims for payments by creditors of the partnership. If a partner is married, whether marital properties are subject to business claims depends on whether the couple resides in a "community property" state, as described in the Sole Proprietorship section earlier in this chapter.

Corporations

A corporation is a legal entity distinct and separate from its owners. In fact, from a legal perspective, a corporation is considered a "person" and has many similar rights and responsibilities, such as entering into contracts, representing itself in a court of law, owning property and borrowing money. A corporation can be a partner, both general and limited, in a partnership and can own stock in another corporation. There is no minimum number of owners for a corporation; a corporation can have just one shareholder and be owned by an individual.

Since starting a corporation requires a set of formal written documents called "articles of incorporation" and "bylaws," it is often considered a more complicated form of business organization than a partnership or sole proprietorship. The statutes governing the formation, reporting requirements, and rights and responsibilities of corporations are state-specific. Hence, the actual amount of paperwork involved depends on each state's statutes and the type of business being launched. In some states, these requirements are relatively simple.

2.4 Corporate Bylaws

Corporate bylaws are written documents that specify how a corporation will be governed. They cover processes for conducting shareholders' meetings, elections of the board of directors, the rights and duties of corporate officers, and specific situations that require direct voting by shareholders, such as the sale of the entire business or changes to the bylaws themselves. To minimize changes to bylaws, imagine how you would like the business to be governed when it has grown to its full potential, not just at the startup stage. Small business owners might think that bylaws are for big corporations only and are caught unprepared when situations arise that are not addressed by their bylaws. For example, your business may reach a stage when outside funding is needed and you want to have different classes of stocks so that the original owners have more voting rights.

A well-written partnership agreement contains much of the same information included in the articles of incorporation and bylaws. For example, most states require the articles of incorporation to contain the corporation's name, its business purpose, and the number of shares that can be issued.

Bylaws are specific to each corporation and are the rules describing how the corporation will be governed. For example, bylaws usually contain voting rights of shareholders, rights and responsibilities of the board of directors and corporate officers, and procedures for electing the board of directors, transferring shares, and conducting shareholders' meetings.

Where to Incorporate

Some states are known to be "business friendly." Delaware used to be the poster child of "corporate friendly," and many large corporations are still resident there. In the past two decades, many states have enacted or modified legislation to become more competitive. In a 2013 survey of nearly 8,000 businesses by Thumbtack.com and the Kaufman Foundation, Utah, Alabama, New Hampshire, Idaho, and Texas scored as the top five in terms of overall small business friendliness (Allen & Daniels, 2013). The factors considered in the survey included:

- overall small business friendliness;
- ease of starting a small business;
- ease of hiring a new employee;
- overall regulatory friendliness;
- friendliness of health and safety regulations;
- friendliness of employment, labor, and hiring regulations;
- friendliness of tax code;
- friendliness of licensing regulations;
- friendliness of environmental regulations;
- friendliness of zoning regulations;
- training and networking programs.

For many small business owners and entrepreneurs, the choice of location for their businesses is governed by family or market factors, and state statutes are often the last item to be considered, if they are considered at all. This could be a missed opportunity if the business climates for adjacent states are radically different. For example, Massachusetts ranked number 30 in the Thumbtack.com survey, whereas New Hampshire ranked number 3. See Appendix 2.1 for the articles of incorporation forms required by New Hampshire and by Massachusetts. The Massachusetts form has eight fields to be completed, while the New Hampshire form has only four fields to be completed:

- name of the corporation;
- number of shares authorized to issue (there is no limit to the number and no minimum price per share);

- name of the initial registered agent and address (this is usually the lawyer or the owner);
- principal purpose or purposes of the corporation.

The most often cited disadvantage of the corporation form of business organization is double taxation. The exception is the S corporation, which is a common choice for many small businesses. The next section will discuss the S corporation in detail. Since a corporation is a separate legal entity, it must file its own tax returns with the IRS and the state, and it pays its own income taxes. In contrast, a partnership must also file its own returns but does not pay any income tax. Unlike a partnership, income and losses of a corporation are not passed through to the owners. Instead, when the corporation pays dividends to the owners, the amount of dividends received is taxable as income to the owners. As a result, the income of a corporation is taxed twice, first as income to the corporation and again as dividends to the shareholders. If the owner also works at the corporation, she must pay herself reasonable wages, which are subject to employment tax.

Consulting an accountant and a lawyer at the startup stage about strategies to minimize tax is one of the best investments for a business owner. A comprehensive discussion is beyond the scope of this text, but you can find clarification in Keir and Tissot (2013) or Freeman (2014). For example, if the owner designates her capital contribution to the business as a loan to the corporation, initial cash payouts from the business will be considered loan repayments and not dividends.

The main advantages of the corporation are limited liability and ease of transferring ownership. Since a corporation is considered a separate legal entity, it is responsible for its own business debts and liabilities. The potential losses of its shareholders are limited to their investments in the corporation. Creditors of the business cannot extract payments from the personal wealth of shareholders. The legal entity status also allows the corporation to continue to operate indefinitely, regardless of changes in the composition of its ownership structure. The process of transferring ownership is usually described in the corporate bylaws, making it straightforward to implement.

2.5 Double Taxation Versus Pass-Through Income

Corporations are considered separate legal entities and must pay taxes on incomes they earned. Taxable incomes are computed as revenues minus expenses. However, dividends are not considered an expense for revenues and are not deducted from them when computing taxable income for the corporation. Shareholders must also pay personal taxes on dividends they receive.

With pass-through income, S corporations do not pay taxes on incomes they earned. Instead, shareholders combine their personal incomes and their share of the S corporation's income and pay personal taxes on the combined total. This means that incomes are taxed only once with S corporations. Note that shareholders of S corporations pay taxes on the company's *incomes*, not *dividends*. Shareholders of regular corporations pay taxes on dividends.

Here is a numerical example:
Sweet Pie, a summer ice cream stand, generated $150,000 in revenues and incurred $120,000 in operating expenses. You are the sole owner of Sweet Pie. You and your spouse are in the 30 percent personal tax bracket.

Taxable income for Sweet Pie = $150,000 − $120,000 = $30,000

S Corporation

If you form an S corporation, the entire $30,000 will be combined with your family's joint income and taxed at 30 percent.

Tax related to Sweet Pie is $30,000 × 0.30 = $9,000

Regular Corporation (C-Corporation)

As a regular corporation, Sweet Pie is taxed for the $30,000 in income. The applicable corporate tax rate is 15 percent. Corporate tax for Sweet Pie is $30,000 × 0.15 = $4,500. Therefore, the net income after tax from Sweet Pie is $30,000 − $4,500 = $25,500.

If you want to spend money from Sweet Pie, you must pay yourself dividends. Assuming that you pay out all net income after tax as dividends, you will receive $25,500, which is taxed at your personal rate of 30 percent. Your personal income tax on these dividends is $25,500 × 0.30 = $7,650.

Total tax related to Sweet Pie is $4,500 (corporate) +
$7,650 (personal) = $12,150

Note that the amount of taxes at the personal level depends on dividends paid. If a company is reinvesting its incomes instead of paying them out as dividends, the total amount of taxes can be much lower. For example, you can choose not to pay out any dividend from Sweet Pie, which means you will not have the cash for personal spending, and taxes related to Sweet Pie will be only $4,500. There are IRS rules limiting how long a company can delay paying dividends.

S Corporations

S corporations (often called S corps) enjoy special tax status from the IRS and avoid double taxation on corporate income. The requirements for an S corporation are:

- a domestic corporation;
- have only allowable shareholders, including individuals, certain trusts, and estates, and may not include partnerships, corporations or non-resident alien shareholders;
- have no more than 100 shareholders;
- have only one class of stock;
- not be an ineligible corporation (i.e. certain financial institutions, insurance companies, and domestic international sales corporations).

Most small businesses and startup companies will qualify for S corporation status. The incomes and losses of an S corporation are treated in the same way as those of a partnership, i.e. they are passed through to the shareholders. The S corporation files a tax return but does not pay any income taxes.

The special tax status of S corporation has another unique advantage in regard to employment tax. Shareholders of S corporations who are also employees pay employment tax only on wages received; the remaining pass-through incomes are considered "distributions" and are taxed at a lower rate. Lastly, shareholders of S corporations enjoy limited liability.

In short, the S corporation avoids double taxation and maintains many of the advantages of a corporation. The restrictions that limit the S corporation to no more than 100 shareholders and one class of stock are typically not important for small businesses. However, the restriction of not allowing non-resident aliens as shareholders will exclude this form as a viable option if one of the owners is not an American citizen.

Limited Liability Companies

The statutes governing the formation and reporting requirements of a limited liability company (LLC) are also state-specific. Owners of an LLC are called members instead of partners or shareholders. There is usually no limit to the maximum or minimum number of members, and an LLC may contain only a single member. An LLC may be classified for federal income tax purposes as a partnership, a corporation, or part of the owner's tax return if the LLC is owned by an individual. To be taxed as a corporation, an LLC must file Form 8832 (Entity Classification Election) with the IRS and its income will then be subject to double taxation. Another way an LLC will be taxed as a corporation is if it possesses three or more of the characteristics of a corporation.

The IRS defines these corporate characteristics as: continuity of life, centralization of management, limited liability, and free transferability of ownership. For example, if each member owns more than 20 percent of the business and elects limited liability then, to avoid being taxed as a corporation, the LLC cannot elect continuity of life or free transferability of ownership. This can make succession planning and the future sale of business difficult. Of course, there are ways to circumvent these limits by creating additional legal entities in the business structure. However, such strategies greatly increase the complexity of setting up the business.

The process of forming an LLC and related registration fees varies significantly state by state. For example, in New Hampshire, the fee is the same whether forming a corporation or an LLC, whereas in Massachusetts, the fee may be lower for forming a corporation than for forming an LLC.[4] In general, the required information to be filed for creating an LLC is less than that required for a corporation but more than that required for a partnership. Recall that a verbal agreement is sufficient in many states to establish a partnership. All states require at least a written document to be filed to create an LLC. Even though not required, a well-written LLC agreement will reduce potential friction among members farther down the road and ensure that a maximum of two corporate characteristics are adopted, avoiding challenges from the IRS in regard to its tax status.

Professional Limited Liability Company

Professionals, such as doctors, dentists, accountants, lawyers, architects, engineers, or business consultants, traditionally form partnerships. A Professional LLC is particularly suitable for these types of business because it provides limited liability and preserves most of the tax advantages and operating characteristics of a partnership. If your business is in one of these professions, a Professional LLC will likely be the best option for you.

LLC versus S corporation

The main advantages of LLC are limited liability and pass-through income and losses for tax purposes. Since S corporations also provide these advantages, it is useful to compare the main differences between these two forms of business organization (Table 2.2).

For many small businesses, the tax advantage of LLC versus S corporation depends on the income level and amount of startup capital required. Even though the reporting requirement is lower for an LLC, a business with good operating procedures will often keep records similar to those required for corporate filing. We cannot emphasize enough that a well-written partnership agreement or LLC agreement will specify procedures for profit distribution, voting, and transfer of ownership. As to regular meetings and minutes,

Table 2.2 LLC and S Corporation Compared

	Limited Liability Company	S Corporation
Limited liability	Yes	Yes
Pass-through incomes and losses	Yes	Yes
Pass-through tax status recognized in all states	Yes	No
Self-employment tax on all pass-through incomes	Yes	No
Limit on the maximum number of owners	No	Yes
Limit on the minimum number of owners	1	1
Limit on non-human legal entity as owners	No	Yes—limited to certain trusts and estates
Allow nonresident aliens as owners	Yes	No
The business allow to own stocks in other businesses	Yes	No
Allow different classes of stocks	Yes	No
Limit on corporate characteristics	Yes	No
Requires board meetings and minutes	No	Yes

sound business practice states that owners need to meet and communicate regularly and have written records of decisions.

The most important advantage of an LLC over an S corporation is the ability to have one or more owners who are non-resident aliens, which would disallow them from qualifying the business as an S corporation. For immigrants, this is a significant advantage. The ability to raise funds with a venture capital firm is also an advantage of LLC. You will learn about raising venture capital funds in Chapter 3.

Appendix 2.1 Business Registration Forms for Massachusetts and New Hampshire

D

The Commonwealth of Massachusetts
William Francis Galvin
Secretary of the Commonwealth
One Ashburton Place, Boston, Massachusetts 02108-1512

FORM MUST BE TYPED · **Articles of Organization** · FORM MUST BE TYPED
(General Laws Chapter 156D, Section 2.02; 950 CMR 113.16)

ARTICLE I
The exact name of the corporation is:

ARTICLE II
Unless the articles of organization otherwise provide, all corporations formed pursuant to G.L. Chapter 156D have the purpose of engaging in any lawful business. Please specify if you want a more limited purpose:

ARTICLE III
State the total number of shares and par value, * if any, of each class of stock that the corporation is authorized to issue. All corporations must authorize stock. If only one class or series is authorized, it is not necessary to specify any particular designation.

WITHOUT PAR VALUE		WITH PAR VALUE		
TYPE	NUMBER OF SHARES	TYPE	NUMBER OF SHARES	PAR VALUE

G.L. Chapter 156D eliminates the concept of par value, however a corporation may specify par value in Article III. See G.L. Chapter 156D, Section 6.21, and the comments relative thereto.

P.C.

c156ds202950c11316 01/13/05

ARTICLE IV

Prior to the issuance of shares of any class or series, the articles of organization must set forth the preferences, limitations and relative rights of that class or series. The articles may also limit the type or specify the minimum amount of consideration for which shares of any class or series may be issued. Please set forth the preferences, limitations and relative rights of each class or series and, if desired, the required type and minimum amount of consideration to be received.

ARTICLE V

The restrictions, if any, imposed by the articles of organization upon the transfer of shares of any class or series of stock are:

ARTICLE VI

Other lawful provisions, and if there are no such provisions, this article may be left blank.

Note: The preceding six (6) articles are considered to be permanent and may be changed only by filing appropriate articles of amendment.

ARTICLE VII

The effective date of organization of the corporation is the date and time the articles were received for filing if the articles are not rejected within the time prescribed by law. If a later effective date is desired, specify such date, which may not be later than the 90th day after the articles are received for filing:

ARTICLE VIII

The information contained in this article is not a permanent part of the articles of organization.

   a.   The street address of the initial registered office of the corporation in the commonwealth:

   b.   The name of its initial registered agent at its registered office:

   c.   The names and street addresses of the individuals who will serve as the initial directors, president, treasurer and secretary of the corporation (an address need not be specified if the business address of the officer or director is the same as the principal office location):

President:

Treasurer:

Secretary:

Director(s):

   d.   The fiscal year end of the corporation:

   e.   A brief description of the type of business in which the corporation intends to engage:

   f.   The street address of the principal office of the corporation:

   g.   The street address where the records of the corporation required to be kept in the commonwealth are located is:

_____ , which is
(number, street, city or town, state, zip code)

☐ its principal office;
☐ an office of its transfer agent;
☐ an office of its secretary/assistant secretary;
☐ its registered office.

Signed this _____ day of _____ , _____ by the incorporator(s):

Signature: _____

Name: _____

Address: _____

COMMONWEALTH OF MASSACHUSETTS

William Francis Galvin
Secretary of the Commonwealth
One Ashburton Place, Boston, Massachusetts 02108-1512

Articles of Organization
(General Laws Chapter 156D, Section 2.02; 950 CMR 113.16)

I hereby certify that upon examination of these articles of organization, duly submitted to me, it appears that the provisions of the General Laws relative to the organization of corporations have been complied with, and I hereby approve said articles; and the filing fee in the amount of $_____ having been paid, said articles are deemed to have been filed with me this _____ day of _____, 20_____ , at _____a.m./p.m.

time

Effective date:_____
(must be within 90 days of date submitted)

WILLIAM FRANCIS GALVIN
Secretary of the Commonwealth

_____
Examiner

_____
Name approval

_____
C

_____
M

Filing fee: $275 for up to 275,000 shares plus $100 for each additional 100,000 shares or any fraction thereof.

TO BE FILLED IN BY CORPORATION
Contact Information:

_____

_____

_____

Telephone: _____

Email: _____

Upon filing, a copy of this filing will be available at www.sec.state.ma.us/cor. If the document is rejected, a copy of the rejection sheet and rejected document will be available in the rejected queue.

D 𝕿𝖍𝖊 𝕮𝖔𝖒𝖒𝖔𝖓𝖜𝖊𝖆𝖑𝖙𝖍 𝖔𝖋 𝕸𝖆𝖘𝖘𝖆𝖈𝖍𝖚𝖘𝖊𝖙𝖙𝖘

William Francis Galvin
Secretary of the Commonwealth
One Ashburton Place, Room 1717, Boston, Massachusetts 02108-1512

Limited Liability Company
Certificate of Organization
(General Laws Chapter 156C, Section 12)

Federal Identification No.: _____

(1) The exact name of the limited liability company:

_____

(2) The street address of the office in the commonwealth at which its records will be maintained:

(3) The general character of the business:

(4) Latest date of dissolution, if specified: _____

(5) The name and street address, of the resident agent in the commonwealth:
  NAME   ADDRESS

(6) The name and business address, if different from office location, of each manager, if any:
  NAME   ADDRESS

(7) The name and business address, if different from office location, of each person in addition to manager(s) authorized to execute documents filed with the Corporations Division, and at least one person shall be named if there are no managers:

NAME   ADDRESS

(8) The name and business address, if different from office location, of each person authorized to execute, acknowledge, deliver and record any recordable instrument purporting to affect an interest in real property recorded with a registry of deeds or district office of the land court:

NAME   ADDRESS

(9) Additional matters:

Signed by *(by at least one authorized signatory)*: _____

Consent of resident agent:

I _____,
resident agent of the above limited liability company, consent to my appointment as resident agent pursuant to G.L. c 156C § 12*

*or attach resident agent's consent hereto.

COMMONWEALTH OF MASSACHUSETTS

William Francis Galvin
Secretary of the Commonwealth
One Ashburton Place, Boston, Massachusetts 02108-1512

Limited Liability Company Certificate
(General Laws Chapter 156C, Section 12)

I hereby certify that upon examination of this limited liability company certificate, duly submitted to me, it appears that the provisions of the General Laws relative thereto have been complied with, and I hereby approve said application; and the filing fee in the amount of $_____ having been paid, said application is deemed to have been filed with me this

_____ day of _____, 20 _____, at _____a.m./p.m.
                                                                time

Effective date:_____

WILLIAM FRANCIS GALVIN
Secretary of the Commonwealth

Filing fee: $500

TO BE FILLED IN BY LIMITED LIABILITY COMPANY
Contact Information:

_____

_____

_____

Telephone: _____

Email: _____

Upon filing, a copy of this filing will be available at www.sec.state.ma.us/cor.
If the document is rejected, a copy of the rejection sheet and rejected document will be available in the rejected queue.

$20.00 filing fee   BUSINESS CERTIFICATE   RENEWAL _____ NEW _____

COMMONWEALTH OF MASSACHUSETTS   Original certificate must be filed

CITY OF PEABODY

In conformity with the provisions of Chapter one hundred and ten, Section five of the General Laws, as amended, the undersigned hereby declare(s) that a business under the title

of ....

.... is conducted at

Number ....

in the City of Peabody, Massachusetts by the following named person(s).

FULL NAME   RESIDENCE

....

....

....

All signatures must be notarized if signed outside of the City Clerk's Office

Signed   ....
                    (SIGNATURE)   SIGNATURE)

                ....
                    (SIGNATURE)   (SIGNATURE)

COMMONWEALTH OF MASSACHUSETTS
CITY OF PEABODY

ESSEX SS.   ....

Personally appeared before me the above-named ....

....

and made oath that the foregoing statement is true. ....

A certificate issued in accordance with this section shall be in force and effect for four years from the date of issue and shall be renewed each four years thereafter so long as such business shall be conducted and shall lapse and be void unless so renewed.

Expiration Date ....

                                                                        City Clerk
(Seal)   A "Form of List" must be filed with the Assessors Office for personal property taxes   TITLE

BUSINESS CERTIFICATE FILINGS ARE NOT A LICENSE TO CONDUCT BUSINESS. ANY PERSON WISHING TO CONDUCT BUSINESS MUST, IN ADDITION TO T HE ABOVE, CONTACT THE BUILDING INSPECTOR TO ENSURE THAT THE BUSINESS LOCATION IS IN COMPLIANCE WITH CITY ZONING LAWS PRIOR TO THE ISSUANCE OF THIS CERTIFICATE AND RECEIVE APPROVAL FROM THE BUILDING INSPECTOR FOR THE SAME.

State of New Hampshire

ARTICLES OF INCORPORATION
INSTRUCTIONS FOR COMPLETING FORM 11 (RSA 293-A:2.02)

NINE STEPS TO AVOID REJECTION

1. The form must be legibly printed or typed *in black ink*; pencil is not acceptable. The form must be single-sided on 8½" x 11" paper and one inch side margins must be maintained. Double-sided pages will not be accepted.

2. Article First: The name must contain a corporation designation. Per RSA 293-A:4.01 the corporate name must contain the word "corporation," "incorporated," or "limited" or the abbreviation "corp.," "inc.," or "ltd.", or words or abbreviations of like import in another language.

3. Article Second: Per RSA 293-A:6.01, all corporations must state how many shares the corporation is authorized to issue. All corporations must have at least one share. RSA 293-A:1.40 (22) defines a share as a unit to which proprietary interests in the corporation are divided (unit of ownership).

4. Article Third: A registered agent and registered office must be provided. The registered agent must reside in New Hampshire. The registered agent is the person who would receive service of process should the corporation be sued. The registered office is the registered agent's business address where the registered agent can be found for in-hand service of process. **A street/physical address must be provided in addition to the post office box.** The sheriff's department must be able to hand the service of process to the registered agent; it cannot be served to a post office box.

5. Article Fourth: The articles of incorporation must contain the following statement: *The sale or offer for sale of any ownership interests in this business will comply with the requirements of the New Hampshire Uniform Securities Act (RSA 421-B).*

6. Article Fifth: This article is not required to be completed. However, purposes may be helpful in determining the availability of corporate name. See RSA 293-A:2.02 (b) for additional articles which may be included.

7. Article Sixth: The name and address of all incorporators must be listed. All incorporators must sign both the articles of incorporation *and the addendum.*

8. Refer to **Instructions for Form SRA – Addendum to Business Organization and Registration Forms** for assistance in completing that form.

9. The total filing fee to incorporate is $100.00. This is comprised of $50.00 for the articles of incorporation plus $50.00 for the SRA form.

PLEASE NOTE: The name will be searched for availability upon receipt of these documents. If the filing has been accepted, you will receive a filed-stamped copy within 30 days. If you do not receive an acknowledgement, please contact our office. Checks are deposited upon receipt. If the check has been cashed, it only indicates we have received the document. A cashed check is not an indication that the document has been accepted and filed.

Mail fees, <u>DATED AND SIGNED ORIGINAL AND FORM SRA</u> to: Corporation Division, Department of State, 107 North Main Street, Concord NH 03301-4989. Physical location: 25 Capitol Street, 3rd Floor, Concord, NH 03301.

Form 11 Instruct

Print	Reset

State of New Hampshire

Filing fee: $50.00
Fee for Form SRA: <u>$50.00</u>
Total fees $100.00
Use black print or type.

Form 11
RSA 293-A:2.02

ARTICLES OF INCORPORATION

The undersigned, acting as incorporator(s) of a corporation under the New Hampshire Business Corporation Act, adopt(s) the following articles of incorporation for such corporation:

FIRST: The name of the corporation is _____

_____ .

SECOND: The number of shares the corporation is authorized to issue: _____

_____ .

THIRD: The name of the corporation's initial registered agent is _____

_____ .

and the **street address**, town/city (including zip code and post office box, if any) of its initial registered

office is (agent's business address) _____

_____ .

FOURTH: The sale or offer for sale of any ownership interests in this business will comply with the requirements of the New Hampshire Uniform Securities Act (RSA 421-B).

FIFTH: The corporation is empowered to transact any and all lawful business for which corporations may be incorporated under RSA 293-A and the <u>principal</u> purpose or purposes for which the corporation is organized are:

[If more space is needed, attach additional sheet(s).]

Page 1 of 2

ARTICLES OF INCORPORATION

SIXTH: The name and address of each incorporator is:

Name	Address
_____	_____
	_____
_____	_____
	_____
_____	_____
	_____

_____
_____
_____
Incorporator(s)

Date signed: _____

To receive your ANNUAL REPORT REMINDER NOTICE by email, please enter your email address here:
_____.

DISCLAIMER: All documents filed with the Corporation Division become public records and will be available for public inspection in either tangible or electronic form.

Mail fees, <u>DATED AND SIGNED ORIGINAL AND FORM SRA</u> to: Corporation Division, Department of State, 107 North Main Street, Concord NH 03301-4989. Physical location: 25 Capitol Street, 3rd Floor, Concord, NH 03301.

Form 11 Pg 2 (5/2007)

Print

Reset

Form SRA – Addendum to Business Organization and Registration Forms
Statement of Compliance with New Hampshire Securities Laws

Part I – Business Identification and Contact Information

Business Name: _____

Business Address (include city, state, zip): _____

Telephone Number: _____ E-mail: _____

Contact Person: _____

Contact Person Address (if different): _____

Part II – Check *ONE* of the following items in Part II. If more than one item is checked, the form will be rejected. [*PLEASE NOTE:* Most small businesses registering in New Hampshire qualify for the exemption in Part II, Item 1 below. *However,* you must insure that your business meets all of the requirements spelled out in A), B), and C)]:

1. ____ Ownership interests in this business are exempt from the registration requirements of the state of New Hampshire because the business meets *ALL* of the following three requirements:
   A) This business has *10 or fewer owners*; and
   B) Advertising *relating to the sale of ownership interests* has not been circulated; and
   C) Sales of ownership interests – if any – will be *completed within 60 days* of the formation of this business.

2. ____ This business will offer securities in New Hampshire under another exemption from registration or will notice file for federal covered securities. Enter the citation for the exemption or notice filing claimed - _____.

3. ____ This business has registered or will register its securities for sale in New Hampshire. Enter the date the registration statement was or will be filed with the Bureau of Securities Regulation - _____.

4. ____ This business was formed in a state other than New Hampshire and will not offer or sell securities in New Hampshire.

Part III – Check *ONE* of the following items in Part III:

1. ____ This business *is not being* formed in New Hampshire.

2. ____ This business *is* being formed in New Hampshire and the registration document states that any sale or offer for sale of ownership interests in the business will comply with the requirements of the New Hampshire Uniform Securities Act.

Part IV – Certification of Accuracy

(NOTE: The information in Part IV must be certified by: 1) all of the incorporators of a corporation to be formed; or 2) an executive officer of an existing corporation; or 3) all of the general partners or intended general partners of a limited partnership; or 4) one or more authorized members or managers of a limited liability company; or 5) one or more authorized partners of a registered limited liability partnership or foreign registered limited liability partnership.)

I (We) certify that the information provided in this form is true and complete. (Original signatures *only*)

Name (print): _____ Signature: _____

Date signed: _____

Name (print): _____ Signature: _____

Date signed: _____

Name (print): _____ Signature: _____

Date signed: _____

Rev. 3/08

Instructions for
Form SRA – Addendum to Business Organization and Registration Forms

Statement of Compliance with New Hampshire Securities Laws

This form is required for all businesses being formed or registering in the state of New Hampshire. New Hampshire law requires that before your application for business registration is accepted, you must provide a statement that your business has complied with the state's securities law. A security is an ownership interest in a business. For example, a share of stock is a security and so is an interest in a limited liability company or a limited partnership. So, for example, if you and your wife own the sole interests in a limited liability company, those interests are securities. Generally, a business that issues securities in New Hampshire must either register the securities with the New Hampshire Bureau of Securities Regulation or claim a valid exemption. There are several exemptions from the requirement to register securities. The most common exemption is the exemption described in Part II, Item 1.

Please read the following instructions for each part of Form SRA. These instruction will help you to provide accurate responses.

Part I: Please provide the complete business name and address, including number, street, city, state and zip code. The name of the business must exactly match the name that is on the business formation or registration document being submitted with the Form SRA. In addition, please provide the businesses telephone number, e-mail address (if any), a contact person's name and the contact person's full address if different from the business address.

Part II: One item in Part II must be checked. Check only **ONE** item in this part.

1. Your business is qualified for the exemption from registration in Item 1 if it meets **ALL** of the requirement listed in A), B), and C) below:

    A) The business has 10 or fewer owners. So, for example, if you and your wife are forming a limited liability company and there are no other owners, you meet this requirement for an exemption; AND

    B) Advertising relating to the sale of ownership interests in your business has not been circulated. Please note that this requirement asks whether you have circulated advertising *related to the offer or sale of ownership interests*. This requirement does not address advertising related to the sale of your products or services. So, for example, if you advertise that you are selling shares of stock in your corporation, then you do not meet this requirement and cannot claim the exemption; AND

    C) Sales of ownership interests – if any – will be completed within 60 days of the formation of the business. If you do not intend to sell any further ownership interests in your business, then you meet this requirement for an exemption. If you intend to sell more ownership interests in your business and will complete all sales within 60 days, then you meet this requirement. However, if the sale of any ownership interests will occur after 60 days of the formation of the business, you do not meet this requirement and cannot claim the exemption.

    If you meet all of these requirements, you may then check off Item 1 and claim this exemption.

2. If you can claim a different registration exemption from the one listed in Item 1 or if you are offering federal covered securities that only require a notice filing in New Hampshire, you should check Item 2. In addition, you must cite the statute for the exemption which you are claiming or for the type of notice filing you are making.

Rev. 5/2007

3. If a New Hampshire business or a business formed in a state other than New Hampshire intends to offer ownership interests for sale and is not subject to any exemption from registration, the securities must be registered with the Bureau of Securities Regulation. If this is the case, you should check Item 3. In addition, you should provide us with the date that you registered the securities or that you intend to register the securities.

4. If your business was formed in a state other than New Hampshire and you will not offer or sell ownership interests in New Hampshire, you should check Item 4. Your securities do not need to be registered nor do you need to seek an exemption from registration.

Part III: One item in Part III must be checked. Check only **_ONE_** item in this part.

1. If your business was *not* formed in New Hampshire, then you should check this item.

2. If your business was formed in New Hampshire, then you should check this item.

Part IV: This is a statement certifying the accuracy of all the information contained in the Form SRA. Part IV must be signed. Please note that we cannot accept photocopied signatures for this filing. All signatures must be original. Also, please make note of all individuals who must sign this document:

1) *ALL* of the incorporators of *a corporation to be formed*; OR
2) *ONE* executive officer of *an existing corporation*; OR
3) *ALL* of the general partners or intended general partners of *a limited partnership*; OR
4) *ONE or MORE* authorized members or managers of *a limited liability company*; OR
5) *ONE or MORE* authorized partners of *a registered limited liability partnership* or *foreign registered limited liability partnership*.

State of New Hampshire

CERTIFICATE OF FORMATION
OF A NEW HAMPSHIRE LIMITED LIABILITY COMPANY
INSTRUCTIONS FOR COMPLETING FORM LLC-1 (RSA 304-C:31)

11 STEPS TO AVOID REJECTION

1. The form must be completed in ink; pencil or erasable ink is not acceptable. A one inch margin must be maintained; the pages cannot be double-sided.

2. Article First: The name must contain one of the following designations: Limited Liability Company, L.L.C., L. L. C. or LLC (per RSA 304-C:32)

3. Article Second: The law requires that the certificate of formation include a primary nature of business, such as "sales and manufacturing of disposable products" or "software consulting and development." We cannot accept a general clause such as "sales and manufacturing", "consulting and development", or "any lawful activity." You need to include a descriptive word. Refer to RSA 304-C:21 for nature of business permitted.

4. Article Third: A registered agent and registered office must be provided. The registered agent must reside in New Hampshire and is the person who would receive service of process should the limited liability company be sued. The registered office is the registered agent's business address where the registered agent can be found for in-hand service of process; it cannot be served to a post office box. **A street address or physical address must be provided in addition to a post office box.**

5. Article Fourth: If a specific date of dissolution is set, a full date (month, day, year) must be stated. We cannot calculate dates. If no specific date of dissolution is set, "none", "perpetual" or "ongoing" is acceptable.

6. Article Fifth: The certificate of formation must state whether or not management is vested in a manager(s). If management is vested in a manager(s), this line must be completed as "is". If management is not vested in a manager(s), this line must be completed with "is not". **"Is" or "is not" are the only two acceptable entries.**

7. Article Sixth: The certificate of formation must contain the following statement: *The sale or offer for sale of any ownership interests in this business will comply with the requirements of the New Hampshire Uniform Securities Act (RSA 421-B).*

8. The title and printed name of the person signing the documents must be stated beside or below his/her signature. RSA 304-C:28 V requires that the documents be signed by a "manager" and if there is no manager, by a "member". **If Article Fifth states "is not", the title of the person signing must be member. If Article Fifth indicates "is", the title must be manager. No other title will be accepted.**

9. Refer to **Instructions for Form SRA – Addendum to Business Organization and Registration Forms** for assistance in completing that form.

10. The total filing fee is $100.00. This is comprised of $50.00 for the certificate of formation plus $50.00 for the addendum.

11. Any other matters the members decide to include may be added. If more space is needed, attach additional pages.

PLEASE NOTE: The name will be searched for availability upon receipt of these documents. If the filing has been accepted, you will receive a filed-stamped copy within 30 days. If you do not receive an acknowledge-ment, please contact our office. Checks are deposited upon receipt. If the check has been cashed, it only indicates we have received the document. A cashed check is not an indication that the document has been accepted and filed.

Mail fees, <u>DATED AND SIGNED ORIGINAL AND FORM SRA</u> to: Corporation Division, Department of State, 107 North Main Street, Concord NH 03301-4989. Physical location: 25 Capitol Street, 3rd Floor, Concord, NH 03301.

Print	Reset

State of New Hampshire

Filing fee: $50.00
Fee for Form SRA: <u>$50.00</u>
Total fees $100.00
Use black print or type.

Form LLC-1
RSA 304-C:31

CERTIFICATE OF FORMATION
NEW HAMPSHIRE LIMITED LIABILITY COMPANY

THE UNDERSIGNED, under the New Hampshire Limited Liability Company Laws submits the following certificate of formation:

FIRST: The name of the limited liability company is _____

_____.

SECOND: The nature of the primary business or purposes are _____

_____

_____.

THIRD: The name of the limited liability company's registered agent is _____

_____

and the **street address**, town/city (including zip code and post office box, if any) of its registered office is

(agent's business address) _____

_____.

FOURTH: The latest date on which the limited liability company is to dissolve is _____.

FIFTH: The management of the limited liability company _____ vested in a manager or
        managers.

SIXTH: The sale or offer for sale of any ownership interests in this business will comply with the requirements of the New Hampshire Uniform Securities Act (RSA 421-B).

*Signature: _____

Print or type name: _____

Title: _____
                        (Enter "manager" or "member")

Date signed: _____

To receive your ANNUAL REPORT REMINDER NOTICE by email, please enter your email address here:

_____.

*Must be signed by a **manager**; if no manager, must be signed by a **member**.

DISCLAIMER: All documents filed with the Corporation Division become public records and will be available for public inspection in either tangible or electronic form.

Mail fees, <u>DATED AND SIGNED ORIGINAL AND FORM SRA</u> to: Corporation Division, Department of State, 107 North Main Street, Concord NH 03301-4989. Physical location: 25 Capitol Street, 3rd Floor, Concord, NH 03301.

Form LLC-1 (1/2013)

Form SRA – Addendum to Business Organization and Registration Forms
Statement of Compliance with New Hampshire Securities Laws

Part I – Business Identification and Contact Information

Business Name: _____

Business Address (include city, state, zip): _____

Telephone Number: _____   E-mail: _____

Contact Person: _____

Contact Person Address (if different): _____

Part II – Check _ONE_ of the following items in Part II. If more than one item is checked, the form will be rejected. [*PLEASE NOTE:* Most small businesses registering in New Hampshire qualify for the exemption in Part II, Item 1 below. *However,* you must insure that your business meets all of the requirements spelled out in A), B), and C)]:

1. _____   Ownership interests in this business are exempt from the registration requirements of the state of New Hampshire because the business meets **_ALL_** of the following three requirements:
    A) This business has **10 or fewer owners**; and
    B) Advertising **relating to the sale of ownership interests** has not been circulated; and
    C) Sales of ownership interests – if any – will be **completed within 60 days** of the formation of this business.

2. _____   This business will offer securities in New Hampshire under another exemption from registration or will notice file for federal covered securities. Enter the citation for the exemption or notice filing claimed - _____.

3. _____   This business has registered or will register its securities for sale in New Hampshire. Enter the date the registration statement was or will be filed with the Bureau of Securities Regulation - _____.

4. _____   This business was formed in a state other than New Hampshire and will not offer or sell securities in New Hampshire.

Part III – Check _ONE_ of the following items in Part III:

1. _____   This business **is not being** formed in New Hampshire.

2. _____   This business **is** being formed in New Hampshire and the registration document states that any sale or offer for sale of ownership interests in the business will comply with the requirements of the New Hampshire Uniform Securities Act.

Part IV – Certification of Accuracy

(NOTE: The information in Part IV must be certified by: 1) all of the incorporators of a corporation to be formed; or 2) an executive officer of an existing corporation; or 3) all of the general partners or intended general partners of a limited partnership; or 4) one or more authorized members or managers of a limited liability company; or 5) one or more authorized partners of a registered limited liability partnership or foreign registered limited liability partnership.)

I (We) certify that the information provided in this form is true and complete. (Original signatures **_only_**)

Name (print): _____   Signature: _____

                                                         Date signed: _____

Name (print): _____   Signature: _____

                                                         Date signed: _____

Name (print): _____   Signature: _____

                                                         Date signed: _____

Rev. 3/08

Instructions for
Form SRA – Addendum to Business Organization and Registration Forms

Statement of Compliance with New Hampshire Securities Laws

This form is required for all businesses being formed or registering in the state of New Hampshire. New Hampshire law requires that before your application for business registration is accepted, you must provide a statement that your business has complied with the state's securities law. A security is an ownership interest in a business. For example, a share of stock is a security and so is an interest in a limited liability company or a limited partnership. So, for example, if you and your wife own the sole interests in a limited liability company, those interests are securities. Generally, a business that issues securities in New Hampshire must either register the securities with the New Hampshire Bureau of Securities Regulation or claim a valid exemption. There are several exemptions from the requirement to register securities. The most common exemption is the exemption described in Part II, Item 1.

Please read the following instructions for each part of Form SRA. These instruction will help you to provide accurate responses.

Part I: Please provide the complete business name and address, including number, street, city, state and zip code. The name of the business must exactly match the name that is on the business formation or registration document being submitted with the Form SRA. In addition, please provide the businesses telephone number, e-mail address (if any), a contact person's name and the contact person's full address if different from the business address.

Part II: One item in Part II must be checked. Check only **ONE** item in this part.

1. Your business is qualified for the exemption from registration in Item 1 if it meets **ALL** of the requirement listed in A), B), and C) below:

    A) The business has 10 or fewer owners. So, for example, if you and your wife are forming a limited liability company and there are no other owners, you meet this requirement for an exemption; AND

    B) Advertising relating to the sale of ownership interests in your business has not been circulated. Please note that this requirement asks whether you have circulated advertising **related to the offer or sale of ownership interests**. This requirement does not address advertising related to the sale of your products or services. So, for example, if you advertise that you are selling shares of stock in your corporation, then you do not meet this requirement and cannot claim the exemption; AND

    C) Sales of ownership interests – if any – will be completed within 60 days of the formation of the business. If you do not intend to sell any further ownership interests in your business, then you meet this requirement for an exemption. If you intend to sell more ownership interests in your business and will complete all sales within 60 days, then you meet this requirement. However, if the sale of any ownership interests will occur after 60 days of the formation of the business, you do not meet this requirement and cannot claim the exemption.

    If you meet all of these requirements, you may then check off Item 1 and claim this exemption.

2. If you can claim a different registration exemption from the one listed in Item 1 or if you are offering federal covered securities that only require a notice filing in New Hampshire, you should check Item 2. In addition, you must cite the statute for the exemption which you are claiming or for the type of notice filing you are making.

Rev. 5/2007

Instructions – Form SRA

3. If a New Hampshire business or a business formed in a state other than New Hampshire intends to offer ownership interests for sale and is not subject to any exemption from registration, the securities must be registered with the Bureau of Securities Regulation. If this is the case, you should check Item 3. In addition, you should provide us with the date that you registered the securities or that you intend to register the securities.

4. If your business was formed in a state other than New Hampshire and you will not offer or sell ownership interests in New Hampshire, you should check Item 4. Your securities do not need to be registered nor do you need to seek an exemption from registration.

Part III: One item in Part III must be checked. Check only _ONE_ item in this part.

1. If your business was *not* formed in New Hampshire, then you should check this item.

2. If your business was formed in New Hampshire, then you should check this item.

Part IV: This is a statement certifying the accuracy of all the information contained in the Form SRA. Part IV must be signed. Please note that we cannot accept photocopied signatures for this filing. All signatures must be original. Also, please make note of all individuals who must sign this document:

    1) **ALL** of the incorporators of *a corporation to be formed*; OR
    2) **ONE** executive officer of *an existing corporation*; OR
    3) **ALL** of the general partners or intended general partners of *a limited partnership*; OR
    4) **ONE or MORE** authorized members or managers of *a limited liability company*; OR
    5) **ONE or MORE** authorized partners of *a registered limited liability partnership* or *foreign registered limited liability partnership*.

Rev. 5/2007

Print	Reset

State of New Hampshire

Filing fee: $50.00
Use black print or type.

Form TN-1
RSA 349

APPLICATION FOR REGISTRATION OF TRADE NAME

(PLEASE TYPE OR PRINT CLEARLY)

1. BUSINESS NAME: _____
   (Name **cannot include "INC."** or other corporate designation)

2. BUSINESS ADDRESS: _____
   No. & Street   City / town   State   Zip

   MAILING ADDRESS (if different): _____
   No. & Street   City / town   State   Zip

3. BRIEF DESCRIPTION OF KIND OF BUSINESS TO BE CARRIED ON: _____
   _____

4. DATE BUSINESS ORGANIZED: _____
   (month / day / year)

5-A. **ENTITY APPLICANT:** IF THE APPLICANT IS A CORPORATION OR OTHER ENTITY, LIST
   CORPORATION'S OR ENTITY'S EXACT NAME AND INCLUDE TITLE OF PERSON SIGNING. If
   more space is needed for additional entity applicants, please attach additional sheet(s).

   _____   _____
   ENTITY NAME (TYPE OR PRINT)   NO.   STREET

   _____   _____
   AUTHORIZED SIGNATURE   TOWN/CITY   STATE   ZIP

   _____
   SIGNER'S NAME AND TITLE (TYPE OR PRINT)

5-B. **INDIVIDUAL APPLICANTS:** PLEASE TYPE OR PRINT APPLICANTS' NAME(S), ADDRESS(ES)
   AND INCLUDE SIGNATURE. If more space is needed for additional individual applicants, please
   attach additional sheet(s).

1. _____   _____
   TYPE OR PRINT NAME   NO.   STREET

   _____   _____
   SIGNATURE   TOWN/CITY   STATE   ZIP

2. _____   _____
   TYPE OR PRINT NAME   NO.   STREET

   _____   _____
   SIGNATURE   TOWN/CITY   STATE   ZIP

3. _____   _____
   TYPE OR PRINT NAME   NO.   STREET

   _____   _____
   SIGNATURE   TOWN/CITY   STATE   ZIP

DISCLAIMER: All documents filed with the Corporation Division become public records and will be
available for public inspection in either tangible or electronic form.

Mail fee and <u>DATED AND SIGNED ORIGINAL</u> to: Corporation Division, Department of State, 107 North
Main Street, Concord, NH 03301-4989. Physical location: 25 Capitol Street, Concord, NH 03301.

Form TN-1 Pg 1 (05/2012)

About Trade Name Registration

New Hampshire law requires that anyone doing business under any name other than his or her own must register that name with the Secretary of State. The fee for registration is $50.00.

The purpose of registration is to let the public know who is transacting business under a particular business name. The Secretary of State will not register a name that might be confused with one already registered.

Filling out the trade name application requires the following:

1. Exact trade name being registered (your name will be checked for **availability** when the application is filed).

   You may call the Secretary of State's Information Line (603-271-3246) to have the business name checked for **availability. However,** even if you have checked your name with the Secretary of State's Information Line, you should **not** consider it finally approved or proceed with printing, advertising, etc. using that name until your application is processed and you receive your trade name certificate. A telephone name check is preliminary only.

2. Complete address of the business. If the mailing address for the business is different from the listed business address, please insert the complete mailing address on the line provided.

3. Brief description of type of business (e.g. real estate, hairdresser, etc.).

4. Date business was organized.

5-A & B. Applicants: may be an individual, corporation, limited liability company, limited liability partnership, group of partners or association.

   Original signatures of all applicants; if a corporation, of an authorized officer; if a limited liability company, by the manager or if no manager, by a member; if a limited liability partnership, by one or more authorized partners.

Case 2.1 Mystic Landscaping: Selecting a Form of Business Ownership

Gina Vega

As a 16-year-old baby-faced boy, Tim was a little different from the other neighborhood kids. Like them, he wanted to make some spending money after school. In Massachusetts, where he lived, the snowy season could extend from November through March, so shoveling snow in the winter and cutting grass in the summer seemed like a good way to pick up a little extra cash. Unlike the other boys, however, Tim quickly graduated from a borrowed lawn mower to a small truck with a plow, a walk-behind mower, and a trailer. By the time he graduated from Salem State University, Tim's plowing and landscaping business was bringing in more than $500,000 per year and employed seven full-time workers.

In his mid-twenties, Tim LeBlanc was still baby-faced. But underestimating him based on his appearance would be a big mistake.

The Startup

In 2005, Tim was picking up spending money by doing what so many teenagers did—mowing two or three neighbor's lawns. He also cut a lawn in a nearby town that his dad drove him to weekly. One of his neighbors took him under his wing and began teaching him the basics of landscaping, and Tim enjoyed the outdoor work. It didn't take too long for his parents to tire of carting Tim around to lawns in different towns. When he saw a small pickup truck for sale, Tim easily persuaded his parents to subsidize its purchase and the initial insurance costs. As a minor, Tim's income and expenses were all subsumed into his parents' taxes and insurance policies.

At 16, Tim was too young to have his driver's license, but he did have his permit and, with his new truck, he was able to learn elements of snow plowing. Another neighbor plowed local driveways and began teaching Tim some of the tricks of the trade. In a short time, Tim was hooked. He took his driver's test in a snowstorm, passed it handily, and he and his father learned snow plowing on the job.

That first winter, they plowed a dozen driveways. The following summer, the landscaping neighbor asked Tim to cover his list for two weeks, and Tim earned $2,000 in that time. Heady stuff for a high schooler.

At the end of that summer, he bought his own walk-behind 36″ mower and a small, closed trailer. He made a conscious decision to reinvest his revenues into the young company rather than spend his profits on fun or save them for future needs. The small business began to grow.

In 2006, still operating under his parents' supervision, Tim ran an ad for Mystic Landscaping (named for the Mystic River north of Boston) in the local Peabody and Lynnfield newspaper, which reached 7,000 houses a week. His mom fielded an average of two calls each day and soon Tim was responsible for 23 lawns. This was his junior year in high school, and classes were over by 1:50 pm. Three days a week he cut lawns from 2:30 to 7:00 pm, and he did other jobs on the remaining days while school was in session. In the summer, he got a job as groundskeeper for a local golf course, where he worked a full week from 6:00 am to 2:30 pm, leaving him time to mow lawns and apply the landscaping lessons he was learning at the golf course to his residential clients. He had too much work to handle on his own, so he hired a friend at $15/hour to help him. The two boys earned more doing their mowing than they earned at the golf course but, according to Tim, "I learned about pricing and estimating time and materials, and that was worth it."

In the fall, Tim used his summer earnings to buy a new enclosed trailer to transport his equipment. One morning, very early, he and his friend were driving to work when suddenly Tim could no longer see the trailer behind his truck. For a terrifying moment, he saw it swing out into the lane for oncoming traffic as the hitch on the ten-year-old vehicle snapped. He was able to bring it under control and call for help, but soon thereafter his dad had to co-sign for a new truck. This time, he bought a showroom vehicle, and he continued to purchase new trucks as needed. No more broken hitches for him.

The new truck came in handy during the winter of 2006–2007, when he plowed 30 driveways. By the time he graduated high school, Tim owned a truck and a trailer, and used his friend's truck when he needed additional transport. The same year, he filed his "doing business as" statement and transferred his records, files, taxes, and insurance to his own business name.

During his first year at Salem State University, his schedule allowed him to go to class, work in his business, go to class, and work in his business. He no longer needed a co-signer to buy his next truck, and he maintained a grueling schedule of school, work, homework, work, a little sleep, and back to work.

He was running his business by instinct and the seat of his pants, coupled with the need for only a small amount of sleep.

Case Questions

1.   What opportunities are available to you for starting a small business that you could run while going to school? Compare your idea with Tim's. What are the key similarities and key differences?
2.   What form of business ownership would you have recommended to Tim when he launched Mystic Landscaping? When, if at all, should he change this form of ownership? Why?

Case 2.2 Information Technology Experts, Inc. of Maryland: Partnerships and Governance: Perils and Pitfalls

Karen Hallows and Sue White

William Peace,[5] CEO of ITE, Inc. had successfully brought his IT consulting firm through a period of rapid growth through acquisition in the 2000s. In 2010, he needed to fully integrate the acquisitions and decide on the best future strategy. William's problem was more than just a decision about growth and financing, however. It was also about how to deal with the dysfunctional dynamics of the three partners who owned the firm. If they could not come to a resolution, William believed his only choices were to look for a buyer, to restructure the firm's debt, to find financing to grow, or to spin off prior acquisitions to solve his governance dilemma.

ITE, Inc. was founded by John Swenson in his garage in the mid-1990s. At this same time, William Peace was earning a degree in engineering and, after graduation in 1997, he met the third partner, Carl Boatwright. These two worked together for two years, always talking about someday having their own company. In 1999, they launched Musicmedia.com, with a quarter of a million dollars raised from friends and family. After two years, they decided to close the doors, and William began looking for new opportunities. He met John at a paintball camp competition in West Virginia. John told William about his small IT company, which was rapidly losing money, and said he needed help. John and William decided to join together as partners, bringing Carl in as chief technology officer. All agreed that each should be an equal partner in the company, but with the proviso that William and Carl needed to turn around the company within the year or lose their shares in the company.

The firm enjoyed rapid growth from 2002 to 2005, followed by a period of multiple acquisitions of smaller firms. But in 2008 the recession hit, and the company experienced a steep drop in business. This left the firm with a declining client base, $500,000 in debt, and little ability to borrow more. The bank debt was secured by collateral put up by William and John, who received cash to compensate them for the stock and bond certificates and real estate collateral that they pledged to their lender. At this point in ITE's life, William was open to all financing options. However, the other two partners were less flexible.

The Partnership Agreement

William, Carl and John had developed a formal, written partners' agreement when they first joined forces. ITE, Inc. was structured as an S corporation according to its shareholders' agreement, dated October 11, 2005 (abbreviated bylaws are given at the end of this case). Each partner would own an equal share of the company, and none of them invested any equity. The company thrived under William's leadership and, at first, the three had an excellent working relationship. The governance structure began to unravel after the company started making acquisitions and the partners began to take on debt to finance those acquisitions.

As is typical with small businesses, the bank required personal guarantees from the three owners. Carl refused to put up any personal collateral. Carl's wife was the primary breadwinner in his family, and he only wanted to do work that was fun for him. William put up some of his stock certificates as collateral, while John's house, a gift from his father-in-law that had been in his wife's family for three generations, served as his collateral. Carl recognized that this meant that William and John were taking on more risk than he was, and to compensate for the higher risk, William and John received a one-time cash payment from profits. John became highly risk-averse. He didn't want to lose his family home and he wouldn't approve any decisions that he thought might put his home at risk. As time went on, John's wife became more adamant that their home be released as loan collateral.

William discovered that the partnership agreement worked fine when things were going well, but after the partners started having disagreements, William saw lots of holes in the agreement. The partners had differing ideas about the best way out of financial problems. William had no discretion to make decisions on his own as CEO. All major and most minor decisions required him to call a formal meeting of all three partners. They were required to follow Robert's Rules of Order, which made the decision-making process cumbersome. They had no operating budget so every expense had to be decided upon by all three partners. William found that he and John were usually on opposite sides of an issue, each trying to convince Carl of the merits of their points of view. Carl became a pinball and it took him weeks to decide on anything. He was not a confrontational person, so he retreated from any issue and became so fed up that he wanted nothing more to do with the company.

At an Impasse

William felt he had to break the logjam somehow. The firm could continue as it had been operating, a frustrating experience for all three partners. The firm could find a buyer and sell out, but market timing for a sale was poor, as most potential buyers were looking for fire sale bargains. One of ITE's biggest liabilities was its "non-owner notes," debt held by the former owners of the companies ITE had acquired. The firm did not have the cash to pay off these notes when they were due. William thought ITE, Inc. could reorganize this debt, if necessary, declaring Chapter 7 or 11 bankruptcies. William wasn't ready to give up on the firm under Chapter 7 liquidation. Chapter 11 might allow the company to shed or renegotiate some of its unsecured debt. Or ITE could find the necessary financing to continue to grow and thrive.

"But, when three owners can't agree, and none of us is willing to walk away, getting financing will be the biggest challenge," William concluded. "Unless we can figure out a better way to solve our problems."

Case Questions

1. What are some of the governance issues in a small firm where the principals cannot agree on a future course of action?
2. What are William's options for ITE, Inc. and what are the pros and cons of each option? (Options may include selling, bankruptcy, or continuing the business through organic growth or growth by acquisition, or other options.)
3. What should William do to alleviate the governance problem of having three owners who have difficulty agreeing?

Bylaws of Information Technology Experts, Inc. of Maryland

Note: Less relevant sections have been redacted.

Section 3 Special Meetings

Special meetings of the shareholders for any purpose or purposes may be called by the president, and must be called by him or her on receipt of a written request from the holders of 25 percent of the shares then outstanding and entitled to vote.

Section 5 Quorum

At any meeting of the shareholders, the holders of a majority of the shares entitled to vote then issued and outstanding shall constitute a quorum, except as otherwise provided by law.

Section 6 Voting

At each meeting of the shareholders, every holder of shares then entitled to vote may vote in person or by proxy, and shall have one vote for each share registered in his or her name.

Section 7 Number of Directors, Tenure, Vacancies

The business and affairs of the corporation shall be managed and controlled by a board of directors of not more than 3 nor less than 1 director, who shall be elected annually by the shareholders at the annual meeting. The number of directors at any given time shall be solely in the discretion of the shareholders, in accordance with the procedures for electing and/or removing directors outlined in these bylaws. Each director shall hold office until the election of his or her successor. Any director may resign at any time. Vacancies occurring among the directors may be filled by the directors or, based on a vote of the shareholders, may be left open until the next annual meeting of the shareholders.

Section 11 Quorum

A majority of the board of directors shall constitute a quorum at all meetings of the board.

Section 12 Officers

The officers of the corporation shall be a president, a vice president, a secretary, and a treasurer, who shall be elected annually by the directors and who shall hold office during the pleasure of the directors, and any other assistants the board of directors may determine to elect at any time. All officer positions may be united in one person. All vacancies occurring among any of the above officers shall be filled by the directors. Any officer may be removed at any time by the affirmative vote of a majority of the board of directors at a special meeting of the board of directors called for that purpose or by a majority vote of the stockholders at a special meeting of the stockholders called for that purpose.

Section 13 Subordinate Officers

The board may appoint such other officers and agents with such powers and duties as it shall deem necessary.

Section 14 The President

The president shall preside at all meetings of the shareholders and directors. He or she shall have general management and control of the business and affairs of the corporation.

Section 15 The Vice President

The vice president shall, in the absence or disability of the president, exercise the powers and perform the duties of the president. He or she shall also generally assist the president and exercise such other powers and perform such other duties as shall be prescribed by the directors.

Section 16 The Treasurer

The treasurer shall have the custody of all funds, securities, evidences of indebtedness and other personal property of the corporation and shall deposit the same in such bank or trust company as shall be designated by the directors of the corporation or the president. He or she shall receive and give receipts and acquaintances for monies paid in on account of the corporation and shall pay out of the funds on hand all bills, payrolls, and other just debts of the corporation of whatever nature upon maturity of the same; he or she shall enter regularly in books of the corporation to be kept by him or her for that purpose full and accurate accounts of all monies received and paid out by him or her on account of the corporation, and he or she shall perform all other duties incident to the office of treasurer.

Section 17 The Secretary

The secretary shall keep the minutes of all proceedings of the directors and the shareholders; he or she shall attend to the giving and serving of all notices to the shareholders and directors, or the notices required by law or these bylaws; he or she shall affix the seal of the corporation to deeds, contracts, and other instruments in writing requiring a seal, when duly signed; he or she shall have charge of the certificate books and stock books, and such other books and papers as the board may direct, and he or she shall perform all other duties incident to the office of secretary.

Section 18 Salaries

The salaries of all officers shall be fixed by the board of directors.

Section 19 Certificates of Stock

Certificates of stock shall be issued in numerical order from the stock certificate book; they shall be signed by the president and by the secretary of the corporation and the corporate seal shall be affixed thereto. A record of each certificate shall be kept on the stub thereof.

Section 20 Transfer of Shares

Shares may be transferred on the books of the corporation by the holder in person or by his or her attorney upon the surrender and cancellation of certificates for a like number of shares. Should the shareholders unanimously enter into a so-called "closed corporation agreement" or other shareholder agreement limiting the transfer of stock, such stock shall be transferred on the books of the corporation only in accordance with the terms of such agreement.

Section 21 Board to Declare Dividends

The directors may from time to time, as they shall see fit, declare dividends upon the capital stock from surplus.

Section 22 Indemnification of Officers, Directors, Employees, and Agents

The corporation hereby indemnifies from liability each of its officers, directors, employees, or agents who is a party or is threatened to be made a party to any threatened, pending or completed action, suit or proceeding ("actions"), whether civil, criminal, administrative, or investigative (other than an action by or in the right of the corporation) by reason of the fact that such person is or was a director, officer, employee, or agent of the corporation, or is or was serving at the request of the corporation as a director, officer, employee, or agent of another corporation, partnership, joint venture, trust, or other enterprise. This indemnification shall include expenses (including attorneys' fees), judgments, fines, and amounts paid in settlement actually and reasonably incurred by the person in connection with such actions. In response to any request for indemnification, the corporation shall promptly make or cause to be made, by any of the methods permitted by law, a determination as to whether each prospective indemnity acted in good faith and in a manner such indemnity reasonably believed to be lawful. Under no circumstances shall the corporation be permitted to make such an indemnification unless it can be determined that such indemnity acted in good faith and in a manner such indemnity reasonably believed to be in or not opposed to the best interests of the corporation, and, in the case of any criminal action or proceeding, had no reasonable cause to believe that his conduct was unlawful.

Section 23 Depositories

The funds of the corporation shall be deposited in such bank or trust company, and checks drawn against such funds shall be signed in such manner, as may be determined from time to time by the directors.

Section 24 Notice and Waiver of Notice

Any notice required to be given by these bylaws may be given by mailing or telegraphing the same to the person entitled thereto at his or her address as shown on the corporation's books and such notice shall be deemed to have been given at the time of such mailing or telegraphing. Any notice required by these bylaws to be given may be waived by the person entitled to such notice.

Section 25 Power of Directors to Amend, etc.

The board of directors shall have power to make, amend, and repeal the bylaws of the corporation by a vote of a majority of all the directors at any regular or special meeting of the board.

Section 26 Power of Shareholders to Amend, etc.

The shareholders may make, alter, amend, and repeal the bylaws of the corporation at any annual meeting or at a special meeting called for the purpose and all bylaws made by the directors may be altered or repealed by the shareholders.

> Adopted at the special meeting of the Board of
> Directors of Information Technology Experts,
> Inc. of Maryland, held on December 16, 2004.
>
> William Peace
> Chair, Board of Directors

Notes

1 Note that each state has different filing requirements for sole proprietorship and different names for the form. For example, in New Hampshire a form called "Application for Registration of Trade Name" needs to be filed with the state. In Massachusetts, registration is at the city level, e.g. the City of Peabody requires a "Business Certificate" to be filed. Forms from these two states are included in Appendix 2.1.
2 "Community property" states include Arizona, California, Idaho, Louisiana, Nevada, New Mexico, Texas, Washington, and Wisconsin. Married couples in Alaska can elect to have their properties treated as community property. All other states are considered "common law" states (http://www.irs.gov/publications/p555/ar01.html).
3 Tax codes for partnerships are very complicated and beyond the scope of this textbook. Consult a tax professional if you plan to set up a partnership.
4 The fee was $100 in 2013 for filing either an Article of Incorporation or an LLC Certificate of Formation in New Hampshire. In Massachusetts, the fee for filing a Certificate of Registration (LLC) was $500 and the fee for filing an Article of Incorporation was $275 for up to 275,000 shares, plus $100 for each additional 100,000 shares.
5 The names of the firm and of the three owners have been changed to protect the privacy of the firm.

Bibliography

Allen, N., & Daniels, S. (2013). *2013 Thumbtack.Com Small Business Friendliness Survey: Methodology & Analysis Conducted in Partnership With the Kauffman Foundation*. San Francisco, CA: Thumbtack.

Anderson, K. E., Pope, T. R., & Rupert, T. J. (2014). *Prentice Hall's Federal Taxation 2014 Corporations, Partnerships, Estates & Trusts*. Upper Saddle River, NJ: Prentice Hall 2014.

Aristotle. *Politics: A Treatise on Government, Book 5*, Chapter 4. (1303b29)

Freeman, L. S. (Ed.). (2014). *The Partnership Tax Practice Series* New York, NY: Practicing Law Institute.

Keir, J., & Tissot, J. (2013). *Income Tax Planning Textbook* Middletown, OH: Keir Educational Resources.

Lorence, R. (1999). The family limited partnership: a planning technique. *The CPA Journal, July 1999.*

Ridgway, S. (2009). Should my company be an LLC, an S-corp or both? *SBA Community Blog* http://www.sba.gov/community/blogs/community-blogs/business-law-advisor/should-my-company-be-llc-s-corp-or-both (accessed 12/6/2013).

US Internal Revenue Service. *Business Structures* http://www.irs.gov/Businesses/Small-Businesses-&-Self-Employed/Business-Structures (accessed 11/11/2013)

US Internal Revenue Service. *Husband and Wife Business* http://www.irs.gov/Businesses/Small-Businesses-&-Self-Employed/Husband-and-Wife-Business (accessed 11/11/2013)

US Internal Revenue Service. *Industries/Professions Tax Centers* http://www.irs.gov/Businesses/Small-Businesses-&-Self-Employed/Industries-Professions (accessed 11/11/2013)

US Internal Revenue Service. *IRS Publication 541—Partnerships* http://www.irs.gov/publications/p541/ar02.html (accessed 11/11/2013)

US Internal Revenue Service. *IRS Publication 555—Community Property* http://www.irs.gov/publications/p555/ar01.html (accessed 11/11/2013)

US Internal Revenue Service. *Partnerships* http://www.irs.gov/Businesses/Small-Businesses-&-Self-Employed/Partnerships (accessed 11/11/2013)

US Internal Revenue Service. *SOI Tax Stats—Integrated Business Data* http://www.irs.gov/uac/SOI-Tax-Stats-Integrated-Business-Data (accessed 11/11/2013)

US Internal Revenue Service. *Sole Proprietorships* http://www.irs.gov/Businesses/Small-Businesses-&-Self-Employed/Sole-Proprietorships (accessed 11/11/2013)

3 Financing a Business

The importance of money essentially flows from its being a link between the present and the future.

John Maynard Keynes

Finding money to fund a business is a challenge for nearly all entrepreneurs. Many business owners use their own savings and borrow from relatives and friends to get started. Some rely on credit cards. The drawbacks of these strategies include limited funds and high interest rates and, sooner or later, a business will need to obtain financing from external sources. This chapter introduces various sources of financing and their pros and cons from the perspective of a small business owner. Before going into specific financing alternatives, it is useful to first consider the characteristics of debt versus equity financing and the different stages of a firm's life cycle.

Life Cycle of a Business

We can compare the life cycle of a business to the stages of human life, except that a business has the option of prolonging its life indefinitely. Each stage presents its own unique operational and financial challenges, as described. Although there are many variations of the life cycle construct, they all include at least five generally recognized stages (Figure 3.1):

1. seed or startup;
2. launch and growth;
3. maturity;
4. expansion or re-visioning;
5. exit or death.

Stage 1—Seed or Startup

In the human life cycle, the initial stage includes conception and birth. For a business, it includes the origination of an idea, development of a plan,

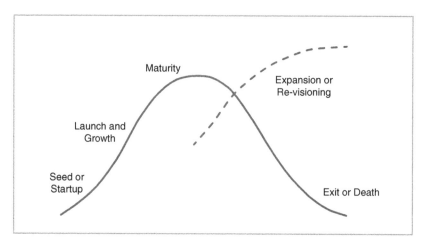

Figure 3.1 Business Life Cycle

obtaining initial capitalization, and all activities prior to the actual launch of the business. For a product-oriented business, such as the manufacture and sales of a new kind of athletic shoe, the entrepreneur will have both a concept and a developed prototype. The entrepreneur will also have obtained a patent to protect the new product from piracy. For a service-oriented business, the entrepreneur has a detailed business model, with concept drawings or mock-up designs of the service to be provided. The business structure is simple and is centered around the owner. The primary task of the owner is to pull together resources, suppliers, vendors, and consultants, and to design the distribution system for the product or service.

Financing at Stage 1 usually comes from the entrepreneur's assets with the assistance of family and personal friends as needed.

Stage 2—Launch and Growth

This stage equates to the long developmental period in a human life that extends from infancy through adolescence and young adulthood. Just as children change dramatically from babyhood to adulthood, so does the small business during this phase of the life cycle. In Stage 2, the business owner produces and launches the product or makes its services available to the public. The founder must contend with numerous developmental and operational issues, some of which may disguise or cloak the financial challenges to be expected.

Rapid growth leads to an increase in the number of employees and complexity of the business structure, along with considerable financial activity during this period. A business at this stage is not necessarily profitable, but it requires access to larger financial resources than a founder can normally supply. Significant debt or formal external equity investment is often needed for the first time.

Stage 3—Maturity

Stage 3 corresponds to the fully adult stage of a human life. You may be married or have a life partner, you may have children or have made the decision not to have children, you are established in your profession, and you can see the progression of your life. By this stage, a business has established itself in the marketplace and has formalized its structure. It may have diversified its product or service line, it may have expanded geographically, and it certainly has developed its own set of administrative (called "bureaucratic" in business) procedures.

The business is now generating revenue and positive cash flow, and financing is needed to maintain the smooth operations of the firm.

Stage 4—Expansion or Re-Visioning

You can compare this stage of development to the person who changes his or her life drastically, either through personal reinvention upon retirement or the sudden career shift that can occur when you are exposed to a new opportunity. These reinventions are often said to "keep a person young" by giving an individual a chance to explore new directions, to refocus on his or her passions, or to gain a second, third, or fourth chance at fulfillment. After the mature stage, a business must re-vision its purpose in order to sustain its viability. Sometimes a business encounters opportunities to expand, sometimes to adapt to a changing market, and sometimes to develop new directions entirely. Without expansion or re-visioning, a business will continue on a downward trajectory. All these changes require significant investment and external financing is often needed again at this stage.

Stage 5—Exit, Harvest, or Death

Death is inevitable in the human life cycle, but it is not inevitable in the business life cycle. Certainly, if an owner skips over Stage 4 and the business does not take the opportunity to redefine itself, it will phase out and die. However, a wise and forward-thinking business owner will develop an exit strategy to protect his or her assets, generate ongoing income, or gain a lump sum to provide for personal expenses.

At this stage, financial decisions have a different purpose and are structured differently. You can learn more about exit strategies in Chapter 10.

Debt Versus Equity—The Capital Structure Decision

3.1 Owner's Debt

For tax purposes, entrepreneurs often classify their cash investment in the business as debt and issue stock with nominal par value to themselves. If the owner's investment is considered debt, when the business starts generating cash flow and the owner withdraws cash from the business, the initial payout can be counted as repayment of the loan principal and, therefore, not taxable. If the owner's investment is considered equity, any cash payout will be considered dividends. The assumption is that the owner wants to retain control of the business and will not want to sell back shares. Debt to the entrepreneur created for tax purposes does not carry the same financial risk as debt to a bank or an outside lender.

In finance, the term "capital structure" refers to the proportion of debt versus equity that a business is carrying. The trade-off between debt and equity is risk versus cost and control (Table 3.1). The financial risk of using debt is well-known to business owners. If a business fails to make interest or principal payments on its loan, it may fall into default, putting itself at risk of bankruptcy. An intangible cost is the added stress on the entrepreneur. On the upside, lenders do not share in the firm's profit and do not have control over how the business is run unless they foreclose on the business in the event of bankruptcy. The cost of debt is usually significantly lower than the cost of equity demanded by venture capital firms or angel investors. In addition, interest on debt is tax deductible as an expense, whereas payments to equity investors are not and come directly out of profits.

Many small businesses follow some form of order of preference for funding, starting with internal funds generated by the business itself, then debt financing,

Table 3.1 Debt and Equity at a Glance

	Benefits	*Disadvantages*
Debt	No sharing of profits No sharing of control Lower cost Interest on debt is tax deductible	Higher financial risk, potentially leading to bankruptcy Stress on the entrepreneur

Equity	Amount of capital available not
	  limited
	Investors provide experience and
	  skills
	Maintain and often decrease
	  financial risk, increasing the
	  business's borrowing ability
		Sharing or loss of control
		Dividends to investors are not tax
		  deductible
		Higher cost
		Sharing future profits

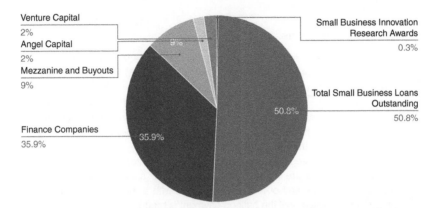

Figure 3.2 Share of Financing by Category, 2012 (Small Business Administration, Office of Advocacy, 2014)

Note: Total small business loans are defined as all loans outstanding under $1 million, including SBA loans. Finance company lending consists of all business receivables outstanding.

and finally moving to external equity financing. According to the Small Business Administration (SBA), in 2012 debt financing represented 85 percent of external funding for small businesses (Figure 3.2). The next section discusses sources of debt financing followed by a section on sources of equity financing. The last part of this chapter examines a new source of financing, crowdfunding.

Sources of Debt Financing

According to a Small Business Administration report (Small Business Administration, Office of Advocacy, 2014), in 2013 total small business loans outstanding were over $1 trillion, with banks providing $585 billion and finance companies providing $422 billion, including real estate mortgages and equipment loans. SBA-guaranteed loans accounted for about $24.5 billion, or about 1/40 of the total.

Types of Loan

Asset-backed loans are secured by real assets and include mortgages, equipment loans and inventory loans. The assets serve as collateral, and if a firm defaults on an asset-backed loan, the lender can sell off or repossess the specific asset as repayment. Unsecured business loans, such as term loans, do not require any real assets as collateral and are often used to finance permanent working capital, business expansion, and acquisition. Both asset-backed and unsecured term loans are generally fixed term amortized loans with either fixed or variable interest rates.

3.2 Amortized Loans

A key feature of an amortized loan is that each payment contains both an interest and a principal component. As a result, each payment repays not just interest, but part of the original loan amount as well. An amortized loan with fixed interest rate has equal payments throughout the life of the loan. Payments on an amortized loan with variable interest rates change when the index interest rate changes. One of the most common index interest rates is the LIBOR (London Inter-bank Offered Rate).

With a fully amortized loan, the loan is fully paid with zero balance when all scheduled payments are made. Some loans require a balloon payment—a lump sum due at the end of the loan. For loans with a balloon payment, the loan is not fully repaid until the balloon payment is made.

Lines of credit are temporary, short-term, unsecured loans that are often used for seasonal cash needs or emergency funds. A main feature of lines of credit is that borrowers only need to make payments when the line is used, that is, when they actually borrow money. Interest rates on lines of credit are variable and are tied to a pre-specified index interest rate, such as LIBOR. An unused line of credit is a promise by a bank to lend up to a specific, identified amount to a business. A line of credit is similar to the overdraft protection for a checking account—it is there when you need it. There are usually no explicit fees associated with a line of credit provided by banks and credit unions. Instead, a minimum combined monthly balance or transaction volume is required to qualify for an open line.

Factoring, the next form of financing, is technically (legally) not a loan. Companies specializing in accounts receivable factoring, purchase order factoring, and business or merchant cash advance (MCA) provide cash to business owners in exchange for future revenues or customer payments. Since these cash advances are not considered loans, such "lenders" are not subject to federal and state financial regulations, including the usury laws that prohibit exorbitant interest rates. Owing to a lack of regulation, contract terms vary greatly between companies. Even within the same company, terms may differ significantly for large versus small businesses. There are no disclosure requirements, and the true costs of borrowing are often obfuscated and buried in fine print. Some businesses consider this source of financing their last resort for necessary cash or emergencies.

Banks

Banks, from large commercial banks to local savings and loans, are traditionally the primary source of financing for small business. A 2004 Kauffman

Table 3.2 Bank Small Business Loans

	Micro business lending (less than $100,000)	Macro business lending ($100,000 to $1 million)	Total
Loan amount	$93,244,690,000	$190,201,717,000	$283,446,407,000
Percentage of total, by amount	33%	67%	100%
Number of loans	18,469,303	791,984	19,261,287
Percentage of total, by number	96%	4%	100%

Source: (US Small Business Administration, Office of Advocacy, 2011).

survey (Table 3.2) found that business loans represented the second largest group of financing dollars for startup firms. The SBA classifies business loans less than $100,000 as micro business lending and loans between $100,000 and $1 million as macro business lending. Table 3.2 shows that the majority of business loans in 2012, 96 percent, were micro business loans, totaling over $93 billion.

The US Chamber of Commerce recommends supplying the following documents when applying for a small business loan for a startup firm:

- a personal financial statement and 1–3 years of personal federal income tax returns;
- projected startup cost estimates;
- projected balance sheets and income statements for at least 2 years;
- projected cash flow statements for at least 1 year;
- if available, assets with evidence of ownership and other collaterals;
- a business plan (see Chapter 11 for a discussion of business plans);
- a break-even analysis that covers loan and interest payments in terms of dollars or units sold.

For a startup business with no history of revenues and profits, banks often require owners to co-sign the business loan. In such cases, the owners remain personally liable for the amount of the loan, and the bank can claim payment against their personal property even if the business is an LLC or a corporation. However, the owners' personal property remains protected against other liabilities, such as lawsuits.

For existing businesses with more than three years of history, banks usually require the following documents when applying for a loan:

- income statements and business balance sheets for the preceding three years;
- projected balance sheets and income statements for the next two years;

- projected cash flow statements for at least the next 12 months;
- personal and business tax returns for the preceding three years;
- intended uses of loan proceeds or a business plan (if the loan is for significant expansion or acquisition of another business);
- asset-specific information for real estate mortgages, equipment loans, and other asset-backed loans.

Small Business Administration Loans

The SBA provides loan guarantees to financial institutions on behalf of small business owners. The loans are provided by regular banks and financial companies. In 2013, the SBA guaranteed over 54,000 loans, totaling $25.5 billion. The definition of a small business varies by industry, and the SBA uses the North American Industry Classification System (NAICS) to make the determination (http://www.census.gov/eos/www/naics/). For some industries, such as contracting, convenience stores and restaurants, the definition is based on annual revenues.[1] For other industries, such as bakeries and breweries, the definition is based on the number of employees. Each sector within an industry may have different size definitions. For example, within the restaurant industry, the size limit for cafeterias and buffets is $25.5 million in revenue, whereas for most other types of restaurants, from full-service to mobile food service, the limit is $7 million in annual revenues. Each state has at least one SBA office, and you can contact them directly for assistance.

The SBA offers many programs to small businesses. The two most popular loan programs are the 7(a) Loan Guaranty Program for general small business loans and the 504 Loan Program for real estate and equipment loans.[2] You can also use 7(a) loans for real estate and equipment purchases, but the 504 loan program provides for a larger combined maximum loan value.

The 7(a) Loan Guaranty Program can be used for many financing needs of small businesses, including loans for long-term and short-term working capital, purchasing equipment and furniture, real estate, acquiring an existing business and, under some conditions, refinancing existing business debt. The terms vary depending on what the loan is used for: 25 years for real estate, up to 10 years for equipment, and generally up to 7 years for working capital. The term for equipment loans depends on the useful life of the equipment.

Most 7(a) loans are fully amortized, i.e. each monthly payment includes both interest and principal, and at the end of the term, the loans will be paid in full. The loans can be fixed-rate, which means that the interest rate stays the same throughout the life of the loan. The payment amount also stays constant. However, many 7(a) loans have variable rates tied to interest rate changes in the financial market. For variable rate loans, the payment amount changes with interest rates. The actual interest rate is negotiated between the borrower and the lender, with maximums set by the SBA. The lender cannot charge prepayment penalties, but the SBA will charge the borrower a prepayment fee if the loan is for longer than 15 years and is prepaid within the first three years. Careful planning can help you avoid such penalties.

An important provision of the 7(a) Loan Guaranty Program is that the SBA expects every 7(a) loan to be fully secured. This means that businesses have to put up collaterals for 7(a) loans. In the case of real estate and equipment loans, the natural collateral is the asset itself. For working capital loans, businesses have to provide other assets as collateral. If a business does not have assets that can be used as collateral, the SBA may require personal assets, such as the owner's residence, to be used. In addition, the SBA requires personal guarantees from all owners who hold 20 percent of more of the equity of the business. Thus, similar to banks requiring owners to co-sign business loans, owners remain personally liable for the amount of the 7(a) loan, and the SBA can claim payment against their personal property even if the business is an LLC or a corporation. Since the SBA provides guarantees to the bank, the bank receives payment even if the business defaults. As a result, businesses that may not qualify for conventional bank loans or may only qualify at higher interest rates can benefit from the SBA loan program.

According to the SBA, to be eligible for the 7(a) Loan Guaranty Program, businesses must:

- operate for profit;
- be small, as defined by the SBA;
- be engaged in, or propose to do business in, the United States or its possessions;
- have reasonable invested equity;
- use alternative financial resources, including personal assets, before seeking financial assistance;
- be able to demonstrate a need for the loan proceeds;
- use the funds for a sound business purpose;
- not be delinquent on any existing debt obligations to the US government.

The second most popular SBA loan program is the CDC/504 program for real estate and equipment loans. CDC stands for Certified Development Companies, which are non-profit corporations certified and regulated by the SBA to process all CDC/504 loans. The eligibility requirements are similar to the 7(a) Loan Guaranty Program, except that the business must have a tangible net worth less than $15 million and an average net income less than $5 million after taxes for the preceding two years. As the program title implies, CDC/504 loan proceeds can only be used for real estate and long-term machinery and equipment. CDC/504 loans are more complicated, and while there is no legal minimum loan amount, many CDCs set a minimum loan amount, ranging from $50,000 to $250,000. A borrower usually provides at least 10 percent of the loan amount as down payment. The loans typically come from two sources: a conventional first mortgage from a bank or credit union and an SBA-guaranteed subordinated debenture, like a second mortgage. The borrower makes a single payment each month to the CDC, which allocates the payment to the bank and the debenture holders. Since the maximum CDC/504 debenture amount is $5 million, when combined with a conventional first mortgage up to $6.5 million, a business can borrow up to $11.5 million through this program.

The SBA also offers a microloan program for very small businesses through special intermediary lenders, which are non-profit community-based organizations. These organizations range from the Disabled Veterans Assistance Foundation, which serves veterans nationwide to regional programs such as the Economic Development Industrial Corporation of Lynn in Massachusetts. The microloan program provides loans up to $50,000. Eligibility requirements vary and are set by the intermediaries. Some borrowers may be required to fulfill business training or planning before their loan applications are considered. Proceeds from microloans can be used for working capital, inventory, supplies, furniture, fixtures, machinery and equipment. These loans cannot be used for real estate or to pay existing debts. The maximum repayment term is six years. Interest rates varies by intermediary and depend on the costs to the intermediary from the US Treasury. Table 3.3 compares the 7(a) loan, CDC/504 loan, and microloan programs.

Alternative Lending Sources

Traditional bank loans, especially those with SBA guarantees, are the least expensive form of business financing. Careful financial planning will greatly enhance a business's ability to obtain funding from these traditional sources. However, sometimes a business may find itself in need of cash and have to resort to alternative lending options. Since many of these alternative sources are not regulated, it is important to examine the terms of the contracts carefully.

Peer-to-Peer Lending

Peer-to-peer (P2P) lending is a relatively new source of debt financing for individuals and businesses. The business model of most P2P lending companies is to match small businesses and individual borrowers directly with investors. Some P2P lending companies also partner with banks. In 2008, the SEC ruled that P2P lending companies must register their securities in accordance with the Securities Act of 1933; the same requirement that applies to investment banks issuing bonds to investors.

One big difference between P2P lending and investment banking is size. In 2013, investment banks helped companies issue $1.11 trillion in bonds,

Table 3.3 SBA Loan Program Comparison

	SBA CDC/504 loan	SBA 7(a) loan	SBA Microloan
Purpose	Commercial real estate and equipment	General purpose	Limited purposes
Loan size	Up to $5,000,000 in SBA subordinated debentures plus up to $6,250,000 in bank loans	Up to $5,000,000 in total loan amount with up to $3,750,000 guaranteed by SBA	Up to $50,000
Interest rate	Fixed rate	Variable rate; some limited fixed-rate options	Variable rate; some limited fixed-rate options
	Interest rates on 504 loans are set at the time the loans are funded. Each month, the rate is set at an increment above the current market rate for five-year and ten-year U.S. treasury issues.	Interest rates are negotiated between the borrower and the lender subject to mandated SBA maximums.	Interest rates are negotiated between the borrower and the lender.
Terms available and amortization periods	20 years fully amortized for real estate loans	Up to 25 years fully amortized for real estate loans	Varies and is negotiated between the borrower and the intermediary
	10 years fully amortized for equipment loans	Up to 10 years fully amortized for equipment and business acquisition loans	
	No balloon payments	No balloon payments	
Provider	Certified development companies (CDCs)	Banks, savings and loans, credit unions and some specialized lenders	Intermediaries approved by the SBA
Loan structure	50% bank loan (traditional loan, not SBA guaranteed).	Loan structure is negotiated between borrower and lender. SBA can guarantee up to 85% on loans up to $150000 and 75% on loans over $150000.	Loan structure is negotiated between borrower and intermediaries.
	40% CDC loan (SBA guaranteed debenture)	10% down payment (minimum)	
	10% borrower down payment		
Use of loan proceeds	Purchase existing building	Expand, acquire, or start a business	Working capital
	Land acquisition and ground-up construction (includes soft cost development fees)	Purchase or construct real estate	Inventory or supplies
	Expansion of existing building	Refinance existing business debt	Furniture or fixtures
	Finance building improvements	Buy equipment	Machinery or equipment
	Purchase equipment	Provide working capital	
		Construct leasehold improvements	
		Purchase inventory	

(Continued)

Table 3.3 SBA Loan Program Comparison (Continued)

	SBA CDC/504 loan	SBA 7(a) loan	SBA Microloan
Loan program requirements	51% owner occupancy required for existing building	51% owner occupancy required for existing building	
	60% owner occupancy required for new construction	60% owner occupancy required for new construction	
	Equipment with a minimum 10 year economic life	All assets financed must be used to the direct benefit of the business	
Collateral	The project assets being financed are used as collateral.	All available assets (both business and personal), up to the loan amount or until all assets have been pledged, are expected to be used as collateral. This includes personal residence unless bank can justify why it is unnecessary.	
	Personal guarantees are required from all owners of 20 percent or more of the equity of the business.	Personal guarantees are required from all owners of 20 percent or more of the equity of the business. Bank may require personal guarantees from owners of less than 20 percent.	
Loan fees	Fees for the bank loans (usually 50%) are negotiated with the borrower.	Loan fees from the lending institution are negotiated with the borrower.	
	Fees total approximately 3% of the SBA guaranteed debenture (usually 40%) and may be financed with the loan.	SBA guarantee fee varies with the size of the guaranteed portion of the loan. Guaranteed amount below $150,000 has no guarantee fee. It goes up to 3% for amount between $150,000 and $700,000 and, 3.5% for amount between $700,000 and $1 million, and 3.75% for amount over $1 million.	
	Servicing fee (lowest allowed by SBA) for CDC 504 plus a legal review fee	SBA guarantee fees can be financed in the 7(a) loan.	

with companies like Verizon borrowing $49 billion and Apple borrowing $17 billion. Peer-to-peer lending companies provide a platform that allows small businesses and individuals to borrow money outside the traditional banking system in a way that was previously only available to large corporations. LendingClub was one of the first P2P lending companies in the USA. The company was founded in 2007, and by February 2014, it had funded $3.6 trillion in loans. For business owners, LendingClub provided personal loans up to $35,000 for their business needs. Because these are personal loans, business owners are personally liable.

One of the advantages of P2P lending companies is speed. Many promise a loan decision within days, instead of the weeks a loan decision can sometimes take through banks. Another feature of P2P lending companies is that they use proprietary credit analysis software that may evaluate a business's credit worthiness differently from banks. They also create loan products for less than prime credit borrowers, albeit at much higher interest rates. For example, LendingClub (https://www.lendingclub.com/public/how-we-set-interest-rates.action) classifies their loans into grades A to G with five subgroups within each grade. At the time of writing, the interest rate for a grade A1 loan was 5.93 percent, while for a grade G5 loan it was 26.06 percent.

Although P2P lending is a new entrant in the lending industry, it has gained a lot of momentum and attention. A number of P2P lending companies, such as Dealstruck and SoMoLend, focus on P2P loans to small businesses. In 2014, Dealstruck offered loans from up to $250,000, including unsecured fixed-rate business term loans, revenue secured term loans, and asset based lines of credit. Dealstruck offers loans only to businesses, and does not offer personal loans. It requires businesses to be profitable, have been in operation for over one year, and have annual sales over $250,000. Many P2P lending companies consider transparency their competitive advantage over other alternative sources of financing. Their websites provide loan grade based interest rates and fees and describe in detail their loan application and approval process.

Accounts Receivable Financing

Accounts receivable financing, also known as invoice financing or accounts receivable factoring, is another source of funds for small businesses. While some large commercial banks also offer accounts receivable factoring, there are companies that specialize in this type of financing. There are two types of accounts receivable financing: non-recourse factoring and recourse factoring.

In non-recourse factoring, the financing company assumes responsibility for collecting payments from the business's customers. The financing company purchases the accounts receivable or 'invoices' from the business and, in the event of customer default, the business does not have to repay the finance company. In recourse factoring, the financing company purchases accounts receivable from the business, but in the event of non-payment by customers, the business has to buy back these bad accounts receivable. Thus, the business retains the risk of non-paying customers. Since the financing company is technically purchasing the accounts receivable, factoring is not considered a loan, and is therefore not regulated.

The actual total cost of accounts receivable financing is complicated. It depends on the factor rate (discount rate), the minimum fee (if applicable), setup fees, which may include credit verification of a business's customers, documentation fees, origination, application, and legal fees, and many other potential charges. Factoring as a form of financing has a long history in import–export and some manufacturing industries and can be a useful source of financing for medium to large businesses. However, it can be very costly for small businesses. As in all loan contracts, beware of the fine print.

3.3 Factor Financing Example

A factor financing company advertised that the factor rate was 3.5 percent for average monthly sales over $50,000 and an average collection period of 30 days with a cash advance rate over 95 percent.[3] Under this contract, a business with $80,000 average monthly sales would receive $73,200 ($80,000 × 95% − $80,000 × 3.5%) at the time of factoring and $4,000 ($80,000 × 5%) when the cash advance rate threshold was met.

Assuming all customers paid off their invoices, the business would have paid $2,800 ($80,000 × 3.5%) for getting $77,200 ($73,200 + $4,000) in cash advance. This financing arrangement translates to 3.63 percent ($2,800/$77,200) every 30 days or 44 percent (3.63% × 365 days / 30 days) per year. This is very expensive financing. This example demonstrates the importance of reading the fine print and applying the contractual agreement to a business's specific conditions.

Merchant Cash Advance

Business or merchant cash advance (MCA) is another source of short-term financing for small businesses. Following the 2008 recession, banks tightened up credit requirements for businesses and eliminated some loan products, focusing primarily on 'A-credit' small businesses. Alternative lenders seized the opportunity and moved into the lending market for non-A-credit small businesses. Technically, a merchant cash advance is not a loan; it is cash in exchange for future credit and debit card sales. This type of financing is usually very expensive compared with loans from traditional lenders. For example, Arturo Calderon, owner of Yucatan Taco Stand in Texas, obtained an $80,000 cash advance. He had to pay back $100,000, and the lender took 12 percent of his credit card sales every day until the entire amount was paid off. At that time, he was averaging over $5,700 per day in credit card sales. So the MCA company took about $684 per day from his sales. Assuming he achieved his average sales consistently with no unexpected interruptions, it would take 146 days (about 5 months) to pay off the $100,000. This cash advance translated into an interest cost of $20,000 ($100,000 − $80,000) or 25 percent ($20,000/$80,000) over 5 months. That represented an interest rate of 60 percent per year.

Almost all MCA companies require direct access to a business's future revenues. The most common arrangement is to require the business to switch its credit card processing service to a provider contracted by the MCA company. This credit card processing provider will split each transaction between the MCA company and the business according to the cash advance contract. Another arrangement is to have the business set up automatic daily or weekly cash transfers from their banking account to the MCA company. The bottom line is that payments to the MCA company take precedence over all other cash outlays.

In addition to being a very expensive source of financing, another danger of MCA is that small businesses can get trapped in a vicious cycle. Since the business is diverting cash flow toward MCA payments first, it may get behind on other bills. By the time the MCA is paid off, the business may find itself in the hole again and need cash to pay vendors it has been neglecting. Once again, it turns to MCA to get the cash it now desperately needs. This cycle is difficult to break. With these significant drawbacks, why would a small business seek cash from an MCA? MCA is clearly a funder of last resort for short-term dollars.

Sources of Equity Financing

Seeking external equity financing is a major step for business owners. When new owners join a business, they share in future profits and all business decisions. Since most small businesses do not have stock traded on an exchange, existing owners have to negotiate the value of their business with potential new owners. Thus, obtaining external financing can be a time-consuming and stressful process. Chapter 9 discusses business valuation methods, Chapter 10 discusses exit and harvest strategies, and Chapter 11 equips you with tools to present your business successfully to different types of investors. This section discusses different types of equity financing, and regulatory requirements.

New owners provide funds needed for the business to realize its full potential, and equity financing does not increase the firm's financial risk. Quite often, new owners bring expertise and experience in managing large companies, which is useful as the business grows. The two main types of private equity investor are angel investors and venture capital firms. Both become actively involved in the operation of the business they invest in and expect to exit the business, that is, sell off their equity holdings, in four to six years. Angel investors tend to invest in the earlier stages of a business and are willing to remain minority owners while acting as mentors to the entrepreneur.

Angel Investors

3.4 Accredited Investors

The US Securities and Exchange Commission defines an accredited investor in Rule 501 of Regulation D (US SEC, 2013) as:

1. a bank, insurance company, registered investment company, business development company, or small business investment company;
2. an employee benefit plan, within the meaning of the Employee Retirement Income Security Act, if a bank, insurance company, or registered investment advisor makes the investment decisions, or if the plan has total assets in excess of $5 million;
3. a charitable organization, corporation, or partnership with assets exceeding $5 million;
4. a director, executive officer, or general partner of the company selling the securities;
5. a business in which all the equity owners are accredited investors;
6. a natural person who has individual net worth, or joint net worth with the person's spouse, that exceeds $1 million at the time of the purchase, excluding the value of the primary residence of such person;
7. a natural person with income exceeding $200,000 in each of the two most recent years or joint income with a spouse exceeding $300,000 for those years and a reasonable expectation of the same income level in the current year; or
8. a trust with assets in excess of $5 million, not formed to acquire the securities offered, whose purchases a sophisticated person makes.

There is no official definition for angel investors. Usually, angel investors meet the definition of accredited investors by the Securities and Exchange Commission (SEC).[4] When a business sells stocks to outside investors, it is subject to SEC regulation unless it qualifies for private placement exemption under Rule 506.[5] To qualify for this exemption, the purchasers of the stocks must have enough knowledge and experience in finance and business matters to be 'sophisticated investors' (able to evaluate the risks and merits of the investment), or be able to bear the investment's economic risk. The purchasers also must agree not to resell the securities to the public. In turn, the business must provide the purchasers access to information that it would normally include in a prospectus,[6] including financial statements and biographies of officers and their compensation. Therefore, an angel investor who is an accredited investor can purchase stocks from a business under the private placement exemption. Qualifying for Rule 506 exemption is an important consideration for entrepreneurs because, without the exemption, the amount of time and expenses required to meet SEC regulations to sell stocks to outside investors can be prohibitive.

3.5 SEC Rule 506 of Regulation D

Rule 506 of Regulation D is considered a "safe harbor" for the private offering exemption of Section 4(2) of the Securities Act. Companies using the Rule 506 exemption can raise an unlimited amount of money. A company can be assured it falls within Section 4(2) exemption by satisfying the following standards:

- The company cannot use general solicitation or advertising to market the securities.
- The company may sell its securities to an unlimited number of "accredited investors" and up to 35 other purchasers. All non-accredited investors, either alone or with a purchaser representative, must be sophisticated—that is, they must have sufficient knowledge and experience in financial and business matters to make them capable of evaluating the merits and risks of the prospective investment.
- Companies must decide what information to give to accredited investors, so long as it does not violate the anti-fraud prohibitions of the federal securities laws. But companies must give non-accredited investors disclosure documents that are generally the same as those used in registered offerings. If a company provides information to accredited investors, it must make this information available to non-accredited investors as well.
- The company must be available to answer questions by prospective purchasers.
- Financial statement requirements:
  - Financial statements need to be certified by an independent public accountant.
  - If a company other than a limited partnership cannot obtain audited financial statements without unreasonable effort or

expense, only the company's balance sheet (to be dated within 120 days of the start of the offering) must be audited.
- ○ Limited partnerships unable to obtain required financial statements without unreasonable effort or expense may furnish audited financial statements prepared under federal income tax laws.
- Purchasers receive "restricted" securities, meaning that the securities cannot be sold for at least a year without registering them.

While companies using the Rule 506 exemption do not have to register their securities and usually do not have to file reports with the SEC, they must file what is known as a "Form D" after they first sell their securities. Form D is a brief notice that includes the names and addresses of the company's owners and stock promoters, but contains little other information about the company.

According to a report by the Center for Venture Research (Sohl, 2013), in 2012 angel investors provided about $23 billion in investment funding to over 67,000 ventures. While software remained the top sector, receiving 23 percent of funding, retail and industrial and energy received 12 percent and 7 percent, respectively. About 35 percent of funding went to seed and startup stage firms and 29 percent went to expansion financing. The average deal size was $341,800, and the average business was valued at $2.7 million. Angel investors accepted 22 percent of proposals they reviewed. In other words, 1 in 5 entrepreneurs received funding. Businesses sold 12.7 percent of equity to angel investors on average, implying that entrepreneurs retained majority ownership for themselves.

Angel investors typically seek active involvement in the business through consulting and mentoring the entrepreneur or become directors on the board. Owing to their involvement, they are often more willing to invest in an earlier stage of a business than are venture capital firms. Businesses receiving funding from angel investors represent many industries, not just technology firms. 'Low-tech' companies can be attractive to angel investors because their businesses are easier to understand, making the 5-minute pitch more effective. Moreover, angel investors may be better able to bring added value through their management and marketing expertise. Geographic proximity can be an important factor for angel investors because they want to be active participants in the business. The 'four-hour rule' got its name because many angel investors only consider companies within a four-hour journey.

Most angel investors are not super-rich individuals. Individuals with more than $1 million in net worth or more than $200,000 in regular income are eligible to become accredited investors. Many professionals, such as doctors, dentists, engineers, and retired business executives, are angel investors. They often join networks or form investment groups in order to pool their capital, diversify risk, share knowledge, workload, and other non-financial resources, and attract more entrepreneurs. Angel networks are run by companies and organizations that provide matching services between angels and entrepreneurs. They may provide additional services such as due diligence.

3.6 Due Diligence

Due diligence refers to the responsibility of investors to investigate all available facts related to an investment. The due diligence process typically takes place after investors sign intent-to-purchase and confidentiality agreements. At this point, entrepreneurs provide potential investors access to financial and business documents that may contain proprietary and privileged information, including detailed background about the management team, their compensation, bylaws, financial, customer, products and services, production, and operations data. Investors, and their accountants and attorneys, verify these data for accuracy and evaluate the investment. The due diligence process is time consuming and requires knowledge of the industry, accounting principles, and corporate laws.

For entrepreneurs seeking equity financing, angel investors are often the first step. Personal referral is still the best way to approach angel investors. The local chamber of commerce, accountants, lawyers, real estate agents, doctors, and bankers are all potential connections to angel investors. Many entrepreneurs turn to online resources to expand beyond their personal network. Angel Capital Association is a trade association for angel investment groups; their website provides a listing of member angel groups. Angel Resource Institute was founded in 2006 with support by the Kauffman Foundation to provide education, training, research, and mentoring on angel investing, as well as a searchable listing of angel groups on their website. A new rule by the SEC, Rule 506(c) under Title II of the JOBS Act of 2012, added even more momentum to online equity funding referrals (http://www.sec.gov/news/press/2013/2013-124-item1.htm). This rule allows private issuers, i.e. businesses that normally qualify for the private placement exemption, to advertise the sale of their stocks to the general public, including online. Note that the actual sales are still limited to accredited investors.

A key to obtaining successful funding is finding a good match between your company's strengths and the angel group's investment criteria. While you need funding from them, also remember that angel investors will actively participate in your business. Consider the experience and skills they can bring to your business. Check references and look at the businesses they have funded in the past. Be sure to look at their exit strategies: how long they expect to stay invested in a business and how they typically sell off their shares.

3.7 Investment Criteria

A well-organized angel group or an experienced angel investor will have clearly stated investment criteria, which usually include:

- a range of funding amounts;
- stage of the firm's life cycle;
- geographic preference or restriction;
- industry preference;
- revenues or cash flow;
- experiences of the management team.

For example, Golden Seeds, an angel group targeting women entrepreneurs, stated their investment criteria as:[7]

Golden Seeds (the angel network and the funds) accepts applications from women-led companies across all sectors. Frequently, companies have a female founder or CEO. We also consider companies with women in other C-level positions. When considering women entrepreneurs, Golden Seeds cares about two things: Does she have power and influence in the company? Does she own a "fair" amount of the company's equity, given her role and the stage of the company when she joined?

In addition, Golden Seeds looks for:

- an extremely capable management team;
- a scalable business model;
- an addressable market of a $1,000,000,000+;
- limited capital expenditure requirements;
- opportunities that can be accelerated with support from our Angel Investors, Fund Partners, and advisors.

Almost all of the companies in which we invest meet these criteria:

- product is in beta (versus alpha) stage of development and has been created with input from clients or potential clients,
- company has some "proof of concept" revenue, except for life science companies;
- a clear, plausible exit strategy within 5–7 years;

- typical valuation at first funding of below $5 million (before new capital is raised);
- typically seeking first-round funding of $250,000 to $2,000,000;
- domiciled in the United States or Canada;
- consumer product companies have run rate revenue over $1,000,000 and gross margins over 40 percent.

SBA—Small Business Investment Companies (SBICs)

In addition to providing loan guarantees directly to small businesses, the SBA partners with private investors to form professionally managed investment funds, known as small business investment companies (SBICs), which provide both equity and loan financing to small businesses.[8] These SBICs are for-profit investment funds and use their own investment criteria and process when making investment decisions. In 2012, SBICs provided $518 million in equity funding, $695 million in debts, and $1,912 million in loans to small businesses. Under their license agreements with the SBA, SBICs can only invest in small businesses, generally defined as firms with tangible net worth of less than $18 million and an average net income of less than $6 million in the preceding two years. Specific industries may be exempted from these size limits. Another important criterion is the limit on foreign operations, which requires businesses to have fewer than 49 percent of their employees or tangible assets located outside the USA. The SBA provides a directory of SBICs on their website and includes the following information to help entrepreneurs find an SBIC that may be a good match for them:

- *Preferred investment size* The amount the SBIC is willing to invest or loan.
- *Investment policy* The type of investment the SBIC is willing to make (for example, loans, equity, or debt with equity features).
- *Investment type* The various stages of financing that the SBIC is willing to fund (for example, seed, startup, early-stage, expansion financing, later-stage financing, or managed buyout, leveraged buyout, or acquisition).
- *Industry preference* The type of industry or industries the SBIC is interested in financing, usually based on the knowledge and experience of the SBIC's management.
- *Geographic preference* The area of the United States where the SBIC prefers to make financing.
- *Description of firm's focus.*

BB&T Capital Partners II, LLC, an SBIC based in North Carolina, provided the following information on the SBA directory:

- *Investment size range* $5 million to $15 million.
- *Type of capital provided* Equity.
- *Funding stage preference* Buyout, acquisitions, recapitalization, consolidation.
- *Industry preference* Cash flow-oriented businesses with critical mass in any industry except high tech, real estate, or financial services.
- *Geographic preference* National.
- *Description of firm's focus* Seeks to invest in companies with experienced management, a demonstrated need for the company's products or services, and sustainable competitive advantages, allowing for profitable growth both organically and through strategic acquisitions.

Businesses that have received funding from BB&T Capital Partners included a firm that provides safety signs to construction companies, a firm that packages specialty beverage and craft beer, and a firm that provides online courses for medical coding and billing. This example illustrates the diversity of businesses that SBICs may invest in.

Venture Capital Firms

Venture capital firms are private equity professional money management firms that specialize in emerging growth companies. When entrepreneurs seek funding from venture capital firms, they interact with professional money managers, not the investors themselves. Compared with angel investors, venture capital firms tend to invest later in the life cycle, invest larger amount of capital, and demand a bigger share of equity stake in the business. Venture capital firms usually invest at least $1 million in a business, whereas the average deal size for angel investors was $341,800 in 2012. The National Venture Capital Association, an industry association, reported that in 2013 venture capital firms participated in 3,995 deals totaling over $29 billion. That put the average deal size for venture firms at over $7 million. Figure 3.3 shows financing by venture capital firms at different stages. Seed stage financing represented only 3 percent of amount invested and 5 percent of the deal. Half of the deals were in early stage financing, representing 33 percent of the amount invested. Expansion financing accounted for 34 percent of the total amount invested and 25 percent of the deals. Later-stage financing made up the last 30 percent of the total amount invested and 20 percent of the deals. Software was by far the top sector in which venture capital firms invested, capturing 37 percent of the amount invested and 38 percent of the deals, followed by media and entertainment and biotechnology.

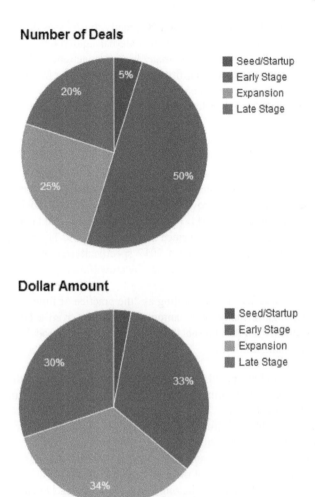

Figure 3.3 Venture Capital Firm Investment in Different Stages

If your business reaches a stage of needing significant equity financing, venture capital firms may be a good option. Large venture capital firms, such as Bain Capital Ventures, Charles River Ventures, and Sequoia Capital, are well-known beyond the investment community. While technology remains the top sector to receive venture financing, there are opportunities for businesses in any industry with strong growth potential and unique competitive advantage. Starbucks and P.F. Chang's were once backed by venture capital. However, finding venture capital financing can be challenging. A Forbes article (Rao, 2013) claimed that only one or two out of 100 business plans submitted to venture capital firms were funded. Typically, businesses do not seek venture financing as their first step toward external equity financing. Angel investors can be valuable mentors and many have connections and past business relationships with venture capital firms. It is very common for small businesses to secure first-round external equity financing with angel investors at the seed and startup stage and then look for venture capital funding at the growth and expansion stage.

Crowdfunding

Crowdfunding is gaining a lot of attention and provides a new financing option for small businesses. The word "crowdfunding" was added to *Oxford Dictionaries Online* in November 2011 (Oxford Dictionaries, 2011) and Kickstarter has become a household name since its launch in 2009. The JOBS act (Jumpstart Our Business Startups Act) of 2012 specifically required the SEC to develop new rules permitting capital raising by crowdfunding. So what is crowdfunding?

The Oxford Dictionary defines crowdfunding as "the practice of funding a project or venture by raising many small amounts of money from a large amount of people, typically via the Internet." There are three basic models of crowdfunding: equity, debt, and other.

- In an equity crowdfunding model, contributors receive ownership in the company. This is the newest form of crowdfunding and was the focus of Title III of the JOBS act.
- The second model, debt crowdfunding, is gaining in popularity. Some peer-to-peer lending platforms utilize a debt crowdfunding model.
- The last crowdfunding model ranges from donation to rewards in exchange for contributions. Many of the best known crowdfunding sites, such as Kickstarter and Indiegogo, belong to this last model. Donation crowdfunding is just what it sounds like: contributors give money to a project or a cause and receive nothing in return. Contributors to a reward-based crowdfunding campaign may receive special discounts, products, or services in exchange for their cash. In many cases, the campaign resembles a form of pre-sale. However, it is not technically a sale and if the product or service does not come to fruition, contributors do not receive refunds.

Which Crowdfunding Model Is Right for Your Business?

If you decide to try crowdfunding to raise money for your business, you must first decide whether you want to raise money through equity, debt, or the donation/reward model. The trade-offs between equity and debt are discussed in an earlier section in this chapter. In general, debt financing carries higher financial risk than equity but has much lower cost, both in terms of required return to investors and reporting and compliance requirements by the business. One form of debt crowdfunding is peer-to-peer lending, discussed previously. Peer-to-peer lending is more expensive than SBA-guaranteed loans and conventional bank loans but less expensive than alternative sources, such as merchant cash advance.

On October 23, 2013, the SEC proposed Regulation Crowdfunding to govern equity crowdfunding. This proposal has not been adopted as of October 2014. Until the regulation is finalized, it is unclear how equity crowdfunding will compare to angel investors and venture capital firms as a source of external equity for small businesses.

The intent of the crowdfunding regulation is to enable small businesses to raise up to $1 million each year from any investors through a funding portal or a broker registered with the SEC and the Financial Intermediary Regulatory Authority (FINRA). Individual investors, i.e. not accredited investors, are limited in the amount they can invest through crowdfunding based on their annual income or net worth. This regulation also reduces the reporting requirements by small businesses compared with publicly traded stocks.

In September 2013, the SEC adopted Rule 506(c), which enables online platforms to advertise and market securities, both stocks and debts, to investors on behalf of businesses. Only accredited investors are allowed to purchase these securities. Rule 506(c) opens the door for a number of funding platforms, such as Gust.com, Startupvalley.com, Crowdfunder.com, and EquityNet.

These platforms work a lot like a dating website for entrepreneurs and accredited investors. Each party fills out a profile. Investors can search for potential investments based on industry, funding amount, geographic location, and keywords. Entrepreneurs can search for investors based on industry, geographic location, and keywords. Actual transactions between entrepreneurs and accredited investors take place outside the online platform and all the provisions of Rule 506 must be met. Crowdnetic (2014) reported that 120 days after the SEC enacted Rule 506(c) it tracked 2,266 ventures that received $80 million in committed funds via online platforms. Some of the accredited investors on these platforms were existing angel investors extending their networks to reach more potential investments. Some were new to investing in startup ventures and might not provide the same degree of involvement and mentoring as angel investors. These new channels for raising capital are exciting and bring new opportunities but also potential downfalls. While accredited investors need to exercise due diligence to understand the investments, entrepreneurs need to learn how much information to disclose to satisfy regulatory and investor demands without compromising operation and trade secrets. This challenge will be magnified if entrepreneurs are raising money from a number of unaffiliated accredited investors.

The donation and reward-based crowdfunding model can be an alternative source of financing for small businesses. Kickstarter is the first and the largest crowdfunding platform in this model. Kickstarter was designed to fund creative projects, not businesses. However, its categories range from games and books to food and technology. For example, OUYA is a company that created and produced a gaming console. It started a Kickstarter campaign to raise money on July 10, 2012. The campaign lasted 29 days. Its goal was $950,000 and it raised almost $8.5 million. Rewards for OUYA backers included:

- $10 or more—a reserved username;
- $25 or more—a reserved username with a founder emblem next to the username;
- $95 or more—an OUYA console and controller for early birds; limited to 1,000 backers;
- $99 or more—an OUYA console and controller guaranteed;
- larger pledge amounts came with more perks.

Another Kickstarter campaign was by The Garret, a restaurant startup in New York City to raise money for operating cash flow. Rewards ranged from burgers, T-shirts, and brass name plates to naming a drink in the backer's honor. The funding goal of this project was $15,000, and the owners exceeded their goal by 172 percent, raising over $25,000.

There are no industry standards or government regulations for the donation- and reward-based crowdfunding model. Each platform operates differently. Table 3.4 compares three popular crowdfunding sites: Kickstarter, IndieGoGo and GoFundMe. Since backers do not receive monetary return on their donation, crowdfunding campaigns offer rewards or perks to attract backers. Usually businesses offer products or services as rewards. The amounts raised through these platforms are small relative to other sources. The OUYA example is a rare exception. Kickstarter reported that the majority of their projects, 63 percent, raised between $1,000 and $10,000 and less than 0.10 percent raised more than $1 million.

Private Equity Markets

Changes in security laws and technology continue to expand financing options for entrepreneurs. NASDAQ, usually known as an exchange for public companies, launched NASDAQ Private Market in March 2013. In September 2013, NYSE Euronext, the largest stock exchange in the world, entered into a strategic partnership with ACE Portal to expand into the private equity market, and in July 2014 VC Experts joined this partnership. In the past, equity of entrepreneurs and early stage investors in private companies was highly illiquid. The lack of liquidity reduces the value of these investments.

Table 3.4 Comparison of Crowdfunding Sites

	Kickstarter	IndieGoGo	GoFundMe
Use of proceeds	Creative project with a clear goal	No restrictions	No restrictions
Partial funding allowed	No: all or nothing	Yes: also allows all or nothing option	Yes: also allows all or nothing option
Fee to platform	5% of funds collected if successful	4% if goal is met 9% if goal is not met for flexible funding 0% if goal is not met for fixed funding, (for non-profits, 3% and 6.75%)	5% of funding amount
Return to backer	Rewards vary: could be nothing	Perks vary: could be nothing	Incentives and perks vary: could be nothing
Limit on amount raised	None	None	None
Minimum amount required	None	None	None
Funding period deadline	Required	Required	Not required
Refund	Required if promised rewards are not delivered	Required if promised rewards are not delivered	Required if promised rewards are not delivered
Eligibility requirements for fundraising entities in the USA	18 years or older, permanent U.S. resident with a social security number, U.S. address, U.S. bank account, U.S. state-issued ID, U.S. credit or debit card	18 years or older or between the ages of 13 and 17 using the website and services with consent and supervision of parental or legal guardian Membership or use has not otherwise been restricted, suspended or terminated Not using another member's account without permission	A Facebook account with photo and "high" friend count

The only way to gain liquidity is to take the company public, a process we will discuss in detail in Chapter 10. Private equity markets provide companies not interested in going public, or not quite ready to go public, with a new alternative to raise equity capital. Under current security laws, only accredited investors can purchase private stocks. In addition to serving as a market between accredited investors and companies raising capital, both NASDAQ Private Market and ACE NYSE also provide equity management services, removing another obstacle for raising equity capital.

Financial markets are constantly evolving with new products and services. Game changing innovations in the past few years include electronic payment options and crowdfunding. Implementation of the JOBS act and regulations on private equity will likely have a significant impact on financial market and entrepreneurs raising capital in the near future.

Case 3.1 Edupass[9]

Jaime Martínez

Industry Background

In 2011, Alejandro Garcia had been the CEO of FS in Mexico for more than eight years. He reported to the headquarters in Miami, Florida. Garcia noticed that the global financial crisis had resulted in a decrease in the number of students served.

According to Garcia, most students eager to study abroad belonged to Mexico's middle class. "For parents, sending their children to study abroad is an aspirational goal," Garcia said to himself. He figured that nearly three million families with an average monthly income equivalent to $4,000 had the potential to send their children to study abroad.

At that time, there were approximately 25 travel agencies offering study-abroad programs, but none of them offered financial aid for students.

While still working for FS, Garcia suggested to his boss in Miami that FS offer some kind of financial aid for parents who couldn't afford to pay for a whole study program in advance. His proposal was rejected. Garcia subsequently quit FS and started his own credit union, named Edupass, to serve this population.

Business Environment

In 2008, as a consequence of the global financial crisis, some financial institutions, such as Lehman Brothers, went bankrupt, reflecting the effects of this "financial tsunami."

According to the Mexican newspaper *La Jornada*, in January 2009, Mexico was hit by this crisis and the Mexican peso devalued more than 25 percent, shrinking to an exchange rate of more than $14 pesos per USD.[10] Mexican gross domestic product (GDP) fell close to 7 percent in that year.[11] Because of this devaluation, in 2009 nearly 45 percent of customers cancelled their studies abroad.

In 2012, the average interest rate for personal credit in Mexico had decreased to a level close to 30 percent, while the average rate offered by Edupass was 18 percent on an annual basis.

Problem Discussion

Owing to the financial situation in Mexico, many parents couldn't afford to send their children to study abroad. Only one bank offered credit for education but it included neither internship programs nor overseas studies support.

The only financial aid available for most students in Mexico was via credit cards, with average interest rates reaching 40 percent.[12] Even this was a limited option, given that only 28 percent of the Mexican population had access to a bank account.[13]

This situation represented an opportunity to start a credit union (Edupass) focused on the international students market, as no other institution in Mexico offered financial aid for students willing to study abroad.

The Business

Garcia launched Edupass as a limited partnership in March, 2012. The first year, they handled 100 credits, averaging $7,700 per student. That amount was transferred directly to the foreign schools, while the parents signed promissory notes to Edupass.

The goal for the second year was to finance 150 credits, increasing to 200 credits in the third year.

Garcia's wife assumed the role of Edupass CEO, as she was not only an investor in this company, but also aligned with her husband's vision.

Their initial capitalization was close to $333,000 but the Garcias thought it insufficient to cover the market requirements. They used $130,000 for basic startup costs, leaving them only $200,000 to lend. They started looking for more capital, but financial credit was not available for a startup with less than two years of operation.

The Challenge

As banks did not want to grant financial aid to the Garcias, they had to find other ways to unlock this issue to get enough capital to finance their credit union. Without additional sources of capital, the number of credits they could finance for students would be severely limited.

Case Questions

1. If you were Alejandro Garcia, what aspects of the business should you focus on to convince potential funders to provide capital for Edupass?
2. If you were a potential investor, what key aspects of the business would you take into account before you agreed to provide funding?
3. What options does Garcia have to finance and grow his business? Identify the pros and cons of each.

Case 3.2 REACH Health, Inc.: A Startup Telemedicine Company at the Funding Crossroads

Simon Medcalfe, William Hamilton, and David Hess

Dr. David Hess (chair of the board and founder), Bill Hamilton (secretary and founder), and Sam Andrews, the Chief Executive Officer of REACH Health, Inc., were traveling from Augusta to Savannah, Georgia, to present at a "pitch" session to an angel investor group. They were seeking $250,000 to finance their company's growth. Discussions had evolved to the point that a voluminous due diligence document had been created, and they hoped that this pitch would seal the deal.

"We really need this investment," said Bill. "Without the Technology Associates of Georgia award of $100,000, we would have made a loss of about $31,000 so far this year. A capital investment of $250,000 will allow us to increase business management and sales support infrastructure, and will provide money for a marketing campaign."

REACH Health, Inc. had been founded in early 2006 (as REACHMD Consult, Inc.) to provide telemedicine to rural Georgia. Telemedicine is the use of medical information exchanged from one site to another via electronic communications to improve a patient's clinical health status. Telemedicine includes a growing variety of applications and services using two-way video, email, smart phones, wireless tools, and other forms of telecommunications technology. The original idea emanated from a group of academic neurologists at the Medical College of Georgia (MCG), in Augusta, Georgia in 2002. The telestroke system called REACH (*r*emote *e*valuation of *a*cute is*ch*emic stroke) was designed and developed in consultation with rural community hospital emergency room staff. The web-based system included custom-built software integrating video conferencing, computed tomography, and patient data into an integrated screen. The system was designed with a drop-down screen to implement the National Institute Health Stroke Scales (NIHSS).

In 2003, MCG instituted the REACH system in two rural Georgia hospitals, McDuffie Regional in Thompson, and Emanuel County Hospital in Swainsboro. The system was well received by the emergency room staff and the network of hospitals that installed telemedicine systems expanded to include seven additional hospitals over the next three years.

The original telestroke system was very effective in rural Georgia. However, to commercialize REACH and scale the technology to be able to accommodate and support hundreds of hospitals, it was necessary to create an updated version, REACH 2.0, which would accommodate a higher volume of consultations, provide additional user-friendly features, and be expandable to include other clinical applications.

It was at this point that REACHMD Consult, Inc. was formed. The company was originally funded by a business launch competition award of $100,000 (Technology Associates of Georgia/Georgia Research Alliance) and by $100,000 equity investment by MCG Health, Inc., a 501(c)3 not-for-profit hospital. The subsequent funding plan was to build "organically" via customer sales, without outside investment. The business model was predicated on a telemedicine software-as-service, monthly recurring revenue model, based on contracts with hospitals and health systems for one-to-three-year terms. From 2006 to 2007, the company was able to maintain slim margins and grow its customer base incrementally. For the first eight months of 2007, revenue was just over $340,000.

"Our business model, while strong, does not support exponential growth," continued Bill. "We cannot grow exponentially relying on current revenue streams."

"I agree that our current business model does not support exponential growth, but I don't like taking outside money at this time. It could be very expensive while also diluting the ownership position of the founders, the option pool for the employees, and the overall construct of the management team," replied Sam. "Most importantly, we would lose control of the direction of the company," Sam continued. "However, I fully understand the need for exponential growth and am very concerned about the financial stability of the company. The small size of the company does not allow me the flexibility to focus on overall growth strategies, but only on day-to-day operations."

"I think we all agree about the fragile financial state of the company, but the way to improve that is through quickly scaling our operations and for that we need this investment," David added.

Sam turned to David and Bill and said, "You know, I am not so sure we need the investment right now. We can continue to grow using current cash flows without the influx of external funding. Bill, why don't you become the chief operating officer and together we will institute a tight financial management system that will balance revenue and expense cash flow and allow for a sustainable organic growth pattern. We will manage a lean sales force, outsource key functions, and use a customer relationship management system to manage the operations of the company, such as sales, accounts payable, and accounts receivable."

"We can protect the interests of the shareholders from unnecessary dilution," continued Sam, "and lay the foundation for a future larger external investment by venture capital firms. REACH will be more attractive without the angel investors and also offer a company that has a growth trajectory, while maintaining a profit."

By this time, David, Bill and Sam were on the outskirts of Savannah. The company was at a crossroads. The board, as a whole—not just David and Bill—had agreed to seek outside funding. Sam was not enamored of this prospect, but had agreed to go down this path, since he served at the pleasure of the board. However, neither party wanted to lose control of the company at this point. They had to make a decision quickly over the future of their company. Should they aggressively pursue investment capital from the angel investors?

Case Questions

1. Evaluate the option of growing the company organically, using current revenue streams.
2. Evaluate the option of taking the angel investment capital of $250,000.
3. Would you pursue the angel investment or grow organically?

Case 3.3 Coos Bay Organic Products, Inc.:
Financing Compost

John Voyer and Frederic Aiello

There is a long composting tradition along Oregon's Pacific Coast, especially among the region's tuna canneries, Pacific whiting and crab processors, and its timber industry. In the mid-1990s, the state formed a compost team to help many of these processors set up successful composting programs. This team was ad hoc, consisting of members of government agencies and universities in Oregon.

One of the composting team's original clients, the Pacific Northwest Mussel Company, had gotten involved in composting because it had been looking for an alternative to waste disposal. However, in 2006 the company had become dissatisfied with the lack of scale of the waste composting efforts. Its management approached Charles Brooks, a former corporate banker who had relocated to Coos Bay to work with a relative's small business, about starting a company that could solve the problem of lack of sufficient composting scale.

Brooks felt that there was an unfulfilled consumer need for a high-quality, organic compost for garden and potting soil enrichment. Having named the new company Coos Bay Organic Products, Inc., he began to confront the challenge of obtaining additional funds to launch the business. He estimated that he would need $100,000 for several reasons: for additional working capital, to finance the development of a compost recipe, to obtain sources of raw materials, and for a marketing campaign. Brooks identified various options:

1. *Bank financing* A few community banks in Coos Bay were supportive of small business development, so it might be possible to obtain a loan or a line of credit for the new business.
2. *Venture capital* There might be venture capitalists in Oregon who would be interested in buying a piece of the new company.
3. *Angel investors* There might be wealthy people in southern Oregon who would be interested in taking on some financial risk in exchange for equity in the company, given the "good cause" it represented.
4. *Friends and family* Brooks had several friends and relatives who owned or ran businesses. He might approach them about financing in exchange for equity or repayment through a loan. Friends and family were second

to personal funds and "sweat equity" in the financing of new ventures. Friends and family funds might come in the form of a loan, investment, or outright gift.

5. *Public or quasi-public grant and loan financing* Several state and federal agencies had missions to provide financing, some in grants and some in loans, to startups in the state. These included the Southern Oregon Tidal Ventures, a non-profit dedicated to economic development in the region, and federal agencies, such as the Small Business Administration (SBA) and the Farmer's Home Administration.

6. *Venture financing from Pacific Northwest Mussel Company (or similar firm in a local industry)* Given that Pacific Northwest Mussel Company was looking for a way to dispose of its waste stream more efficiently and effectively, it might be interested in providing startup funding to Coos Bay Organic Products. Doing so might provide it with a solution to its waste problem.

7. *Crowdfunding* Brooks heard about the concept of crowdfunding, which involved using the Internet to raise small amounts of money from a large number of individual "investors."

As he sat in his home office, Brooks mulled over which of these options to undertake.

Case Questions

1. Evaluate the various options for financing.
2. What process should Brooks follow to get the startup financing?

Notes

1　The term "annual receipts" is used to mean "annual revenues" in many SBA documents.
2　The SBA website (www.sba.gov) has a wealth of information for small business owners, including details on their loan programs.
3　http://www.usafactoring.com/Factoring-Rates.html
4　SEC Rule 501 of Regulation D defines the term accredited investor. See https://www.sec.gov/answers/accred.htm and https://www.sec.gov/info/smallbus/qasbsec.htm#capital
5　If a business does not qualify for the private placement exemption, the security sale will be considered a public placement. Public placement is often referred to as "going public" and is a costly and time-consuming process. It is discussed in detail in Chapter 10. Rules 504 and 505 also allow private placement but these rules are more restrictive in terms of dollar amounts that can be raised and do not preempt state blue sky registration requirements. Rule 506 does not have limit on dollar amount raised and contains provisions that preempt state blue sky registration and review. Therefore, most private placements are issued under Rule 506.
6　A prospectus is the first part of the 'Registration Statements' required by law for any companies selling stocks to the public. A prospectus must contain important

facts about the company, including its business, properties, competitions, risk factors, management, and their compensation, intended use of money raised from sale of new stocks, audited financial information, and more. See https://www.sec. gov/info/smallbus/qasbsec.htm#capital for more information.

7 http://www.goldenseeds.com/entrepreneurs/investment-criteria

8 An SBIC licensee raises equity for the investment company from private investors and the SBA provides loan guarantees up to three times the private equity raised to the licensee. For example, if a licensee raises $10 million from private investors, the SBA will commit up to $30 million of loan guarantee, totalling $40 million in funding to the SBIC.

9 All personal names have been disguised.

10 Jornada.unam.mx (January 31, 2009).

11 *The Seattle Times* (January 29, 2010).

12 Jornada.unam.mx (November 20, 2008).

13 Eluniversal.com.mx (March, 27, 2008).

Bibliography

Angel Capital Association. http://www.angelcapitalassociation.org/ (accessed 2/22/2014).

Angel Resource Institute. http://www.angelresource.org/ (accessed 2/22/2014).

Barnett, C. (2013, May 8). Top 10 crowdfunding sites for fundraising. *Forbes* http://www.forbes.com/sites/chancebarnett/2013/05/08/top-10-crowdfunding-sites-for-fundraising/ (accessed 1/24/2014).

Barth, C. (2012, June 6). Looking for 10 percent yields? Go online for peer to peer lending. *Forbes* http://www.forbes.com/sites/chrisbarth/2012/06/06/looking-for-10-yields-go-online-for-peer-to-peer-lending/ (accessed 2/15/2014).

BB&T Capital Partners http://www.bbtcp.com/ (accessed 2/22/2014).

Bennett, E. S., & Tiku, N. (2008, April 1). Thanks, but no thanks: Why to avoid taking out a merchant cash advance. *Inc.* http://www.inc.com/magazine/20080401/thanks-but-no-thanks.html (accessed 2/17/2014).

Blake, B. (2013, October 21). Small business lending: banks and credit unions are getting left behind. *Forbes* http://www.forbes.com/sites/brockblake/2013/10/21/small-business-lending-banks-and-credit-unions/ (accessed 2/14/2014).

Castrataro, D. (2011, December 12). A social history of crowdfunding. *Social Media Week* http://socialmediaweek.org/blog/2011/12/a-social-history-of-crowdfunding/#.Uu1jEbTuqKg (accessed 2/1/2014).

Cherney, M. (2013, December 31). Companies sell record $1.111 trillion of bonds in 2013: higher yields, economic growth attract investors. *The Wall Street Journal* http://online.wsj.com/news/articles/SB10001424052702304361604579292453595212672 (accessed 2/15/2014).

Clark, P. (2013, October 16). Here come LendingClub's small business loans. *Bloomberg Business, The New Entrepreneur* http://www.bloomberg.com/bw/articles/2013-10-16/here-come-lendingclubs-small-business-loans (accessed 2/14/2014)

Conner, C. (2013, April 10). "Money, money"—how alternative lending could increase your company's revenue in 2013. *Forbes* http://www.forbes.com/sites/cherylsnapp-conner/2013/04/10/money-money-how-alternative-lending-could-increase-your-companys-revenue-in-2013/ (accessed 2/15/2014)

Crowdnetic. (2014). *JOBS Act Title II: The First 120 Days in Review.* http://www.crowdnetic.com/data-report (accessed 2/22/2014).

Davidoff Solomon, S. (2013, October 30). Trepidation and restrictions leave crowd-funding rules weak. *Dealbook, The New York Times* http://dealbook.nytimes.com/2013/10/29/trepidation-and-restrictions-leave-crowdfunding-rules-weak/?_r=0 (accessed 2/22/2011).

Deluca, M. (2011, September 21). How risky are cash advances? *Inc.* http://www.inc.com/guides/201109/how-risky-are-cash-advances.html (accessed 2/14/2014).

DeGennaro, R. P. (2012). Angel investors: who they are and what they do; can I be one, too? In R. P. DeGennaro (Ed.), *Principles of Financial Management.* San Diego, CA: Cognella Academic Publishing.

Gardella, A. (2011, January 20). How a low-tech soap maker raised $400,000 from investors. *You're the Boss, The New York Times* http://boss.blogs.nytimes.com/2011/01/20/how-a-low-tech-soap-maker-raised-400000-from-investors/ (accessed 2/17/2014).

Golden Seeds. (2014). *Investment Criteria* http://www.goldenseeds.com/entrepreneurs/investment-criteria (accessed 2/22/2014).

Goodman, M. (2012, June 11). Case study: how a merchant cash advance worked in a pinch. *Entrepreneur* http://www.entrepreneur.com/article/223523# (accessed 2/14/2014).

Guzik, S. S. (2014, January 15) Regulation A+ offerings—a new era at the SEC. *The Harvard Law School Forum on Corporate Governance and Financial Regulation* https://blogs.law.harvard.edu/corpgov/2014/01/15/regulation-a-offerings-a-new-era-at-the-sec/#more-57459 (accessed 1/24/2014).

Keynes, J. M. (1936). *The General Theory of Employment, Interest and Money.* London, UK: Macmillan & Co.

Kickstarter. *Stats* https://www.kickstarter.com/help/stats (accessed 2/23/2014).

Klein, K. E. (2013, March 14). How are the SBA's loan programs doing? *Bloomberg Business, Smart Answers* http://www.bloomberg.com/bw/articles/2013-03-14/how-are-the-sbas-loan-programs-doing (accessed 2/8/2014).

LendingClub. *Interest Rates and How We Set Them* https://www.lendingclub.com/public/how-we-set-interest-rates.action (accessed 2/15/2014)

Mandelbaum, R. (2011, October 6). SBA-Backed Lending Set a Record in 2011. *You're the Boss, The New York Times* http://boss.blogs.nytimes.com/2011/10/06/s-b-a-backed-lending-set-a-record-in-2011/ (accessed 2/8/2014).

Mitra, T., & Gilbert, E. (2014, February) The language that gets people to give: phrases that predict success on Kickstarter, *Proceedings 17th ACM Conference on Computer Supported Cooperative Work and Social Computing*, New York, NY: Association for Computing Machinery. pp. 49–61.

National Venture Capital Association. *Venture Capital Disbursements (MoneyTree data).* http://www.nvca.org/index.php?option=com_content&view=article&id=344&Itemid=103 (accessed 2/22/2014).

Neiss, S. (2014, January 2). It might cost you $39K to crowdfund $100K under the SEC's new rules. *VB* http://venturebeat.com/2014/01/02/it-might-cost-you-39k-to-crowdfund-100k-under-the-secs-new-rules/ (accessed 2/22/2014).

Outlaw, S. (2013, October 3). Which type of crowdfunding is best for you? *Entrepreneur* www.entrepreneur.com/article/228524 (accessed 2/1/2014).

Outlaw, S. (2013). *Cash From the Crowd.* Irvine, CA: Entrepreneur Press

Oxford Dictionaries. (2011, December 2). Slactivism, dadrock, and bibimbap: ODO quarterly update November 2011. *OxfordWords Blog* http://blog.oxforddictionaries.com/2011/12/odo-quarterly-update-november-2011/ (accessed 2/1/2014).

Prive, T. (2013, March 12). Angel investors: How the rich invest. *Forbes* http://www.forbes.com/sites/tanyaprive/2013/03/12/angels-investors-how-the-rich-invest/ (accessed 2/17/2014).

Rao, D. (2013, July 22). Why 99.95 percent of entrepreneurs should stop wasting time seeking venture capital. *Forbes* http://www.forbes.com/sites/dileeprao/2013/07/22/why-99-95-of-entrepreneurs-should-stop-wasting-time-seeking-venture-capital/ (accessed 2/22/2014).

Sohl, J. (2013, April 25). The angel investor market in 2012: a moderating recovery continues. *Center for Venture Research* paulcollege.unh.edu/sites/default/files/2012_analysis_report.pdf (accessed 7/2/2013).

Solman, P. (2014, January 1). How to rate the risks of peer-to-peer lending, the newest bubble. *PBS Newshour, Making Sense* http://www.pbs.org/newshour/making-sense/how-to-rate-the-risks-of-peer-to-peer-lending-the-newest-bubble/ (accessed 2/15/2014).

Thorpe, D. (2014, February, 1). Where does crowdfunding go from here? Experts explain. *Forbes* http://www.forbes.com/sites/devinthorpe/2014/02/01/where-does-crowdfunding-go-from-here-experts-explain/ (accessed 2/22/2014).

Uong, M. (2014. January 23). Crowdfunding tips for turning inspiration into reality. *Personal Tech, The New York Times* http://www.nytimes.com/2014/01/23/technology/personaltech/crowdfunding-tips-for-turning-inspiration-into-reality.html (accessed 1/24/2014).

USA Factoring. *Factoring Rates as Low as .59%* http://www.usafactoring.com/Factoring-Rates.html (accessed 2/15/2014).

US Census Bureau. *North American Industry Classification System.* http://www.census.gov/eos/www/naics/ (accessed 2/6/2015)

US Chamber of Commerce. *Bank Loan Documentation.* https://www.uschamber smallbusinessnation.com/toolkits/guide/P10_3500 (accessed 2/7/2014).

US Securities and Exchange Commission. *Accredited Investors.* https://www.sec.gov/answers/accred.htm (accessed 2/17/2014)

US Securities and Exchange Commission. (2013) Crowdfunding SEC Open Meeting. *SEC Fact Sheet.* https://www.sec.gov/News/PressRelease/Detail/PressRelease/1370540017677#.UwoFglKIC-0 (accessed 2/23/2014).

US Securities and Exchange Commission. (2013, July 10). *Eliminating the Prohibition on General Solicitation and General Advertising in Certain Offerings.* SEC Fact Sheet. http://www.sec.gov/news/press/2013/2013-124-item1.htm (accessed 2/1/2014.)

US Securities and Exchange Commission. (2013, September 23). Investor Bulletin: Accredited Investors http://www.investor.gov/news-alerts/investor-bulletins/investor-bulletin-accredited-investors (accessed 2/9/2015)

US Securities and Exchange Commission. *Small Business and the SEC.* https://www.sec.gov/info/smallbus/qasbsec.htm (accessed 2/17/2014).

US Small Business Administration. *Directory of SBIC Licensees.* http://www.sba.gov/content/sbic-directory (accessed 2/22/2014).

US Small Business Administration. *SBIC Program FY 2012 Annual Report.* Washington, DC: US SBA https://www.sba.gov/content/sbic-program-annual-report-fy-2012 (accessed 3/23/2014).

US Small Business Administration, Office of Advocacy. (2011, September) *Frequently Asked Questions about Small Business Finance* http://www.sba.gov/sites/default/files/files/Finance%20FAQ%208-25-11%20FINAL%20for%20web.pdf (accessed 2/7/2014).

US Small Business Administration, Office of Advocacy. (2014, February). *Frequently Asked Questions*. https://www.sba.gov/sites/default/files/2014_Finance_FAQ.pdf (accessed 2/7/2014).

Wortham, J., & Miller, C. C. (2013, April 28). Venture capitalists are making bigger bets on food start-ups, *Business Day, The New York Times*. http://www.nytimes.com/2013/04/29/business/venture-capitalists-are-making-bigger-bets-on-food-start-ups.html?pagewanted=all (accessed 7/2/2015)

Module 3
Measuring Performance in the Short Term

4 Financial Statements and Analysis

The naked truth is always better than the best-dressed lie.

Ann Landers

Financial statements are to an entrepreneur as gauges on the dashboard are to a driver. They tell you how fast your car is going, how much gas is left, how hot the engine is, and so forth. No rational person would think of driving without knowing how to read the gauges. The purpose of this chapter is to introduce you to key financial statements so you can monitor the health and progress of your business successfully.

Financial Statements

Accounting is about recording and organizing important financial data into categories that provide useful information. Accounting is also the common language of business. Without a common language, financial records in one business would not be understood by anyone outside the firm, including new employees. Thus, having a uniform standard increases efficiency and promotes easy exchange of information. In the USA, the Financial Accounting Standards Board (FASB), a private non-profit organization, is designated by the Securities and Exchange Commission (SEC) to develop and update accounting standards called "Generally Accepted Accounting Principles" (GAAP). Companies that sell shares to the public must have their financial statements audited based on the GAAP framework. Although private businesses are not required to have audited financial statements, they should still follow GAAP so that their statements can be evaluated easily by banks and outside investors. An academic study (Minnis, 2011) found that private companies with audited financial statements could lower their borrowing interest rate by about three-quarters of a percentage point. Perhaps more interesting was the finding that even firms with average annual revenues of $500,000 were sometimes asked to provide audited statements by banks.

4.1 Audited Financial Statements

While a business is responsible for preparing financial statements, sometimes an external audit of these statements is needed. An auditor must be an outsider and credentialed by the state to perform financial audit. If a business hires an accounting firm to prepare its statements, the same company cannot perform the audit. In the USA, a certified public accountant (CPA) is qualified to audit financial statements and is expected to follow auditing standards set by the American Institute of CPAs (AICPA). Following the audit, the CPA expresses an opinion on whether the financial statements as a whole are free from material misstatement and are fairly presented in accordance with Generally Accepted Accounting Principles (GAAP). The auditor issues a "clean" opinion when the conclusion is that the financial statements are free from material misstatement. If there is any doubt or concern, or if the auditor is unable to gather all evidence needed to be conclusive, the auditor issues a "qualified" opinion.

Performing a formal audit of financial statements can be expensive (AICPA, 2010). Sometimes banks and suppliers will accept reviewed financial statements instead of audited statements. In a review, the CPA follows the standards for accounting and review services, and reports whether there are material modifications that should be made to the financial statements for them to conform with the applicable financial reporting framework. Performing a review is substantially cheaper than an audit because it is both less comprehensive and cannot provide a "clean" opinion.

Chart of Accounts

The chart of accounts forms the basic building block of the accounting system. It is a list of all the accounts in the business. Hiring a certified public accountant (CPA) to set up the chart in an accounting software package is a worthwhile one-time investment. Appendix 4.1 contains selected sections from the GAAP-recommended chart of accounts. For financial statements to be useful, the chart of accounts must accurately reflect how the business operates. For example, GAAP requires revenues for goods and services to be recorded separately, therefore there are two accounts for revenues, one each for revenues from sale of goods and from services provided. For many businesses, additional subcategories of revenues are needed to provide useful information to the entrepreneur. A retail business might want to keep track of its online sales versus in-store sales. A restaurant might want to know how much revenues come from dine-in, take-out, catering, etc. Similar considerations should be given to expenses. For businesses that manufacture products, the cost of goods sold includes both materials and labor. Retail businesses might want to track the costs of goods sold for different product lines that have significantly different markups. Restaurants typically record food costs, alcoholic beverage costs, and non-alcoholic beverage costs separately. Each subcategory of revenues and expenses requires a unique account in the chart. The entrepreneur and her accountant should prepare as complete a list of subcategories as possible at the launch of the business. Setting up the chart of accounts is a valuable exercise for the entrepreneur, because she has to articulate detailed aspects of the business's operation.

Each account should be assigned a unique name and a unique number in the accounting software. A more detailed chart will provide more information but result in a longer list of accounts. Table 4.1 contains sample accounts for a restaurant.

Although the list can grow very quickly, setting up the chart of accounts is a one-time event and it is worth the investment to have a well-designed system. The time and effort involved in training employees and the entrepreneur to adhere to the system must also be considered. A more complex chart of accounts increases the amount of training required and the opportunity for error. For example, if a coffee shop sets up a separate account for each flavor of coffee it sells, an employee will have to record each sale accordingly. This system can slow down customer service, employees might not adhere to the system as a result, and the records will then be incorrect. Conversely, if there is only one account for all sales, from coffee to pastries, data entry and recording will be very simple. However, the entrepreneur cannot obtain much useful information from a chart of accounts that is this simple. Like many aspects of running a small business, setting up the chart of accounts is a balancing act.

Accounting Methods

Choosing either a cash or an accrual accounting method is another important decision entrepreneurs make. The *cash accounting method* records revenues when cash is received and expenses when bills are paid. This sounds simple and straightforward. However, cash accounting can distort the true picture of a business's operation. For example, if in one month a business makes a lot of sales but collects few receivables from its customers and pays a lot of bills, it will show big losses for the month. Another business may collect cash from customers on sales it generated long ago and delay paying bills, thus showing big profits for a month in which it actually generated few sales.

In *accrual accounting*, revenues are recorded when a sale is made, even if no cash is received at the time of sale, such as a sale on credit to a customer. Operating expenses are recorded when services are provided by a vendor and used by the business. A good example to demonstrate how accrual operating expenses will be recorded is an insurance premium. Insurance premiums are

Table 4.1 Sample Accounts for a Restaurant Business

Account number	Account title	Description of account
40000	Revenues	Amounts earned from providing goods and services. Combines revenues from all sub-accounts of revenues. This is the primary level of revenue accounts for this restaurant.
40100	Revenues from sale of goods	Amounts earned from sale of goods to customers. This is the second level of revenue accounts and includes food and alcohol revenues for this restaurant.
40110	Food revenues	Amounts earned from sale of food items. This is the third level of revenue accounts and includes all food revenues for this restaurant.
40120	Alcohol revenues	Amounts earned from sale of alcoholic beverages.
40130	Non-alcoholic beverage revenues	Amounts earned from sale of non-alcoholic beverages.
40111	Lunch food revenues	Amounts earned from sale of food items during lunch. This is the lowest level of food revenue account for this restaurant. All food sales during lunch will be entered into this account.
40112	Dinner food revenues	Amounts earned from sale of food items during dinner. This is the lowest level of food revenue account for this restaurant. All food sales during dinner will be entered into this account.
40113	Catering food revenues	Amount earned from sale of food items from catering. This is the lowest level of food revenue account for this restaurant. All food sales from catering will be entered into this account.
40121	Lunch alcohol revenues	Amount earned from sale of alcohol during lunch. This is the lowest level of alcohol revenue account for this restaurant. All alcohol sales during lunch will be entered into this account.

usually paid once a year or once every six months. If a business pays a one-year insurance premium, using the accrual accounting method it will record one-twelfth of the premium as an expense each month. Under the cash method, the entire amount will be recorded as an expense in one month and there will be no insurance expense recorded in other months.

Another common expense that differs between the accrual and cash methods is *cost of goods sold* (*COGS*). The accrual method tries to match COGS to revenues generated in the same period. A seasonal business sells golf equipment and supplies in the summer and skiing products in the winter. It will purchase golf-related inventory beginning in February and skiing inventory beginning in September. For one or two months each year, there will likely be significant product mismatch between inventory purchases and sales. The advantage of accrual accounting is that it provides a more accurate picture of the operation of a business by matching expenses to purchases. However, an entrepreneur has to pay close attention to cash flows and cash balances in addition to profits because profits under accrual accounting does not equal to cash flows.

The Internal Revenue Service (IRS) requires businesses with more than $5 million in revenues to use the accrual method.[1] Firms below the $5 million threshold can elect to use cash basis accounting for tax purposes and the accrual method for internal decision-making. Even firms with revenues above the threshold may choose one accounting policy, such as the accelerated depreciation method, for tax purposes and a different policy, such as the straight-line depreciation method, to evaluate operation performance.[2] Since the accrual accounting method provides much better information for decision-making, a business should maintain its records on an accrual basis. A tax accountant can prepare financial statements in accordance with IRS requirements from the firm's records when filing for taxes. The rest of this chapter discusses how to use financial statements prepared using the accrual method.

Financial Statements

Financial statements provide vital information about the financial health of a business. There are four main financial statements:

1. income statement;
2. balance sheet;
3. statement of cash flow;
4. statement of owners' equity (or statement of partner's equity, statement of stockholders' equity).

A balance sheet is a snapshot of a firm's assets, liabilities, and owner's equity at a specific point in time. The other three statements show the cumulative effects of a firm's activities over a period of time. An income statement shows a firm's revenues and expenses, and a statement of cash flow shows where a firm's cash came from and where it went. A statement of owners' equity shows changes in the book value of equity. Each of these statements contains different types of information. When analyzed jointly, the statements provide a comprehensive picture of a firm's financial performance.

Income Statement

The income statement is also called the *profit and loss* (*P&L*) *statement*, or *statements of revenues and expenses*. It records revenues and expenses for

Table 4.2 Sample Income Statement: LCG Innovations LLC Income Statement for the Year January 1 Through December 31, 2013

Gross revenues	$700,000
Less: allowances for doubtful accounts	50,000
Net revenues	650,000
Cost of goods sold	415,000
Gross profit	235,000
Operating expenses	
Selling expenses	
Advertising expense	8,300
Promotional expenses	3,500
Administrative expenses	
Office supplies	7,050
Office communication expenses	6,000
Total operating expenses	24,850
Earnings before interest, taxes, depreciation and amortization	210,150
Depreciation expenses	28,750
Earnings before interest and taxes	181,400
Non-operating revenues and expenses	
Interest revenues	1,800
Interest expenses	147,000
Total non-operating income	−145,200
Earnings before tax	36,200
Taxes	14,480
Net income	$21,720

a business over a period of time, usually monthly, quarterly, and annually. Table 4.2 provides a sample income statement.[3]

Revenues or *sales* are generated from sale of products and services by the business. With accrual accounting, revenues do not equal cash receipts if a business allows customers to buy on credit.[4] Revenues include both cash and credit sales. If a large portion of sales is on credit and there is a history of non-payment by some proportion of customers, a business should create an account called *allowance for doubtful accounts* or *bad debt*.

Another provision under accrual accounting relates to potential returns, refunds, and warranties. If there is a history that a certain proportion of sales will be returned or that customers will demand refund for services, a business should create an account that provides *reserves for returns or refunds and warranties*. The goal of these allowance and reserve accounts is to help create a realistic picture of the business. The term *net revenues* or *net sales* refers to the amount of revenues with all allowances and reserves subtracted. It is what a business estimates its true revenues to be, based on past experience.

Net revenues = Gross revenues − Allowance for doubtful accounts − Reserves for returns

Expenses includes all costs associated with generating revenues during the same time period as the sales are recorded. The income statement arranges expenses according to the degree they can be attributed directly to sales. Therefore, *cost of goods sold*[5] (COGS) is the first expense item on an income statement.

4.2 Cost of Goods Sold (COGS)

Cost of goods sold reflects the cost to produce or procure products for sale to customers. In a restaurant, COGS will consist of food and beverage costs. In a retail business, COGS will be the cost of merchandise. In a manufacturing business, COGS will include labor, materials, and supplies used directly in the production process. COGS is calculated as follows.

For non-manufacturing businesses:

COGS = Beginning inventory + Purchases – Ending inventory

For manufacturing businesses:

COGS = Beginning inventory + Cost of labor + Cost of materials and supplies – Ending inventory

---

Under accrual accounting, COGS does not typically equal purchases or payments on purchases. Instead, the goal is to match COGS as closely to sales as possible. Recall the example of the ski and golf retail store. To provide useful information to the entrepreneur, the accounting system should match sales of skis to cost of skis, not cost of golf clubs. One way to do this is to keep track of each set of skis and golf clubs. This approach may be feasible for low transaction businesses, such as car dealers, but impossible for high-volume businesses, such as convenience stores. The general approach is to infer COGS from the value of the ending inventory.[6]

Generally Accepted Accounting Principles provides a number of methods for determining inventory value: specific identification, average cost, first-in-first-out (FIFO), and last-in-first-out (LIFO). A business can use one method to minimize tax and a different method for internal use. The purpose of this chapter is to show entrepreneurs how to use financial statements to manage their businesses, and all discussions will focus on internal use rather than tax minimization.

- The specific identification method requires individual items to be tracked and is only feasible for businesses with few transactions, such as car dealers.

- The FIFO method assumes that oldest inventory will be used up first so that ending inventory reflects the most recent purchase cost. This is typical of a provider of perishable items.
- The LIFO method assumes that newest inventory will be used first, and ending inventory reflects the oldest purchase cost. This method is sometimes used for tax purposes to reduce taxable income because the newest inventory may have the highest cost.
- In the average cost method, ending inventory reflects average purchase cost.

If purchase costs vary minimally, all the methods result in similar ending inventory value. For internal use, the choice of inventory valuation method should reflect the actual inventory management process of the business. Many businesses use the FIFO method, i.e. they sell older inventory before new ones.

Gross profit is defined as net revenues less COGS. This is an important income statement item. If a business does not have positive gross profit, it is losing money on an average transaction! We will return to gross profit as a key performance indicator many times throughout this book.

Gross profit = Net revenues – COGS

The next category of expenses is *operating expenses*, which include overhead costs that are fixed and do not vary with sales. *Selling, general, and administrative (SG&A) expenses* typically fall into this category. Selling expenses may include advertising, special promotion events, or sales materials. General and administrative expenses may include rent, utilities, office supplies, and salary for managers. These expenses are essential to the smooth operation of the business. *Research and development (R&D) expenses* also fall under operating expenses. A business does not have to be in high tech to have R&D expenses. The key factor is using experimentation to improve or develop a product. To claim R&D expenses, there has to be a trial and error process in product development. *Earnings before interest, taxes, depreciation, and amortization (EBITDA)* is usually calculated as gross profits less SG&A and R&D; it is another important metric because it shows whether the business is generating enough revenues to cover overheads, i.e. pay the rent and keep the heat and lighting on.

EBITDA = Gross profits – Selling, general and administrative expenses – R&D expenses

Depreciation and *amortization* expenses fall into the category of *non-cash* expenses. Because expenses are recorded when services are provided by a vendor and used by the business under accrual accounting, capital expenditures such as equipment and building purchases are depreciated over the useful life of these assets. For tax purposes, the IRS has issued specific rules regarding depreciation that may or may not reflect the average useful life of an asset. A business can use one depreciation method to minimize tax and another method for internal use. The Generally Accepted Accounting Principles provide guidelines for four depreciation methods: *straight-line, unit of production, sum of year digits,* and *double declining balance.* The last two methods, sum of year digits and double declining balance, are acceler-ated methods. This means that depreciation expenses in earlier years are higher than in later years. These methods are appropriate for assets whose values drop rapidly initially and stabilize in later years, such as a new car. We know that a car loses 10 percent of its book value as soon as it leaves the dealership, so our depreciation method should reflect that.

The straight-line depreciation method assigns the same amount of depre-ciation to each year, resulting in a constant depreciation expense throughout the life of the asset. This method may be appropriate for a building, the value of which remains constant over a long period of time.

The unit of production method assigns the same amount to each unit owned and is appropriate for machinery whose useful life depends on actual usage rather than time.

These expenses are considered non-cash because the assets have been purchased in prior years. For example, a business does not pay depreciation expenses on a building to anyone. Instead, the net book value of the building is reduced annually by the approved depreciation amount. Amortization expense is a similar concept to depreciation, except that it applies to intangi-ble assets, such as a patent, which is amortized over the life of the patent.

The usefulness of these non-cash expenses and net book values depends on how much the market values of these assets fluctuate. The more market values remain constant, the more useful are these measures. The greatest impact of non-cash expenses is on taxes, regardless of market values. Since the IRS considers depreciation an operating expense, taxable incomes are reduced, lowering taxes. For tax-minimization purposes, businesses should follow IRS guidelines on depreciation.

Earnings before interest and taxes (EBIT), also called *operating income,* is computed as EBITDA less depreciation and amortization expenses.

$$EBIT = EBITDA - \text{Depreciation expenses} - \text{Amortization expenses}$$

If market values of depreciated fixed assets and amortized intangible assets are fairly constant, operating income (EBIT) reflects the business's ability to pay off direct costs (COGS) and overhead, and replenish long-term assets. Even though EBITDA and EBIT are non-GAAP measures, they are impor-tant performance indicators for internal use. Some outside investors and banks also compute these measures when they evaluate a business for loans and equity investments.

4.3 GAAP and Non-GAAP Financial Measures

Since Generally Accepted Accounting Principles (GAAP) apply to businesses in many industries, the guidelines are intentionally broad. For example, GAAP require COGS to be separated from other expenses and gross profit to be computed. Gross profit is a GAAP measure. However, GAAP do not require cash and non-cash expenses to be separated. Therefore, EBITDA and EBIT are considered non-GAAP measures because they are not required calculations under GAAP. These measures provide useful information to the entrepreneur if non-cash expenses are significant for a business. Since specific guidelines for computing these measures are not provided by GAAP, your accountant may choose to follow industry conventions.

Non-operating (or *other*) *revenues and expenses* include *interest expenses* on loans directly related to the business and the *interest revenue* a business earns on its bank accounts and security holdings. If a business owns a minority interest in other businesses, income from these investments will be included here as well. *Total non-operating income* equals the sum of these revenues net of expenses.

Total non-operating income = Non-operating revenues −
Non-operating expenses

Earnings before taxes or *taxable income* equals EBIT plus total non-operating income (loss). This item is also called *income from continuing operations before provision for taxes.* If the business is a partnership, an LLC, or an S corporation, no income tax is filed by the business, and *provision for taxes* will be zero. Instead, the owners report their proportional share of the business's taxable income on their personal tax forms. For a C-corporation, provision for taxes is computed based on the amount of taxable income and the corporate tax schedules by the IRS. *Net income* equals taxable income less taxes. This is the bottom line for a business.

Earnings before taxes = EBIT + Total non-operating income

Net income = Earnings before taxes − provision for taxes

Balance Sheet

A balance sheet is organized into three broad categories: *assets, liabilities,* and *equity.* Table 4.3 contains a sample balance sheet for two years. The accounting identity states that total assets equal the sum of total liabilities and equity.

Total assets = Total liabilities + Total equity

Table 4.3 Sample Balance Sheet

Assets	December 31, 2013	December 31, 2012	Liabilities	December 31, 2013	December 31, 2012
Current assets			*Current liabilities*		
Cash	$3,070	$2,850	Accounts payable	$11,500	$10,600
Petty cash	500	500	Wages payable	8,500	9,200
Short-term investments	2,500	2,500	Current maturity of mortgage	27,500	27,500
Accounts receivable–net	28,600	24,500	Taxes payable	9,600	8,800
Inventory	12,800	14,200	Other current liabilities	6,300	6,300
Supplies	3,100	2,900	Total current liabilities	63,400	62,400
Prepaid insurance	1,500	1,500			
Other current assets	600	750	*Long-term liabilities*		
Total current assets	52,670	49,700	Notes payable	125,000	125,000
			Mortgage	500,000	527,500
Long-term investments	26,000	26,000	Total long-term liabilities	625,000	652,500
Long-term assets			Total liabilities	688,400	714,900
Fixed assets			*Stockholders' equity*		
Land	125,000	125,000	Common stock—par value	10,000	10,000
Land improvements	80,000	80,000	Common stock—additional paid-in capital	250,000	250,000
Buildings	365,000	365,000	Accumulated retained earnings	84,770	63,050
Equipment	279,000	258,000	Total stockholders' equity	344,770	323,050
Less: accumulated depreciation	–65,000	–36,250			
Net fixed assets	784,000	791,750	**Total liabilities & stockholders' equity**	$1,033,170	$1,037,950
Intangible assets					
Trademark	58,000	58,000			
Goodwill	100,000	100,000			
Total intangible assets	158,000	158,000			
Other assets	12,500	12,500			
Total assets	$1,033,170	$1,037,950			

Assets are resources owned by the firm so that it can operate and generate revenues. *Current assets* are short-term assets that are expected to be used up or converted into cash within one year. Examples of current assets are inventory and accounts receivable. Cash is also a current asset. It is important to remember that values recorded on the balance sheet are for a specific day and are referred to as the book value. For example, cash is the amount of cash balance on that day. In the sample balance sheet, you can compare the values between the two years and gain more information about the business's performance.

Long-term assets are assets that are not expected to be used up or converted into cash in the near future. Examples of long-term assets include *fixed assets*, such as equipment and buildings, and *intangible assets*, such as goodwill, trademarks, and patents. *Net fixed assets* is the book value of fixed assets after accumulated depreciation expenses are deducted. *Net intangible assets* is the book value of intangible assets after accumulated amortization expenses. There is often an 'other' category to capture items that do not fit into one of the existing categories or items of which there are too few to warrant creating a new category. A balance sheet is arranged in order of liquidity. Liquidity refers to how fast an asset can be converted into cash. The first item on the balance is typically cash, followed by current assets. Fixed assets will come before intangible assets. Goodwill is often the last asset listed.

Total assets = Total current assets + Net fixed assets + Net intangible assets

Liabilities are classified into *current liabilities* and *long-term liabilities*. Current liabilities include accounts payable, wages payable, and notes payable (loans that are due within one year). Those long-term liabilities due in the coming year are classified as current liabilities. As with the asset section, the accounts are arranged in order of liquidity. Hence, a balance sheet tells an entrepreneur which payments are coming due; the higher a liability is listed on the balance sheet, the sooner it is due.

Total liabilities = Total current liabilities + Long-term liabilities

The title of the equity section varies depending on the form of organization the firm has chosen (Table 4.4). For sole proprietorships, it will be *owner's equity*; for partnerships, it will be *partners' equity*; for corporations, it will be *stockholders' equity*.

The two main categories of *equity* keep track of contributions from owners to the business and accumulated earnings generated by the business. Contributions to partnerships are recorded in the *capital account,* and contributions to corporations are recorded in the *common stock account.* The common stock account may include a par value section and an additional paid-in capital section. *Par value* is a notional number specified in the articles

Table 4.4 Balance Sheets for Different Forms of Business Organization

a Balance Sheet, Equity, Sole Proprietorship

For the year ended December 31	2013	2012
Owner's equity	$344,770	$323,050

b Balance Sheet, Equity, Partnership

For the year ended December 31	2013	2012
Partners' equity		
Joan Smith		
Joan Smith—capital account	$30,000	$30,000
Joan Smith—current account	21,716	18,458
Joan Smith—equity	51,716	48,458
Sarah Goldberg		
Sarah Goldberg—capital account	45,000	45,000
Sarah Goldberg—current account	23,954	19,610
Sarah Goldberg—equity	68,954	64,610
Liam O'Keefe		
Liam O'Keefe—capital account	60,000	60,000
Liam O'Keefe—current account	26,192	20,762
Liam O'Keefe—equity	86,192	80,762
Ann George		
Ann George—capital account	80,000	80,000
Ann George—current account	57,908	49,220
Ann George—equity	137,908	129,220
Total partners' equity	$344,770	$323,050

c Balance Sheet, Equity, Corporation

For the year ended December 31	2013	2012
Shareholders' equity		
Common stock—par value	10,000	10,000
Common stock—additional paid-in capital	250,000	250,000
Accumulated retained earnings	84,770	63,050
Total stockholders' equity	$344,770	$323,050

of incorporation and does not represent the actual contribution. The articles of incorporation in most states require that the number of shares and par value per share be specified at the time that the corporation is first established. Since the value of the stocks and total startup costs are usually unknown at that time, a common practice is to set the par value at $0.01. When an entrepreneur contributes money to the business, any amount above the par value will be recorded as additional paid-in capital. The actual contribution is the sum of par value and additional paid-in capital.

Total common stock = Par value + Additional paid-in capital

Earnings generated by the business that are retained by the business are recorded in the *current account* in partnerships and in the *accumulated retained earnings account* in corporations.
  For partnerships:

Total equity = Partner's capital account + Partner's current account

For corporations:

Total equity = Total common stock + Accumulated retained earnings

The primary characteristic of a partnership's equity accounts is that there is a capital account and a current account for each partner. A partnership with four partners will have eight equity accounts. For corporations, there is no separate account for each shareholder. The equity accounts show the book value of equity. The informational content of equity book value is a topic of hot debate in academic studies.[7] The most important message for entrepreneurs is that book value is not market value. In other words, if an entrepreneur wants to sell a business or part of a business, outside investors will not base their offer price on the existing book value. Chapter 9 provides detailed discussions of business valuation.

Statement of Cash Flows

The statement of cash flow contains three main segments: *cash flow from operating activities*, *cash flow from investing activities*, and *cash flow from financing activities*. The change in a firm's cash holding on the balance sheet from one period to the next is the sum of these three types of cash flow.

Change in cash on balance sheets = Cash flow from operating activities + Cash flow from investing activities + Cash flow from financing activities

Cash flow from investing activities includes cash from liquidation or sale of long-term assets minus cash used in purchasing long-term assets. Cash flow from financing activities includes cash raised from issuing new equity and new long-term loans minus cash used to pay off long-term loans, dividends to shareholders, or withdrawals by partners, and to buy back stocks that have been issued. Cash flow from investing and financing activities reveals strategic decisions made by a business.
  A business owner can choose to compute *cash flows from operating activities* in two ways: direct and indirect. The direct method presents a

Table 4.5 Sample Statement of Cash Flows—Direct Method: LCG Innovations LLC Statement of Cash Flows (Direct Method) for the Year January 1 Through December 31, 2013

Cash flows from operating activities	
Add: Cash received from customers	645,900
Less: Cash paid to suppliers	412,700
Less: Cash paid to other vendors	25,600
Add: Interest received	1,800
Less: Interest paid	147,000
Less: Taxes paid	13,680
Net cash flows provided by operating activities	48,720
Cash flows from investing activities	
Add: Sale of fixed assets	0
Less: Purchase of equipment	21,000
Net cash flows from investing activities	−21,000
Cash flows from financing activities	
Add: New borrowing with notes	0
Less: Principal repayment on mortgage	27,500
Net cash flows from financing activities	−27,500
Net change in cash	220
Cash balance as of December 31, 2012	$2,850
Net change in cash	220
Cash balance as of December 31, 2013	$3,070

summary of cash inflows and outflows and is more intuitive to understand. Table 4.5 shows a sample statement of cash flows prepared using the direct method. Cash flows from operating activities include cash received from customers minus cash paid to suppliers and other vendors. Other cash flows include interest received, less interest and taxes paid. In a nutshell, the direct method of cash flows from operating activities shows whether a business is generating enough cash to pay all its bills.

Although the direct method is intuitive to understand, it does not connect back to the income statement and balance sheets. The indirect method starts with net income from the income statement, adjusts for non-cash items, such as depreciation and amortization expenses, and reconciles changes in current assets and current liabilities to arrive at cash flows from operating activities. The indirect method is less intuitive and requires solid understanding of accounting concepts. Its advantage is that it connects explicitly to the income statement and balance sheets. In fact, if a business follows GAAP when preparing its financial statements, even if it uses the direct method, it still needs to include a reconciliation schedule showing the indirect method.[8] Table 4.6 shows a sample statement of cash flows prepared using the indirect

Table 4.6 Sample Statement of Cash Flows—Indirect Method: LCG Innovations LLC Statement of Cash Flows (Direct Method) for the Year January 1 Through December 31, 2013

Cash flows from operating activities	
Net income	$21,720
Add: Depreciation	28,750
Add: Increase in current liabilities—accounts payable	900
Add: Increase in current liabilities—taxes payable	800
Add: Decrease in current assets—inventory	1,400
Add: Decrease in other current assets	150
Less: Increase in current assets—accounts receivable	4,100
Less: Increase in current assets—supplies	200
Less: Decrease in current liabilities—wages payable	700
Net cash flows provided by operating activities	$48,720
Cash flows from investing activities	
Add: Sale of fixed assets	0
Less: Purchase of equipment	21,000
Net cash flows from investing activities	−21,000
Cash flows from financing activities	
Add: New borrowing with notes	0
Less: Principal repayment on mortgage	27,500
Net cash flows from financing activities	−27,500
Net change in cash	220
Cash balance as of December 31, 2012	$2,850
Net change in cash	220
Cash balance as of December 31, 2013	$3,070

method. Of course, the amount of net cash flow provided by operating activities is the same using either method.

Statement of Changes in Equity

The format of the statement related to equity depends on the form of business organization: *Statement of Owner's Equity* for sole proprietorships; *Statement of Partners' Equity* for partnerships; *Statement of Stockholders' Equity* for corporations. The purpose of this statement is to keep track of the owner's book value equity in the business. While the information content of book value equity is in debate, book value can impact the amount of tax an entrepreneur may have to pay if she decides to sell the business. Table 4.7 provides sample statements of owner's equity, partners' equity, and stockholders' equity.

To prepare this statement, start with the beginning book value of equity, add any additional investments and net income for the year, and subtract withdrawals or dividend distributions.

Table 4.7 Statements of Owner's, Partners', and Shareholders' Equity

a Statement of Changes in Owner's Equity

Owner capital, December 31, 2012	$323,050
Add: New owner capital	0
Add: Year-to-date net income	21,720
Less: Owner draws	0
Owner capital, of December 31, 2013	$344,770

b Statement of Changes in Partners' Equity

	Joan Smith	Sarah Goldberg	Liam O'Keefe	Ann George	Total capital
Partner capital account, December 31, 2012	$30,000	$45,000	$60,000	$80,000	$215,000
Add: New contribution to partner capital	0	0	0	0	0
Partner capital account, December 31, 2013	30,000	45,000	60,000	80,000	215,000
Partner current account, December 31, 2012	18,458	19,610	20,762	49,220	108,050
Add: Year-to-date net income	3,258	4,344	5,430	8,688	21,720
Less: Partner draws	0	0	0	0	0
Partner current account, December 31, 2013	21,716	23,954	26,192	57,908	129,770
Total partners' equity, December 31, 2013	$51,716	$68,954	$86,192	$137,908	$344,770

c Statement of Changes in Shareholders' Equity

Common stock—par value, December 31, 2012	$10,000
Add: Par value of new stocks issued	0
Common stock—par value, December 31, 2013	10,000
Common stock—additional paid-in capital, December 31, 2012	250,000
Add: Additional paid-in capital of new stocks issued	0
Common stock—additional paid-in capital, December 31, 2013	250,000
Retained earnings, December 31, 2012	63,050
Add: Year-to-date net income	21,720
Less: Year-to-date dividends	0
Additions to retained earnings	21,720
Retained earnings, December 31, 2013	84,770
Total stockholders' equity	$344,770

For sole proprietorships:

Ending owner's capital = Beginning owner's capital + Net income –
Owner's drawings

For partnerships:

Ending partners' capital account = Beginning partners' capital account +
New partners' capital contribution

Ending partners' current account = Beginning partners' current account +
Net income – Partners' withdrawal

For corporations:

Ending par value = Beginning par value + Par value of new stocks issued

Ending additional paid-in capital = Beginning additional paid-in capital +
Additional paid-in capital of new
stocks issued

Ending retained earnings = Beginning retained earnings + Net income –
Dividends

In summary, the income statement shows whether a business is profitable over the operating period, and the balance sheet shows how much assets, including cash, a business has on hand and how many liabilities it has to pay. The statement of cash flow shows how much cash has been generated and used over the operating period. The three statements together provide a comprehensive picture of a business. The next section discusses additional tools for analyzing these statements, to help entrepreneurs make informed decisions.

Financial Statement Analysis

While financial statements provide basic data about a business, additional analysis is needed if an entrepreneur wants to extract more information to help in effective business decision-making. Just as when the fuel gauge reads empty, the driver knows she needs to stop and refuel. However, if the speedometer reads 30 mph, the driver needs more data to decide if she needs to speed up, slow down, or stay the course. This section introduces the essential dashboard of financial ratios that will help entrepreneurs get the most out of financial statements.

Common Size Financial Statements

Common size or *standardized* income statements and balance sheets present financial data as percentages instead of total dollar amounts. Transforming dollar amounts into percentages allows meaningful comparison over time and against

Table 4.8 Sample Common Size Income Statement: LCG Innovations LLC Common Size Income Statement for the Year January 1 Through December 31, 2013 (in percent)

Gross revenues	100.00
Less: Allowances for doubtful accounts	7.14
Net revenues	92.86
Cost of goods sold	59.29
Gross profit	33.57
Operating expenses	
Selling expenses	
Advertising expense	1.19
Promotional expenses	0.50
Administrative expenses	
Office supplies	1.01
Office communication expense	0.86
Total operating expenses	3.55
Earnings before interests, taxes, depreciation and amortization	30.02
Depreciation expenses	4.11
Earnings before interests and taxes	25.91
Non-operating revenues and expenses	
Interest revenues	0.26
Interest expenses	21.00
Total non-operating income	−20.74
Earnings before tax	5.17
Provisions for taxes	2.07
Net income	3.10

competitors or industry averages. To compute common size income statements, divide all its items by revenues. Table 4.8 presents the income statement from Table 4.2 in a common size format. From Table 4.8, the entrepreneur can see that the two largest expenses are COGS (59 percent of revenues) and interest expenses (21 percent of revenues). In fact, these two items comprised 80 percent of revenues. Taxes represent only 2 percent.

To compute the common size balance sheet, divide all its items by total assets. Table 4.9 presents the balance sheets for both years from Table 4.3 in common size format. The firm's relative financial position remained stable over the two years. Fixed assets represent about 76 percent of total assets, and debt ratio decreased from almost 69 percent to 66.6 percent. The common size statements are a good starting point for financial analysis. An entrepreneur can focus on items that have changed significantly over time or deviate greatly

Table 4.9 Sample Common Size Balance Sheet: LCG Innovations LLC Balance Sheet As of December 31, 2013 and 2012

Assets	As of December 31, 2013 (%)	As of December 31, 2012 (%)	Liabilities	As of December 31, 2013 (%)	As of December 31, 2012 (%)
Current assets			*Current liabilities*		
Cash	0.30	0.27	Accounts payable	1.11	1.02
Petty cash	0.05	0.05	Wages payable	0.82	0.89
Short-term investments	0.24	0.24	Current maturity of mortgage	2.66	2.65
Accounts receivable—net	2.77	2.36	Taxes payable	0.93	0.85
Inventory	1.24	1.37	Other current liabilities	0.61	0.61
Supplies	0.30	0.28	Total current liabilities	6.14	6.01
Prepaid insurance	0.15	0.14			
Other current assets	0.06	0.07	*Long-term liabilities*		
Total current assets	5.10	4.79	Notes payable	12.10	12.04
			Mortgage	48.39	50.82
Long-term investments	2.52	2.50	Total long-term liabilities	60.49	62.86
Long-term assets			Total liabilities	66.63	68.88
Fixed assets					
Land	12.10	12.04	Stockholders' Equity		
Land improvements	7.74	7.71	Common stock—par value	0.97	0.96
Buildings	35.33	35.17	Common stock—additional paid-in capital	24.20	24.09
Equipment	27.00	24.86	Accumulated retained earnings	8.20	6.07
Less: Accumulated depreciation	−6.29	−3.49	Total stockholders' equity	33.37	31.12
Net fixed assets	75.88	76.28			
			Total liabilities & stockholders' equity	100.00	100.00
Intangible assets					
Trademark	5.61	5.59			
Goodwill	9.68	9.63			
Total intangible assets	15.29	15.22			
Other assets	1.21	1.20			
Total assets	100.00	100.00			

from industry averages. The next section introduces financial ratio analysis, another set of tools that works hand-in-hand with common size statements.

Financial Ratios

Financial ratios are usually divided into four categories: *liquidity ratios, financial leverage ratios, turnover ratios,* and *profitability ratios.* The first two categories provide information about financial risks facing the firm in the short-term (liquidity) and long-term (financial leverage). Turnover ratios tell the entrepreneur how well the firm is utilizing its assets. They also provide early warnings on whether the firm is nearing its capacity. Profitability ratios are often the focus of entrepreneurs, but they should be interpreted in the context of the other categories, to provide a more complete picture of the firm.

Liquidity Ratios

Liquidity ratios include *current ratio, quick ratio,* and *cash ratio.* These ratios provide information about a firm's ability to meet its current liabilities, i.e. liabilities that are due within one year. The terms "liabilities," "debts," and "loans" will be used interchangeably. Therefore, the denominator for all these ratios is current liabilities.

Current Ratio

The current ratio is the most commonly used measure for short-term financial risk. Many banks and suppliers use current ratio as one of the factors in credit decisions. The current ratio is defined as:

$$\text{Current ratio} = \frac{\text{Current assets}}{\text{Current liabilities}}$$

Using values from the sample balance sheet in 2013, the current ratio is:

$$\text{Current ratio} = \frac{\text{Current assets}}{\text{Current liabilities}} = \frac{52,670}{63,400} = 0.83$$

Recall that current assets are expected to be converted into cash within one year. The current ratio represents the firm's ability to pay off its current liabilities without additional cash flow from the operation. What is a good current ratio? The answer depends on the industry. The rule of thumb is that the current ratio should be at least 1 and generally over 2. A current ratio of 1 means that the firm will be able to pay off its current liabilities by converting all its current assets into cash. A current ratio of 2 provides some margin of safety. The sample firm has a current ratio of 0.83, which is troubling and warrants more in-depth analysis. However, a current ratio of less than 1 does not necessarily mean that a firm is in immediate danger of bankruptcy. The sample firm had a current ratio of 0.80 in 2012 and 0.83 in 2013. It stayed in business during 2013 and even generated a profit; however, a low current ratio will limit its ability to borrow funds if needed, and it is likely that the owners will have to raise additional equity capital.

Quick Ratio

The quick ratio, also called the acid-test ratio, recognizes that some current assets, especially inventory and prepaid expenses, cannot be converted into cash easily if a business faces hard times. The nickname "acid-test" implies that this is a more rigorous test of a firm's short-term financial risk. The quick ratio is defined as:

$$\text{Quick ratio} = \frac{\text{Current assets} - \text{Inventory} - \text{Prepaid expenses}}{\text{Current liabilities}}$$

$$= \frac{(52,670 - 12,800 - 1,500)}{63,400} = 0.61$$

Unlike the current ratio, there is no simple rule of thumb for assessing the quick ratio. Comparing against industry averages is particularly important because inventory may be an important factor in some industries and not in others. For our sample firm, a quick ratio of 0.61 in 2013 means that the firm will cover only 61 percent of its current liability by liquidating all remaining current assets without bringing in additional cash and not selling any existing inventory.

Cash Ratio

Cash includes cash on hand, cash balance in bank accounts, and short-term investments. Using values from the sample balance sheet as of December 31, 2013, we calculate cash ratio as:

$$\text{Cash Ratio} = \frac{\text{Cash} + \text{Short-term investments}}{\text{Current liabilities}}$$

$$= \frac{(3,070 + 500 + 2,500)}{63,400} = 0.0957$$

This firm's cash ratio implies that available cash covers less than 10 percent of its current liabilities, which is not much at all. However, keeping cash on hand is expensive because cash does not generate revenues. Cash flow management is the most important financial decision of a small business and the next chapter is devoted to this topic. For our sample firm, the three liquidity ratios all point to a very high level of current liabilities relative to current assets. A more in-depth look at the balance sheet of the sample firm, Table 4.3, reveals that a large part of its current liabilities is the current portion of its mortgage. A competitor may have higher liquidity ratios because it rents instead of owning its building. Rent reduces profit but does not affect a firm's balance sheet. This firm chose to own its building and finance using a mortgage. While this may be a correct strategic decision, these ratios show that the entrepreneur may need to consider investing more cash to strengthen the firm's short-term liquidity.

Financial Leverage Ratios

Financial leverage ratios measure a firm's long-term financial risk. These ratios look at a firm's ability to support its loan obligations beyond the current year. We include five ratios in this category: *Total debt ratio, debt-to-equity ratio, equity multiplier, times interest earned ratio* and *cash coverage ratio.* The first three ratios are based on balance sheet items and reflect the financial standing of a firm at a given point in time. The last two ratios are based on income statement items and look at a firm's ability to support its interest obligations from its day-to-day operation.

Total Debt Ratio

Sometimes total debt ratio is simply referred to as debt ratio and is defined as:

$$\text{Total debt ratio} = \frac{\text{Total liabilities}}{\text{Total assets}} = \frac{688,400}{1,033,170} = 0.67$$

In other words, our sample firm uses 67 percent debt. The choice of debt level is partly a strategic decision by management and partly constrained by the structural characteristics of an industry. For example, in 2013, the average total debt ratio was 81.5 percent for the airline industry and 42.9 percent for restaurants.[9] If the sample firm is a restaurant, its debt ratio of 67 percent, more than 1.5 times the industry average, would be a red flag for investors and banks. Since use of debt increases the financial risk of a firm, financial ratios that are substantially higher than industry averages signal greater risk.

Debt-To-Equity Ratio

The debt-to-equity ratio is defined as:

$$\text{Debt-to-equity ratio} = \frac{\text{Total debt}}{\text{Total equity}} = \frac{688,400}{344,770} = 2.00$$

The debt-to-equity ratio of the sample firm shows that for every dollar of equity contributed by the entrepreneur in 2013, the firm borrowed two dollars.

Equity multiplier

Equity multiplier is defined as:

$$\text{Equity multiplier} = \frac{\text{Total assets}}{\text{Total equity}} = \frac{1,033,170}{344,770} = 3.00$$

The equity multiplier indicates that in 2013 every dollar of equity was leveraged to support three dollars of assets. The three ratios are based on the same items from the balance sheet and provide the same basic information. Banks, suppliers and outside investors will use these ratios to determine the credit risk of a business.

Times Interest Earned and Cash Coverage Ratios

$$\text{Times interest earned ratio} = \frac{\text{Earnings before interest and taxes}}{\text{Interest expense}}$$

$$= \frac{181,400}{147,000} = 1.23$$

$$\text{Cash coverage ratio} = \frac{\text{Earnings before interest, taxes, depreciation, and amortization}}{\text{Interest expense}}$$

$$= \frac{210,150}{147,000} = 1.43$$

The times interest earned ratio of our sample firm shows that its EBIT were 1.23 times that of its interest expense. Since non-cash expenses are deducted when computing EBIT, the actual amount of cash available for interest payment may be higher. The cash coverage ratio uses EBITDA, which excludes non-cash expenses. In general, the higher these ratios, the better, and banks will be more willing to lend to the business. In personal finance, banks typically look for an income-to-debt payment ratio of 3 to 4. Business finance is more complicated and banks look at more factors but the coverage ratios of the sample firm are quite low. If EBITDA decreased by 30 percent, the firm would not be able to make interest payments.

Turnover Ratios

Turnover ratios reveal the efficiency of a firm's operation. Items used in computing turnover ratios are based on both the income statement and the balance sheet. Using data from both financial statements presents a new challenge. The balance sheet measures a firm's financial position at a single point in time, whereas the income statement measures a firm's financial results over a period of time. A landscaping business started the year with one truck. It was so successful that the owner purchased a second truck six months later. Total assets on the balance sheet at the beginning of the year would show the value of one truck. The balance sheet at the end of the year would show two trucks. The income statement showed total revenue generated for the entire year. Did the business generate these revenues with one truck or two trucks? The answer is neither! As a general rule, instead of using the beginning value or the ending value, we use the average value when computing turnover ratios. The average value is:

$$\text{Average balance sheet value} = \frac{\left(\begin{array}{c}\text{Beginning balance sheet value} + \\ \text{Ending balance sheet value}\end{array}\right)}{2}$$

Inventory Turnover and Days Sales in Inventory

Inventory turnover measures how many times a firm turnover its inventory each year and days sales in inventory is the average number of days a firm carries its inventory before selling it. Since inventory is a balance sheet item, we first need to compute average inventory:

$$\text{Average inventory} = \frac{\left(\text{Beginning inventory} + \text{Ending inventory}\right)}{2}$$

$$= \frac{\left(14,200 + 12,800\right)}{2}$$

$$= \$13,500$$

$$\text{Inventory turnover} = \frac{\text{Cost of goods sold}}{\text{Average inventory}} = \frac{415,000}{13,500} = 30.74$$

$$\text{Days sales in inventory} = \frac{365\,\text{days}}{\text{Inventory turnover}} = \frac{365}{30.74} = 11.87\,\text{days}$$

Turnover ratios tend to be industry-specific. For example, the retail apparel industry has an average inventory turnover ratio of 5.03.[10] By comparison, the restaurant industry has an average inventory turnover ratio of 29.05. A business wants to keep as low an inventory level as possible but not so low as to risk running out of product and losing sales.

Receivables Turnover and Average Collection Period

The receivables turnover and average collection period measure how fast a firm collects from its customers who purchase on credit. As with inventory, accounts receivable is a balance sheet item, so we first compute average accounts receivable:

$$\text{Average accounts receivable} = \frac{\left(\begin{array}{c}\text{Beginning accounts receivable} + \\ \text{Ending accounts receivable}\end{array}\right)}{2}$$

$$= \frac{(24,500 + 28,600)}{2} = \$26,550$$

$$\text{Receivable turnover} = \frac{\text{Net revenues}}{\text{Average accounts receivable}} = \frac{650,000}{26,550} = 24.48$$

$$\text{Average collection period} = \frac{365\,\text{days}}{\text{Receivables turnover}} = \frac{365}{24.48} = 14.91\,\text{days}$$

Industry convention again plays an important role when evaluating your firm's performance using receivable turnover and average collection period. If other firms in the industry are offering 15-day terms to customers, you may need to offer similar terms to stay competitive. Accounts receivable financing is a valuable current asset and, as shown in Chapter 3, can be used as collateral for short-term loans or be sold to special financing companies through factoring.

Payables Turnover and Accounts Payables Period

Payables turnover measures how often a firm pays its suppliers and accounts payables period shows the number of days it takes the firm to pay its invoices.

$$\text{Average accounts payable} = \frac{\left(\begin{array}{c}\text{Beginning accounts payable} + \\ \text{Ending accounts payable}\end{array}\right)}{2}$$

$$= \frac{(11,500 + 10,600)}{2} = \$11,050$$

$$\text{Purchases} = \text{COGS} + \text{Ending Inventory} - \text{Beginning Inventory}$$

$$= \$415,000 + \$14,200 - \$12,800 = \$416,400$$

$$\text{Payable turnover} = \frac{\text{Purchases}}{\text{Average accounts payable}} = \frac{416,400}{11,050} = 37.68$$

$$\text{Average payable period} = \frac{365\,\text{days}}{\text{payable turnover}} = \frac{365}{37.68} = 9.69\,\text{days}$$

In this example, the firm takes almost 10 days on average to pay its suppliers. It can compare this ratio against the industry average. If the normal term in the industry is net 15, implying most firms have 15 days to pay its suppliers, it may be able to negotiate longer terms with its suppliers. If this firm's suppliers typically offer a cash discount for payment within 10 days, this ratio implies that the firm have been paying within the discount period.

Total Asset Turnover

Total asset turnover is an overall efficiency measure and is defined as:

$$\text{Average total assets} = \frac{\left(\text{Beginning total assets} + \text{Ending total assets}\right)}{2}$$

$$= \frac{\left(1,037,950 + 1,033,170\right)}{2}$$

$$= \$1,035,560$$

$$\text{Total asset turnover} = \frac{\text{Net revenues}}{\text{Average total assets}} = \frac{650,000}{1,035,560} = 0.63 \text{ times}$$

In general, a higher total asset turnover than the industry average means that a firm is using its assets more efficiently. However, if total asset turnover is too high, it may signal that a firm is reaching its capacity or that the book values of assets have been depreciated and the assets are old. Both scenarios mean that the firm will need significant capital investment in the near future. Conversely, if total asset turnover is too low because a firm just acquired a lot of new assets, the low ratio is not a cause for alarm.

Profitability Ratios

We include four popular measures of profitability: *gross margin, profit margin, return on assets (ROA)*, and *return on equity (ROE)*. The first two margin measures assess the profitability of the business's operation and are based on items from the income statement only. The last two return measures assess how profitable the firm's investment is as a whole without leverage (ROA) and how profitable is the owners' investment with leverage included (ROE). Since assets and equity are balance sheet items, we use average total assets and average equity when computing these ratios to address the dilemma of different beginning and ending values, as discussed earlier.

Gross Margin

Gross margin tells a business how much gross profit is generated from each dollar in net revenue. It is defined as:

$$\text{Gross margin} = \frac{\text{Gross profit}}{\text{Net revenues}} = \frac{235,000}{650,000} = 0.36 = 36\%$$

Thus, for the sample firm, each dollar in net revenue brought in 36 cents of gross profit in 2013. Comparing this ratio against the industry average will provide more meaning. A gross margin of 36 percent may be reasonable for retail businesses but will be low for service industries.

Profit Margin

Profit margin is often the focus of any business owner. It shows how much net profit (net income) is generated from each dollar in net revenue and is defined as:

$$\text{Profit margin} = \frac{\text{Net income}}{\text{Net revenues}} = \frac{21,720}{650,000} = 0.03 = 3\%$$

Recall that many expense items are deducted to arrive at net income. Turning a profit is highly desirable and a business cannot survive if it remains unprofitable for a long time. However, it is also important to caution against overemphasis on short-term profits. For example, a business may strategically choose to sacrifice profit margin to gain higher volume.

Return on Assets (ROA)

The ROA measures the amount of profit generated per dollar of assets and is defined as:

$$\text{Return on assets}(\text{ROA}) = \frac{\text{Net income}}{\text{Average total assets}} = \frac{21,720}{1,035,560} = 0.02 = 2\%$$

Return on Equity (ROE)

The ROE measures the amount of profit generated per dollar of total equity and is defined as:

$$\text{Average total equity} = \frac{\left(\text{Beginning total equity} + \text{Ending total equity}\right)}{2}$$

$$= \frac{\left(323,050 + 344,770\right)}{2}$$

$$= 333,910$$

$$\text{Return on equity}(\text{ROE}) = \frac{\text{Net income}}{\text{Average total equity}} = \frac{21,720}{333,910} = 0.07 = 7\%$$

Both ROA and ROE are measures of return on investment. The ROA looks at return from the perspective of the entire firm based on total assets. Since ROA is not affected by financial leverage, it is a particularly useful measure for comparing profitability of the business against industry averages and competitors. Outside investors will also likely use ROA to evaluate a business. The ROE measures return from the perspective of the owners based on total equity and is the most commonly referenced profitability ratio. When a firm uses debt, financial leverage magnifies ROE. In the sample firm, ROE is 7 percent compared with ROA at 2 percent, about 3.1 times larger. Notice that the average equity multiplier for this firm is also around 3.1. This is no coincidence. The equity multiplier measures the magnifying effect of financial leverage. The ROE is one of the most scrutinized financial ratios and an important profitability measure for owners. It is much less useful as a comparative measure because different firms tend to have different financial leverage. Outside investors also tend to rely on ROA more than ROE because they expect the capital structure of a firm to change when outside equity is added.

More Financial Ratios

The ratios discussed in this chapter are the most commonly used financial ratios. There are other ratios unique to specific industries that are not included in this chapter. As new business models emerge, entrepreneurs and financial analysts may develop additional ratios. For example, if a business is considering developing a website for online sales, a useful ratio will be revenue per "click," which is computed as total revenues divided by number of clicks. The goal of financial statement and ratio analysis is to enable meaningful comparisons over time and against external benchmarks. Industry trade groups and their magazines often publish industry averages and benchmarks annually. A few online websites, such as the Yahoo Industry Center, provide key industry financial ratios for free. Check out your local library and school library, which often subscribe to financial and accounting databases and books (e.g. Troy, 2014).

Appendix 4.1 Chart of Accounts

Table 4.10 shows selected account titles and numbers based on the Generally Accepted Accounting Principles.

Table 4.10 Selected Chart of Accounts Titles and Account Names Based on GAAP

Account title	Account number
Assets	10000
Current assets	10100
Cash and short-term investments	10101
Receivables	10102
Inventory	10103
Accrued, deferred, and other current assets	10104
Long-lived assets	10200
Investments and financial instruments	10201
Property plant and equipment	10202
Intangible assets (excluding goodwill)	10204
Goodwill	10205
Other long-lived assets	10206
Liabilities	20000
Short-term liabilities	20100
Payables	20101
Accrued and deferred liabilities	20102
Current portion of long-term debt	20103
Other short-term liabilities	20104
Long-term liabilities	20200
Debts	20201
Other non-current liabilities	20204
Stockholders' equity	30000
Paid-in capital	30100
Common stock	30101
Preferred stock	30102
Additional paid-in capital	30103
Retained earnings	30200
Revenues	40000
Revenues from goods	40100
Revenues from products and merchandise	40101
Allowances and discounts	40102
Revenues from services	40200
General services	40201
Allowances and discounts	40202
Other operating revenues	40300
Other operating income	40400
Expenses	50000
Cost of sales	50100
Cost of goods sold	50101

Account title	Account number
Cost of services rendered	50102
Selling, general, and administrative	50200
Selling expenses	50201
General and administrative expenses	50202
Other selling, general, and administrative expenses	50203
Non-operating items	60000
Gains and losses	60100
Business combination, acquisition related costs	60107
Income (loss) from equity method investments	60108
Gain (loss) related to litigation settlement	60109
Non-operating revenues and expenses	60200
Other revenues	60201
Other expenses	60202
Income tax	70000
Income tax benefit	70100
Income tax expense	70200

Appendix 4.2 Financial Statement Calculations

Income Statement

- Net revenues = Gross revenues − Allowance for doubtful accounts − Reserves for returns
- Gross profits = Net revenues − COGS
- EBITDA = Gross profits − Selling, general, and administrative expenses − R&D expenses
- *Earnings before interest and taxes (EBIT)*, also called *operating income*, is computed as EBITDA less depreciation and amortization expenses.
- EBIT = EBITDA − Depreciation expenses − Amortization expenses
- Total non-operating income = Non-operating revenues − Non-operating expenses
- Earnings before taxes = EBIT + Total non-operating income
- Net income = Earnings before taxes − provision for taxes

Balance Sheet

- Total assets = Total liabilities + Total equity
- Total assets = Total current assets + Net fixed assets + Net intangible assets
- Total liabilities = Total current liabilities + Long-term liabilities
- For partnerships: Total equity = Partners' capital account + Partners' current account
- For corporations: Total equity = Total common stock + Accumulated retained earnings
- Total common stock = Par value + Additional paid-in capital

Statement of Cash Flow

- Change in cash on balance sheets = Cash flow from operating activities + Cash flow from investing activities + Cash flow from financing activities

Statement of Equity

For sole proprietorships:
- Ending owner's capital = Beginning owner's capital + Net income − Owner's drawings

For partnerships:

- Ending partners' capital account = Beginning partners' capital account + New partners' capital contribution
- Ending partners' current account = Beginning partners' current account + Net income − Partners' withdrawal

For corporations:

- Ending par value = Beginning par value + Par value of new stocks issued
- Ending additional paid-in capital = Beginning additional paid-in capital + Additional paid-in capital of new stocks issued
- Ending retained earnings = Beginning retained earnings + Net income − Dividends

Appendix 4.3 Financial Ratios

Liquidity Ratios

$$\text{Current ratio} = \frac{\text{Current assets}}{\text{Current liabilities}}$$

$$\text{Quick ratio} = \frac{\text{Current assets} - \text{Inventory} - \text{Prepaid expenses}}{\text{Current liabilities}}$$

$$\text{Cash ratio} = \frac{\text{Cash} + \text{Short-term investments}}{\text{Current liabilities}}$$

Financial Leverage Ratios

$$\text{Total debt ratio} = \frac{\text{Total liabilities}}{\text{Total assets}}$$

$$\text{Debt-to-equity ratio} = \frac{\text{Total debt}}{\text{Total equity}}$$

$$\text{Equity multiplier} = \frac{\text{Total assets}}{\text{Total equity}}$$

$$\text{Times interest earned ratio} = \frac{\text{Earnings before interests and taxes}}{\text{Interest expense}}$$

$$\text{Cash coverage ratio} = \frac{\text{Earnings before interests, taxes, depreciation and amortization}}{\text{Interest expense}}$$

Turnover Ratios

$$\text{Average inventory} = \frac{\left(\text{Beginning inventory} + \text{Ending inventory}\right)}{2}$$

$$\text{Inventory turnover} = \frac{\text{Cost of goods sold}}{\text{Average inventory}}$$

$$\text{Days Sales in inventory} = \frac{365\,\text{days}}{\text{Inventory turnover}}$$

$$\text{Average accounts receivable} = \frac{\left(\begin{array}{c}\text{Beginning accounts receivable} + \\ \text{Ending accounts receivable}\end{array}\right)}{2}$$

$$\text{Receivable turnover} = \frac{\text{Net revenues}}{\text{Average accounts receivable}}$$

$$\text{Average collection period} = \frac{365\,\text{days}}{\text{Receivables turnover}}$$

$$\text{Average accounts payable} = \frac{\left(\begin{array}{c}\text{Beginning accounts payable} + \\ \text{Ending accounts payable}\end{array}\right)}{2}$$

$$\text{Purchases} = \frac{\left(\begin{array}{c}\text{Beginning accounts payable} + \\ \text{Ending accounts payable}\end{array}\right)}{2}$$

$$\text{Purchases} = \text{COGS} + \text{Ending Inventory} - \text{Beginning Inventory}$$

$$\text{Payable turnover} = \frac{\text{Purchases}}{\text{Average accounts payable}}$$

$$\text{Average payable period} = \frac{365\,\text{days}}{\text{Payable turnover}}$$

$$\text{Average total assets} = \frac{\left(\begin{array}{c}\text{Beginning total assets} + \\ \text{Ending total assets}\end{array}\right)}{2}$$

$$\text{Total asset turnover} = \frac{\text{Net revenues}}{\text{Average total assets}}$$

Profitability Ratios

$$\text{Gross margin} = \frac{\text{Gross profit}}{\text{Net revenues}}$$

$$\text{Profit margin} = \frac{\text{Net income}}{\text{Net revenues}}$$

$$\text{Average total assets} = \frac{\left(\begin{array}{c}\text{Beginning total assets} + \\ \text{Ending total assets}\end{array}\right)}{2}$$

$$\text{Return on assets}\left(\text{ROA}\right) = \frac{\text{Net income}}{\text{Average total assets}}$$

$$\text{Average total equity} = \frac{\left(\begin{array}{c}\text{Beginning total equity} + \\ \text{Ending total equity}\end{array}\right)}{2}$$

$$\text{Return on equity}\left(\text{ROE}\right) = \frac{\text{Net income}}{\text{Average total equity}}$$

Case 4.1 Making the Numbers Work for Decisions: Eco Excellence Express Cleaners, LLC

Caroline Glackin

Business plan written? Check. Financials complete? Check. Finals of business plan competition? Check. Ready to start the business? No check.

Jason Martin was a 26-year old senior at Shepherd University in the Eastern Panhandle of West Virginia when he entered Eco Excellence Express Cleaners, LLC (E^3C) into the statewide business plan competition. He had completed his marketing and entrepreneurship coursework between stints as a truck driver, employee at a beer and wine distributor, and salesperson. He grew up surrounded by family members who owned businesses ranging from a fine dining restaurant and a gourmet gift shop to a beer and wine distributor. He knew that he wanted to start and grow an entrepreneurial venture, but was not certain what that might be.

During the fall semester, he identified an opportunity to create an eco-friendly dry cleaning and laundry service for the local area, which provided pickup and delivery to homes and places of employment. He entered his idea in the business plan competition and succeeded in advancing to the semi-final and final rounds. He continued to develop and test the concept into the spring. The value proposition evolved into saving time, improving family health, and being eco-friendly.

As the plan evolved, Jason's financial projections became increasingly detailed and fact-based. He secured quotations for many of his startup costs and benchmarked against other dry cleaning, laundry, and mobile dry cleaning services. He found an existing local eco-friendly dry cleaner as a supplier and located a leasing opportunity for the laundry facility. Family and friends stepped forward and committed funds to the proposed business. Jason received feedback from judges and coaches during the competition as well as from his classmates and faculty advisor.

Because Jason had some savings, substantial equity, and a current job, he could pursue financing through a microloan program to bring E^3C into existence. However, he was not certain that he was ready to do so. His financial projections showed that the company would be profitable in the second year and that he would live off of his savings in the first year and earn about $84,000 in the third year. Jason also knew that by working for an employer he could garner commissions as a salesman that would far exceed his early earnings from the business. He also recognized that the financial projections were just that... projections... and he had heard his advisor say, "A business plan is a creative work of fiction that is the story of your expectations." He knew that even with the best of plans the business would not evolve exactly as described.

Jason was convinced that he could promote the business and that there was an ample market for it, but he was less certain of the financial projections and the opportunity costs of deciding to move forward upon graduation. Also, he was counting on the $10,000 business plan prize for a significant portion of his equity. Without that funding, he would have to add debt to his financials and revisit the numbers. Graduation was rapidly approaching, and Jason had not begun to line up the business or to search for a full-time job. He faced some difficult choices.

Case Questions

1. Review the financial statements in Tables 4.11 to 4.15. What issues, questions, and concerns do you have about them?
2. How would the statements change if Jason decided to secure an additional $10,000 in debt to replace the planned equity from the competition?
3. What do the key ratios tell us about the proposed venture?
4. What factors should Jason consider when deciding whether to proceed with the efforts required to launch E³C? Why?
5. What do you recommend that Jason do and why?

Table 4.11 Eco Excellence Express Cleaners LLC Projected Start-Up Costs

Item	Cost	Estimate or Actual
Start-Up Expenses		
Expensed Equipment	$500	estimate
Financial Institution Fees	$1,500	estimate
Fuel	$400	estimate
Identity Set/Stationary	$500	estimate
Insurance	$1,000	estimate
Licenses	$150	estimate
Marketing Materials	$1,200	estimate
Payroll (with taxes)	$–	
Professional Fees – Accounting	$–	
Professional Fees – Legal	$–	
Rent	$630	actual
Supplies – Office	$200	estimate
Supplies – Cleaning	$400	estimate
Utilities	$500	estimate
Web Fees	$250	estimate
Total Start-Up Expenses	$7,230	
Start-Up Assets		
Cash on Hand	$200	actual
Equipment (including installation)	$60,500	actual
Furniture and Fixtures	$4,500	estimate
Leasehold Improvements	$1,000	estimate
Rent Deposit	$630	actual

Table 4.11 Eco Excellence Express Cleaners LLC Projected Start-Up Costs (Continued)

Item	Cost	Estimate or Actual
Signage	$750	estimate
Utility Deposits	$1,800	estimate
Vehicle(s)	$35,000	actual
Total Start-Up Assets	$104,380	
Total Start-Up Requirements	**$111,610**	
Contingency Funds (10%)	$11,161	
Start-Up with Contingency	**$122,771**	

Equipment = washer 35# ($9000), washer 50# ($11000), 4 dryers ($18000), press ($3200), hot water heater ($1200), 25 storage units ($3300), miscellaneous ($4000)

Equipment

Washer, 35lbs	$9,000
Washer, 50lbs	$11,000
4 Dryers ($4500 ea.)	$18,000
Press	$3,200
Hot water heater	$12,000
25 Rubbermaid storage sheds	$3,300
Miscellaneous	$4,000
	$60,500

Furniture and Fixtures

Office Furniture & Furnishings	$1,000
Fixtures	$2,000
Work Tables	$1,500
	$4,500

Table 4.12 Eco Excellence Express Cleaners LLC Sales Projections

	Month 1	Month 2	Month 3	Month 4	Month 5	Month 6	Month 7
Laundry							
# of customers	35	45	60	65	70	75	80
Loads (4.3 wks)	150.5	193.5	258	279.5	301	322.5	344
Price per 20lbs	$24.00	$24.00	$24.00	$30.00	$30.00	$30.00	$30.00
Gross Sales	$3,612	$4,644	$6,192	$8,385	$9,030	$9,675	$10,320
Returns & allowances	$–	$–	$–	$–	$–	$–	$–
Net Laundry Sales	**$3,612**	**$4,644**	**$6,192**	**$8,385**	**$9,030**	**$9,675**	**$10,320**
Quarterly Net Laundry Sales			$14,448			$27,090	
Dry Cleaning							
Customers	30	40	52	65	78	90	108
Units (4.3)	64.5	86	111.8	139.75	167.7	193.5	232.2
Price per order	$35.00	$35.00	$35.00	$35.00	$35.00	$35.00	$35.00
Gross Sales	$2,258	$3,010	$3,913	$4,891	$5,870	$6,773	$8,127
Returns & allowances							
Net Dry Cleaning Sales	**$2,258**	**$3,010**	**$3,913**	**$4,891**	**$5,870**	**$6,773**	**$8,127**
Quarterly Net Dry Cleaning Sales			$9,181			$17,533	
Repairs & Alterations							
Net Repairs and Alterations Sales	$–	$–	$–	**$100**	**$100**	**$100**	**$500**
Quarterly Net Repairs and Alterations Sales						300	
Quarterly Total Sales	**$5,870**	**$7,654**	**$10,105** $23,629	**$13,376**	**$15,000**	**$16,548** $44,923	**$18,947**

Month 8	Month 9	Month 10	Month 11	Month 12	Year 1	Year 2	Year 3
85	90	95	100	105		1000	1200
365.5	387	408.5	430	451.5	xxxxxxxx xxxxxxxx	4300	5160
$30.00	$30.00	$30.00	$30.00	$30.00	xxxxxxxx xxxxxxxx	$30.00	$30.00
$10,965	$11,610	$12,255	$12,900	$13,545	$1,13,133	$1,29,000	$1,54,800
$–	$–	$–	$–	$–	$–	$–	$–
$10,965	**$11,610**	**$12,255**	**$12,900**	**$13,545**	**$1,13,133**	**$1,29,000**	**$1,54,800**
	$32,895			$38,700	$1,13,133		
130	156	190	228	250	1417	3300	3500
279.5	335.4	408.5	490.2	537.5	xxxxxxxx xxxxxxxx	7095	7525
$35.00	$35.00	$35.00	$35.00	$35.00	xxxxxxxx xxxxxxxx	$35.00	$35.00
$9,783	$11,739	$14,298	$17,157	$18,813	$1,06,629 $–	$2,48,325	$2,63,375
$9,783	**$11,739**	**$14,298**	**$17,157**	**$18,813**	**$1,06,629**	**$2,48,325**	**$2,63,375**
	$29,649			$50,267			
$500	**$500**	**$500**	**$500**	**$500**	**$3,300**	**$6,000**	**$7,500**
	1500			1500			
$21,248	**$23,849**	**$27,053**	**$30,557**	**$32,858**	**$2,23,062**	**$3,83,325**	**$4,25,675**
	$64,044			$90,467			

Table 4.13 Eco Excellence Express Cleaners LLC Income Statement For the Period Ending

	1Q	2Q	3Q	4Q	Year 1	Year 2	Year 3
Total Net Sales	$23,629	$44,923	$64,044	$90,467	$2,23,063	$3,83,325	$4,25,675
Cost of Goods Sold							
Laundry	$11,068	$14,211	$16,184	$18,158	$59,621	$63,860	$72,632
Dry Cleaning	$5,509	$10,520	$17,789	$30,160	$63,978	$1,48,995	$1,58,025
Repairs & Alterations	$–	$210	$1,050	$1,050	$2,310	$4,200	$5,250
Total COGS	$16,577	$24,940	$35,024	$49,368	$1,25,909	$2,17,055	$2,35,907
GROSS PROFIT	$7,052	$19,983	$29,020	$41,099	$97,154	$1,66,270	$1,89,768
Operating Expenses							
Advertising & Promotion	$2,400	$2,400	$2,400	$2,400	$9,600	$10,000	$11,000
Depreciation – Equipment	$2,358	$2,358	$2,358	$2,358	$9,431	$16,163	$11,543
Depreciation – Vehicle	$1,750	$1,750	$1,750	$1,750	$7,000	$11,200	$6,720
Insurance expense	$3,000	$3,000	$3,000	$3,000	$12,000	$12,000	$12,000
Office supplies expense	$100	$100	$100	$100	$400	$500	$550
Rent expense	$1,890	$1,890	$1,890	$1,890	$7,560	$7,560	$7,560
Repairs & Maintenance	$125	$125	$125	$125	$500	$500	$500
Salaries, Wages Comprehensive	$–	$–	$–	$–	$–	$24,000	$24,000
Travel	$2,000	$2,000	$2,000	$2,000	$8,000	$8,000	$8,000
Utilities expense	$10,800	$10,800	$10,800	$10,800	$43,200	$43,200	$43,200
Total Operating Expenses	$24,423	$24,423	$24,423	$24,423	$97,691	$1,33,123	$1,25,073

Earnings Before Interest and Taxes (EBIT)	$(17,371)	$(4,440)	$4,597	$16,676	$(537)	$33,147	$64,695
Other Expenses:							
Interest expense – vehicle	$517	$495	$472	$448	$1,932	$1,550	$1,145
Interest expense – equip	$894	$878	$861	$844	$3,477	$3,199	$2,903
Total Other Expenses	$1,411	$1,373	$1,333	$1,292	$5,409	$4,749	$4,048
Net Income before Taxes	$(18,782)	$(5,813)	$3,264	$15,384	$(5,946)	$28,398	$60,647
(Loss Carry Forward)						$(5,946)	0
Taxes (25%)*	$–	$–	$–	$–	$–	$5,613	$15,162
Net Income	$(18,782)	$(5,813)	$3,264	$15,384	$(5,946)	$22,785	$45,485

Table 4.14 Eco Excellence Express Cleaners LLC Cash Flow Statement For the Period Ending

	Start-up	1Q	2Q	3Q	4Q	Year 1	Year 2	Year 3
Starting Cash	$–	$36,770	$19,420	$15,039	$19,735	$36,770	$36,551	$75,334
Cash in from Operations (Sales)	$–	$23,629	$44,923	$64,044	$90,467	$2,23,063	$3,83,325	$4,25,675
Cash out from Operations (COGS, Expenses, Taxes)	$7,230	$36,892	$45,255	$55,339	$69,683	$2,07,169	$3,28,428	$3,57,879
Cash in from Investing (equity infusions, earnings on investments)	$50,000			$–	$–	$–	$–	$–
Cash out from Investing (equipment purchases, repaying investors)	$1,01,000	$1,411	$1,373	$1,333	$1,292	$5,409	$4,749	$4,048
Cash in from Financing (loans)	$95,000			$–	$–	$–	$–	$–
Cash out for Financing (repayment of debt)	$–	$2,676	$2,676	$2,676	$2,676	$10,704	$11,365	$12,065
Ending Cash Balance (= starting balance for next period)	$36,770	$19,420	$15,039	$19,735	$36,551	$36,551	$75,334	$1,27,017

Table 4.15 Eco Excellence Express Cleaners LLC Balance Sheet As of

	Starting Balances	1Q	2Q	3Q	4Q	Year 1	Year 2	Year 3
ASSETS								
Current Assets								
Cash	$36,770	$19,420	$15,039	$19,735	$36,551	$36,551	$75,334	$1,27,017
Marketable Securities	$–	$–	$–	$–	$–	$–	$–	$–
Accounts Receivable	$–	$–	$–	$–	$–	$–	$–	$–
Inventory	$–	$–	$–	$–	$–	$–	$–	$–
Pre-paid Expenses	$7,230	$7,230	$7,230	$7,230	$7,230	$7,230	$7,230	$7,230
Total Current Assets	$44,000	$26,650	$22,269	$26,965	$43,781	$43,781	$82,564	$1,34,247
Long-Term Assets								
Capital Equipment (net of depr)	$66,000	$63,642	$61,284	$58,926	$56,568	$56,568	$40,405	$28,862
Vehicle	$35,000	$33,250	$31,500	$29,750	$28,000	$28,000	$16,800	$10,080
Total L–T Assets	$1,01,000	$96,892	$92,784	$88,676	$84,568	$84,568	$57,205	$38,942
TOTAL ASSETS	$1,45,000	$1,23,542	$1,15,053	$1,15,641	$1,28,349	$1,28,349	$1,39,769	$1,73,189
LIABILITIES								
Current Liabilities								
Accounts Payable – Trade	$–	$–	$–	$–	$–	$–	$–	$–
Compensation Payable	$–	$–	$–	$–	$–	$–	$–	$–
Taxes Payable	$–	$–	$–	$–	$–	$–	$–	$–
Current Portion of L–T Liabilities	$10,704	$8,028	$5,352	$2,676	$–	$11,365	$12,065	$12,809
Total Current Liabilities	$10,704	$8,028	$5,352	$2,676	$–	$11,365	$12,065	$12,809

(Continued)

Table 4.15 Eco Excellence Express Cleaners LLC Balance Sheet As of (Continued)

	Starting Balances	1Q	2Q	3Q	4Q	Year 1	Year 2	Year 3
Long-Term Liabilities (net of current portion)								
Vehicle Loan Payable	$28,812	$28,812	$28,812	$28,812	$28,812	$22,242	$15,267	$7,862
Notes Payable – Bank	$46,236	$46,236	$46,236	$46,236	$46,236	$42,241	$37,999	$33,495
Note Payable – Private	$9,248	$9,248	$9,248	$9,248	$9,248	$8,448	$7,600	$6,700
Total Long-Term Liabilities	$84,296	$84,296	$84,296	$84,296	$84,296	$72,931	$60,866	$48,057
Total Liabilities	$95,000	$92,324	$89,648	$86,972	$84,296	$84,296	$72,931	$60,866
Equity								
Paid-in-Capital	$50,000	$50,000	$50,000	$50,000	$50,000	$50,000	$50,000	$50,000
Retained Earnings	$–	$(18,782)	$(24,595)	$(21,331)	$(5,947)	$(5,947)	$16,838	$62,323
Total Equity	$50,000	$31,218	$25,405	$28,669	$44,053	$44,053	$66,838	$1,12,323
TOTAL LIABILITIES & EQUITY	$1,45,000	$1,23,542	$1,15,053	$1,15,641	$1,28,349	$1,28,349	$1,39,769	$1,73,189

Notes

1 There are special exemptions to this rule for farming business.
2 The accelerated depreciation method allows a firm to write off a larger portion of a fixed asset's value in its earlier life, as compared with the straight line method, thus reducing a firm's tax liability in these earlier years. The total amount of depreciation over the asset's entire life is the same under both methods.
3 The sample income statement in Table 4.2 is called a multiple-step income statement because expenses are grouped into subcategories.
4 Credit sales here refer to credits given to customers directly, not credit card sales. With credit card sales, a business typically receives cash from the bank within days of the transaction with minimum risk.
5 The term "cost of sales" is sometimes used to refer to cost of goods sold.
6 COGS = Beginning inventory + Purchases − Ending inventory
7 For example, see Roychowdhury & Watts (2007) and Barth et al. (1998).
8 FASB 95 permits both direct and indirect methods for determining net cash flow from operating activities. If the direct method is used, a schedule showing the indirect method must be provided.
9 Industry average debt ratios are taken from CSIMarket.com.
10 Industry average turnover ratios are for 2013 and are taken from CSIMarket.com.

Bibliography

American Institute of CPAs. (2010). *What is the Difference Between a Compilation, a Review and an Audit?* Washington, DC: AICPA.

Barth, M. E., Beaver, W. H., & Landsman, W. R. (1998). Relative valuation roles of equity book value and net income as a function of financial health. *Journal of Accounting and Economics, 25*(1), 1–34.

Chasan, E. (2013, June 25). Four reasons non-GAAP metrics are exploding. *CFO Journal. The Wall Street Journal* http://blogs.wsj.com/cfo/2013/06/25/four-reasons-non-gaap-metrics-are-exploding/ (accessed 3/9/2014).

CSIMarket.com. *Airline Industry: Financial Strength Information & Trends* http://csimarket.com/Industry/industry_Financial_Strength_Ratios.php?ind=1102 (accessed 27/4/2014).

CSIMarket.com. *Restaurants Industry: Financial Strength Information & Trends* http://csimarket.com/Industry/industry_Financial_Strength_Ratios.php?ind=914 (accessed 27/4/2014).

Downs, P. (2013, March 25). What you need to know about credit card processing. *You're the Boss: The New York Times* http://boss.blogs.nytimes.com/2013/03/25/what-you-need-to-know-about-credit-card-processing (accessed 3/8/2014).

Landers, A. (1996). *Wake Up and Smell the Coffee!* New York, NY: Villard.

Minnis, M. (2011). The value of financial statement verification in debt financing: evidence from private US firms, *Journal of Accounting Research, 49*(2), 457–506.

Moran, G. (2012, March 19). Looking to borrow? An audited financial statement can help. *Entrepreneur* http://www.entrepreneur.com/article/222806 (accessed 3/1/2014).

Roychowdhury, S., & Watts, R. L. (2007). Asymmetric timeliness of earnings, market-to-book and conservatism in financial reporting. *Journal of Accounting and Economics, 44*(1–2), 2–31.

Smetanka, R. (2012, November). Financial Report: GAAP or Non-GAAP? *Financial Executive Magazine* http://www.financialexecutives.org/KenticoCMS/Financial-Executive-Magazine/2012_11/GAAP-or-Non-GAAP-.aspx#ixzz2vPUKVPBf (accessed 2/21/2014).

Troy, L. (2013). *2014 Almanac of Business and Industrial Financial Ratios*. Chicago, IL: Wolters Kluwer.

Yahoo Finance. *Industry Center* http://biz.yahoo.com/ic/index.html (accessed 3/20/2014).

5 Cash and Working Capital Management

Cash is king.

David Evans

One of the most important principles in financial management is the trade-off between risk and return and it applies to managing cash and working capital. Current assets, also known as *gross working capital*, include inventory, accounts receivable financing, prepaid expenses, and of course, cash. Current liabilities are debts that are due within one year and usually include accounts payable, accrued payroll, accrued taxes, and portions of long-term amortized debt. If a business has insufficient cash or inventory on hand, it may lose sales or incur penalties for bounced checks. However, if the business carries too much cash or inventory, it is not putting costly resources to good use, and inventory may become obsolete and lose value. Managing cash flows, therefore, includes managing current assets, such as accounts receivable and inventory, and current liabilities, such as accounts payable. The difference between current assets and current liabilities is called *net working capital*.

Net working capital = Current assets − Current liabilities

The goal of cash flow management is to ensure that a business has sufficient cash to make all its payments.

Change in cash balance = Net cash flow = Sources of cash − Uses of cash

In Chapter 4, we discussed the statement of cash flow. Sources of cash include cash sales, collections from accounts receivable, other income, and borrowing. Uses of cash include expenses such as payroll, inventory purchases, utilities, benefits, taxes, and loan repayments. Therefore, cash flow management includes managing cash from sales, monitoring spending, and deciding the best form of financing for current assets. The keys to cash flow management are simple: get your customers to pay as soon as possible and delay payments to suppliers as long as possible without hurting your business relationships or incurring penalties.

In practice, this is one of the most difficult tasks for an entrepreneur. Your chances of success will increase significantly if you develop a disciplined approach to cash flow management and devote at least an hour a day working on cash flow. This chapter is organized into three parts: types of current assets, techniques for managing them, and the cash conversion cycle.

Cash

Cash balance includes petty cash, cash balance in checking and savings accounts, and marketable securities, and, for retail businesses, cash on hand.

Petty Cash

While it is important for a business to keep track of its cash transactions, there is a balance between the need for real-time record keeping and the efforts required to maintain it. Therefore, almost all businesses keep a petty cash fund for small expenditures. Since the amounts of these expenditures are, by definition, small, they are recorded in batches rather than individually into the formal accounting system. Petty cash items may include coffee and dough-nuts, one emergency ream of paper, and a tip for the person who delivers a package. Even though the amount in petty cash is small, it is good operating procedure to keep it in a secure place with restricted access. A simple paper notebook, pen, calculator, and plastic zip-lock bag will usually be sufficient to keep track of transactions, the running balance, and to store receipts. The notebook should record the date, amount, employee name, a simple descrip-tion of the transaction, and the remaining balance.

How much should a business keep as petty cash? A rule of thumb is to set the balance such that petty cash will need to be replenished at most weekly or bi-weekly. A business can decide to replenish petty cash based on a fixed time schedule or when the balance reaches a certain threshold. If a business uses petty cash regularly, a fixed schedule will work better. When petty cash

Table 5.1 Petty Cash Example

Date	Amount	By	Description	Balance
1/1/2015			Beginning balance	$100.00
1/5/2015	$14.50	Joe Smith	Coffee and doughnuts for team meeting	$85.50
1/6/2015	$4.50	Jane Wood	Marker for whiteboard	$81.00
1/6/2015	$35.00	Joe Smith	Taxi	$46.00
1/8/2015	($54.00)	Gina Vega	Replenish petty cash (total verified)	$100.00

is replenished to the pre-set level, the transactions will be grouped and the subtotals posted to the business's expense accounts. The receipts should be totaled to verify that they equal the amount of petty cash used.

Cash on Hand

Cash on hand includes change funds kept in registers for cashiers. If you have several cashiers working during the day or several registers, you will need a set of change funds for each shift at each register. This also includes daily sales that have not been deposited at the bank. The greatest risk with cash on hand is robbery and theft. Common sense suggests that an entrepreneur make regular deposits at the bank to avoid a large amount of cash on hand. It is also a good habit to change the times for taking deposits to the bank on a random schedule and to use different routes as a security precaution.

Checking and Savings Accounts and Marketable Securities

Choosing a bank is an important decision. Factors to consider include convenience, fees, and the ability to grow with your business. Local and regional banks are often more convenient, friendlier, and better connected with other local businesses. By contrast, national and international banks have branches in vast geographic regions and the capacity to support your business as it grows. When comparing bank fees, be sure to read the contract carefully. Most banks waive monthly fees if you keep a minimum balance, usually between $2,000 and $5,000. Transaction fees vary greatly. Banking transactions include *automated clearing house* (ACH) transfers, such as direct payroll deposits or automated withdrawals, paper checks, electronic online payments, *automated teller machine* (ATM) deposits and withdrawals, and deposits at the bank's teller window. Most banks allow 200–300 free transactions per month and then charge a per-transaction cost, ranging from $0.20 to $0.60 or more per-transaction. If yours is a retail business, such as a restaurant, cash handling fees can be important. Some banks do not have cash handling fees while others allow $5,000 to $30,000 of cash deposits per month for free and then charge 0.10 percent to 0.30 percent on deposits over the maximum free amount.

Since checking accounts typically pay very low or zero interest, a business should keep the majority of its cash reserve in a savings account, money market account, certificates of deposit or marketable securities. Savings accounts are fairly standard and provide relatively low interest rates. Money market accounts typically pay slightly higher interest rates and provide a limited check writing service, but require a higher minimum balance. Certificates of deposit have more restrictions on cash withdrawal, and require higher balances, but also offer higher interest rates. All three types of account are insured by the Federal Deposit Insurance Corporation. Marketable securities may include bonds and stocks of other companies, institutions, and governments, as long as the intention is to sell them within one year. Bonds and stocks provide higher returns than money markets and certificates of deposits but also carry higher risks. To classify stocks and bonds as marketable securities, a business must clearly demonstrate that the intention is to sell them within one year. Purchasing stock of controlling interest is a long-term investment, not marketable securities.

Non-Cash Payment Methods

A study by the Federal Reserve System (2011) showed that checks continued to decline in popularity while automated clearing house (ACH), debit card and prepaid card gained both in number and value of transactions (Table 5.2). Credit card usage remained stable throughout the study period. Credit, debit, and prepaid cards totaled more than 50 percent of the transaction volume in the study. Although greater dollar values were paid through checks and ACH, these payments included direct deposits such as payroll, whereas credit, debit, and prepaid cards were primarily retail and small business-to-business (B2B) transactions.

Credit and Debit Card Processing

Accepting credit and debit cards is essential to any retail business and an important payment method for small and medium size B2B merchants. Credit card processing is part of merchant banking services. The choice of a credit and debit card merchant service provider affects the total cost and speed of

Table 5.2 Non-Cash Payment Methods

	Number of transactions (in billions)			Value (in trillion dollars)		
	2006	2009	Compound annual growth rate	2006	2009	Compound annual growth rate
Checks (paid)	30.5	24.5	−7.1%	41.60	31.60	−8.8%
Automated clearing house (ACH)	14.6	19.1	9.4%	30.97	37.16	6.3%
Credit card	21.7	21.6	−0.2%	2.12	1.95	−3.4%
Debit card	25.0	37.9	14.8%	0.97	1.42	13.5%
Prepaid card	3.3	6.0	21.5%	0.08	0.14	22.9%
Total	95.2	109.0	4.6%	75.74	72.27	−1.6%

Source: Federal Reserve System (2011).

payment to the business. Paul Downs, a master carpenter, wrote in a New York Times blog in 2013 that he spent more than $27,000 on credit card processing fees for $600,000 in transactions in one year. That is over 4 percent of revenue, making it an expense item worth paying attention to. To put this in perspective, rent typically averages 5 to 8 percent of restaurant revenues. In addition, delays in credit card processing could create significant cash flow problems. Card processing fee structures reached such complexity and abuse that the Durbin Amendment was passed as part of the Dodd–Frank Wall Street Reform and Consumer Protection Act of 2010 to limit swipe fees on debit cards.[1] *Business News Daily* offered three tips to getting the best card processing deal:

1. Be prepared: business owners should become familiar with the card processing industry; how these providers operate; and understand the terms, fees, rates and affiliated parties.
2. Negotiate: card processing fees are not set in stone; you should obtain quotes from more than one provider.
3. Follow up: monitor bills from card processing providers to ensure that fees are not raised without your knowledge.

In a credit card transaction, there are at least four parties: the customer, an issuing bank (issuer), the business (merchant), and an acquiring bank (acquirer). There are usually additional participants, providing processing, reporting, technology, legal, and financial consulting services. This section explains how card processing is conducted and the roles of these parties.

5.1 Participants in Processing Credit and Credit Payments

Issuing Bank

Issuing banks are financial institutions, such as the Bank of America and Capital One, that issue credit and debit cards to consumers, who sign contracts that specify terms, interest rates, and promise to repay charges made on these cards.

Acquiring Bank

Acquiring banks are financial institutions that offer merchant accounts and provide payment processing services to businesses. The contract of a merchant account is technically a line of credit and deposits into the merchant account are considered a loan from the acquiring bank to the business.

Although acquiring banks contract directly with some large businesses, they typically use independent sales organizations (ISOs) and merchant service providers (MSPs) to sell card payment processing services to small and medium size businesses. Acquiring banks may have an internal underwriting department or use external underwriters when determining the final terms of a merchant account contract once a completed application is submitted by a business.

Independent Sales Organizations (ISOs) and Merchant Service Providers (MSPs)

The ISOs and MSPs are contracted by acquiring banks to solicit businesses on behalf of acquiring banks. Salespeople from ISOs and MSPs are considered independent contractors and usually work for commissions. Services provided by ISOs and MSPs vary. Some are involved only in contacting new businesses, explaining terms and rates of merchant accounts, and submitting applications to acquiring banks for approval. Some provide ongoing merchant support. Salespeople from ISOs and MSPs are often the key contact person for small businesses.

Payment Brands

Payment brands are household names, such as Visa, MasterCard, and Discover Card. These companies do not interact directly with consumers or businesses. They operate more like an association with financial institutions as members. Credit cards are issued by member financial institutions (issuing banks), except for American Express, which issues credit cards directly to consumers. Disbursements to merchants are also handled by member financial institutions (acquiring banks). Payment brands also set rules to issuing banks and acquiring banks. Issuing and acquiring banks may have additional rules and conditions but they must enforce the rules of the payment brands. Some, such as MasterCard, also act as processors and provide the technological infrastructure for authorizing a transaction at the point of sale, clearing a transaction to confirm that the purchase information is valid, and calculating net payments due to acquiring banks.

When a customer presents a card to make a purchase, the business sends an authorization request to the acquiring bank or the processor, which forwards the request to the issuing bank via the card payment network. Figure 5.1 shows the sequence of activities in a card transaction.

In a credit card transaction, the issuing bank provides credit to the customer, who pays the issuing bank upon receiving the monthly statement.

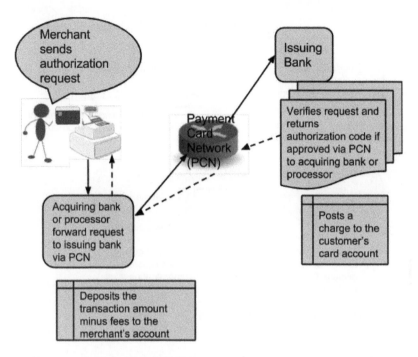

Figure 5.1 Activity Sequence in a Card Transaction

In the case of a debit card, the issuing bank deducts the transaction amount from the customer's checking account automatically at the time of purchase. An issuing bank may be a large retail bank such as the Bank of America, a small local bank, or an online-only bank, but they all issue the same brands of cards: Visa, MasterCard, etc.

The risk to the issuing bank is default by the customer in the case of credit cards. The acquiring bank provides a merchant bank account to the business and collects payment for the card transaction from the issuing bank. The acquiring bank may be operated by the same bank in which a business conducts all its banking services or it may be a bank that specializes in card payment processing. Note that the merchant account service is a separate legal entity even if it is operated by the same bank holding company. When the acquiring bank deposits payments from the card transaction to the business's merchant account, it is technically providing a loan to the business. The acquiring bank receives payments from the issuing bank that pay off this "loan," except in cases of disputed payment leading to chargebacks. When a chargeback occurs, the business has to pay the acquiring bank back for the disputed amount. Thus the risk to the acquiring bank is the merchant's

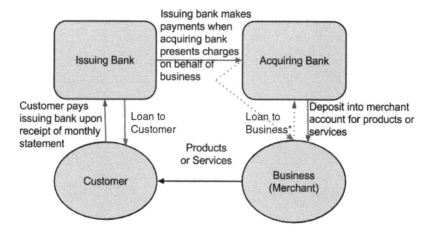

* Business becomes liable and has to repay acquiring bank if issuing bank refuses payment due to customer dispute. Otherwise, payment from issuing bank pays off the loan.

Figure 5.2 Flow of Funds in Card Transaction

inability to repay chargebacks. Figure 5.2 shows the flow of money in a credit card transaction.

Costs of Credit and Debit Card Processing

The costs of credit and debit card processing generally fall into two categories. One category includes variable costs that are charged per transaction. These include interchange fees and assessments fees charged by the banks and brand companies such as Visa, MasterCard, and markups charged by processors. Note that the acquiring bank and the processor may be the same entity in some cases. Interchange fees typically represent the largest portion of the transaction fees and they vary greatly depending on a number of factors, such as:

- Processing method, e.g.:
  - Card presented and physically swiped through a card reader;
  - Card number collected (usually by phone) and entered manually;
  - Online or e-commerce.
- Amount of customer and transaction information, e.g.:
  - Phone number or zip code;
  - Merchandise or service information.

- Types of business;

  o   Merchant category code (a four-digit classification code assigned by a payment card organization).

- Types of cards, e.g.:

  o   Reward points;
  o   Business cards;
  o   Consumer cards.

This is only a partial list of factors considered by processors when setting interchange fees. Some processors use tier pricing, which means that the same business will pay a different fee depending on the tier a particular transaction falls into. In fact, complex and sometimes excessive interchange fees prompted the US Congress to include rules in the Dodd–Frank Wall Street Reform and Consumer Protection Act in 2011 that specifically addressed these concerns. These new rules include limits on interchange fees for debit card transactions and the networks available on a debit card for routing transactions. Here is some advice from the Federal Trade Commission (FTC), which is responsible for enforcing these rules:

> Talk to your acquirer or processor about how you can take advantage of lower debit card interchange fees. Go over your invoice together to see how these and other fees are reflected in your monthly statement, and discuss what you can do to reduce them. And shop around; you may find a better deal.[2]

The other fee category includes monthly fees and other non-recurring fees. There is no industry standard for many of these fees and some may be negotiable. Typical monthly fees and non-recurring fees may include:

- Monthly statement fee;
- Monthly minimum fee;
- Equipment rental fee:

  o   A business can choose to purchase the equipment instead of renting.
  o   Beware of 'free equipment', as this often comes with hidden charges.

- Payment Card Industry (PCI) Data Security Standards (DSS) compliance fee and non-compliance fee:

  o   Some processors provide PCI DSS support and service and charge a PCI compliance fee to help business owners comply with PCI DSS requirements.

- o   Some processors levy a penalty (non-compliance fee) if a business does not meet PCI compliance requirements.
- o   Since business owners are not data security experts, it is important to make sure that you are getting the right support for what you pay. If your business accepts online payments, part of the PCI DSS requirements include network vulnerability scans on a regular basis. The next section will discuss more about online payments. For a business that does not include online payments, the PCI DSS requirements include conducting business process audits and completing self-assessment questionnaires.

- Retrieval fee:

  - o   This is not a recurring fee but is charged each time a customer's issuing bank requests a copy of a sales receipt to confirm a transaction, usually in response to a customer disputing the transaction.

- Chargeback fee:

  - o   If a customer disputes a charge successfully, a business will pay a chargeback fee in addition to repaying the transaction amount to the acquiring bank.

The acquiring bank often uses an underwriting company to access chargeback risks when setting interchange and assessment fees. The underwriting company considers such factors as merchant category code, whether a card is presented in person by the customer, time between payment and delivery, and transaction size. In a typical credit card processing agreement, the merchant provides personal guarantees plus a reserve amount as collateral. The reserve amount is usually taken out of credit card transactions. For example, if an acquiring bank requires $20,000 in reserve, it may deduct 10 percent from each transaction until it has accumulated $20,000 to keep in the reserve. Personal guarantee also means that limited liability protection does not apply to chargeback claims through the acquiring bank. The interchange, assessment, and markup fees are usually included in the initial credit card processing application, but the reserve requirement, some monthly fees and number of days before cash is deposited to the merchant are usually provided only after the application process is completed and subject to change at the discretion of the acquiring bank. The time between when a transaction is submitted and when funds are available to a business is an important factor to consider, and a business should include that consideration when shopping for a card processor. Even after you have chosen a processor, continue to review the statements on a regular basis.

5.2 Payment Card Industry Data Security Standard (PCI DSS)

The PCI Security Standards Council is a global forum that is responsible for the development, management, education, and awareness of the PCI Security Standards, including Data Security Standard (PCI DSS), Payment Application Data Security Standard (PA-DSS) and PIN Transaction Security (PTS) requirements. The Council was originally founded jointly by five payment brands: American Express, Discover Financial Services, JCB International, MasterCard, and Visa. The goal of PCI DSS is to ensure that businesses are taking necessary steps to safeguard credit and debit card information of customers. The enforcement of compliance and determination of non-compliance penalties vary by payment brands. If a processor charges a PCI compliance fee, the processor should provide support to help a business owner understand and comply with PCI DSS. If a processor does not charge a PCI compliance fee, a business owner is still expected to comply with PCI DSS. Verification of PCI compliance is up to the credit card processor.

Online and Mobile Payment Processing

The popularity of credit and debit cards and online shopping has dramatically changed consumer behavior. Businesses increasingly find they need to accept payments online to stay competitive. This trend prevails across industries and businesses of all sizes, from micro-firms to global enterprises. For example, retailers will naturally want to expand their sales channels and a website with online sales capability is often an integral part of the business model. Restaurants that offer a take-out service find growing popularity with online orders.

The best known online payment gateways are VeriSign and Authorize.net. In many ways, online payment gateways are extensions of credit card processing, and they will work with a business's existing merchant accounts. For businesses without merchant accounts, these gateways can set up new merchant accounts, and the application process is similar to that of card processors. Therefore, just as when choosing a card processor, business owners need to pay attention to the fee structure and total costs of payment gateways and be prepared to negotiate to get the best deal. For example, VeriSign do not sell their services directly but work through providers who charge a markup fee and handle most merchant support issues. Authorize.net also relies primarily on third-party resale partners but allows businesses the option of subscribing to their service directly. The costs of setting up online payments usually include a one-time setup fee, monthly gateway fee, monthly statement fee or maintenance fee, monthly minimum fee, and transaction fees.

An alternative to using online payment gateways is to use online payment services, such as PayPal, Amazon, or Google Wallet. One disadvantage of using these services is that customers are redirected to their website to complete a transaction, which may be confusing to customers new to online shopping. Transaction fees are usually higher with these services. The setup process for these services is a lot simpler and does not require a business to have a merchant account.

A relatively new payment option is mobile payment, which allows a business or an individual to accept card payments via a mobile phone or tablet. The ability to accept card payments anywhere can be a great advantage for some businesses, especially those providing direct services (such as therapeutic massage or beauty salons), operating at the level of door-to-door sales, or those that sell primarily at specialized fairs. The largest providers of mobile payment include Square, PayPal Here, Intuit GoPayment, and Bank of America Mobile Pay on Demand. Most of these providers charge a per-transaction fee that is a percentage of the payment amount. They offer a lower rate for transactions completed by swiping a card through their device, which is plugged into a mobile phone or tablet, and a higher rate for transactions manually entered into their system. Transaction fees are relatively high compared with traditional card processors. However, the setup process for these services is a lot simpler and does not require a business to have a merchant account. Since there is virtually no setup fee and many of these services do not charge monthly fees, businesses only pay when they use the service. For very small businesses, online payment or mobile payment gateways may be a viable alternative to traditional card processing during their startup phrase.

Accounts Receivable Financing

The adage "an ounce of prevention is worth a pound of cure" certainly applies to accounts receivable management. Collecting past due payments from customers is one of the most dreaded chores of business owners. Slow collections impose stress on the owners, extra time spent on chasing down customers, cash flow problems, and uncertainty in cash flow forecasts and planning. This section discusses techniques for managing accounts receivable.

Terms of Payment and Customer Credit Screening

Providing credits to customers is part of your business model and competitive strategy. The first step in managing accounts receivable is to establish clear payment terms and have a written agreement with each customer. Every industry usually has accepted practices that serve as good starting points for developing your own specific terms. In general, terms of payment should state the following:

- When a customer will be billed, for example:

    o The billing frequency for repeat customers may be weekly or monthly.
    o A contractor may bill a customer when parts for a project are ordered.
    o A web designer may bill a customer at different stages of development, with clearly specified deliverables.

- When the invoice becomes due

    o You may allow a customer 15 days or 30 days to pay you after receiving the invoice.
    o You may offer a cash discount to encourage early payment.
    o You may include a late payment fee to discourage overdue payment.

Review the agreement with customers in person before signing. This is actually a good opportunity to build relationships with your customers because expectations on both sides are clearly communicated.

Credit screening is especially important for business clients. Require a credit application and check references or use a credit bureau such as Experian or Dun & Bradstreet. Templates of business credit applications are available at office supply stores and in popular word processing software such as MS Office. Having a formal credit screening process demonstrates professionalism to your clients.

Invoicing and Continuous Monitoring

Establish accounting standards for yourself and your employees to ensure accurate and timely invoicing. Errors in an invoice will delay payment and harm your relationship with customers. Include detailed information on the invoice, such as description and date of service or product and terms of payment. Set aside dedicated time for invoicing daily or at least weekly.

Use an aging of accounts receivable report to monitor payments from customers. The sooner you identify a payment problem, the easier it is to resolve. Table 5.3 shows a sample aging of accounts receivable report.

In this example, the business needs to improve its collections. It has $14,000 in past due invoices, with $7,000 overdue for more than 61 days. The amount of past due invoices represents 16 percent of its total accounts receivable. Two other useful metrics are accounts receivable turnover and average

Table 5.3 Aging Accounts Receivable Report Example

Customer information	Terms of sale	Invoice date	Invoice due date	Amount out-standing	Current— not yet due	1–30 days past due	31–60 days past due	61+ 61+ days past past due
Jane Panzer	Net 15	June 3	June 18	$2,000		$2,000		
	Net 15	June 10	June 25	$3,800	$3,800			
Subtotal for Jane Panzer				$5,800	$3,800	$2,000		
Total for business				$86,000	$72,000	$4,000	$3,000	$7,000

collection period, as introduced in Chapter 4. If credit sales are an important part of your business, be sure to choose accounting software that includes features for updating customer information, automated invoice generation, and aging of accounts receivable reports.

Setting up protocols to handle overdue payments is another essential component of accounts receivable management. In general, payments should be received within 7 to 10 days after the due date. The protocols may start with a reminder notice when an invoice is 10 days past due. Be sure to include any applicable late fees. If payment is not received 10 days after the reminder notice, the next actions may include: phone call, personal visit, or suspending order or service delivery. Entrepreneurs may be uncomfortable about collecting overdue payments or may be afraid to lose customers if they press for payments. The truth is that customers who routinely pay late are not profitable in the long run. When calling a customer for payment, be polite and use the opportunity to get to know the customer better so you can determine if this is a customer you want to keep. Take legal action only as a last resort in accounts receivable collection.

In summary, effective accounts receivable management starts with establishing and communicating clear payment terms, performing credit screening on customers, sending out timely and accurate invoices, continuously monitoring payments using an accounts receivable aging report, and following protocols for collection.

Inventory

Inventory management is a critical aspect of the overall operation of retail and manufacturing businesses. The first step in inventory accounting is to determine the quantity of goods on hand. The second step is to assign value to the goods. According to Generally Accepted Accounting Principles (GAAP), there are two inventory accounting systems for determining the quantity of inventory: the perpetual inventory system and the periodic inventory system. Methods for valuing inventory include first-in-first-out (FIFO), last-in-first-out (LIFO), average costing, and specific identification.

Perpetual Inventory System

Advances in inventory tagging technology, such as barcodes and scanners, make perpetual inventory systems much easier to implement. With the perpetual system, inventory quantities are increased when goods arrive from suppliers, reduced when goods are sold, and increased if a customer returns merchandise. The advantage of the perpetual system is that a business owner knows exactly how much inventory is on hand at any moment and how many products are sold. Without a computerized point of sale system, scanner, and barcodes, record keeping will be very labor intensive for the perpetual system. Today, there are inventory management apps that run on mobile phones, and some can be integrated with popular accounting software, enabling small businesses to employ a perpetual inventory system at relatively low cost.

Periodic Inventory System

As the name implies, under the periodic system, inventory quantity is updated periodically. The update frequency may be weekly, monthly, quarterly, or annually. Purchases are tracked in a purchase account during the time interval between updates. Sales of individual items are not tracked. At the end of each period, inventory on hand is tallied and becomes the new ending inventory. Quantity of goods sold is computed as the change in inventory level plus purchases:

$$\text{Quantity Sold} = \text{Beginning Inventory Quantity} + \text{Purchased Quantity} - \text{Ending Inventory Quantity}$$

Inventory Valuation Methods

There are four inventory valuation methods: first-in-first-out (FIFO), last-in-first-out (LIFO), average cost, and specific identification. The last method, specific identification, is less common and used primarily in businesses with high value per item and relatively low transaction volume, such as jewelry stores and car dealerships. Each car has a unique vehicle identification number, and the actual cost of a specific car will be attributed to a sales transaction. Most businesses do not keep track of each individual product, and the other three valuation methods are more applicable. Under the FIFO method, inventory with the oldest costs are assumed to be sold first. Under LIFO, inventory with the newest costs are assumed to be sold first. In a period of rising costs, the LIFO method will result in higher costs and therefore lower taxes than the FIFO method. Note that the valuation methods determine costs associated with inventory, not actual physical movement of inventory. Whether a business uses the perpetual system or the periodic system also affects inventory valuation.

Table 5.4 shows an example of inventory valuation using FIFO, LIFO, and average cost with the perpetual system. Note that the quantity sold is the same, 130 units, under all three valuation methods. With FIFO, the first 100 units were valued at $5.00 (goods from beginning inventory) and the next 30 units at $5.50 (goods purchased on January 3rd). With LIFO, the first 60 units were valued at $5.00 (goods from beginning inventory), the next 30 units at $5.50 (goods purchased on January 3rd), and the next 40 units at $5.75 (goods purchased on January 5th). With the average cost method, a new average cost was computed after each purchase. The COGS of each sale transaction is based on the most recent average cost. Therefore, the first 60 units were valued at $5.00, the next 30 units at $5.28 and the last 40 units at $5.49. Since cost had risen steadily throughout the period, COGS was highest under LIFO, $695, followed by average cost, $678, and lowest under FIFO, $665. For tax purposes, the LIFO valuation resulted in the highest COGS and therefore the lowest taxes paid.

Since the periodic inventory system does not keep track of units on hand continuously, valuation of COGS is inferred from the value of ending inventory. There is no direct calculation of COGS. Table 5.5 shows an example of inventory valuation using FIFO, LIFO, and average cost with the periodic system. Note that the costs of total purchases, $863, and the number of units in the ending inventory, 120 units, were the same under all three methods. Under FIFO, ending inventory consisted of 20 units at $5.50, 50 units at $5.75, and 50 units at $6.00, totaling $698. Under LIFO, ending inventory consisted of 100 units at $5.00 and 20 units at $5.50, totaling $610. With the average cost method, the first step is to compute total goods available for sale.

$$\text{Total goods available for sale} = \text{Beginning inventory} + \text{Total purchases}$$

$$\text{Average cost per unit} = \frac{\text{Value of total goods available for sale}}{\text{Total units available for sale}}$$

In this example, there were 250 units available for sales, totaling $1,363. The average cost per unit was $5.45, which was the value used for computing ending inventory. With 120 units as ending inventory, the value was $654. COGS is computed as the difference between total goods available for sale and ending inventory.

$$\text{COGS} = \text{Total goods available for sale} - \text{Ending inventory}$$
$$\text{COGS} = \text{Beginning inventory} + \text{Total purchases} - \text{Ending inventory}$$

Therefore, COGS with the periodic system was $665 under FIFO, $753 under LIFO, and $709 under the average cost method. Once again, in a time period

Table 5.4 Perpetual Inventory Systems

a Perpetual Inventory System With First-In-First-Out Valuation

Date	Purchases			Cost of goods sold			Balance	
	Quantity purchased	Unit cost	Total cost of purchases	Quantity sold	Unit cost	Total cost of goods sold	Quantity on hand	Total inventory value
Jan 1							100	$500
Jan 2				60	$5.00	$300	40	$200
Jan 3	50	$5.50	$275				90	$475
Jan 4				30	$5.00	$150	60	$325
Jan 5	50	$5.75	$288				110	$613
Jan 6				10	$5.00	$50	100	$563
Jan 6				30	$5.50	$165	70	$398
Jan 7	50	$6.00	$300				120	$698
Total for week Jan 1–7	**150**		**$863**	**130**		**$665**	**120**	**$698**

←
20 @ $5.50
50 @ $5.75
50 @ $6.00

(Continued)

Table 5.4 Perpetual Inventory Systems (Continued)

b Perpetual Inventory System With Last-In-First-Out Valuation

Date	Purchases			Cost of Goods Sold			Balance	
	Quantity purchased	Unit cost	Total cost of purchases	Quantity sold	Unit cost	Total cost of goods sold	Quantity on hand	Total inventory value
Jan 1							100	$500
Jan 2				60	$5.00	$300	40	$200
Jan 3	50	$5.50	$275				90	$475
Jan 4				30	$5.50	$165	60	$310
Jan 5	50	$5.75	$288				110	$598
Jan 6				40	$5.75	$230	70	$368
Jan 7	50	$6.00	$300				120	$668
Total for week Jan 1–7	**150**		**$863**	**130**		**$695**	**120**	**$668**

↑

**40 @ $5.00
20 @ $5.50
10 @ $5.75
50 @ $6.00**

c Perpetual Inventory System With Average Cost Valuation

Date	Purchases			Cost of goods sold			Balance		
	Quantity purchased	Unit cost	Total cost of purchases	Quantity sold	Unit cost	Total cost of goods sold	Quantity on hand	Total inventory value	Average cost
Jan 1							100	500	$5.00
Jan 2				60	$5.00	$300	40	$200	$5.00
Jan 3	50	$5.50	$275				90	$475	$5.28
Jan 4				30	$5.28	$158	60	$317	$5.28
Jan 5	50	$5.75	$288				110	$604	$5.49
Jan 6				40	$5.49	$220	70	$384	$5.49
Jan 7	50	$6.00	$300				120	$684	$5.70
Total for week Jan 1–7	**150**		**$863**	**130**		**$678**	**120**	**$684**	

120 @ $5.70

Table 5.5 Periodic Inventory Systems

a Periodic Inventory System with First-In-First-Out Valuation

Date	Purchases		
	Quantity purchased	*Unit cost*	*Total cost of purchases*
January 3	50	$5.50	$275
January 5	50	$5.75	$288
January 7	50	$6.00	$300
Total for week Jan 1–7	150		$863

Inventory account in balance sheet	*Balance*		
	Quantity on hand	*Total inventory value*	
January 1	100	$500	
January 7	120	$698	20 @ $5.50 50 @ $5.75 50 @ $6.00

Cost of goods sold calculation

	Quantity	*Total value*	
Beginning inventory (Jan 1)	100	$500	
Add: Purchases	150	$863	
Total goods available for sale	250	$1,363	
Less: Ending inventory (Jan 7)	120	$698	
Cost of goods sold	130	$665	

b Periodic Inventory System with Last-In-First-Out Valuation

Date	Purchases		
	Quantity purchased	*Unit cost*	*Total cost of purchases*
January 3	50	$5.50	$275
January 5	50	$5.75	$288
January 7	50	$6.00	$300
Total for week Jan 1–7	150		$863

Inventory account in balance sheet	*Balance*		
	Quantity on hand	*Total inventory value*	
January 1	100	$500	
January 7	120	$610	100 @ $5.00 20 @ $5.50

Table 5.5 Periodic Inventory Systems (Continued)

Cost of goods sold calculation			
	Quantity	Total value	
Beginning inventory (Jan 1)	100	$500	
Add: Purchases	150	$863	
Total goods available for sale	250	$1,363	
Less: Ending inventory (Jan 7)	120	$610	
Cost of goods sold	130	$753	

c Periodic Inventory System with Average Cost Valuation

Date	Purchases		
	Quantity purchased	Unit cost	Total cost of purchases
January 3	50	$5.50	$275
January 5	50	$5.75	$288
January 7	50	$6.00	$300
Total for week Jan 1–7	150		$863

Inventory account in balance sheet	Balance		
	Quantity on hand	Total inventory value	
January 1st	100	$500	
January 7th	120	$654	

Cost of goods sold calculation			
	Quantity	Average unit cost	Total value
Beginning inventory (Jan 1st)	100	$5.00	$500
Add: Purchases	150	$5.75	$863
Total goods available for sale	250	$5.45	$1,363
Less: Ending inventory (Jan 7)	120	$5.45	$654
Cost of goods sold	130	$5.45	$709

with rising costs, the LIFO method would result in the highest COGS and the lowest taxes.

In addition to illustrating different valuation methods, the examples in Tables 5.4 and 5.5 also highlight differences between the perpetual and periodic systems. In particular, the goods purchased on January 7, 50 units at $6.00, were not involved in computing COGS under any valuation method with the perpetual system because the last sale occurred on January 6. Under the periodic system, COGS were inferred from inventory balance at the end of the period and therefore included the purchase made on January 7.

The focus of this book is on managing businesses and not tax planning. For management purposes, a valuation method that matches the physical movements of goods will best reflect the actual state of the business. For businesses where obsolescence and spoilage are concerns, the oldest goods are usually sold first, implying that FIFO valuation will match the business process. For businesses with high transaction volume and price fluctuations, the average cost method may provide the most unbiased valuation. As owner, you want to see an accurate picture of your business.

Inventory Control

Waste and theft can have high potential costs for any business, but especially so for small businesses where margins are low. The main tool for monitoring errors and potential thefts is physical verification. If your company uses the perpetual inventory system, at least once per year, you should conduct a physical count of inventory on hand and check the quantity against the records in the accounting system. With the periodic system, after counting physical inventory you should compare the implied quantity of goods sold against sales records. Counting inventory is a time-consuming process, so it makes sense to focus your efforts on items that are important. The ABC inventory analysis refers to a method of grouping inventory into "A", "B", and "C" items.

- "A" items are very important to the operation and of relatively high value. A rule of thumb is that "A" items account for 65–70 percent of COGS value but may only represent 10–20 percent in unit quantity. An example of an "A" item is cigarettes in a convenience store.
- "B" items are important and account for 20–25 percent of COGS value but 20–30 percent in unit quantity. An example will be bakery and dairy items in a convenience store.
- "C" items are relatively less important and account for 5–10 percent of COGS value but 50–70 percent in unit quantity. An example will be candies in a convenience store.

The physical counts often do not match exactly to the recorded amounts. The difference may be due to counting errors, theft, spoilage, or damage. Comparing the discrepancy against historic and industry averages will highlight unusual situations. For example, the USDA uses 12 percent as the estimated average spoilage rate for fresh fruits (Burzby et al., 2009). If you found a difference of 10 percent between the counted item and the recorded amount for fresh fruits, it would be within the average spoilage rate. If you keep a historic record for your own company, you will get a better estimate than a national average. For example, you may decide to conduct a recount if the error is more than 5 percent for an "A'" item, and you may be willing to ignore errors up to 10 percent for a "C" item. If recounting confirms the physical counts, the next step is to decide whether corrective action is needed. Sad but true, internal theft is more common than theft by outsiders. Business owners often have some ideas of potential thefts but are unwilling to take action until they have evidence. If the situation is serious, outside help may be needed.

Inventory turnover and days' sales in inventory (from Chapter 4) are additional tools for managing inventory. Recall that inventory turnover measures how many times inventory turns over in one year and days' sales in inventory measures the average length of time an item sits on the shelf. For example, low inventory turnover may be a cause of excessive spoilage. Identifying which items are the culprits may not be easy. You can use the ABC analysis to help focus your efforts. You also want to keep track of inventory shortages to avoid losing sales. Comparing inventory turnover and days' sales in inventory with your ordering routine will identify potential problems ahead of time. For example, if you usually order an item once per week and you notice the item has 8 days' sales in inventory, it may be time to increase ordering frequency to once every 5 or 6 days.

Accounts Payable

You want to collect receivables as soon as possible from your customers, but you want to delay payments as long as possible to your suppliers without damaging the relationship. You also do not want to forgo cash discounts. For example, if your supplier offers terms of 2/10 net 30, you receive a 2 percent discount if you pay within 10 days, and the full amount is due in 30 days. This term is equivalent to a loan of 20 days because you can pay on the 10th day and get the discount or wait till the 30th day and forgo 2 percent. The approximate annualized cost of forgoing this discount is over 37 percent (2 percent per 20 days, 37 percent per year).[3] Therefore, missing out on cash discounts is actually an expensive form of financing, as is paying after the due date and incurring late payment fees. Not only are late payment fees expensive; not making payments on time can damage your business's credit scores. If you plan ahead appropriately you will likely be able to obtain a line of credit or short-term loan at a lower interest rate.

To find out if your business is managing its accounts payable effectively, compute the accounts payable period discussed in Chapter 4 and compare it with the industry average. Finding out the industry average may also help you negotiate terms with your suppliers. Organization is the key for accounts payable management. Prioritize your payments to take advantage of cash discounts and avoid late payment fees. Avoid late payments to maintain or improve your business's credit score and build good relationships with your suppliers.

Cash Conversion Cycle

The cash conversion cycle, often simply called the cash cycle, is the time between when you pay your suppliers and when you receive cash from your customer. This period is critical and it depends on how long inventory sits on the shelf, how many days you have before you pay your suppliers, and how many days it takes your customers to pay you. In the example from Chapter 4, the firm has days' sales in inventory of 11.88 days, an average collection period of 14.91 days, and an accounts payable period of 9.69 days. We can use this information to compute this firm's cash conversion cycle.

Cash conversion cycle = Days' sales in inventory + Average collection period − Accounts payable period

In the example,

Cash conversion cycle = 11.88 + 14.91 − 9.69 = 17.10 days

Large retailers like Walmart, CostCo, and Amazon.com are legendary for their short cash cycles. In 2012, Walmart achieved a cash cycle of less than 10 days, but was still bested by CostCo at 4.5 days and Amazon.com, which reported a cash cycle of −14 days. In other words, Amazon.com was able to receive cash from its customers 14 days before it had to pay its suppliers. These retail giants are vigilant about their cash cycles because they recognize the cost of financing this time gap. You can determine the financing cost for the cash cycle as follows:

$$COGS \text{ per day} = \frac{COGS}{365 \, days}$$

COGS that needs financing over the cash cycle = COGS per day ×
    Cash conversion cycle

Total financing cost for the cash cycle = COGS that needs financing ×
    interest rate

$$\text{Savings from reducing cash cycle by one day} = \frac{\begin{array}{c} \text{Total financing cost} \\ \text{for the cash cycle} \end{array}}{\text{Cash conversion cycle}}$$

COGS of the firm in Chapter 4's example were $415,000. If we assume that it could borrow at 6 percent per year, the financing cost of the cash cycle would be as follows:

$$COGS \text{ per day} = \frac{\$415,000}{365} = \$1,137$$

COGS that needs financing over the cash cycle = $1,137 × 17.1 = $19,442

Total financing cost for the cash cycle = $19,442 × 6% = $1,167

$$\text{Savings from reducing cash cycle by one day} = \frac{\$1,167}{17.1} = \$68$$

These calculations provide a great deal of useful information. First, they tell the owner that she will need to borrow $19,442 to finance the cash cycle. This amount should be included in forecasting and financial planning, a topic that will be addressed in detail in Chapter 6. Second, they provide an estimate of savings from reducing the cash cycle. There are three ways to shorten the cash cycle: (1) increase inventory turnover, i.e. reduce the number of days inventory sits on the shelf; (2) speed up accounts receivable collection; and (3) increase the number of days it takes to pay suppliers. The pros and cons of each of these approaches have been discussed in earlier sections of this chapter. Having a quantitative estimate of potential savings will enable you, the business owner, to make better informed decisions about whether to pursue these strategies.

Case 5.1 Integrated Communications Inc. of Virginia: The Cost of Factoring

Susan White

Bills to pay, and little cash coming in! Andrew Lowry,[4] chief financial officer for Integrated Communications Inc. of Virginia (ICV), saw his fledgling firm's slow accounts receivable and wondered if there was a way to make the funds come in faster. As CFO (and chief operating officer and chief technology officer), Andrew was responsible for daily operations and for the financial health of the consulting firm that he and chief executive officer and wife, Jennifer, had founded. The firm was a certified 8a, woman-owned company, which meant that the firm received preference in obtaining government contracts, which were the bread and butter of the firm. Jennifer owned 51 percent of the firm's stock and Andrew owned the remaining 49 percent. ICV currently had contracts or had completed contracts with the federal agency clients, such as the Departments of Agriculture, Defense, Labor, Homeland Security, Energy, and Treasury, and Transportation, the Office of Personnel Management, USAID, the Federal Deposit Insurance Corporation, and the Food & Drug Administration. In recent years, government agencies had provided about 85 percent of ICV revenues. Services provided by ICV included developing organizational plans, products, and programs for clients; taking clients' communications and creating a consistent and integrated message, voice look and fee; employee training; motivational programs; and developing and implementing creative solutions to effect change within a firm.

Andrew said ICV planned to focus on its federal government practice to fuel its projected expansion. He expected revenues to be $8 million in 2014 and to grow to $10 million in 2015, a 25 percent increase realized largely by a larger government consulting practice. Andrew had forecast revenues in 2015 of $15 million, an even greater increase of 50 percent. The greatest impediment to the firm's growth was access to financing.

ICV had a line of credit that was adequate for its current needs, but Andrew was looking for a way to get paid faster in order to put that money to work more quickly. Government clients were reliable, but slow to pay; exactly when the money would arrive was the big question. For example, ICV had yet to be paid in 2013 for a contract it had completed in 2012, because the hiring agency had not filled out the necessary paperwork properly. Andrew was researching factoring as a way to bring in accounts receivable cash sooner, working with a local company that specialized in factoring government accounts receivable. His concern was that this would be a very expensive form of financing and could impact profits adversely. At present, the firm had only 20 percent in equity, with the remainder current liabilities and the bank line of credit. Selected financial information is contained in Table 5.6.

Table 5.6 Integrated Communications of Virginia, Selected Financial Information

Income statement	2013	2012	2011	2010	2009	2008
Revenue	6,848,413	4,763,910	2,687,599	3,254,256	1,027,417	1,204,455
Cost of goods sold	4,375,568	1,075,253	516,088	521,446	224,668	364,507
Selling and administrative expenses	2,313,033	3,175,886	2,517,747	2,346,797	1,027,754	742,176
Income from operations	159,812	512,771	−346,236	386,013	−225,006	97,772
Other expenses	(65,345)	(11,073)	(63,157)	(122,352)	(76,258)	(36,525)
Net income	94,467	501,698	−409,393	263,661	−301,264	61,247
Balance sheet						
Assets						
Cash	32,646	6,279	40,915	1,413	14,262	600
Accounts receivable	2,095,496	1,032,792	562,200	631,324	173,608	245,776
Total current assets	2,128,142	1,039,071	603,115	632,737	187,870	246,376
Fixed assets	112,618	49,823	33,306	25,596	54,469	74,413
Other assets	13,231	5,228	5,228	5,228	5,228	101,062
Total assets	2,253,991	1,094,122	641,649	663,561	247,567	421,851
Current liabilities	2,069,836	1,277,398	1,053,505	659,838	645,819	384,362

Andrew had investigated factoring and found that with factoring, ICV could sell the accounts receivable that were approved for payment. The factoring contract that Andrew was offered would give the firm a loan amount of 80 percent of accounts receivable with interest at 1.5 percent per month. There were no fees in addition to the interest, due monthly. The initial loan was based on a 60-day payback period, although the loan due date could be extended if ICV wanted more time. If any of the receivables being factored went beyond 90 days, they were considered to be past due. Like 70 percent of factoring contracts, this was a "recourse" contract, which meant that ICV would need to supply new receivables to replace the stale accounts receivable. In other words, ICV would pay interest on the original amount of the receivables loan, even though it had ultimately supplied receivables worth more than 100 percent of the value of the original loan. This was equivalent to paying interest on loan funds that were not received.

In particular, Andrew was looking at a contract from a government agency that was especially slow to pay and was considering factoring. The contract would bring in $125,000 in revenues and provide ICV with $6,000 in profit. He thought he would be able to pay back the factoring loan after two months when he expected payment from a different, larger contract to come in, but it was possible that he might have to stretch the factoring loan to four months.

If this worked well, he would consider factoring all of 2013's accounts receivable for a four month period.

Case Questions

1. Did Andrew have enough of a "slow payment" problem to make factoring worthwhile?
2. What would be the impact on profits of factoring the $125,000 contract and 2013 revenues?
3. Why might a firm use factoring in spite of the cost?

Case 5.2 Coos Bay Organic Products, Inc.: Managing Cash Flows in a Seasonal Business

John Voyer and Frederic Aiello

The need for large-scale composting in southern Oregon led to the founding of Coos Bay Organic Products, Inc. in early 2006. The company's purpose was to coordinate the region's composting efforts better, by investing in quality and especially *capacity* and *scale*. Charles Brooks, hired to manage the company, also hoped to develop markets for distinctive composts.

During the peak gardening season in 2006, Coos Bay Organic Products, Inc. used $100,000 in equity and loans for a number of things. It formulated a compost recipe and designed a "really good bag" for retail distribution. It used a subcontractor to manufacture and fill 100 pallets of the newly designed bags with its new recipe. Lastly, it conducted an extensive sales campaign aimed at independent garden centers in the Pacific Northwest. It sold its 100 pallets in two weeks.

This success led to a joint venture with one of its biggest customers, the Pacific Northwest Mussel Company, and an investment of $100,000 from Southern Oregon Tidal Ventures, a non-profit dedicated to economic development in the region, in exchange for 33 percent of the company's equity. By late 2006, Coos Bay Organic Products, Inc. had taken over the management of a county-owned salmon composting facility located in south-westernmost Coos County, Oregon. The site was convenient to the region's salmon and oyster aquaculture farms, tuna, Pacific whiting, and crab fisheries, and vast softwood forests that together yielded the ingredients needed for its compost recipes.

One challenge Brooks faced at Coos Bay Organic Products was the extreme seasonality of its industry, especially since the company distributed to the Midwest and not only along the Pacific Coast. The selling season in most of Coos Bay Organic Products' markets began in the second half of February and most of March, as garden centers began to prepare for their customers' growing season, and it was over by July 4. Yet Brooks had to keep the composting facility open all year, and had to make sure that his customers (all of which were independent garden centers) had inventory at the beginning of their customers' growing season.

Brooks thought about the issues Coos Bay's seasonality raised:

1. How would the company handle its inventory and expenses over the winter?

    a. Should the company deplete its inventory of finished, bagged product over the winter, going into hyperproduction mode just prior to the selling season? Alternatively, should it make and keep enough on hand to supply its customers' early-season needs?
    b. Should the company lay off any employees, or should it keep everyone employed, over the winter?

2. What would the company do for working capital over the winter?

    a. Should it rely on its cash flow?
    b. Should it rely on its equity owner for cash?
    c. Alternatively, should it take out a line of credit?

3. How would the company handle its bagging, shipping, and cash management during the growing season?

    a. Should Coos Bay Organic Products begin its bagging and shipping during the winter? Alternatively, should it wait until the selling season has begun?
    b. How should it handle its cash during the selling season? Should it rely entirely on cash flow? Alternatively, should it take out a line of credit?

As he sat in his office, Brooks thought about how to meet these challenges.

Case Questions

1. What approaches should Brooks use for handling inventory and expenses over the winter?
2. How should Brooks finance working capital over the winter?
3. How should the company handle its bagging, shipping, and cash management during the busy selling season?

Notes

1 US Securities and Exchange Commission.
2 Federal Trade Commission (2011).

3 The implied annual interest of the trade credit can be computed as: Annual rate =
$\dfrac{\text{Discount}}{\left(1 - \text{Discount}\right)} \times \dfrac{365 \, \text{days}}{\text{Days till net}}$. In the example: Annual rate $= \dfrac{0.02}{\left(1 - 0.02\right)} \times \dfrac{365}{20} = 0.37$

= 37%. Note that this calculation does not take into account compounding frequency.

4 The names of the firm and of the two owners have been changed to protect the privacy of the firm.

Bibliography

Brooks, C. (2013, August 27). 3 Tips to Getting the Best Credit Card Processing Deal. *Business News Daily* http://www.businessnewsdaily.com/4984-credit-card-processing-best-deal.html (accessed 4/21/2014).

Brooks, C. (2013, November 15). Accepting Credit Cards: A Small Business Guide. *Business News Daily* http://www.businessnewsdaily.com/4394-accepting-credit-cards.html (accessed 4/21/2014).

Burg, N. (2013, June 10). The 5 Best Inventory Management Apps. *Forbes Brand Voice* http://www.forbes.com/sites/ups/2013/06/10/the-5-best-inventory-management-apps/

Burzby, J., Wells, H., Axtman, B., & Mickey, J. (2009, March). Supermarket Loss Estimates for Fresh Fruit, Vegetables, Meat, Poultry, and Seafood and Their Use in the ERS Loss-Adjusted Food Availability Data. USDA Economic Research Service. *Economic Information Bulletin Number 44.*

Downs, P. (2013, March 25). What you need to know about credit card processing. *The New York Times Boss Blog* http://boss.blogs.nytimes.com/2013/03/25/what-you-need-to-know-about-credit-card-processing/ (accessed 4/19/2014).

Downs, P. (2013, March 26). My Search for Reasonable and Understandable Credit Card Processing. *You're the Boss: The New York Times* http://boss.blogs.nytimes.com/2013/03/26/my-search-for-reasonable-and-understandable-credit-card-processing/?_r=0 (accessed 4/19/2014).

Evans, D. (2012, April 30). Cash is king: 5 simple rules for creating a cash flow plan. *Accounting, Inc.* http://www.inc.com/david-evans/5-rules-for-making-cash-a-figurehead-king.html (accessed 3/9/2015).

Federal Reserve System. (2011). *The 2010 Federal Reserve Payments Study: Noncash Payment Trends in the United States: 2006–2009.* Washington, DC: Federal Reserve System.

Federal Trade Commission. (2011, September). *FTC Facts for Business: New Rules on Electronic Payments; Lower Costs for Retailers.* Washington, DC: Federal Trade Commission.

Lagorio-Chafkin, C. (2010, February 18). How to Handle Online Credit Processing. *Inc.* http://www.inc.com/guides/credit-card-payment-online.html (accessed 6/3/2014).

Moran, G. (2011, February 22). How to Check a Customer's Credit Worthiness. *Entrepreneur* http://www.entrepreneur.com/article/218126 (accessed 6/4/2014).

Sekar, A. (2013, June 5). Study: For Small Businesses, Big-Name Mobile Payments Aren't Always Best. *nerdwallet* http://www.nerdwallet.com/blog/current-events/study-small-businesses-bigname-mobile-payments/ (accessed 6/3/2014).

Shapiro, D. (2013, April 10). Driving Revenues & Relationships: Smart Cash Management Strategies. *The TJE American Business Magazine* http://www.americanbusinessmag.com/2013/04/driving-revenues-relationships-smart-cash-management-strategies/ (accessed).

US Securities and Exchange Commission. *Implementing the Dodd–Frank Wall Street Reform and Consumer Protection Act* http://www.sec.gov/spotlight/dodd-frank.shtml (accessed 4/21/2014).

Wang, Z. (2012). Debit Card Interchange Fee Regulation: Some Assessments and Considerations. *Economic Quarterly*, *98*(3) 159–183.

Wang, Z., & Wolman, A. (2014, April). Payment Choice and the Future of Currency: Insights from Two Billion Retail Transactions. *Working Paper Series, No 14–9*. Richmond, VA: Federal Reserve Bank of Richmond.

Module 4
The Mechanics of Finance

6 Forecasting Cash Flows

> The future is not some place we are going to, but one we are creating. The paths are not to be found, but made, and the activity of making them changes both the maker and the destination.
>
> John Schaar

When entrepreneurs think finance, they are often thinking about cash. Making sure that there is enough cash for payroll and bills is on top of every business owner's stress list. This chapter provides tools that enable entrepreneurs to be in control of their cash flows. We discussed the statement of cash flow in Chapter 3. In this chapter, we will use the direct method as the framework for forecasting cash flow. Table 6.1 shows the basic cash flow calculations.

When cash receipts do not include sale of equipment and fixed assets, and cash disbursements do not include planned capital investments, the resulting net cash flows are called "net cash flows from operations."

Cash flow forecasting and cash budget development are iterative processes. You should focus on estimating net cash flows from operations first. After you are satisfied that you have incorporated all important assumptions about the company's future strategies and factored in trends in the industry and economy, the next step is to include planned sales and purchases of equipment and fixed assets. The last step is to examine different financing options. Occasionally, if financing is not available, you may need to revise the company's strategies or timing of sales and purchases of equipment. You can improve your chances of obtaining financing by planning ahead.

Cash Ledger

Successful entrepreneurs manage cash flows proactively. This means that they know the cash position of their companies on any given day. The first step to gain proficiency in cash management is to become familiar with your company's cash flow pattern. The cash ledger details all cash receipts and disbursements, transaction by transaction. A good habit to establish is to review the cash ledger at least once a week. Table 6.2 shows an example of a cash ledger for a cleaning company.

Table 6.1 Cash Flow Calculation

	Cash receipts from cash sales and accounts receivable collections
add	Cash from sale of equipment and fixed assets
equals	Total cash receipts
	Cash disbursements to suppliers, wages, taxes, etc.
add	Equipment and fixed assets purchased with cash
equals	Total cash disbursements
	Total cash receipts
less	Total cash disbursements
equals	Net cash flow
	Cash balance at beginning of period
add	Total cash receipts
equals	Total cash available
less	Total cash disbursements
equals	Cash available before financing transactions
add	Cash from new borrowing
less	Cash payments for interest on debt
less	Cash repayments of debt principal
less	Cash dividends or owner's draw
equals	Cash balance at end of period

Table 6.2 Cash Ledger

Date	Reference	Name	Description	Amount paid	Amount received	Balance
Jan 1			Beginning balance			$2,000
Jan 3	3520002	Organic Cleaning Supplies	Cleaning supplies	$600		$1,400
Jan 4	201312005	Springfield Dental	Customer payment of December invoice		$800	$2,200
Jan 5	201401001	John Hartfeld	Customer payment for one time post-party clean up		$200	$2,400
Jan 5	8426500	Main Street Property	Rent for January	$1,500		$900
Jan 6	201312008	Melissa Tower	Customer payment of December invoice		$500	$1,400
Total for week Jan 1–7				**$2,000**	**$1,500**	**$1,400**

Over the week, the cash balance of this firm ranged from $900 to $2,400. In this example, the entrepreneur was lucky. Payments from two customers were received prior to rent being paid. Were those payments to have arrived a couple of days later, the business would not have had sufficient cash to pay the rent on January 5. To reduce the probability of running into cash flow problems, entrepreneurs should prepare a cash budget that estimates future cash flows and seek financing ahead of time if necessary. Setting a minimum target cash balance and being disciplined in adhering to the target are keys to successful cash management. The next section focuses on the cash budget.

Cash Budget

A cash budget computes cash balance based on estimated future cash inflows and outflows. Entrepreneurs need to decide upon time frequencies (daily, weekly, monthly, quarterly) and planning horizons (e.g. 1 quarter, 1 year, 3 years) that best fit the need of their businesses. For an existing business, historic cash flows are a good starting point for the budget. Historic values should be modified to factor in estimated changes, such as expected increases in rent and insurance premiums. For a new business, you will need to provide detailed assumptions about sales and costs.

Two examples that illustrate the cash budgeting process follow. The first example is a weekly cash budget for a startup restaurant for 1 quarter. The second example is a monthly cash budget for an established retailer for one year. Once the cash budget is developed, the entrepreneur can examine the impact of different financing options. The challenge is that banks are eager to loan to businesses that are cash rich and much less willing to extend credit when cash is most needed. The trade-off is between higher interest expenses and the risk of running out of cash. Entrepreneurs can be better prepared if they consider more than one possible scenario.

Cash Flow Forecast for a New Business

Forecasting sales for a new business is an art rather than a science. It is also a key step in preparing a cash budget. Techniques for forecasting sales depend on the industry. For retail businesses, dollar per square foot is a commonly used measure. eMarketer (2014) reported that in 2013 the average sales per square foot was $468 for shopping malls. Apple ranked as the highest sales per square foot retailer in 2013, averaging $4,551 per square foot. Stores like Walmart and Target averaged $430 and $300 per square foot (Polson, 2013; Thau, 2014). Restaurants usually base their sales forecasts on average checks and table turnovers. Many industries have trade associations that compile statistics useful for forecasting sales. For example, the National Restaurant Association (2014) reported that the average check per person for

Table 6.3 Assumptions Used in Forecasting Sales for Tasty Taco

	Sunday	Monday	Tuesday	Wednesday	Thursday	Friday	Saturday
Lunch average check	$20	$15	$15	$15	$15	$15	$20
Dinner average check	$25	$25	$25	$25	$25	$30	$30
Take-out average check	$20	$20	$20	$20	$20	$20	$20
Lunch drink/food mix	10%/90%	10%/90%	10%/90%	10%/90%	10%/90%	10%/90%	10%/90%
Dinner drink/food mix	25%/ 5%	25%/75%	25%/75%	25%/75%	25%/75%	40%/60%	40%/60%
Lunch turnover	1	1.5	1.5	1.5	1.5	1.5	1
Dinner turnover	1	1	1.5	1.5	2	2.5	2.5
Number of take-out orders	20	30	30	30	30	50	50

Number of days of operation: 360 days (closed Christmas Eve, Christmas day, Good Friday through Easter Sunday)
Number of tables: 20

a full-service restaurant was just below $15 in 2014. Trade magazines are another good resource of sales data.

Listing all the assumptions of the operation explicitly is an often overlooked benefit of preparing a sales forecast. This process help new entrepreneurs identify potential flaws in their business model. In the first example, Tasty Taco is a small new restaurant. Table 6.3 lists the assumptions used in preparing its sales forecast.

Tasty Taco's assumptions include days the restaurant will be open, average checks for lunch, dinner, and take-out, and table turnover. These values vary throughout the week, reflecting customers' dine-out patterns. They also include the sales mix of food and alcoholic drinks. The level of detail in the assumptions paints a clear picture of how the restaurant will perform according to the entrepreneur's vision, and enables the entrepreneur to articulate the forecast process to banks and outside investors when needed. If actual sales deviate significantly from what was envisioned, the entrepreneur could identify the source of the shortfall and make strategic changes. Table 6.4 shows the projection of weekly sales based on these assumptions. The calculations are as follows.

Projected lunch
food sales for Sunday = Lunch average check for Sunday ×
  Number of tables × Lunch turnover for Sunday ×
  Lunch food mix for Sunday
  = $20 × 20 × 1 × 0.90
  = $360

Table 6.4 Weekly Sales Forecasts for Tasty Taco ($)

	Sunday	Monday	Tuesday	Wednesday	Thursday	Friday	Saturday	Weekly total
Projected lunch food sales	360	405	405	405	405	405	360	2,745
Projected lunch drink sales	40	45	45	45	45	45	40	305
Projected dinner food sales	375	375	563	563	750	900	900	4,426
Projected dinner drink sales	125	125	188	188	250	600	600	2,076
Projected take-out food sales	400	600	600	600	600	1,000	1,000	4,800
Total projected food sales	1,135	1,380	1,568	1,568	1,755	2,305	2,260	11,971
Total projected drink sales	165	170	233	233	295	645	640	2,381
Total projected sales	**1,300**	**1,550**	**1,801**	**1,801**	**2,050**	**2,950**	**2,900**	**14,352**

Projected lunch
drink sales for Sunday = Lunch average check for Sunday ×
Number of tables × Lunch turnover for Sunday ×
Lunch drink mix for Sunday
= $20 × 20 × 1 × 0.10
= $40

Projected dinner
food sales for Sunday = Dinner average check for Sunday ×
Number of tables × Dinner turnover for Sunday ×
Dinner food mix for Sunday
= $25 × 20 × 1 × 0.75
= $375

Projected dinner
drink sales for Sunday = Dinner average check for Sunday ×
Number of tables × Dinner turnover for Sunday ×
Dinner drink mix for Sunday
= $25 × 20 × 1 × 0.25
= $125

Projected take-out
sales = Take-out average check for Sunday ×
Take-out orders for Sunday
= $20 × 20
= $400

Total projected
food sales for Sunday = Projected lunch food sales for Sunday +
                         Projected dinner food sales for Sunday +
                         Projected take-out sales
                       = $360 + $375 + $400
                       = $1,135

Total projected drink
sales for Sunday   = Projected lunch drink sales for Sunday +
                         Projected dinner drink sales for Sunday
                       = $40 + $125
                       = $165

Total projected
sales for Sunday   = Total projected food sales for Sunday +
                         Total projected drink sales for Sunday
                       = $1,135 + $165
                       = $1,300

Tasty Taco's estimated weekly total sales would be about $14,350. Seasonality might be an important factor for some businesses. For Tasty Taco, the preceding projections were based on the peak tourist season in July and August; sales in June would only be 80 percent of the peak. Factoring in seasonality, the sales projections would be:

Weekly sales in June = $14,350 × 0.80 = $11,480

Weekly sales in July = $14,350

Weekly sales in August = $14,350

The next step is to forecast expenses and planned investments in fixed assets. The major types of expense are cost of goods sold, payroll, and overhead. Table 6.5 shows the assumptions for Tasty Taco's expenses.

A carefully prepared cash budget would include all expected cash disbursements. The assumptions for Tasty Taco reflect the business model (quick service with 3 or 4 employees per shift) and business strategies for advertising and equipment rental. Future expenses can be computed based on these assumptions.

Weekly costs of food = Cost of food percentage × Total projected food sales

Weekly costs of alcoholic beverage = Cost of drink percentage × Total projected drink sales

Weekly total cost of goods sold = Weekly costs of food + Weekly costs of alcoholic beverage

Table 6.5 Assumptions Used in Forecasting Expenses for Tasty Taco

Days of operation	360	days per year
Number of tables	20	tables
Kitchen and waiting staff employees, weekly hours	562	two 8 hour shifts × 4 employees Sun–Thur, two 8 hour shifts × 6 employees Fri–Sat
Kitchen and waiting staff, hourly rate	$8	per hour
Owner's salary	$60,000	per year, payable fortnightly on Monday
Costs of food	33.80%	of food revenue
Costs of alcoholic beverage	29.00%	of alcoholic drink revenue
Employee benefits	$12,000	per year, health insurance premium payable on the 1st of each month
Payroll taxes	12.42%	for all employees
Advertising	$500	per month, payable on the 15th
Rent	$5,000	per month, payable on the 1st
Utilities	$1,000	per month, payable on the 15th
Insurance	$10,000	per year, payable on Jan 15th
Workmen's compensation insurance	$10,000	per year, payable quarterly on the 1st
Licensing	$2,600	per year, payable on July 1st
Office, accounting and technology	$200	per month, payable on the 1st
Credit card charges	2.00%	of sales, payable immediately
Percentage of sales through credit card	40%	of total sales
Supplies	$5,000	per year, estimated to be paid once per month on the 1st
Equipment lease	$10,000	per year, payable monthly on the 15th

Weekly wages for
kitchen and waiting staff = Kitchen and waiting staff weekly hours × hourly rate

$$\text{Owner's salary} = \frac{\text{Owner's annual salary}}{26} \text{ (there are 26 biweekly payments per year)}$$

Total wages
and salary = Wages for kitchen and waiting staff + owner's salary

Payroll taxes = Payroll tax percentage × Total wages and salary

Using the first week of June as a demonstration, these calculations are as follows.

Weekly costs of food = 0.3380 × $9,576 = $3,237

Weekly costs of alcoholic beverage = 0.29 × $1,904 = $552

Weekly total cost of goods sold = $3,237 + $552 = $3,789

Weekly wages for kitchen and waiting staff = 512 × $8 = $4,096

Fortnightly owner's salary = $60,000 / 26 = $2,308 (occurs biweekly)

Total wages and salary = $4,096 + $2,308 = $6,404

Payroll taxes = 0.1242 × $6,404 = $795

The other expenses were due at different times of the month. It is important to include payment details with the assumptions. Table 6.6 shows detailed week by week cash receipts and disbursements for June, July, and August.

The cash receipts and disbursements forecast for Tasty Taco reveal that there was a great deal of variability in cash outflow. Over the three-month period, weekly cash disbursements range from $8,485 to almost $24,000. A lot of expenses fell due in the first week of July. In fact, that week had a projected net cash flow of −$9,417. Should the owner be alarmed? It depends on the total amount of cash available. To answer this question, we use the projections from Tables 6.5 and 6.6 and the basic cash flow calculations from Table 6.1 to develop a cash budget. Information from Table 6.6 is also useful for determining the minimum target cash balance.

A common rule of thumb is to have one to three months' expenses as cash reserve. For Tasty Taco, total cash expenses for the three-month period are around $170,000, averaging over $56,000 per month.

Another approach is to consider a worst-case scenario. For example, the owner believed the worst case would be for sales to be 30 percent below forecast and expenses to be 20 percent higher than expected. This meant that cash inflow could be $52,521 below the forecasted amount and outflow could be $33,830 higher than expected, resulting in a total shortfall of $86,351 over the three-month period. Based on this analysis, Tasty Taco should have a minimum target cash balance of between $60,000 and $90,000. The owner decided to start the business with $80,000 cash on hand and maintain a target minimum balance of $70,000. Table 6.7 shows the cash budget for Tasty Taco before any additional financing.

The cash balance for Tasty Taco ranged from $68,421 to $85,914 during the three-month period and was below the original balance of $80,000 in all but the last two weeks in August. Cash balance dropped below the minimum target of $70,000 in the first week of July when many bills were due. While the situation was not dire, the owner of Tasty Taco should take action to stay on target. One option would be to raise additional startup funds and increase the beginning cash balance to $85,000. Another would be to arrange for a line of credit of $10,000. The owner could also plan to borrow $5,000 at the end of June and repay the loan in August. The last option would have the lowest interest costs but would require an investment of time by the owner to deal with the bank during the first few months of starting a new business. Option two, arranging for a line of credit, might not be available to a new business. Given this is a new startup, raising an additional $5,000 prior to opening would be the best option.

Table 6.6 Cash Receipts and Disbursement Projections for Tasty Taco

	June: 80% of peak season				July: 100% of peak season					August: 100% of peak season			
	Jun 1 to Jun 7	Jun 8 to Jun 14	Jun 15 to Jun 21	Jun 22 to Jun 28	Jun 29 to Jul 5	Jul 6 to Jul 12	Jul 13 to Jul 19	Jul 20 to Jul 26	Jul 27 to Aug 2	Aug 3 to Aug 9	Aug 10 to Aug 16	Aug 17 to Aug 23	Aug 24 to Aug 30
Cash receipts													
Total projected food sales	$9,576	$9,576	$9,576	$9,576	$11,970	$11,970	$11,970	$11,970	$11,970	$11,970	$11,970	$11,970	$11,970
Total projected drink sales	$1,904	$1,904	$1,904	$1,904	$2,380	$2,380	$2,380	$2,380	$2,380	$2,380	$2,380	$2,380	$2,380
Total projected sales receipts	**$11,480**	**$11,480**	**$11,480**	**$11,480**	**$14,350**	**$14,350**	**$14,350**	**$14,350**	**$14,350**	**$14,350**	**$14,350**	**$14,350**	**$14,350**
Cash disbursements													
Cost of goods sold													
Costs of food	$3,237	$3,237	$3,237	$3,237	$4,046	$4,046	$4,046	$4,046	$4,046	$4,046	$4,046	$4,046	$4,046
Costs of alcoholic beverages	$552	$552	$552	$552	$690	$690	$690	$690	$690	$690	$690	$690	$690
Total costs of goods sold	**$3,789**	**$3,789**	**$3,789**	**$3,789**	**$4,736**	**$4,736**	**$4,736**	**$4,736**	**$4,736**	**$4,736**	**$4,736**	**$4,736**	**$4,736**
Wages and salaries													
Wages for kitchen and waiting staff	$4,096	$4,096	$4,096	$4,096	$4,096	$4,096	$4,096	$4,096	$4,096	$4,096	$4,096	$4,096	$4,096
Owner's salary	$2,308	$2,308	$2,308		$2,308		$2,308		$2,308		$2,308		$2,308
Total wages and salary	**$6,404**	**$6,404**	**$6,404**	**$4,096**	**$6,404**	**$4,096**	**$6,404**	**$4,096**	**$6,404**	**$4,096**	**$6,404**	**$4,096**	**$6,404**
Payroll taxes	$795	$509	$795	$509	$795	$509	$795	$509	$795	$509	$795	$509	$795
Employee benefits	$1,000				$1,000				$1,000				
Advertising			$500				$500				$500		

(Continued)

Table 6.6 Cash Receipts and Disbursement Projections for Tasty Taco (Continued)

	June: 80% of peak season				July: 100% of peak season					August: 100% of peak season			
	Jun 1 to Jun 7	Jun 8 to Jun 14	Jun 15 to Jun 21	Jun 22 to Jun 28	Jun 29 to Jul 5	Jul 6 to Jul 12	Jul 13 to Jul 19	Jul 20 to Jul 26	Jul 27 to Aug 2	Aug 3 to Aug 9	Aug 10 to Aug 16	Aug 17 to Aug 23	Aug 24 to Aug 30
Rent	$5,000				$5,000					$5,000			
Utilities			$1,000				$1,000					$1,000	
Insurance													
Workmen's compensation insurance					$2,500								
Licensing					$2,600								
Office, accounting and technology	$200				$200				$200				
Credit card charges	$92	$92	$92	$92	$115	$115	$115	$115	$115	$115	$115	$115	$115
Supplies	$417				$417				$417				
Equipment lease			$833				$833				$833		
Total cash disbursements	$17,697	$8,486	$13,413	$8,486	$23,767	$9,456	$14,383	$9,456	$18,667	$9,456	$14,383	$9,456	$12,050
Net cash flows	−$6,217	$2,994	−$1,933	$2,994	−$9,417	$4,894	−$33	$4,894	−$4,317	$4,894	−$33	$4,894	$2,300

Table 6.7 Cash Budget Before Additional Financing for Tasty Taco

	June: 80% of peak season				July: 100% of peak season					August: 100% of peak season			
	Jun 1 to Jun 7	Jun 8 to Jun 14	Jun 15 to Jun 21	Jun 22 to Jun 28	Jun 29 to Jul 5	Jul 6 to Jul 12	Jul 13 to Jul 19	Jul 20 to Jul 26	Jul 27 to Aug 2	Aug 3 to Aug 9	Aug 10 to Aug 16	Aug 17 to Aug 23	Aug 24 to Aug 30
Cash, beginning balance	$80,000	$73,783	$76,777	$74,844	$77,838	$68,421	$73,315	$73,282	$78,176	$73,859	$78,783	$78,720	$83,614
Total projected sales receipts	$11,480	$11,480	$11,480	$11,480	$14,350	$14,350	$14,350	$14,350	$14,350	$14,350	$14,350	$14,350	$14,350
Total cash available	*$91,480*	*$85,263*	*$88,257*	*$86,324*	*$92,188*	*$82,771*	*$87,665*	*$87,632*	*$92,526*	*$88,209*	*$93,103*	*$93,070*	*$97,964*
Total cash disbursements	$17,697	$8,486	$13,413	$8,486	$23,767	$9,456	$14,383	$9,456	$18,667	$9,456	$14,383	$9,456	$12,050
Cash available before financing transactions	*$73,783*	*$76,777*	*$74,844*	*$77,838*	*$68,421*	*$73,315*	*$73,282*	*$78,176*	*$73,859*	*$78,753*	*$78,720*	*$83,614*	*$85,914*
Cash from new borrowing													
Cash payments for debt interest													
Cash repayments on debt principal													
Cash for owner's draw													
Ending cash balance	**$73,783**	**$76,777**	**$74,844**	**$77,838**	**$68,421**	**$73,315**	**$73,282**	**$78,176**	**$73,859**	**$78,753**	**$78,720**	**$83,614**	**$85,914**

Cash Flow Forecast for an Established Business

For established businesses, a cash flow forecast usually starts with historic financial data. Assuming there are no extraordinary events, the most recent year's financials or the average of the recent two years can be used as the base values. The most important and difficult task is estimating which values will change over the planning horizon and by how much. A few key variables, such as sales, cost of goods sold (COGS) or inventory purchases, and labor costs are critical for most businesses and should always be analyzed individually.

The next step will be to identify key variables specific to your business, as not all variables have the same impact on different industries. For example, gas expense will be a key variable for a taxi company but might not be significant for a restaurant. The growth rate for each key variable can then be estimated based on the entrepreneur's experience and research findings of the industry group, combined with the economic outlook for the local area. Sometimes, changes to expenses are known in advance. For example, when a business signs a new lease, rent for the next two years is fixed. These changes should be incorporated into the forecast. Remaining variables can be divided into two groups. The first group is assigned a general rate of increase, such as the rate of inflation. The second group is assumed to remain as a fixed percentage of another key variable. For example, credit card service payment is assumed to be a fixed percentage of credit card sales and FICA is assumed to be a fixed percentage of payroll.

We will use Peace Blossom, a floral and landscaping business, to illustrate cash flow forecasting for an established business. Peace Blossom was a seasonal business, with spring and fall being its busy seasons. In addition to retail sales, it provided landscaping services, which were billed to customers with a 30-day credit period. A large portion of its purchases were cash on delivery, with only a handful of suppliers allowing them to pay 15 days net. Table 6.8 shows historic cash receipts and disbursements over the preceding 12 months.

The impact of the seasonal nature of the business on cash flows is obvious. Net cash flow for Peace Blossom ranged from −$60,975 to $173,902. The largest cash deficit occurred in March, when sales were still relatively low but the business was purchasing inventory in preparation for the spring season. Given the large variability, this company decided to prepare a monthly forecast of its cash flows for the following year. The key variables for Peace Blossom were sales, purchases, and labor costs. Massachusetts, where Peace Blossom was located, had just passed legislation to increase the minimum wage for the coming year from $8 to $9 per hour, a 12.5 percent increase. This would significantly affect hourly employee wages. Table 6.9 lists the forecast assumptions for these key variables.

Peace Blossom expected increases in cash sales to lag behind credit card and credit sales in the following year. The owner planned to obtain credit purchase terms with some suppliers, increasing purchases with accounts payable and reducing cash purchases. The increase in wages reflected changes in the minimum wage law for the state. The next step was to identify variables with known changes or linked directly to other variables. For Peace Blossom, these

Table 6.8 Cash Receipts and Disbursements in the Past 12 Months for Peace Blossom

	Jan	Feb	Mar	Apr	May	Jun	Jul	Aug	Sep	Oct	Nov	Dec	Year's total
Cash receipts													
Cash sales	$1,008	$2,088	$4,608	$89,652	$175,512	$172,992	$86,504	$66,444	$161,568	$152,976	$22,776	$5,616	$941,744
Credit card sales deposit from merchant account	$504	$1,044	$2,304	$44,826	$87,756	$86,496	$47,202	$33,222	$80,784	$76,488	$11,388	$2,808	$474,822
Cash collection from accounts receivable	$1,736	$204	$330	$806	$14,942	$30,650	$28,430	$11,074	$10,830	$29,012	$25,096	$3,560	$156,670
Total cash receipts	**$3,248**	**$3,336**	**$7,242**	**$135,284**	**$278,210**	**$290,138**	**$162,136**	**$110,740**	**$253,182**	**$258,476**	**$59,260**	**$11,984**	**$1,573,236**
Cash disbursements													
Purchases—cash on delivery	$1,152	$2,512	$40,870	$97,928	$115,888	$67,974	$44,296	$86,574	$93,894	$24,118	$4,558	$1,696	$581,460
Payment of accounts payable	$424	$288	$628	$10,217	$24,482	$28,972	$16,993	$11,074	$31,643	$15,973	$11,029	$1,889	$153,612
Hourly employee wages	$0	$0	$6,240	$7,200	$14,880	$14,880	$7,200	$7,440	$14,880	$14,880	$13,920	$7,200	$108,720
Manager's salary	$4,800	$4,800	$9,600	$9,600	$9,600	$14,400	$14,400	$14,400	$14,400	$14,400	$14,400	$9,600	$134,400
Total wages and salary	**$4,800**	**$4,800**	**$15,840**	**$16,800**	**$24,480**	**$29,280**	**$21,600**	**$21,840**	**$29,280**	**$29,280**	**$28,320**	**$16,800**	**$243,120**
FICA	$367	$367	$1,212	$1,285	$1,873	$2,240	$1,652	$1,671	$2,240	$2,240	$2,166	$1,285	$18,598
Workmen's compensation insurance	$320	$320	$1,056	$1,120	$1,632	$1,952	$1,440	$1,456	$1,952	$1,952	$1,888	$1,120	$16,208
Advertising, website hosting	$200	$200	$200	$200	$200	$200	$200	$200	$200	$200	$200	$200	$2,400
Credit card service payment	$60	$70	$94	$902	$1,718	$1,693	$681	$648	$1,585	$1,503	$266	$103	$9,323

(Continued)

Table 6.8 Cash Receipts and Disbursements in the Past 12 Months for Peace Blossom (Continued)

	Jan	Feb	Mar	Apr	May	Jun	Jul	Aug	Sep	Oct	Nov	Dec	Year's total
Rent	$6,800	$6,800	$6,800	$6,800	$6,800	$6,800	$6,800	$6,800	$6,800	$6,800	$6,800	$6,800	$81,600
Insurance	$400			$400			$400			$400			$1,600
Water	$65	$68	$85	$98	$92	$126	$240	$285	$143	$95	$72	$64	$1,433
Electricity	$185	$176	$184	$186	$168	$174	$246	$284	$182	$168	$174	$182	$2,309
Phone	$250	$250	$250	$250	$250	$250	$250	$250	$250	$250	$250	$250	$3,000
Repairs and maintenance	$60	$485	$124	$60	$260	$60	$86	$124	$240	$168	$174	$204	$2,045
Gas for trucks and equipment	$120	$142	$180	$146	$846	$978	$625	$547	$963	$784	$135	$168	$5,634
Legal, accounting and professional services	$500	$500	$500	$500	$500	$500	$500	$500	$500	$500	$500	$500	$6,000
Total cash disbursements	$15,963	$17,223	$68,217	$137,045	$179,309	$141,288	$96,077	$132,325	$169,956	$84,574	$56,718	$31,515	$1,130,210
Net cash flows	−$12,715	−$13,887	−$60,975	−$1,761	$98,901	$148,850	$66,059	−$21,585	$83,226	$173,902	$2,542	−$19,531	$443,026

Table 6.9 Forecast Assumptions of Key Variables for Peace Blossom

Key variables	Forecast assumptions
Cash sales	Cash sales will grow at 4%
Credit card sales	Credit card sales will grow at 5%
Sales on credit to customers (accounts receivable)	Sales on credit will grow at 5%
Cash purchases	Cash purchases will grow at 3%
Purchases on credit (accounts payable)	Purchases on credit will grow at 10%
Hourly employee wages	Hourly employee wages will increase by 12.5%
Manager salary	Manager salary will increase by 3%

variables included rent, FICA, workmen's compensation insurance premiums, and credit card service expense. The current lease still had one more year to run, so rent would remain the same. FICA included 6.2 percent of Social Security and 1.45 percent of Medicare. Hence FICA, would be 7.65 percent (6.2% + 1.45%) of total wages and salary. Peace Blossom received a quotation for next year's workmen's compensation premium for 80 cents per dollar per year on total wages and salary. The merchant account contract included a $50 monthly flat fee plus 3.8 percent of credit card sales. All other expenses were assumed to increase at 3 percent, the expected rate of inflation. Table 6.10 summarizes forecast assumptions for these variables.

Monthly cash receipts and disbursements for the following year were estimated based on the historic data in Table 6.8 combined with the assumptions listed in Tables 6.9 and 6.10. Since cash sales were expected to grow at 4 percent, cash sales for the following January were calculated as January cash sales for the

Table 6.10 Forecast Assumptions of Other Variables for Peace Blossom

FICA	6.2% Social Security and 1.45% Medicare, totaling 7.65% of total wages and salary
Workmen's compensation insurance	80 cents per dollar of total wages and salary per year
Credit card service payment	$50 monthly fee + 3.8% of credit card sales
Rent	no change
Advertising, website hosting	increase by 3%
Insurance	increase by 3%
Water	increase by 3%
Gas heating	increase by 3%
Electricity	increase by 3%
Phone	increase by 3%
Repairs and maintenance	increase by 3%
Gas for trucks and equipment	increase by 3%
Legal, accounting and professional services	increase by 3%

past year × (1 + 4%), $1,048 = $1,008 × 1.04. June cash sales for the following year were estimated to be $179,912 ($172,992 × 1.04). Credit card sales were assumed to grow at 5 percent. Hence, credit card sales for January and June were calculated to be $529 ($504 × 1.05) and $ 90,821 ($86,496 × 1.05) respectively. Table 6.11 provides a side-by-side comparison of forecasted values for January and June for the following year and historic values from the past year.

FICA was assumed to be 7.65 percent of total wages and salary. For January, total wages and salary was estimated to be $4,944, resulting in FICA expense of $378 ($4,944 × 0.0765). Workmen's compensation insurance for the Therefore, the workmen's compensation premium for January was estimated to be $330 ($0.80 × $4,944/12). Credit card service fees included a flat fee of $50

Table 6.11 Historic and Estimated Cash Receipts and Disbursements in January and June for Peace Blossom

	Jan this Year	Jan next year	Jun this year	Jun next Year
Cash Receipts				
Cash sales	$1,008	$1,048	$172,992	$179,912
Credit card sales deposit from merchant account	$504	$529	$86,496	$90,821
Cash collection from accounts receivable	$1,736	$1,823	$30,650	$32,183
Total cash receipts	$3,248	$3,400	$290,138	$302,916
Cash Disbursements				
Purchases–cash on delivery	$1,152	$1,187	$67,974	$70,013
Payment of accounts payable	$424	$424	$28,972	$31,869
Hourly employee wages	$0	$0	$14,880	$16,740
Manager salary	$4,800	$4,944	$14,400	$14,832
Total wages and salary	$4,800	$4,944	$29,280	$31,572
FICA	$367	$378	$2,240	$2,415
Workmen's compensation insurance	$320	$330	$1,952	$2,105
Advertising, website hosting	$200	$206	$200	$206
Credit card service payment	$60	$70	$1,693	$3,501
Rent	$6,800	$6,800	$6,800	$6,800
Insurance	$400	$412	$0	$0
Water	$65	$67	$126	$130
Gas heating	$260	$268	$89	$92
Electricity	$185	$191	$174	$179
Phone	$250	$258	$250	$258
Repairs and maintenance	$60	$62	$60	$62
Gas for trucks and equipment	$120	$124	$978	$1,007
Legal, accounting and professional services	$500	$515	$500	$515
Total cash disbursements	$15,963	$16,236	$141,288	$150,724
Net cash flows	**−$12,715**	**−$12,836**	**$148,850**	**$152,192**

Table 6.12 Cash Receipts and Disbursements Forecast for Peace Blossom

	Jan	Feb	Mar	Apr	May	Jun	Jul	Aug	Sep	Oct	Nov	Dec	Year Total
Cash receipts													
Cash sales	$1,048	$2,172	$4,792	$93,238	$182,532	$179,912	$89,964	$69,102	$168,031	$159,095	$23,687	$5,841	$979,414
Credit card sales deposit from merchant account	529	1,096	2,419	47,067	92,144	90,821	49,562	34,823	84,823	80,312	11,957	2,948	498,561
Cash collection from accounts receivable	1,823	214	347	846	15,689	32,183	29,852	11,628	11,372	30,463	26,351	3,738	164,506
Total cash receipts	**$3,400**	**$3,482**	**$7,558**	**$141,151**	**$290,365**	**$302,916**	**$169,378**	**$115,613**	**$264,226**	**$269,870**	**$61,995**	**$12,527**	**$1,642,481**
Cash disbursements													
Purchases—cash on delivery	1,187	2,587	42,096	100,866	119,365	70,013	45,625	89,171	96,711	24,842	4,695	1,747	598,905
Payment of accounts payable	424	317	691	11,239	26,930	31,869	18,692	12,181	34,807	17,570	12,132	2,078	168,930
Hourly employee wages	0	0	7,020	8,100	16,740	16,740	8,100	8,370	16,740	16,740	15,660	8,100	122,310
Manager salary	4,944	4,944	9,888	9,888	9,888	14,832	14,832	14,832	14,832	14,832	14,832	9,888	138,432
Total wages and salary	4,944	4,944	16,908	17,988	26,628	31,572	22,932	23,202	31,572	31,572	30,492	17,988	260,742
FICA	378	378	1,293	1,376	2,037	2,415	1,754	1,775	2,415	2,415	2,333	1,376	19,945
Workmen's compensation insurance	330	330	1,127	1,199	1,775	2,105	1,529	1,547	2,105	2,105	2,033	1,199	17,384
Advertising, website hosting	206	206	206	206	206	206	206	206	206	206	206	206	2,472
Credit card service payment	70	92	142	1,839	3,551	3,501	1,933	1,376	3,273	3,102	504	162	19,545
Rent	6,800	6,800	6,800	6,800	6,800	6,800	6,800	6,800	6,800	6,800	6,800	6,800	81,600
Insurance	412	0	0	412	0	0	412	0	0	412	0	0	1,648
Water	67	70	88	101	95	130	247	294	147	98	74	66	1,477
Gas heat	268	252	200	158	124	92	70	74	87	147	192	262	1,926
Electricity	191	181	190	192	173	179	253	293	187	173	179	187	2,378
Phone	258	258	258	258	258	258	258	258	258	258	258	258	3,096
Repairs and maintenance	62	500	128	62	268	62	89	128	247	173	179	210	2,108
Gas for trucks and equipment	124	146	185	150	871	1,007	644	563	992	808	139	173	5,802
Legal, accounting and professional services	515	515	515	515	515	515	515	515	515	515	515	515	6,180
Total cash disbursements	**$16,236**	**$17,576**	**$70,827**	**$143,361**	**$189,596**	**$150,724**	**$101,959**	**$138,383**	**$180,322**	**$91,196**	**$60,731**	**$33,227**	**$1,194,138**
Net cash flows	*−$12,836*	*−$14,094*	*−$63,269*	*−$2,210*	*$100,769*	*$152,192*	*$67,419*	*−$22,770*	*$83,904*	*$178,674*	*$1,264*	*−$20,700*	*$448,343*

per month plus 3.8 percent of credit card sales. Payments to credit card service in January were $70 ($50 + $529 × 0.038) and in June were $3,501 ($50 + $90,821 × 0.038). Rent would stay at $6,800 per month under the existing lease. All other expenses were assumed to increase by 3 percent, the estimated rate of inflation. Figure 6.12 presents the complete cash flows forecast for next year.

Net cash flows from operations for next year followed a similar seasonal pattern to the one shown in the historic data. The lowest net cash flow was −$63,269, which occurred in March, a month with low receipts and relatively high disbursements, owing to inventory build-up for April. The largest net cash flows were expected in October, $178,674. Compared with the past year's cash receipts and disbursements (Table 6.8), the following year's projections showed greater variability and range, implying more uncertainty. The owner of Peach Blossom decided to increase the minimum target cash balance by $5,000 as a result. The new minimum target balance would be $180,000.

Planned Capital Expenditures and New Financing

The next step after estimating net cash flows from operations is to include any planned capital expenditure and new financing. Peace Blossom planned to purchase another delivery truck in March. The truck was estimated to cost $85,000, and the dealer required 10 percent down and would finance the balance at 4 percent per year over five years. In other words, Peace Blossom would have a net cash outflow of $8,500 ($85,000 × 0.10) for the down payment in March and a $76,500 ($85,000 − $8,500) amortized loan with fixed monthly payments beginning in April.

6.1 Amortized Loan

An amortized loan is a common type of loan for both consumers and businesses. Real estate mortgages and automobile loans are two examples. Most amortized loans are fixed payment loans. An important feature of an amortized loan is that each payment includes both an interest portion and a principal portion. The borrower repays part of the principal in each payment, lowering the remaining loan balance. With a fixed payment amortized loan, since the payment amount remains the same throughout the life of the loan, the interest portion decreases while the principal portion increases over time. By the end of the loan, nearly the entire payment will represent principal, while in the beginning, most of the payment represents interest.

You can compute the fixed payment amount of an amortized loan using an online loan payment calculator, a financial calculator or a spreadsheet, such as the PMT function in Microsoft Excel®.[1] The monthly payment for this loan was $1,408.86. A useful tool for managing and understanding an amortized loan is an amortization table, which shows the remaining balance, the interest portion and the principal portion of each payment.

6.2 Amortization Table

An amortization table shows the remaining balance, the interest portion, and the principal portion of each payment. The formulas for computing the amortization table are:

Interest portion = Previous ending balance × interest rate
Principal portion = Fixed payment − interest portion
Current ending balance = Previous ending balance − Principal portion

Since Peace Blossom planned to purchase the truck in March, the ending balance of the loan in March was $76,500. The first payment would be due in April and the payment amount would remain $1,408.86 throughout the life of the loan. For the April payment, the interest portion would be $255 ($76,500 × 0.04 /12) and the principal portion would be $1,153.86 ($1,408.86 − $255). The new ending balance was $75,346.14 ($76,500 − $1,153.86). Table 6.13 shows the amortization table of this loan from March through December. By the end of the next year, Peace Blossom will have paid off more than $10,000 of the loan, with an ending balance of $65,975.68.

The Cash Budget

Now we have all the elements needed to prepare the cash budget for Peace Blossom.[2] We will use the basic cash flow calculations listed in Table 6.1. The cash balance was $250,000 at the beginning of the forecast period. In January and February, the only items are estimated cash receipts and disbursements from operation. Cash receipts in January were $3,400 but disbursements were projected to be $16,234, reducing the cash balance to $237,164 ($250,000 + $3,400 − $16,236) by the end of the month. Table 6.14 shows the first iteration of the cash budget from January through May. By the end of February, the cash balance decreased to $223,070. In March, Peace Blossom planned to purchase the truck. The cash budget showed the total cost of $85,000 as an outflow and the loan amount of $76,500 as an inflow. The net cash impact of the truck purchase was an outflow of $8,500 (−$85,000 + $76,500), which was the down payment amount. The cash balance in March further decreased to $151,301 ($223,070 + $7,558 − $70,827 − $85,000 + $76,500). Payments on the loan began in April. The cash budget included the interest portion and the principal portion of the loan payment as two separate lines. This presentation

Table 6.13 Amortization Table for Peace Blossom's Truck Loan

a Payment Details

Truck cost	$85,000
Down payment	$8,500
Loan amount	$76,500
Interest rate	4.00% per year (1/3% per month)
Loan term	5 years (60 months)
Fixed monthly payment	$1,408.86

b Amortization Table

Month	Payment	Interest	Principal	Ending balance
March				$76,500.00
April	$1,408.86	$255.00	$1,153.86	$75,346.14
May	$1,408.86	$251.15	$1,157.71	$74,188.43
June	$1,408.86	$247.29	$1,161.57	$73,026.86
July	$1,408.86	$243.42	$1,165.44	$71,861.42
August	$1,408.86	$239.54	$1,169.33	$70,692.09
September	$1,408.86	$235.64	$1,173.22	$69,518.87
October	$1,408.86	$231.73	$1,177.13	$68,341.73
November	$1,408.86	$227.81	$1,181.06	$67,160.67
December	$1,408.86	$223.87	$1,185.00	$65,975.68

format shows any additional principal payments clearly if Peace Blossom decide to make extra payments to pay off the loan earlier. The separation of interest and principal payments is also important when preparing a pro forma income statement, a topic covered in Chapter 7. Interest expense is part of the income statement and affects a firm's taxable income and net income. Principal repayment is not considered an expense. We will discuss this distinction in more detail in Chapter 7.

Recall that the owner of Peace Blossom decided to set the target minimum cash balance to $180,000, owing to increased variability in forecasted net cash flows. The cash budget in Table 6.14 shows that the projected cash balance in March and April would fall below the target. Would delaying the truck purchase helped achieve this target? When preparing the cash budget, we knew that the net cash impact of the truck purchase in March was $8,500. So delaying the truck purchase would only increase the cash balance in March to $159,801, still more than $20,000 below the target. The total car payment in April would be $1,409 ($255 + $1,154) and delaying this payment would not make a material difference in its cash balance. Since the truck purchase would help the business grow and achieve its projected sales increase, postponing this capital investment would limit its growth without

Table 6.14 Cash Budget (First Iteration) From January Through May for Peace Blossom

	Jan	*Feb*	*Mar*	*Apr*	*May*
Cash, beginning balance	$250,000	$237,164	$223,070	$151,301	$147,682
Total projected cash receipts	$3,400	$3,482	$7,558	$141,151	$290,365
Total cash available	$253,400	$240,646	$230,628	$292,452	$438,047
Total projected cash disbursements	$16,236	$17,576	$70,827	$143,361	$189,596
Planned capital expenditure			$85,000		
Cash available before financing transactions	$237,164	$223,070	$74,801	$149,091	$248,451
Cash from new borrowing			$76,500		
Cash payments for debt interest				$255	$251
Cash repayments on debt principal				$1,154	$1,158
Cash for owner's draw					
Ending cash balance	$237,164	$223,070	$151,301	$147,682	$247,042

helping improve its cash balance significantly. For a seasonal business like Peace Blossom, a line of credit would be the best option.

The company had a profitable year with annual total net cash flows of $438,157 (see Table 6.8). It should apply for a line of credit from its bank. Assume that Peace Blossom was able to obtain a $50,000 line of credit at prime plus 2 percent. Currently prime rate was at 4 percent. This means that the company could borrow up to $50,000 when it needed cash and only paid interest on the amount it actually borrowed. The interest rate would be 2 percent higher than the prime rate, which would be 6 percent per year currently. The original projection from Table 6.14 shows that Peace Blossom would need $30,000 in new funding before March and an additional $10,000 before April. The owner decided to draw $30,000 from the line of credit at the end of February and another $10,000 at the end of March and repay the entire $40,000 at the end of May. Interest expense related to the line of credit would be $150 (($30,000 × 0.06)/12) in March and $200 (($40,000 × 0.06)/12) in April and May. The total interest expense for the three months would be $550 ($150 + $200 + $200). Since the cash need was very short in duration, a line of credit was an effective and relatively inexpensive financing option for Peace Blossom. In fact, cash surplus by the end of June would allow the company to pay off the truck loan. Table 6.15 shows the one-year cash budget with borrowing from the line of credit and early repayment of the car loan at the end of June.

Table 6.15 Cash Budget for Peace Blossom With a Line of Credit and Early Repayment of Car Loan

	Jan	Feb	Mar	Apr	May	Jun	Jul	Aug	Sep	Oct	Nov	Dec
Cash, beginning balance	$250,000	$237,164	$253,070	$191,151	$187,332	$246,492	$324,249	$391,668	$368,898	$452,802	$631,476	$632,740
Total projected cash receipts	3,400	3,482	7,558	141,151	290,365	302,916	169,378	115,613	264,226	269,870	61,995	12,527
Total cash available	$253,400	$240,646	$260,628	$332,302	$477,697	$549,408	$493,627	$507,281	$633,124	$722,672	$693,471	$645,267
Total projected cash disbursements	16,236	17,576	70,827	143,361	189,596	150,724	101,959	138,383	180,322	91,196	60,731	33,227
Planned capital expenditure	—	—	85,000	—	—	—	—	—	—	—	—	—
Cash available before financing transactions	$237,164	$223,070	$104,801	$188,941	$288,101	$398,684	$391,668	$368,898	$452,802	$631,476	$632,740	$612,040
Cash from new borrowing	—	30,000	86,500	—	—	—	—	—	—	—	—	—
Cash payments for debt interest	—	—	150	455	451	247	—	—	—	—	—	—
Cash repayments on debt principal	—	—	—	1,154	41,158	74,188	—	—	—	—	—	—
Cash for owner's draw	—	—	—	—	—	—	—	—	—	—	—	—
Ending cash balance	$237,164	$253,070	$191,151	$187,332	$246,492	$324,249	$391,668	$368,898	$452,802	$631,476	$632,740	$612,040

New borrowing in February was $30,000 and in March was $86,500 ($10,000 from the line of credit + $76,500 from the truck loan). The interest expense in March was $150 on the line of credit and in April and May interest expense included both interest on the line of credit and on the truck loan. The principal repayment in April was the principal portion of the truck loan and in May included both the principal portion of the car loan and the $40,000 repayment on the line of credit. In June, the interest expense was on the car loan only, and the principal repayment included both the principal portion of the June payment and the remaining balance of the car loan. The ending cash balance of these combined financing strategies was projected to stay above the target minimum of $180,000.

These two examples illustrate the mechanics of preparing cash flow forecasts, constructing a cash budget, and using a cash budget to manage cash flows proactively. These tools are the basic building blocks for financial planning, capital budgeting, and business valuations. Typically, the cash budget is prepared for one to three years with weekly or monthly projections and is part of short- and intermediate-term financial planning. The next chapter covers annual pro forma financial statements, which are usually prepared for three to five years and are part of long-term financial planning.

Case 6.1 Breakfast Hill Golf Course's New Membership Plan: The Impact on Cash Flow

Edward Desmarais and Christine Andrews

It was approximately 10 years since Mark had converted his ancestral farm in Greenland NH into the Breakfast Hill Golf Course (BHGC). The course opening coincided with a decline in the number of people playing golf in the United States. The decline in the quantity of golfers coupled with competition from 12 other golf courses in a 15 mile radius further impacted overall sales.

Mark poked his head into Chris's (the club's general manager) office. Mark began: "Chris, I've been looking at the income statements for the past several years and the pro forma income statement you and Kerry [the head golf pro] recently compiled for your membership category expansion. Based on the year-to-year review, I see a definite trend in decreasing revenues and increasing costs. These trends are leading to increasingly thin operating margins. I know you and Kerry worked on ideas to increase revenues and improve cash flows. Your proposal to expand the categories for golf club membership options is interesting. I was particularly intrigued by the significant increase in potential revenues shown on the pro forma income statement. Before we go ahead with your proposal, I would like to review the impact on cash flow. Over the next couple of days, I would like you and Kerry to prepare a cash flow statement to go along with the proposed expansion of membership categories. Let's plan to meet in a few days to take a look at what you prepared."

Breakfast Hill Golf Course had a two-tier membership plan that offered players reduced rates in exchange for advanced payments and, in some cases, restricted playing times. Chris and Kerry used the following assumptions in developing the plan:

Competitive context planning assumptions

- The golf industry is in the mature to early decline phase of its life cycle. For the past ten years, the quantity of golfers across the country has declined and about 15 percent of golf courses across the country have closed owing to decreased revenues.
- Competition is fierce. The New Hampshire and Maine sea coasts have 12 golf courses within a 15 mile radius of the BHGC.
- The New Hampshire sea coast is once again ranked as one of the best retirement locations in the USA. The retired demographic market segment make up the majority of new memberships (many "baby-boomers" are taking up golf when they retire).
- Vacationers and casual golfers comprise the majority of non-member revenue.
- Memberships are attractive to the local market because of the reduced cost to play on a per-round basis.

- There are 65 full annual pass (every day, any time) members and 40 weekday pass (Monday to Thursday, any time) members. The overwhelming majority of the pass holders play during the morning and, by noon, nearly all pass holders are on the course. The course is underutilized weekday (Monday to Thursday) afternoons and weekend evenings.
- The big advantage of pass revenue from members is that BHGC receives cash before the season starts in late March. (Fifty percent of membership fees are due at sign up on December 1st, with the balance due by March 31st.) Membership revenue increases cash flow early in the season when it is needed to ready the course.
- Use of the range is included in membership. Rival courses charge an additional fee for an annual range pass. Fifty percent of the membership would likely purchase the range pass.
- Primarily, non-members rent golf carts.
- The majority of non-member golfers play during the afternoons and all day Friday. Perhaps these players might not want to pay the full price for an annual pass but might be interested in an afternoon or weekday pass for a reduced fee.

Using these assumptions, Chris and Kerry developed a new membership category proposal (Table 6.16).

Chris emailed Kerry. "Hi Kerry. Before you tell me about the children's golf school, let's finish the preparations for our meeting with Mark. I am hoping that after we meet with him, we will be able to proceed with the proposal. We should anticipate his questions and concerns about improving

Table 6.16 Proposed Membership Structure for Breakfast Hill Golf Course

Membership maximum	Annual pass (every day, any time)	Weekday (Monday to Thursday, any time)	Weekday plus (Monday to Friday, any time)	Afternoon (Monday to Thursday, after 1:00 pm)	Afternoon plus (Monday to Friday, after 1:00 pm)
Current	100	100	n/a	n/a	n/a
Proposed	100	100	50	100	50
Fee structure					
Current	$1,900	$900	n/a	n/a	n/a
Proposed	$1,670	$950	$1,150	$680	$950
Proposed range fee	$250	$250	$250	$250	$250
Projected revenue based on new membership categories and range fees					
Memberships					
Expected	65	40	50	100	50
Revenue					
Membership	$108,550	$38,000	$57,500	$68,000	$47,500
Range fees	$ 8,125	$5,000	$6,250	$12,500	$6,250

cash flow. To get us started, I prepared a quarterly cash flow statement (Table 6.17) based on current operations and the following assumptions.

- We receive payments from full pass and weekday pass revenue on or before December 1st (50 percent) and March 31st (50 percent).
- We receive payments from non-pass revenue ratably from May 1st through September 30th.
- We receive golf cart rental revenue ratably from July 1st through September 30th.
- Non-members pay range fees ratably from July 1st through September 30th.
- We recognize tournaments, special events, and league revenues ratably from July 1st through September 30th.
- We recognize revenues from merchandise sales ratably from April 1st through October 31st.
- We incur 10 percent of our personnel expenses from January 1st through March 31st and the remaining personnel expenses at 30 percent per quarter for the year.
- We incur operations support expenses ratably from March 1st through October 31st. For planning purposes, we should include a 5 percent

Table 6.17 Cash Flows from Current Operating Activities for Breakfast Hill Golf Club for the Fiscal Year Ended September 30, 2013 (Amounts to the Nearest Whole Dollar)

	First quarter, 10/1 to 12/31	Second quarter, 1/1 to 3/31	Third quarter, 4/1 to 6/30	Fourth quarter, 7/1 to 9/30	Total
Full pass fees	$61,750	61,750			123,500
Weekday pass fees	18,000	18,000			36,000
Non-pass golf fees			152,800	229,200	382,000
Total golf cash inflows	*79,750*	*79,750*	*152,800*	*229,200*	*541,500*
Golf cart rental fees				93,000	93,000
Range fees				17,175	17,175
Tournaments, special events and leagues				106,700	106,700
Merchandise, net	3,286		9,858	9,858	23,002
Total operating cash inflows	*83,036*	*79,750*	*162,658*	*455,933*	*781,377*
Personnel expense	177,900	59,300	177,900	177,900	593,000
Operations support	7,625	22,875	22,875	7,625	61,000
Administrative expense	29,250	29,250	29,250	29,250	117,000
Total operating cash outflows	*214,775*	*111,425*	*230,025*	*214,775*	*771,000*
Net cash flow from operating activities	$ (131,739)	(31,675)	(67,367)	241,158	10,377

increase in operating costs to cover potential cost increases due to the changes in membership levels.

- We incur administrative expenses ratably throughout the year.

"Kerry, I would like you to prepare a quarterly pro forma statement of cash flows for the proposed new membership categories using the preceding cash flow statement for current operations and assumptions as a template. When we have the 'before and after pictures' of income and cash flows, we will be ready to meet Mark. Thanks for your input and contributions, I think we are moving us in the right direction."

Case Questions

1. Prepare a quarterly pro forma statement of cash flows based on the cash flow statement for current operations and the assumptions. What is the effect of new membership categories on quarterly cash flow receipts?
2. What is the effect of the new membership categories on quarterly cash flow receipts?
3. What other ways could Breakfast Hill Golf Course use to move cash receipts to earlier in the year?

Case 6.2 Coos Bay Organic Products, Inc.: Financing Growth

John Voyer and Frederic Aiello

Coos Bay Organic Products, Inc. was founded in 2006 to enhance the capacity and scale of processing southern Oregon's natural resource waste materials into high-quality composts for garden and potting soils. Having successfully penetrated regional markets through retail garden centers, the company's CEO, Charles Brooks, turned his attention to developing a strategy to grow sales beyond its current markets.

In early- and mid-2006, Coos Bay Organic Products had successfully completed a 100-pallet demonstration project, having sold out in two weeks. This led to a joint venture with one of its biggest customers, the Pacific Northwest Mussel Company, and an investment of $100,000 from Southern Oregon Tidal Ventures, a non-profit dedicated to economic development in the region, in exchange for 33 percent of the company's equity.

By late 2006, Coos Bay Organic Products, Inc. had taken over the management of a county-owned salmon composting facility located in south-westernmost Coos County, Oregon. The site was convenient for the region's salmon and oyster aquaculture farms, tuna and Pacific whiting fisheries, and vast softwood forests that together yielded the ingredients needed for its compost recipes. What followed were approximately five years of unprofitable and then five years of break-even financial results before the company finally broke through to profitability in 2008.

In late 2008, Coos Bay Organic Products purchased the 26-acre site from Coos County and began a significant expansion. Starting in 2010, the company worked closely with other composters in California, Oregon, and Washington, and added kelp, crab, hen manure, and redwood bark to its ingredient list. It completed its new bagging and office facility in 2013, making it much more efficient. The company's management thought that its expanding line of organically approved plant food and compost-based soils represented a real environmental and commercial win-win. The company had found important new uses for the region's natural resources and had introduced its customers to a cost-effective alternative for growing beautiful, healthy, and pest-resistant plants. Furthermore, the company had started to

Table 6.18 Coos Bay Organic Products Financial Statements

Income statement	2009	2010	2011	2012	2013
Total income	$2,432,348	$2,940,946	$3,449,067	$4,082,430	$4,397,676
Gross profit	$770,860	$995,831	$1,069,836	$1,325,564	$1,286,510
Total selling, general, and administrative expenses	$546,199	$678,416	$875,964	$905,367	$987,767
Net operating income	$224,661	$317,416	$193,872	$420,197	$298,743
Other income or expense	$142,320	$138,415	$148,626	$173,683	$192,617
Net profit before taxes	$82,341	$179,000	$45,246	$246,514	$106,126
Net profit after taxes[1]	$82,341	$179,000	$45,246	$246,514	$106,126
Earnings before interest, taxes, depreciation and amortization	$233,756	$317,623	$200,076	$428,043	$305,232

Balance sheet	2009	2010	2011	2012	2013
Total current assets	$975,498	$1,063,438	$1,168,093	$1,164,437	$1,492,387
Of which inventory	$795,758	$805,233	$904,415	$836,025	$1,090,730
Of which cash	$179,740	$258,205	$263,678	$328,412	$401,657
Total property and equipment	$289,915	$255,777	$396,811	$313,032	$281,421
Other assets	$258,846	$282,162	$336,030	$379,724	$423,751
Depreciation	($151,974)	($169,546)	($199,717)	($257,226)	($296,842)
Total other assets	$106,872	$112,616	$136,313	$122,498	$126,909
Total assets	$1,372,284	$1,431,831	$1,701,217	$1,599,966	$1,900,717
Total liabilities	$781,819	$794,709	$1,130,048	$960,247	$1,246,166
Of which long term liabilities	$413,377	$657,841	$785,986	$741,818	$692,454
Total capital	$590,465	$637,122	$571,169	$639,719	$654,551
Total liabilities & capital	$1,372,284	$1,431,831	$1,701,217	$1,599,966	$1,900,717

[1]Prior to 2008, the company had sustained several years of losses. Carrying these losses forward resulted in zero tax liability through 2013.

make profits, after years of losses. (See Table 6.18 for the company's financial statements.)

Charles Brooks thought it was time to expand Coos Bay Organic Products' markets beyond its traditional Pacific Coast and Midwest markets and perhaps to the East Coast and Southeast. However, financing such an expansion, which would require more production capacity and a larger distribution system, would be challenging. Furthermore, because compost is a high bulk and relatively low unit-value product, shipping costs made the product prohibitively expensive at the retail level. Brooks estimated that increasing Coos Bay Organic Products' sales by 25 percent, to approximately $5.5 million, would require an additional $750,000 to $800,000 in capital. Brooks considered various options:

1. *Equity investments* Coos Bay Organic Products had had several equity infusions over the years, starting with the Southern Oregon Tidal Ventures investment back in 2006. Given the possibility of additional returns from sales in new markets, previous and new equity partners might be interesting in additional investments. However, new equity would dilute the ownership value of the older equity.
2. *Borrowing* Coos Bay Organic Products had not shied away from debt, as shown by the near doubling of its long-term liabilities from 2009 to 2011. It could certainly consider borrowing the money to finance an expansion of capacity and distribution. The question was whether Coos Bay's balance sheet could withstand additional debt.
3. *Financing from cash flow* Coos Bay Organic Products had begun to earn profits, and it now had positive cash flows. It might be possible to finance the capacity and distribution expansion from those. Brooks would have to take a closer look at the firm's free cash flow to see if it was sufficient to fund the amount needed.
4. *Selling excess assets* Coos Bay had just purchased the former county composting facility and expanded its bagging building. It might be possible to sell those and lease them back. However, it was not clear that such a sale would bring in the needed amount.
5. *"Co-packing"* There were other large-scale composting companies operating in the areas where Coos Bay Organic Products had considered expanding. Some of them might be interested in a strategic alliance in the form of "co-packing." Using this approach, in exchange for a share of the revenues, the company would issue its partners Coos Bay branded bags and the license to its compost recipes. This financing method would have minimal startup costs, but would have sharply reduced revenue.

As he sat in his office in the new Coos Bay Organic Products building, Brooks mulled over which of these options to undertake.

Case Questions

1. What criteria should Brooks use to evaluate the various options for expansion?
2. Applying those criteria, evaluate the various options for financing the capacity and distribution expansion.

Notes

1   To use the PMT function in Excel to compute monthly payments, you need the loan amount today, the interest rate per month, and the total number of payments. In the Peace Blossom example, the original loan amount was $76,500. The interest rate was 4 percent per year, which equaled 1/3 percent per month. The term of the loan was 5 years, which equaled 60 months. The Excel function, =PMT(interest rate, number of payments, loan amount), =PMT(1/300, 60, 76500), returned a monthly payment amount of $1408.86. Note that Excel returned this value as a negative number by default.
2   Cash receipts and disbursements were computed in Table 6.12. Loan interest and principal repayments were computed in Table 6.13.

Bibliography

eMarketer. (2014, May). *eMarketer Retail Roundup: A Look at the World of Brick & Mortar Retail.* New York, NY: eMarketer, Inc.

National Restaurant Association. (2014). *Restaurant Operations Report 2013–2014* Washington, DC: National Restaurant Association http://www.restaurant.org/News-Research/Research/Operations-Report (accessed 6/30/2014).

Polson, B. (2013, December 9) The simplicity of sales per square foot. *Napa Valley Register* http://napavalleyregister.com/business/columnists/burt-polson/the-simplicity-of-sales-per-square-foot/article_fa20ba56-615b-11e3-af74-0019bb2963f4.html (accessed 6/25/2014).

Stautberg, S., & Behrendt, T. (2012). *Selected Quotations That Inspire Us to Think Bigger, Live Better and Laugh Harder.* West Palm Beach, FL: Quotation Media.

Thau, B. (2014, May 20). Apple and the other most successful retailers by sales per square foot. *Forbes* http://www.forbes.com/sites/barbarathau/2014/05/20/apple-and-the-other-most-successful-retail-stores-by-sales-per-square-foot/ (accessed 6/25/2014).

7 Pro Forma Financial Statements

Good fortune is what happens when opportunity meets with planning.
Thomas Edison

Pro forma financial statements are an integral part of any business plan, from startups to mature firms seeking external financing. Potential investors, including banks, use pro forma statements to assess a firm's value and ability to generate future returns. To convince outside investors, it is important to articulate sales and operation strategies clearly and show that the projected numbers are logically consistent with stated assumptions and overall economic and industry forecasts. Include projections for at least three years and consider multiple scenarios, such as best-case, worst-case, and most likely case. When preparing pro forma statements, it is common for an entrepreneur to discover that some assumptions contradict each other or that a particular strategy does not match market conditions, thus requiring changes. This iterative process helps entrepreneurs refine their strategies. Examining multiple scenarios and developing alternate plans enable the entrepreneur to be better prepared and practice adapting the business to different environmental events. Therefore, pro forma statements are valuable to both external investors and entrepreneurs themselves.

The first step in preparing pro forma statements is to estimate future sales. Chapter 6 introduces sales forecasting techniques for startups and existing businesses and includes two examples, Tasty Taco and Peace Blossom, as illustrations. We will continue using these two examples in this chapter to demonstrate pro forma statements.

Compared with cash budgets, which typically use daily, weekly, or monthly sales forecasts, the time interval for pro forma statements is usually annual with a three-to-five-year horizon. However, sales forecasts still need to incorporate daily variations and seasonal trends. If a cash budget has been prepared, its sales forecasts can be aggregated into annual totals for use in pro forma statements. Experienced investors know that sales forecasts seldom match actual outcomes exactly, especially for startups. Instead of focusing on precision, they look at the thought process, and reasons and assumptions behind the forecast to determine whether the entrepreneur truly understands her business model and the industry.

In addition to the techniques introduced in Chapter 6, other tools that are useful in forecasting sales are market research and industry analysis. Market research includes both secondary research conducted by specialized firms or industry groups and primary research through direct survey, focus groups, and conversations with potential customers in the target market. These tools are particularly valuable for a new product or service that does not yet have an existing market. Secondary market research can be used to determine the overall size of the market and the degree of competition, which helps inform the potential percentage of the market that a business might capture. Primary market research often includes surveys that ask potential customers about their consumption habits and the likelihood of their purchasing the new product or service.

When conducting industry analysis, narrow down the segment in an industry and, if available, find an existing firm that best matches your business. You can then use historic data from the existing firm in your sales forecast. If a matching firm is not available, you can use historic averages of the industry segment as a starting point. Even if you use your own assumptions, as described in Chapter 6, in your forecast, it is a good idea to cross-check your estimates against data from market research and industry analysis. For example, you may have made an error if your sales forecast implied you would capture more than 80 percent of the target market, a highly unlikely event.

Table 7.1 contains sales forecasts for Tasty Taco, a fast casual restaurant startup located in a tourist town in New England. In Chapter 6, we estimate total food sales for Tasty Taco to be $11,970 and total drink sales to be $2,380 per week. These projections are based on the number of seats and hours of operation and take into account table turnover and average check, which vary according to the meal (lunch versus dinner) and day of the week. The range of average checks, $15 to $20, is consistent with industry averages and local competitions. In addition to daily fluctuations, Tasty Taco also expects sales to follow a seasonal pattern, with the summer months being the busiest and late winter to early spring the slowest.

Given that there are approximately 4.33 weeks per month (52/12), estimated monthly food sales will be $51,830 ($11,970 × 4.33) and estimated monthly drink sales will be $10,305 ($2,380 × 4.33). These estimates are for the peak season in July and August. Estimates for other months are adjusted by a seasonality factor. For example, the seasonality factor for January is 60 percent, which means that sales in January are expected to be 60 percent of peak season sales. Therefore, food sales in January are estimated to be $31,098 ($51,830 × 0.60) and drink sales are $6,183 ($10,305 × 0.60). Tasty Taco's sales forecast process enables the entrepreneur to explain the reasons behind the projected numbers easily. Remember that the purpose of the pro forma financial statement is to provide a general outlook of the future; it is

Table 7.1 Sales Forecast for Tasty Taco

a Projected Weekly Sales

Month	Percentage of monthly sales from peak level	Projected monthly food sales	Projected monthly drink sales	Projected total monthly sales
January	60%	$31,098	$6,183	$37,281
February	60%	$31,098	$6,183	$37,281
March	60%	$31,098	$6,183	$37,281
April	70%	$36,281	$7,214	$43,495
May	80%	$41,464	$8,244	$49,708
June	80%	$41,464	$8,244	$49,708
July	100%	$51,830	$10,305	$62,136
August	100%	$51,830	$10,305	$62,136
September	90%	$46,647	$9,275	$55,922
October	80%	$41,464	$8,244	$49,708
November	80%	$41,464	$8,244	$49,708
December	90%	$46,647	$9,275	$55,922
Total projected sales for year 1		$492,386	$97,901	$590,287

Peak weekly projected food sales	$11,970
Peak weekly projected drink sales	$2,380
Assume 4.33 weeks per month on average:	
Peak monthly projected food sales	$51,830 = $11,970 × 4.33
Peak monthly projected drink sales	$10,305 = $2,380 × 4.33

b Growth Rate Assumption

	Year 1	Year 2	Year 3
Revenues—food	$492,386	$526,853	$563,733
Revenues—drink	$97,901	$104,754	$112,087
Total revenues	$590,287	$631,607	$675,820

Sales growth rate is assumed to be 7 percent for years 2 and 3.

not intended to be a precise prediction. The payoff from spending too much time on minute details, such as forecasting down to the exact number of Mondays, Tuesdays, etc. in each month, is usually not worth the effort. After ensuring that the sales forecast reflects all available information, we are ready to prepare the pro forma statements. Starting with sales forecast before building the rest of the pro forma statements is called the top-down approach. The other factors, such as expenses and capital investments, should derive from sales. When outside investors, especially banks, review a company's financials, they look for whether the business has sufficient cash flow to service its debts and provide adequate return on investment. It may be tempting to adjust sales forecast to show higher cash flows, but that would be fooling oneself because the inflated numbers could not be realized. Instead, the pro forma statements provide signals that tell entrepreneurs whether they need to adjust business strategies by cost cutting or different methods of financing. The next section will walk you through preparing pro forma statements using two examples.

Pro Forma Financial Statements

Pro forma financial statements include the income statement, balance sheet, and statement of cash flows. Chapter 4 discusses financial statements and ratio analysis in detail. Formulas for pro forma statements are the same as those for regular financial statements. Estimation for pro forma statements and long-term financial planning are often done simultaneously and will usually require at least two iterations. In the first iteration, long-term debt and equity are assumed to remain the same. The pro forma statement of cash flows will provide an initial estimate of future cash balances, which are needed to make long-term financing decisions. If cash shortfalls are projected, additional borrowing or new equity will be needed. If cash surpluses are expected, early repayment of debt or extra dividends should be considered. The second iteration incorporates these long-term financing decisions and all the pro forma statements are updated to reflect additional interest expenses or dividend payouts. If changing long-term financing options is not sufficient to ensure adequate cash for the business, other alternatives, such as cost cutting, may be required. It often takes several iterations to arrive at a strategy that will satisfy the needs of the business, the entrepreneur, and all investors.

After the sales forecast has been completed, assumptions about expenses are needed to prepare the pro forma income statement. It is crucial that assumptions about expenses are consistent with assumptions about sales. For example, if a sales forecast is based on operating 10 hours per day, labor costs should reflect sufficient staffing for the entire day.

It is sensible to use historic financial data as a good starting point in projecting future expenses for an existing business. One approach is to assume that all expenses will remain a fixed percentage of sales. Preparing a common size income statement will provide the percentages needed for this approach. See Chapter 3 for how to compute common size financial statements. Future expenses are estimated by multiplying the corresponding percentage with forecast sales. For example, if the historic average cost of goods sold is 30 percent and sales are estimated to be $400,000, the projected future cost of goods sold is estimated as $120,000 ($400,000 × 0.30). Another approach is to assume that all expenses will increase at specific percentages from the current level. For example, if wages are expected to increase by 3 percent and last year's wages totaled $150,000, projected wages will be $154,500 ($150,000 × 1.03).

In practice, a combination of these approaches is most common. The percentage-of-sales approach is best suited for estimating variable costs, such as sales commissions and cost of goods sold. The percentage increase approach is usually applicable to fixed costs. Expenses that are governed by specific contracts, such as lease agreements and government regulations, should reflect the actual known amounts. For startups, a combination of these approaches also works well. Industry averages or data from a comparable firm can be used in place of historic financial ratios.

The pro forma balance sheet includes projected changes in current assets and current liabilities, planned capital investments that would impact fixed assets, and changes in long-term financing. Since cash balance, a part of current assets, is estimated in the statement of cash flows, these two statements are prepared concurrently. First, estimates for all balance sheet items except cash are calculated. Second, future cash balances are computed in the pro forma statement of cash flows. Third, values of cash balances from the pro forma statement of cash flow are used as values for the cash account in the balance sheet. Both statements are now complete.

Current assets and current liabilities are usually estimated as a percentage of sales. For existing firms, historic percentages are often used for estimating pro forma values based on projected sales. Of course, any known changes should be incorporated. For example, a company has signed a new contract with its largest customer and agreed to extend credit terms from 15 days to 30 days. It should then increase its accounts receivable percentage from its historic average to reflect the new terms.

Startups can use industry or comparable firm ratios as a starting point and make adjustments to reflect their specific situations. For example, a startup may not be able to obtain credit terms from its suppliers, and its accounts payables ratio will be zero because it has to pay cash for all its purchases. Remember that cash, though part of current assets, will be estimated in the statement of cash flows. Changes in long-term assets include future depreciation of existing assets, planned disposal of fixed assets and acquisition of new fixed assets. Of these items, depreciation is usually known and the costs of acquiring new assets also involve few uncertainties.

The difficulty of estimating proceeds from disposing fixed assets depends on the types of assets. As an example, a limousine service routinely renews its fleet. Given its longstanding relationships with car dealers and auction firms and a robust market for used vehicles, estimating resale values of its cars is relatively easy. Conversely, a custom-built wood-fire pizza oven will have fewer potential buyers and its resale value is difficult to estimate. For startups, long-term assets include initial investments in fixed assets and organizational expenses. Outside investors usually require detailed descriptions of how funds raised will be used. The pro forma balance sheet should provide this information.

The next part of the pro forma balance sheet includes long-term debt and equity. This will be completed after the pro forma statement of cash flows is prepared and entrepreneurs have decided whether to finance any projected cash shortfall using debt or raising more equity and whether to pay out surplus cash as dividends. Preparing pro forma statements is an iterative process because after estimating the amount of new long-term debt or equity, the other statements must be updated to reflect additional interest expenses or higher equity. If projected cash flow is not adequate to support additional borrowing or projected return on equity is too low, it may become necessary to reduce costs or delay capital expenditures.

The pro forma statement of cash flows can be prepared using the direct or the indirect method. If the statements are for external investors, the indirect method is preferred because its format is the same as that used for audited financial statements and is more familiar to investors. For the entrepreneur, the direct method is more intuitive and its format is similar to the cash budget. The pro forma statement of cash flows provides important information to both outside investors and the entrepreneur. It shows whether the business will generate sufficient cash flows to pay its debt obligations and provide returns to investors and the entrepreneur. Financial ratios are also useful indicators. The analysis described in Chapter 4 can be applied to pro forma statements to gain insight on the firm's proposed strategies.

After reviewing the base case projections, the next step is to consider other possible scenarios. As a minimum, include projections for best-case, worst-case, and most likely case. If you do not provide multiple scenarios, an outsider will assume that the projection is the best case and make arbitrary adjustments for the worst case that may not reflect your business at all. Some banks use the worst-case scenario in loan decisions and will only lend to businesses that can make debt payments even in the worst case. Failure to provide your own worst-case estimates may result in a bank's rejecting your loan application. If initial projections show that the business falls short of its target return on investment or fails to meet its debt obligation, the business must revise its strategies. Changes may include cost reduction and different forms of financing. All the pro forma statements need to be updated to reflect the new strategies. You should use spreadsheet software to prepare pro forma statements so that each update and iteration is computed automatically. The next sections provide two extensive examples: Tasty Taco, a startup, and Peace Blossom, an established business, to illustrate the steps involved in creating pro forma financial statements.

Pro Forma Financial Statements Example for a Startup Business

Box 7.1 lists assumptions for forecasting expenses for Tasty Taco. Since Tasty Taco is a startup it does not have historic financial data. Instead, the owner obtains cost information from a comparable restaurant owned by a friend and supplements this with secondary research.

7.1 Assumptions for Estimating Expenses for Tasty Taco

Cost of goods sold

- Cost of food: 33.80 percent of food revenue;
- Cost of alcoholic beverages: 29.00 percent of alcoholic drink revenue;
- Primary source: Comparable restaurant, friend of owner;
- Secondary source: *Restaurant Report* (Gorodesky & Lange).

Other expenses directly related to sales

- Percentage of sales through credit cards will be 40 percent of total sales;
- Credit card service fees will be 2 percent of credit card sales, payable immediately;
- Primary source: Comparable restaurant, friend of owner;
- Secondary source: *Forbes* articles on card service providers (Farrell, 2007; Erb, 2014).

Wages, salary and related expenses

- Kitchen and waiting staff employees:

  - 512 hours per week (May to December), based on two 8 hour shifts with four employees Sunday to Thursday and two 8 hour shifts with six employees Friday to Saturday;
  - 256 hours per week (January to April), based on two 8 hour shifts with two employees Sunday to Thursday and two 8 hour shifts with three employees Friday to Saturday;
  - $8 per hour.

- Owner's salary: $60,000 per year, payable fortnightly on Monday;
- Payroll taxes will be 12.42 percent of all wages and salary;
- Primary source: Comparable restaurant, friend of owner;
- Secondary source: Minimum wage, IRS publication on payroll taxes (Internal Revenue Service, 2014).

Expenses that will remain constant throughout forecast horizon

- Rent: $5,000 per month, payable on the 1st of each month;
- Workmen's compensation premium: $10,000 per year, payable quarterly;
- Licensing: $2,600 per year, payable on July 1st;

- Equipment leasing: $10,000 per year, payable monthly on the 15th;
- Primary source: quotations from vendors.

Other expenses

- Employee benefits: $12,000 per year;
- Advertising: $500 per month, payable on the 15th;
- Utilities: $1,000 per month, payable on the 15th;
- Insurance: $10,000 per year, payable on Jan 15th;
- Office, accounting and technology: $200 per month, payable on the 1st of each month;
- Supplies: $5,000 per year;
- Primary source: Comparable restaurant, friend of owner.

Additional information

- Income tax rate: 25.00 percent of taxable income;
- Estimated increase in wages: 3 percent per year for kitchen and waiting staff;
- Estimated increase in other expenses: 2 percent per year.

The costs of food and alcoholic beverages and credit card service fees are computed as a percentage of sales. Wages for kitchen and waiting staff in the first year are estimated based on hours of operations and seasonal and daily trends. Other expenses are based on tentative agreements and quotes from potential vendors. Notice that in addition to estimated values, Box 7.1 includes sources of information. Having both secondary and primary sources increases the credibility of the pro forma numbers. Expenses in years 2 and 3 are extrapolated from values in year 1. Table 7.2 shows a three-year pro forma income statement for Tasty Taco based on these assumptions.

Estimation of the pro forma income statement for Tasty Taco uses a combination of percentage-of-sales approach and fixed-percentage-increase approach. As noted in the assumptions, the cost of food and alcoholic beverages is computed as a percentage of sales. For example, the cost of food in year 3 is $190,542 ($563,733 × 0.338 = Food revenue × cost of food percentage) and the cost of alcoholic beverages is $32,505 ($112,087 × 0.29 = Drink revenue × cost of alcoholic beverages). Wages in year 1 given estimated labor hours are estimated to be $163,840 (512 hours per week × $8 per hour × 4 weeks × 8 months + 256 hours per week × $8 per hour × 4 weeks × 4 months). In years 2 and 3, wages are expected to increase by 3 percent per year. Thus, year 2 wages will increase to $168,755 ($163,840 × 1.03). Payroll taxes are assumed to be a percentage of wages and salary. For example, in year 3, payroll taxes are expected to be $29,040 ($233,818 × 0.1242 = Total

Table 7.2 Pro Forma Income Statement for Tasty Taco (Base Case)

	Year 1	Year 2	Year 3
Revenues—food	492,386	526,853	563,733
Revenues—drink	97,901	104,754	112,087
Total revenues	590,287	631,607	675,820
Cost of goods sold			
Cost of food	166,426	178,076	190,542
Cost of alcoholic beverages	28,391	30,379	32,505
Total cost of goods sold	194,817	208,455	223,047
Wages and salary			
Wages for kitchen and waiting staff[1]	163,840	168,755	173,818
Owner's salary	60,000	60,000	60,000
Total wages and salary	223,840	228,755	233,818
Payroll taxes	27,801	28,411	29,040
Employee benefits	12,000	12,000	12,000
Total wages and benefits	263,641	269,166	274,858
Advertising[2]	6,000	6,120	6,242
Rent	60,000	60,000	60,000
Utilities[2]	12,000	12,240	12,485
Insurance[2]	10,000	10,200	10,404
Workmen's compensation	10,000	10,000	10,000
Licensing[2]	2,600	2,652	2,705
Office, accounting, and technology[2]	2,400	2,448	2,497
Credit card service fees	4,722	5,053	5,407
Supplies[2]	5,000	5,100	5,202
Equipment leasing	10,000	10,000	10,000
Depreciation and amortization	10,534	10,534	10,534
Total expenses	591,714	611,968	633,381
Earnings before interests and taxes	−1,427	19,639	42,439
Interest	0	0	0
Taxable income	−1,427	19,639	42,439
Taxes	0	4,910	10,610
Net income	−1,427	14,729	31,829

[1]Wages are assumed to increase at 3 percent per year.
[2]Advertising, utilities, insurance, licensing, office, accounting and technology, and supplies are assumed to increase at 2 percent per year.

wages and salary × Payroll tax percentage). As noted in Table 7.2, rent, workmen's compensation insurance, and equipment lease are assumed to remain constant throughout the 3 years. Other expenses, such as advertising, are expected to increase by 2 percent per year in years 2 and 3. Thus, advertising expense in year 2 is $6,120 ($6,000 × 1.02). Credit card service fees are computed as a percentage of credit card sales. To illustrate, credit card service fees in year 3 are $5,407 ($675,820 × 0.40 × 0.02 = Total revenues × percentage of sales through credit cards × credit card service fee percentage). Depreciation expense is computed using the straight-line method. Office equipment ($4,500) is depreciated over 5 years; leasehold improvement ($50,000) is depreciated over 39 years and organizational costs ($125,280) are depreciated over 15 years. Total annual depreciation expenses totaled $10,534 ($4,500/5 + $50,000/39 + $125,280/15).

The values in Table 7.2 represent the most likely case. Projected revenues in year 1 total $590,287 with $591,714 in expenses, resulting in a net loss of $1,427. Since this is the company's first year in business, it will not have to pay income tax with a net loss and there is no prior income to claim tax credits. Increases in revenue are expected to exceed increases in expenses in years 2 and 3, resulting in taxable income of $19,639 and $42,439, respectively. Income tax is assumed to be 25 percent of taxable income and, ignoring any loss carried forward, tax in year 2 will be $4,910 ($19,639 × 0.25) and net income will be $14,729 ($19,639 − $4,910). The same calculations apply to year 3.

It is not uncommon for a new business to have a net loss in the first year, but it is not a promising start. More important than net income are cash flows in the initial years when depreciation expenses tend to be high. Chapter 4 provides formulas and discussions on how to construct the statement of cash flows using the indirect method. Cash flows from operations include net income plus depreciation from the income statement and changes in current assets (except cash) and current liabilities from the balance sheet.

The pro forma statement of cash flows and pro forma balance sheet must be constructed simultaneously. First, all items except cash for the pro forma balance sheet are estimated. For Tasty Taco, the pro forma balance sheet is relatively simple. Its current assets include inventory (approximately 2 weeks of COGS), supplies (approximately 1 week of supply expenses), and prepaid insurance (1 year of insurance premiums). Note that petty cash remains unchanged throughout the forecast period. Current liabilities include only wages payable (approximately 1 week of wages and salary). There is no planned capital investment for the next three years. In the base case, Tasty Taco will be financed 100 percent by equity. Table 7.3 contains the pro forma statement of cash flows and estimated current assets and current liabilities for Tasty Taco.

The impacts from changes in current assets and current liabilities on cash flow are not significant for Tasty Taco. The largest item, inventory, is estimated to require $440 in year 1, $561 in year 2 and $601 in year 3. Table 7.3 shows that when depreciation, a non-cash expense, is added to operating cash flows, even though the business has a net loss in year 1 it expects to generate positive cash flows every year. From a cash flow perspective, Tasty Taco is a much more promising venture.

Table 7.3 Estimated Current Assets and Liabilities and Cash Flows for Tasty Taco (Base Case)

a Estimated Current Assets and Current Liabilities for Tasty Taco

Values at the start of business January 1, Year 1		*Estimated balance sheet values as of December 31*		
		Year 1	*Year 2*	*Year 3*
Current assets				
Petty cash	$500	$500	$500	$500
Inventory	7,578	8018	8579	9180
Supplies	417	425	434	443
Prepaid insurance	10,000	10200	10404	10612
Current liabilities				
Wages payable	4,304	4,399	4,497	4,632
Changes in current assets and liabilities		Year 1	Year 2	Year 3
Inventory		440	561	601
Supplies		8	9	9
Prepaid insurance		200	204	208
Wages payable		95	97	135

b Pro Forma Statement of Cash Flows for Tasty Taco (Base Case)

Cash flows from operating activities	*Year 1*	*Year 2*	*Year 3*
Net income	−1,427	14,729	31,829
Add: depreciation	10,534	10,534	10,534
Add: Increase in current liabilities—wages payable	95	97	135
Less: Increase in current assets—inventory	440	561	601
Less: Increase in current assets—supplies	8	9	9
Less: Increase in current assets—prepaid insurance	200	204	208
Net Cash Flow from Operations	*8,552*	*24,586*	*41,680*
Cash flows from investing activities			
Add: Sale of fixed assets			
Less: Purchase of equipment			
Cash flows from financing activities			
Add: New borrowing with notes			
Less: Principal repayment on mortgage			
Net change in cash	8,552	24,586	41,680
Beginning cash balance	$84,500	$93,053	$117,640
Net change in cash	8,552	24,586	41,680
Ending cash balance	$93,052	$117,639	$159,320

Now we have all the elements needed to complete the pro forma balance sheet (Table 7.4). The ending cash balance from the pro forma statement of cash flows becomes the value for the cash account at the end of each year. The other current assets and long-term assets have already been described.

Table 7.4 Pro Forma Balance Sheet for Tasty Taco (Base Case)

Assets	As of January 1	As of December 31		
	Year 1	Year 1	Year 2	Year 3
Current assets				
Cash	$84,500	$93,053	$117,639	$159,320
Petty cash	500	500	500	500
Short-term investments	0	0	0	0
Accounts receivables	0	0	0	0
Inventory	7,578	8,018	8,579	9,180
Supplies	417	425	434	443
Prepaid insurance	10,000	10,200	10,404	10,612
Other current assets	0	0	0	0
Total current assets	102,994	112,196	137,556	180,055
Long-term investments	0	0	0	0
Long-term assets				
Equipment	4,500	4,500	4,500	4,500
Fixture & furniture	0	0	0	0
Leasehold improvement	50,000	50,000	50,000	50,000
Organization costs	125,280	125,280	125,280	125,280
Less: accumulated depreciation	0	−10,534	−21,068	−31,602
Net fixed assets	179,780	169,246	158,712	148,178
Total assets	$282,774	$281,442	$296,269	$328,233

Liabilities	As of January 1	As of December 31		
	Year 1	Year 1	Year 2	Year 3
Current liabilities				
Accounts payable	$0	$0	$0	$0
Wages payable	4,304	4,399	4,497	4,632
Current maturity of long-term liabilities	0	0	0	0
Taxes payable	0	0	0	0
Other current liabilities	0	0	0	0
Total current liabilities	4,304	4,399	4,497	4,632
Long-term liabilities				
Notes payable	0	0	0	0
Mortgage	0	0	0	0
Total long-term liabilities	0	0	0	0
Total liabilities	4,304	4,399	4,497	4,632
Stockholders' equity				
Common stock—par value	100	100	100	100
Common stock—additional paid-in capital	278,370	278,370	278,370	278,370
Accumulated retained earnings	0	−1,427	13,302	45,131
Total stockholders' equity	278,470	277,043	291,772	323,601
Total liabilities & stockholders' equity	$282,774	$281,442	$296,269	$328,233

Accumulated depreciation is the sum of all previous depreciation expense. In year 1 it is the total depreciation expense ($10,534); it increases to $21,068 in year 2 ($10,534 + $10,534) and to $31,602 in year 3 ($21,068 + $10,534). In the base case, Tasty Taco is financed 100 percent by equity. The owner's initial investment totals $278,470, of which $100 is considered par value of common stocks and the remaining $278,370 is called additional paid-in capital. Since Tasty Taco does not plan to pay out any dividends in the next 3 years, accumulated retained earnings are simply accumulated net income (loss), which equals −$1,427 in year 1 (the net loss from the income statement), $13,302 (−$1,427 + $14,729) in year 2, and $45,131 ($13,302 + $31,829) in year 3. Table 7.4 shows that the book value of Tasty Taco is expected to increase over the next 3 years from $282,774 to $328,233 and its cash balance is expected to reach over $150,000 by the end of year 3. Given the healthy cash flow projections, the base case scenario is acceptable to the entrepreneur.

Next we consider the best and worst scenarios for Tasty Taco. The owner believes that revenues could be 30 percent over or under the original projection. Expenses that are not tied to sales or governed by contracts and government regulations may vary by 20 percent. These expenses include employee benefits, advertising, utilities, insurance, supplies, and office, accounting and technology. Table 7.5 contains the best-case pro forma income statement and pro forma statement of cash flows.

In this scenario, revenues are assumed to be 30 percent higher than the base case and expenses are 20 percent lower than the base case. In fact, Tasty Taco will generate over $100,000 in cash flow each year under the best case. However, most investors and banks are not concerned with what may happen in the best case. Their focus is the firm's ability to survive and meet its debt obligation under the worst case. Table 7.6 presents the worst-case pro forma incomes and cash flows for Tasty Taco.

In the worst case, revenues are 30 percent lower and expenses not tied to revenues or contracts are 20 percent higher than the base case. In this scenario, Tasty Taco will experience net losses in all three years. Of even greater concern are projected cash flows which are negative in all three years. Total net cash flow in year 1 is estimated to be −$118,151. At this cash burn rate, the initial cash balance of $84,500 will support the business for only about 8 months. That is not much time for a new business to get its feet on the ground and build a client base. The owner of Tasty Taco decides to revise her strategies in view of projections in the worst-case scenario. There are only a limited number of factors that can be changed. She begins with her own salary and reduces it from $60,000 to $40,000 per year. Though that is a substantial reduction, $40,000 is still sufficient for her to maintain her current standard of living, given her other sources of income. She reviews staffing assumptions and decides that she could reduce employee hours during the busier months from 512 hours to 400 hours per week. This new strategy will

Table 7.5 Pro Forma Financial Statements for Tasty Taco (Best Case)

a Pro Forma Income Statement for Tasty Taco (Best Case)

	Year 1	Year 2	Year 3
Revenues—food	640,102	684,909	732,852
Revenues—drink	127,272	136,181	145,713
Total revenues	767,374	821,090	878,565
Cost of goods sold			
Costs of food	216,354	231,499	247,704
Costs of alcoholic beverage	36,909	39,492	42,257
Total costs of goods sold	253,263	270,991	289,961
Wages and salary			
Wages for kitchen and waiting staff	163,840	168,755	173,818
Owner's salary	60,000	60,000	60,000
Total wages and salary	223,840	228,755	233,818
Payroll taxes	27,801	28,411	29,040
Employee benefits	9,600	9,600	9,600
Total wages and benefits	261,241	266,766	272,458
Advertising	4,800	4,896	4,994
Rent	60,000	60,000	60,000
Utilities	9,600	9,792	9,988
Insurance	8,000	8,160	8,323
Workmen's comp	10,000	10,000	10,000
Licensing	2,600	2,652	2,705
Office, accounting, and technology	1,920	1,958	1,998
Credit card charges	6,139	6,569	7,029
Supplies	4,000	4,080	4,162
Equipment leasing	10,000	10,000	10,000
Depreciation and amortization	10,534	10,534	10,534
Total expenses	642,097	666,398	692,152
Earnings before interests and taxes	125,277	154,692	186,413
Interest	0	0	0
Taxable income	125,277	154,692	186,413
Taxes	31,319	38,673	46,603
Net income	93,958	116,019	139,810

Best case assumptions:
- Revenues are assumed to be 30 percent higher than the base case.
- Employee benefits, advertising, utilities, insurance, office, accounting and technology, supplies are assumed to be 20 percent lower than the base case.

b Pro Forma Statement of Cash Flows for Tasty Taco (Best Case)

Cash flows from operating activities	Year 1	Year 2	Year 3
Net income	93,958	116,019	139,810
Add: Depreciation	10,534	10,534	10,534
Add: Increase in current liabilities— accounts payable	$0	$0	$0
Add: Increase in current liabilities—taxes payable	0	0	0

Table 7.5 Pro Forma Financial Statements for Tasty Taco (Best Case) (Continued)

b Pro Forma Statement of Cash Flows for Tasty Taco (Best Case)

Cash flows from operating activities	Year 1	Year 2	Year 3
Add: Increase in current assets—wages payable	95	97	135
Less: Increase in current assets—inventory	440	561	601
Less: Increase in current assets—supplies	8	9	9
Less: Increase in current assets—prepaid insurance	200	204	208
Net cash flow from operations	103,938	125,876	149,661
Cash flows from investing activities			
Add: Sale of fixed assets			
Less: Purchase of equipment			
Cash flows from financing activities			
Add: New borrowing with notes			
Less: Principal repayment on mortgage			
Net change in cash	103,938	125,876	149,661
Beginning cash balance	$84,500	$188,438	$314,314
Net change in cash	103,938	125,876	149,661
Ending cash balance	$188,438	$314,314	$463,975

Table 7.6 Pro Forma Financial Statements for Tasty Taco (Worst Case)

a Pro Forma Income Statement for Tasty Taco (Worst Case)

	Year 1	Year 2	Year 3
Revenues—food	344,670	368,797	394,613
Revenues—drink	68,531	73,328	78,461
Total revenues	413,201	442,125	473,074
Cost of goods sold			
Cost of food	116,498	124,653	133,379
Cost of alcoholic beverages	19,874	21,265	22,754
Total cost of goods sold	136,372	145,918	156,133
Wages and salary			
Wages for kitchen and waiting staff	163,840	168,755	173,818
Owner's salary	60,000	60,000	60,000
Total wages and salary	223,840	228,755	233,818
Payroll taxes	27,801	28,411	29,040
Employee benefits	14,400	14,400	14,400
Total wages and benefits	266,041	271,566	277,258
Advertising	7,200	7,344	7,490
Rent	60,000	60,000	60,000
Utilities	14,400	14,688	14,982
Insurance	12,000	12,240	12,485
Workmen's comp	10,000	10,000	10,000
Licensing	2,600	2,652	2,705

(Continued)

Table 7.6 Pro Forma Financial Statements for Tasty Taco (Worst Case) (Continued)

a Pro Forma Income Statement for Tasty Taco (Worst Case)

	Year 1	Year 2	Year 3
Office, accounting and technology	2,880	2,938	2,996
Credit card charges	3,306	3,537	3,785
Supplies	6,000	6,120	6,242
Equipment leasing	10,000	10,000	10,000
Depreciation and amortization	10,534	10,534	10,534
Total expenses	541,333	557,537	574,610
Earnings before interests and taxes	−128,132	−115,412	−101,536
Interest	0	0	0
Taxable income	−128,132	−115,412	−101,536
Taxes	0	0	0
Net income	−128,132	−115,412	−101,536

b Pro Forma Statement of Cash Flow for Tasty Taco (Worst Case)

Cash flows from operating activities	Year 1	Year 2	Year 3
Net income	−$128,132	−$115,412	−$101,536
Add: Depreciation	10,534	10,534	10,534
Add: Increase in current liabilities— accounts payable	—	—	—
Add: Increase in current liabilities— taxes payable	—	—	—
Add: Increase in current liabilities— wages payable	95	97	135
Less: Increase in current assets— inventory	440	561	601
Less: Increase in current assets— supplies	8	9	9
Less: Increase in current assets—prepaid insurance	200	204	208
Net cash flow from operations	−118,151	−105,555	−91,685
Cash flows from investing activities			
Add: Sale of fixed assets			
Less: Purchase of equipment			
Cash flow from financing activities			
Add: New borrowing with notes			
Less: Principal repayment on term loan			
Net change in cash	−118,151	−105,555	−91,685
Beginning cash balance	84,500	−33,651	−139,206
Net change in cash	−118,151	−105,555	−91,685
Ending cash balance	−33,651	−139,206	−$230,891

reduce wages by $28,672 ($163,840 − $135,168) in year 1. The last change she decides on is to purchase used equipment and furniture instead of leasing new. She originally chose the leasing option because she wanted to have new equipment. Used equipment and furniture must be purchased instead of leased and she plans to finance the purchase with a $60,000, 7-year term loan at 6 percent per year, using the assets as collateral. This will be an amortized loan with a fixed monthly payment of $876.51, totaling $10,519 per year. Even though the total annual loan payments are similar to the $10,000 lease payments, under the loan option, only the interest portion will be included as an expense on the income statement. The interest portions in year 1 total $3,407. The principal portion of the loan will be considered debt repayment and reduced long-term debt on the balance sheet, but will not affect net income. An amortization table as described in Chapter 4 is used to determine the interest and principal portions of each payment. Another benefit of purchasing the equipment and furniture is higher depreciation, which helps reduce income taxes. The net results of these strategic changes are higher net income and higher cash flows. The revised pro forma financial statements are presented in Table 7.7.

The pro forma income statement shows that under the new strategies net income will be positive in all years in the base case. Projected net income for year 1 is $36,490, which implies that even if wages for kitchen and waiting

Table 7.7 Pro Forma Financial Statements with Revised Assumptions for Tasty Taco

a Pro Forma Income Statement for Tasty Taco

	Year 1	Year 2	Year 3
Revenues—food	492,386	526,853	563,733
Revenues—drink	97,901	104,754	112,087
Total revenues	590,287	631,607	675,820
Cost of goods sold			
Cost of food	166,426	178,076	190,542
Cost of alcoholic beverages	28,391	30,379	32,505
Total costs of goods sold	194,817	208,455	223,047
Wages and salary			
Wages for kitchen and waiting staff	135,168	139,223	143,400
Owner's salary	40,000	40,000	40,000
Total wages and salary	175,168	179,223	183,400
Payroll taxes	21,756	22,259	22,778
Employee benefits	12,000	12,000	12,000
Total wages and benefits	208,924	213,482	218,178
Advertising	6,000	6,120	6,242
Rent	60,000	60,000	60,000

(Continued)

Table 7.7 Pro Forma Financial Statements with Revised Assumptions for Tasty Taco (Continued)

a Pro Forma Income Statement for Tasty Taco

	Year 1	Year 2	Year 3
Utilities	12,000	12,240	12,485
Insurance	10,000	10,200	10,404
Workmen's compensation	10,000	10,000	10,000
Licensing	2,600	2,652	2,705
Office, accounting and technology	2,400	2,448	2,497
Credit card charges	4,722	5,053	5,407
Supplies	5,000	5,100	5,202
Depreciation and amortization	21,764	21,764	21,764
Total expenses	538,227	557,514	577,931
Earnings before interest and taxes	52,060	74,093	97,889
Interest	3,407	2,968	2,502
Taxable income	48,653	71,125	95,387
Taxes	12,163	17,781	23,847
Net income	36,490	53,344	71,540

b Pro Forma Statement of Cash Flow for Tasty Taco

Cash flows from operating activities	Year 1	Year 2	Year 3
Net income	36,490	53,344	71,540
Add: Depreciation	21,764	21,764	21,764
Add: Increase in current liabilities—accounts payable	—	—	—
Add: Increase in current liabilities—taxes payable	—	—	—
Add: Increase in current liabilities—wages payable	78	80	106
Less: Increase in current assets—inventory	440	561	601
Less: Increase in current assets—supplies	8	9	9
Less: Increase in current assets—prepaid insurance	200	204	208
Net cash flow from operations	57,684	74,414	92,592
Cash flows from investing activities			
Add: Sale of fixed assets			
Less: Purchase of equipment			
Cash flows from financing activities			
Add: New borrowing with notes			
Less: Principal repayment on term loan	7,112	7,550	8,016
Net change in cash	50,572	66,864	84,576
Beginning cash balance	84,500	135,072	201,936
Net change in cash	50,572	66,864	84,576
Ending cash balance	135,072	201,936	286,512

Table 7.7 Pro Forma Financial Statements with Revised Assumptions for Tasty Taco (Continued)

c Pro Forma Balance Sheet for Tasty Taco

Assets	As of January 1 — Year 1	As of December 31 — Year 1	As of December 31 — Year 2	As of December 31 — Year 3
Current assets				
Cash	$84,500	$135,072	$201,936	$286,512
Petty cash	500	500	500	500
Short-term investments	0			
Accounts receivables	0			
Inventory	7,578	8018	8579	9180
Supplies	417	425	434	443
Prepaid insurance	10,000	10200	10404	10612
Other current assets	0	0	0	0
Total current assets	102,995	154,215	221,853	307,247
Long-term assets				
Fixed assets				
Total equipment	49,950	49,950	49,950	49,950
Total fixture & furniture	10700	10700	10700	10700
Leasehold improvement	50,000	50,000	50,000	50,000
Organization costs	125,280	125,280	125,280	125,280
Less: accumulated depreciation	0	−21,764	−43,528	−65,292
Net fixed assets	235,930	214,166	192,402	170,638
Total assets	$338,924	$368,381	$414,255	$477,885

Liabilities	As of January 1 — Year 1	As of December 31 — Year 1	As of December 31 — Year 2	As of December 31 — Year 3
Current liabilities				
Accounts payable	$0	$0	$0	$0
Wages payable	3,369	3,447	3,527	3,633
Taxes payable	0	0	0	0
Other current liabilities	0	0	0	0
Total current liabilities	3,369	3,447	3,527	3,633
Long-term liabilities				
Notes payable	60,000	52,888	45,338	37,322
Mortgage	0	0	0	0
Total long-term liabilities	60,000	52,888	45,338	37,322
Total liabilities	63,369	56,335	48,865	40,955
Stockholders' equity				
Common stock—par value	100	100	100	100
Common stock—additional paid-in capital	275,455	275,455	275,455	275,455
Accumulated retained earnings	0	36,491	89,835	161,375
Total stockholders' equity	275,555	312,046	365,390	436,930
Total liabilities & stockholders' equity	$338,924	$368,381	$414,255	$477,885

staff are restored to the original budget, Tasty Taco will still make money in the first year. Recall that principal payments on the term loan are not included in the income statement. To evaluate Tasty Taco's ability to service its debt, we must also examine the pro forma statement of cash flows. The principal portion of loan payments in year 1 totaled $7,112. Net cash flows (net change in cash) after including loan repayments are estimated to be $50,572, $66,864, and $84,576 in years 1, 2, and, 3, respectively. Both projected net incomes and projected cash flows suggest that the revised strategy greatly enhanced Tasty Taco's ability to thrive. Since this is a startup, the pro forma balance sheet includes the firm's beginning financial position as of January 1 in year 1, in addition to traditional year-end values. Investors and banks are interested in how funds raised will be used. Table 7.8 shows a detail listing of startup costs. We will relate these startup costs to the January pro forma balance sheet.

Total assets must equal total startup costs of $338,925 exactly. Current assets include cash on hand (petty cash + cash = $85,000), initial inventory ($7,578), supplies ($417), and prepaid insurance premiums ($10,000), totaling $102,994. Fixed assets include total equipment (kitchen + office = $45,450 + $4,500 = $49,950), furniture ($10,700), and leasehold improvements ($50,000). Organization costs ($125,280) include qualified expenses approved by the Internal Revenue Service that are incurred prior to the official launch of a business. Current liability includes only wages payable ($3,369), since the business currently does not have any supplier that allows it to buy on credit. The term loan for equipment and furniture ($60,000) is listed as notes payable, part of long-term liabilities. The owner invested $275,555 as equity, of which $100 is considered par value and the remaining $275,455 is considered additional paid-in capital.

In the Tasty Taco example, it takes two iterations to arrive at a set of strategies, cutting wages and salary and borrowing with a term loan instead of leasing, that are acceptable to the entrepreneur. When reviewing the worst-case scenario under the new strategies, the business will still experience net losses in all three years (−$78,051, −$63,926, −$48,589), but projected cash flow balances ($20,530, −29,876, −$65,429) indicate a slower cash burn rate. The initial cash balance of $85,000 will enable the business to operate for more than 5 quarters, giving the entrepreneur a chance to establish a customer base and make additional changes. In the next example, we go through preparing the pro forma statements for an existing business.

Pro Forma Financial Statements Example for an Existing Business

Peace Blossom is a floral, garden, and landscaping business that has been in operation for over 20 years. It is located in the Northeastern United States and its sales are highly seasonal. Table 7.9 contains the most recent year's income

Table 7.8 Startup Costs of Tasty Taco

	Unit cost	Units	Total costs
Grill	$1,500	2	$3,000
Range	2,600	1	2,600
Multipurpose range	5,500	1	5,500
Refrigeration	10,000	1	10,000
Preparation table	500	2	1,000
Fryer	2,000	1	2,000
Steamer	1,000	2	2,000
Quesadilla press	800	2	1,600
Hot food table	1,250	2	2,500
Cold food table	1,000	2	2,000
Hood	1,500	2	3,000
Freezer	3,000	1	3,000
Ice machine	1,500	1	1,500
Dishwasher	5,000	1	5,000
Sink	750	1	750
Total kitchen equipment			$45,450
Tables	$125	20	$2,500
Chairs	50	100	5,000
Tableware for eating in	10	120	1,200
Point of sale equipment	2,000	1	2,000
Total fixtures and furniture			$10,700
Leasehold improvements (renovations)			$50,000
Software			$2,500
Office equipment			2,000
Total office equipment			$4,500
Pre-launch employee training			$1,280
Pre-launch advertising			3,000
Legal expenses to set up LLC			1,000
Licensing and permits			120,000
Organization costs			$125,280
Initial inventory (two weeks' COGS)			$7,578
Cash on hand			85,000
Insurance			10,000
Supplies			417
Total current assets			$102,995
Total startup costs			$338,925

statement. In addition to dollar values, it also provides the common size format, which states each item as a percentage of total sales. For example, COGS is 46.68 percent of total sales. It also shows that the majority of sales (59.93 percent) were cash sales.

Table 7.9 Historic Income Statement for Peace Blossom (in Dollars and Percentages)

Sales	Most recent year	Common size
Cash sales	941,744	59.93%
Credit card sales	474,822	30.22%
Sales on customer credit	154,846	9.85%
Total sales	1,571,412	100.00%
COGS	733,607	46.68%
Hourly employee wages	108,720	6.92%
Manager salary	134,400	8.55%
Total wages and salary	243,120	15.47%
FICA	18,891	1.20%
Workmen's compensation insurance	16,464	1.05%
Advertising, website hosting	2,400	0.15%
Credit card service payment	9,323	0.59%
Rent	81,600	5.19%
Insurance	1,600	0.10%
Water	1,433	0.09%
Gas heating	1,868	0.12%
Electricity	2,309	0.15%
Phone	3,000	0.19%
Repairs and maintenance	2,045	0.13%
Gas for trucks and equipment	5,634	0.36%
Legal, accounting, and professional services	6,000	0.38%
Total expenses	1,129,294	71.85%
Earnings before interests, taxes, depreciation, and amortization	442,118	28.14%
Depreciation expense	50,150	3.19%
Earnings before interests and taxes	391,968	24.94%
Interest expense	–	0.00%
Taxable income	391,968	24.94%
Taxes	137,189	8.73%
Net income	254,779	16.21%

Historic statement of owner's equity for Peace Blossom

Beginning accumulated retained earnings	732,569
Add: net income	254,779
Less: cash dividends	250,000
Ending accumulated retained earnings	737,348

In addition to computing the ratios for the most recent year, Peace Blossom also looks at year-by-year changes on key variables. Since the business has been in operation for a long time, the owner has deep knowledge of both the market and risk. He expects that credit card sales and sales on credit will outpace cash sales in the next three years. Table 7.10 shows the assumptions of

Table 7.10 Base Case Assumptions for Peace Blossom

Key variables	Forecast assumptions (base case)
Sales variables	
Cash sales	Cash sales will grow at 4% per year
Credit card sales	Credit card sales will grow at 5% per year
Sales on credit to customers	Sales on credit will grow at 5% per year
Expenses	
COGS	COGS will grow at 5.5% per year
Hourly employee wages	Hourly employee wages will increase by 12.5% in year 1 and 5% in years 2 and 3
Manager salary	Manager salary will increase by 3% in year 1 and 5% in years 2 and 3
FICA	6.2% Social Security and 1.45% Medicare, totaling 7.65% of total wages and salary
Workmen's compensation insurance	80 cents per dollar of total wages and salary per year
Rent	No change for another year, then a 10% increase in year 2 and stay the same in year 3
Credit card service payment	$50 monthly fee + 3.8% of credit card sales
Income taxes	35% of taxable income
All other expenses	
Advertising, website hosting	Increase by 3% per year
Insurance	Increase by 3% per year
Water	Increase by 3% per year
Gas heat	Increase by 3% per year
Electricity	Increase by 3% per year
Phone	Increase by 3% per year
Repairs and maintenance	Increase by 3% per year
Gas for trucks and equipment	Increase by 3% per year
Legal, accounting, and professional services	Increase by 3% per year

the base case for Peace Blossom. Cost of goods sold has increased at a faster rate than other expenses and is expected to continue to increase by 5.5 percent per year. The biggest change is the new state minimum wage, which will increase hourly wages by 12.5 percent next year. To accommodate this impact, manager's salary will increase by only 3 percent next year. Both hourly wages and manager's salary are expected to increase by 5 percent in years 2 and 3. There are also expense items governed by signed contracts. Rent will remain the same for the year until the lease expires and will likely increase by 10 percent in year 2 and remain the same amount in year 3. The credit card service agreement specifies a $50 monthly fee and averages historically to about 3.8 percent of credit card sales. The quote from the insurance company for workmen's compensation is 80 cents per year per dollar of wages and salary. This rate is assumed to remain constant for the next 3 years. FICA is expected to be 7.65 percent of total wages and salary. None of the employees, including managers, is expected to exceed the social security maximum taxable

7.2   Capital Budget and Financing Plan for Peace Blossom

Peace Blossom plans to purchase a new truck ($85,000) in year 1 and a new backhoe ($125,000) in year 3. These capital expenditures will impact depreciation expenses and long-term financing.

Depreciation

Additional depreciation from the new truck =
$85,000 / 5 = $17,000 per year for 5 years
Additional depreciation from the new backhoe =
$125,000 / 5 = $25,000 per year for 5 years

Long-Term Financing Plan

In year 1, Peace Blossom conducts a month-by-month cash flow forecast, as described in Chapter 6. It will obtain a line of credit of $30,000 in February, $10,000 in March and a truck loan of $76,500 in March. The line of credit will be fully repaid in May and the truck loan will be paid off in June. In other words, it will have total debt from the line of credit of $30,000 for 1 month and $40,000 for 3 months. The $76,500 truck loan is an amortized loan and the principal and interest portion calculations are discussed in Chapter 6.

In year 2, based on past experience and the projections for year 1, Peace Blossom estimates it may need a line of credit of $60,000 for 4 months. In year 3, additional financing will be needed for the new backhoe. Peace Blossom plans to borrow $160,000 for 4 months. All borrowings are expected to be fully repaid by June. The interest rate is expected to be 6 percent per year.

The owner plans to draw $250,000 in dividends each year for the next 3 years.

earnings. The other expenses are assumed to increase by 3 percent per year. Box 7.2 describes planned equipment purchases and new borrowing.

Table 7.11 presents the pro forma income statement prepared using these assumptions and historic values from the most recent year. Cash sales in year 1 are projected to be $979,414 (941,744 × 1.04); credit card sales are $498,563 ($474,882 × 1.05); and sales on customer credit are $162,588 ($154,846 × 1.05), resulting in total sales of $1,640,565 ($979,414 + $498,563 + $154,846). COGS in year 1 will increase to $773,955 ($733,607 × 1.055). Hourly employee wages jump to $122,310 ($108,720 × 1.125) and manager's salary will be $138,432 ($134,400 × 1.03). FICA based on total wages and salary will be $19,947 ($260,742 × 0.0765) and workmen's compensation insurance will be $17,391 ($260,742 × 0.0667). The other expenses except

Table 7.11 Pro Forma Income Statement for Peace Blossom

Sales	Year 1	Year 2	Year 3
Cash sales	979,414	1,018,591	1,059,335
Credit card sales	498,563	523,491	549,666
Sales on customer credit	162,588	170,717	179,253
Total sales	1,640,565	1,712,799	1,788,254
COGS	773,955	816,523	861,432
Hourly employee wages	122,310	128,426	134,847
Manager's salary	138,432	145,354	152,622
Total wages and salary	260,742	273,780	287,469
FICA	19,947	20,944	21,991
Workmen's compensation insurance	17,383	18,252	19,165
Advertising, website hosting	2,472	2,546	2,622
Credit card service payment	19,545	20,493	21,487
Rent	81,600	89,760	89,760
Insurance	1,648	1,697	1,748
Water	1,476	1,520	1,566
Gas heating	1,924	1,982	2,041
Electricity	2,378	2,449	2,522
Phone	3,090	3,183	3,278
Repairs and maintenance	2,106	2,169	2,234
Gas for trucks and equipment	5,803	5,977	6,156
Legal, accounting, and professional services	6,180	6,365	6,556
Total expenses	1,200,249	1,267,640	1,330,027
Earnings before interests, taxes, and amortization	440,316	445,159	458,227
Depreciation expense	67,150	67,150	92,150
Earnings before interests and taxes	373,166	378,009	366,077
Interest expense	1,303	1,200	3,200
Taxable income	371,863	376,809	362,877
Taxes	130,152	131,883	127,007
Net income	241,711	244,926	235,870
Statement of owner's equity for Peace Blossom			
Beginning accumulated retained earnings	737,348	729,059	723,985
Add: net income	241,711	244,926	235,870
Less: cash dividends	250,000	250,000	250,000
Ending accumulated retained earnings	729,059	723,985	709,855

rent will increase by 3 percent. For example, advertising increases to $2,472 ($2,400 × 1.03). Similar calculations apply to years 2 and 3. Rent remains at $81,600 in year 1, then increases to $89,760 ($81,600 × 1.1) in year 2 and stays at $89,760 in year 3. Depreciation expense in years 1 and 2 will be $67,150 ($50,150 + $17,000) and in year 3 will be $92,150 ($67,150 + $25,000). Projected interest expense for year 1 ($1,303) is from Chapter 6 (Table 6.15) and is based on the assumptions that Peace Blossom will obtain a line of credit of $30,000 in February, $10,000 in March, and a truck loan of $76,500 in March. The line of credit will be fully repaid in May and the truck loan will be paid off in June. For year 2, the owner plans to borrow $60,000 at 6 percent for 4 months with $1,200 ((($60,000 × 0.60)/12) × 4) in interest expense. In year 3, Peace Blossom needs to finance both its seasonal needs and the new backhoe. In the base case, it assumes that it will borrow $160,000 at 6 percent for 4 months with $3,200 in interest expense.

The pro forma income statement shows steady and healthy growth in sales for Peace Blossom. Net income is expected to increase in years 1 and 2, with a slight dip in year 3 when the business plans to purchase a new backhoe. However, net income in all 3 years is less than the planned dividend payout of $250,000 per year, and ending accumulated retained earnings decrease over this period as a result. Next, we look at the pro forma statement of cash flows to determine whether Peace Blossom can support these dividend payouts. Recall that the pro forma statement of cash flows and pro forma balance sheet are prepared in tandem.

Table 7.12 shows the historic balance sheet for the most recent year (year 0) and the year before (year −1). It includes the actual values, as a percentage of total assets (the common size format), and as a percentage of total sales. The common size format shows that Peace Blossom has traditionally carried a high cash reserve in the form of short-term investments. This is consistent with the seasonal nature of the business. The company uses debt sparingly and is financed over 90 percent by equity.

For the purpose of forecasting, Peace Blossom decides to use a percentage-of-sales approach to estimate current assets and current liabilities because these items tend to fluctuate with sales. Table 7.13 shows projected values for current assets except cash and current liabilities. For convenience, we include two additional columns with values from Table 7.12. The first contains values of these balance sheet items from the most recent year (year 0) and the second is these items expressed as a percentage of total sales. The next three columns show the projected values for years 1 through 3. Because year 1 total sales are estimated to be $1,640,565 (from Table 7.11), accounts receivable in year 1 will be $17,513 ($1,640,565 × 0.0204). Similar calculations apply to the other items in all years. The second half of Table 7.13 shows the year-to-year change in values.

Recall that increases in current assets and decreases in current liabilities are cash outflows, and decreases in current liabilities and increases in current liabilities are cash inflows. Therefore, annual changes are needed when prepar-

Table 7.12 Historic Balance Sheet for Peace Blossom

a In Dollar Values

Assets	End of year −1	End of year 0	Liabilities	End of year −1	End of year 0
Current assets			*Current liabilities*		
Cash	$49,000	$49,000	Accounts payable	$6,113	$7,947
Petty cash	1,000	1,000	Wages payable	9,351	13,559
Short-term investments	189,560	239,833	Taxes payable	30,948	40,232
Accounts receivable	12,904	16,775	Other current liabilities	9,428	8,768
Inventory	40,756	52,168	Total current liabilities	55,840	70,506
Supplies	20,428	23,901			
Prepaid expenses	8,400	8,400	*Long-term liabilities*		
Other current assets	7,071	7,637	Notes payable	0	0
Total current assets	329,119	398,714	Mortgage	0	0
			Total long-term liabilities	0	0
Long-term assets					
Fixed assets			Total liabilities	55,840	70,506
Total equipment	685,000	685,000			
Total fixture & furniture	25,000	25,000	Stockholders' equity		
Leasehold improvement	38,000	38,000	Common stock—par value	100	100
Organization costs	5,000	5,000	Common stock—additional paid-in capital	15,000	15,000
Less: accumulated depreciation	−278,610	−328,760	Accumulated retained earnings	732,569	737,348
Net Fixed Assets	474,390	424,240	Total stockholders' equity	747,669	752,448
Total assets	$803,509	$822,954	Total liabilities & stockholders' equity	$803,509	$822,954

(Continued)

Table 7.12 Historic Balance Sheet for Peace Blossom (Continued)

b As a Percentage of Total Assets (Common Size Format)

Assets	End of year −1	End of year 0
Current assets		
Cash	6.10%	5.95%
Petty cash	0.12%	0.12%
Short-term investments	23.59%	29.14%
Accounts receivable	1.61%	2.04%
Inventory	5.07%	6.34%
Supplies	2.54%	2.90%
Prepaid expenses	1.05%	1.02%
Other current assets	0.88%	0.93%
Total current assets	40.96%	48.45%
Long-term assets		
Fixed assets		
Total equipment	85.25%	83.24%
Total fixture & furniture	3.11%	3.04%
Leasehold improvement	4.73%	4.62%
Organization costs	0.62%	0.61%
Less: accumulated depreciation	−34.67%	−40.92%
Net fixed assets	59.04%	51.55%
Total assets	100%	100%

Liabilities	End of year −1	End of year 0
Current liabilities		
Accounts payable	0.76%	0.97%
Wages payable	1.16%	1.65%
Taxes payable	3.85%	4.89%
Other current liabilities	1.17%	1.07%
Total current liabilities	6.95%	8.57%
Long-term liabilities		
Notes payable	0.00%	0.00%
Mortgage	0.00%	0.00%
Total long-term liabilities	0.00%	0.00%
Total liabilities	6.95%	8.57%
Stockholders' equity		
Common stock—par value	0.01%	0.01%
Common stock—additional paid-in capital	1.87%	1.82%
Accumulated retained earnings	91.17%	89.60%
Total stockholders' equity	93.05%	91.43%
Total liabilities & stockholders' equity	100%	100%

c As a Percentage of Total Sales

Assets	End of year −1	End of year 0	Liabilities	End of year −1	End of year 0
Current assets			*Current liabilities*		
Cash	3.12%	3.12%	Accounts payable	0.39%	0.51%
Petty cash	0.06%	0.06%	Wages payable	0.60%	0.86%
Short-term investments	12.06%	15.26%	Taxes payable	1.97%	2.56%
Accounts receivable	0.82%	1.07%	Other current liabilities	0.60%	0.56%
Inventory	2.59%	3.32%	Total current liabilities	3.55%	4.49%
Supplies	1.30%	1.52%			
Prepaid expenses	0.53%	0.53%	*Long-term liabilities*		
Other current assets	0.45%	0.49%	Notes payable	0.00%	0.00%
Total current assets	20.94%	25.37%	Mortgage	0.00%	0.00%
			Total long-term liabilities	0.00%	0.00%
Long-term assets					
Fixed assets			Total liabilities	3.55%	4.49%
Total equipment	43.59%	43.59%			
Total fixture & furniture	1.59%	1.59%	*Stockholders' equity*		
Leasehold improvement	2.42%	2.42%	Common stock—par value	0.01%	0.01%
Organization costs	0.32%	0.32%	Common stock—additional paid-in capital	0.95%	0.95%
Less: accumulated depreciation	−17.73%	−20.92%	Accumulated retained earnings	46.62%	46.92%
Net fixed assets	30.19%	27.00%	Total stockholders' equity	47.58%	47.88%
Total assets	51.13%	52.37%	Total liabilities & stockholders' equity	51.13%	52.37%

Table 7.13 Estimated Changes in Current Assets and Current Liabilities for Peace Blossom

Current assets	Year 0	As a percentage of sales	Year 1	Year 2	Year 3
Accounts receivable	16,775	1.07%	17,513	18,284	19,090
Inventory	52,168	3.32%	54,464	56,862	59,367
Supplies	23,901	1.52%	24,953	26,051	27,199
Prepaid expenses	8,400	0.53%	8,770	9,156	9,559
Other current assets	7,637	0.49%	7,973	8,324	8,691
Current liabilities					
Accounts payable	6,113	0.37%	8,297	8,662	9,044
Wages payable	9,351	0.60%	14,156	14,779	15,430
Taxes payable	30,948	2.56%	42,002	43,852	45,784
Other current liabilities	9,428	0.60%	9,154	9,557	9,978

Current assets	Changes from Year 0	Changes from Year 1	Changes from Year 2
Accounts receivable	738	771	806
Inventory	2,296	2,398	2,505
Supplies	1,052	1,098	1,148
Prepaid expenses	370	386	403
Other current assets	336	351	367
Current liabilities			
Accounts payable	350	365	382
Wages payable	597	623	651
Taxes payable	1,770	1,850	1,932
Other current liabilities	386	403	421

ing the statement of cash flows. Table 7.14 contains the pro forma statement of cash flows for Peace Blossom in an indirect format. Cash flows from operating activities include net income plus depreciation, both from the pro forma income statement (Table 7.11) and changes in current assets and current liabilities from the second half of Table 7.13. Net cash flows from operating activities are projected to be over $300,000 in years 1 through 3 in the base case. Peace Blossom has made capital investment plans for a new truck in year 1 and a new backhoe in year 2 and tentative long-term financing plans for borrowing and dividend payouts (Table 7.10). The pro forma statements of cash flows reflect Peace Blossom's plan to repay all borrowing within the same year, using its line of credit and truck loans as temporary sources of financing. It expects to use cash flows from operating activities to pay for the new truck ($85,000) and backhoe ($125,000) and dividend payouts of $250,000 per year. Over the 3 years, these strategies result in a decrease in cash balance of about $17,000, from $289,833 to $273,495, with negative cash flows in years 1 and 3 due to equipment purchases and positive cash flows in year 2.

Table 7.14 Pro Forma Statement of Cash Flows for Peace Blossom

Cash flows from operating activities	Year 1	Year 2	Year 3
Net income	241,711	244,926	235,870
Add: Depreciation	67,150	67,150	92,150
Add: Increase in current liabilities—accounts payable	350	365	382
Add: Increase in current liabilities—taxes payable	597	623	651
Add: Increase in current liabilities—wages payable	1,770	1,850	1,932
Less: Decrease in current liabilities—other current liabilities	386	403	421
Less: Increase in current assets—accounts receivables	(738)	(771)	(806)
Less: Increase in current assets—inventory	(2,296)	(2,398)	(2,505)
Less: Increase in current assets—supplies	(1,052)	(1,098)	(1,148)
Less: Increase in current assets—prepaid expenses	(370)	(386)	(403)
Less: Increase in current assets—other current assets	(336)	(351)	(367)
Net cash flows from operating activities	307,172	310,313	326,177
Cash flows from investing activities			
Add: Sale of fixed assets			
Less: Purchase of equipment	(85,000)		(125,000)
Cash flows from financing activities			
Add: New borrowing (line of credit and car loans)	116,500	60,000	160,000
Less: Principal repayment on debt (line of credit and car loans)	(116,500)	(60,000)	(160,000)
Add: New stocks issued			
Less: Cash dividends paid	(250,000)	(250,000)	(250,000)
Less: Stocks repurchased			
Net change in cash	(27,828)	60,313	(48,823)
Beginning cash balance (cash, petty cash, short-term investment)	289,833	262,005	322,318
Net change in cash	(27,828)	60,313	(48,823)
Ending cash balance (cash, petty cash, short-term investment)	262,005	322,318	273,494

Now that we have projected cash balances, we can complete the pro forma balance sheet (Table 7.15). The cash balances in Table 7.14 include cash on hand, petty cash, and short-term investments. Peace Blossom's policy is always to have $49,000 in cash on hand and $1,000 in petty cash. In year 1, the total projected cash balance is $262,005 (from Table 7.14). Subtracting cash on hand and petty cash implies that $212,005 ($262,005 − $49,000 − $1,000) will be kept in short-term investments. Calculations for the values of current assets and current

Table 7.15 Pro Forma Balance Sheet for Peace Blossom

Assets	End of year 1	End of year 2	End of year 3
Current assets			
Cash on hand	$49,000	$49,000	$49,000
Petty cash	1,000	1,000	1,000
Short-term investments	212,005	272,318	223,494
Accounts receivables	17,513	18,284	19,090
Inventory	54,464	56,862	59,367
Supplies	24,953	26,051	27,199
Prepaid expenses	8,770	9,156	9,559
Other current assets	7,973	8,324	8,691
Total current assets	375,678	440,995	397,400
Long-term assets			
Fixed assets			
Total equipment	770,000	770,000	895,000
Total fixture & furniture	25,000	25,000	25,000
Leasehold improvement	38,000	38,000	38,000
Organization costs	5,000	5,000	5,000
Less: Accumulated depreciation	−395,910	−463,059	−555,209
Net fixed assets	442,090	374,941	407,791
Total assets	$817,768	$815,936	$805,191

Liabilities	End of year 1	End of year 2	End of year 3
Current liabilities			
Accounts payable	8,297	8,662	9,044
Wages payable	14,156	14,779	15,430
Taxes payable	42,002	43,852	45,784
Other current liabilities	9,154	9,557	9,978
Total current liabilities	73,609	76,850	80,236
Long-term liabilities			
Notes payable	0	0	0
Mortgage and car loan	0	0	0
Total long-term liabilities	0	0	0
Total liabilities	73,609	76,850	80,236
Stockholders' equity			
Common stock—par value	100	100	100
Common stock—additional paid-in capital	15,000	15,000	15,000
Accumulated retained earnings	729,059	723,985	709,855
Total stockholders' equity	744,159	739,085	724,955
Total liabilities & stockholders' equity	$817,768	$815,935	$805,191

liabilities are presented in Table 7.13. Total equipment in year 1 increases to $770,000 ($685,000 + $85,000 = Total equipment in year 0 + New truck). In year 3, it increases to $895,000 ($770,000 + $125,000 = Total equipment in year 2 + New backhoe). Accumulated depreciation in year 1 increases to $395,910 ($328,760 + $67,150 = Accumulated depreciation in year 0 + Depreciation expense in year 1). Values for years 2 and 3 are computed using the same approach. On the liability side, since Peace Blossom pays off all its loans within the year, the balance sheet does not show any outstanding loans. There is no plan to issue new stocks, so common stock par value and additional paid-in capital remain unchanged. Ending values of accumulated retained earnings are computed in Table 7.11. Preparing the pro forma balance sheet involves gathering information from both the income statement and the statement of cash flows.

Peace Blossom's owner feels that the fluctuations in cash balances are acceptable for two reasons. The first is the company's ability to repay all borrowing within the same year. The second is that the biggest non-operating cash flow item, dividend payout, is discretionary. In fact, by changing from a uniform payout of $250,000 per year to $220,000 in year 1, $310,000 in year 2, and $200,000 in year 3, Peace Blossom will have positive cash flows in all 3 years. The average payout of this strategy is $243,333. Before finalizing the strategies, Peace Blossom considers the best- and worst-case scenarios. Table 7.16 presents the assumptions under each case and selected key items from the pro forma statements. Under the best-case scenario, sales growth will be higher and increases in expenses will be lower than the base case. Notice that the best and worst cases are not symmetrical. For example, under the best case, sales growth rates are 2 percent higher than in the base case but under the worst case, sales growth rates are assumed to be 0 percent, a −4 percent deviation for cash sales and −5 percent deviation for credit card and customer credit sales compared with the base case. With hourly employee wages, since the increase of 12.5 percent is due to change in the state's minimum wage, it will remain 12.5 percent even under the best case. Instead of reproducing the entire pro forma income statement and statement of cash flows, Table 7.16 selects key items: total sales, total expenses, net income, accumulated retained earnings, cash flows from operations, and cash balances at year end. This is an effective way to present financial data to banks and external investors. You should have the entire statements available upon request.

In the best-case scenario, Peace Blossom shows consistent increase in sales, net income, and cash balances in years 1 through 3. In the worst case, sales will remain flat throughout the 3 years, while expenses increase each year. Net income, cash flows, and cash balances steadily decrease, resulting in negative cash balance at the end of year 3. Negative cash balance means that the company has run out of cash. After reviewing the base-, best-, and worst-case scenarios, the owner decides to stay with the current strategies and re-evaluate dividend payout at the end of year 1.

Table 7.16 Best- and Worst-Case Scenarios for Peace Blossom

a Assumptions

Assumptions	Base case	Best case	Worst case
Cash sales growth rate	4.0%	6.0%	0.0%
Credit card sales growth rate	5.0%	7.0%	0.0%
Customer credit sales growth rate	5.0%	7.0%	0.0%
COGS growth rate	5.5%	4.5%	6.5%
Hourly employee wages growth rate in year 1	12.5%	12.5%	14.5%
Manager salary growth rate in year 1	3.0%	3.0%	4.0%
Growth rate for hourly wages and manager's salary in years 2 and 3	5.0%	3.0%	7.0%
Credit card service fees	3.80%	2.80%	5.30%
Rent increase for new lease beginning in year 2	10%	6%	14%
Workmen's compensation insurance premium (cents per $ of wages and salary per year)	6.67c	6.25c	7.50c
Growth rate for all other expenses	3%	2%	5%
Interest rate on short-term loan in year 3	6%	4%	8%
Duration of short-term loan in year 3	4 months	3 months	6 months

b Base Case

Base case	Year 1	Year 2	Year 3
Total sales	1,640,565	1,712,799	1,788,254
Total expenses	1,200,249	1,267,640	1,330,027
Net income	241,711	244,926	235,870
Accumulated retained earnings	729,059	723,985	709,855
Cash flows from operation	307,172	310,313	326,177
Cash balance at year end	262,005	322,318	273,495

c Best Case

Best case	Year 1	Year 2	Year 3
Total sales	1,671,994	1,779,051	1,893,004
Total expenses	1,186,845	1,236,679	1,283,520
Net income	270,852	308,114	335,227
Accumulated retained earnings	758,200	816,314	901,541
Cash flows from operation	335,545	372,651	424,594
Cash balance at year end	290,378	413,029	462,623

d Worst Case

Worst case	Year 1	Year 2	Year 3
Total sales	1,571,412	1,571,412	1,571,412
Total expenses	1,220,556	1,305,444	1,383,769
Net income	183,562	128,452	57,910
Accumulated retained earnings	670,910	549,362	357,272
Cash flows from operation	250,712	195,602	150,060
Cash balance at year end	205,545	151,147	(73,793)

This chapter provides a detailed step-by-step guide with two extensive examples to demonstrate how to prepare pro forma statements and use them to make strategic decisions. Combined with cash flows forecasting discussed in Chapter 6, you now have been exposed to the fundamental tools of finance. The next module discusses capital budgeting and business valuation. Both topics will require cash flows and income statement projections.

Case 7.1   Breakfast Hill Golf Course's New Membership Plan: Revenue and Income Impacts

Edward Desmarais and Christine Andrews

Mark walked his two dogs between the 9th and 18th fairways of the Breakfast Hill Golf Course (BHGC) while gazing at the last of New Hampshire's fall foliage. It was approximately 10 years since he had converted his ancestral farm in Greenland NH into the BHGC. Mark's thoughts turned to his conversation earlier that day with Chris, the club's general manager. "Chris, I was reviewing the current financial statements and I am concerned with revenue and cash flows from the golf course. I would like you and Kerry to discuss possible changes in membership levels that could help increase revenues and cash flows. When you are ready, let's meet and discuss our options and their respective ramifications."

Later that day, Chris poked his head into Kerry's office. Kerry was the head pro at BHGC. "Kerry, Mark is concerned about revenues and cash flow and wants us to brainstorm ideas for golf operations. After you take a look at the 2013 revenues and costs for our golf operations, you'll see why he is concerned. Here is a copy of an income statement I prepared using last season's data. Please review the statement and prepare recommendations to increase revenues and cash flows. You might want to include the pros, cons and implications of your recommendations, as well as assumptions and competitive context."

Table 7.17 Income Statement: Breakfast Hill Golf Course for the Fiscal Year Ended December 31, 2013

Full pass revenue	$123,500	
Weekday pass revenue	36,000	
Non-pass golf revenue	382,000	
Total golf revenue		*$541,500*
Golf cart rental	93,000	
Range (pre-golf warm-up and practice)	17,175	
Tournaments, special events, and leagues	106,700	
Merchandise, net	23,002	
Total revenue		*781,377*
Personnel expense	593,000	
Operations support	61,000	
Administrative expense	117,000	
Total expense		*771,000*
Net income		*$10,377*

After reviewing the income statement (Table 7.17), Kerry jotted down some points on how they might restructure golf operations.

Competitive context planning assumptions

- The golf industry is in the mature to early decline phase of its life cycle. For the past ten years, the quantity of golfers across the country has declined and about 15 percent of golf courses across the country have closed, owing to decreased revenues.
- Competition is fierce. The New Hampshire and Maine sea coasts have 12 golf courses within a 15 mile radius of the BHGC.
- The retired demographic market segment comprise the majority of new memberships (many "baby-boomers" are taking up golf when they retire).
- Vacationers and casual golfers comprise the majority of non-member revenue.

Revenue and cash flow assumptions based on current golf course usage

- Memberships are attractive to the local market because of the reduced cost to play on a per-round basis.
- There are 65 full annual pass (every day, any time) members and 35 weekday pass (Monday to Thursday, any time) members. The overwhelming majority of the pass holders play during the morning and by noon, nearly all pass holders are on the course. Therefore, the course is underutilized weekday (Monday to Thursday) afternoons and weekend evenings.
- The big advantage of pass revenue from members is that BHGC receives cash before the season starts in late March. (50 percent of membership fees are due at signup on December 1st, with the balance due by March 31st.) Membership revenue increases cash flow early in the season when it is needed to ready the course.
- Currently, use of the range is included in membership. Our rivals charge an additional fee for an annual range pass. We could assume that 50 percent of our members would purchase the range pass.
- Since primarily non-members rent golf carts, we should not expect any changes in this revenue line.
- The majority of non-member golfers play during the afternoons and all day Friday, when they can get a tee time. Perhaps these players might not want to pay the full price for an annual pass but might be interested in an afternoon or weekday pass for a reduced fee.
- Current green fees for non-members are $44.00 per person per round on weekdays (Monday to Thursday) and $54.00 per person per round on weekends (Friday to Sunday).

Table 7.18 Breakfast Hill Golf Course: Preliminary Proposal for New Memberships and Fee Structure

	Annual pass (every day, any time)	Weekday (Monday to Thursday, any time)	Weekday plus (Monday to Friday, any time)	Afternoon (Monday to Thursday, after 1:00 pm)	Afternoon plus (Monday to Friday, after 1:00 pm)
Membership					
Current actual	65	40	n/a	n/a	n/a
Current maximum	100	100	n/a	n/a	n/a
Proposed maximum	100	100	50	100	50
Fee structure					
Current	1,900	900	n/a	n/a	n/a
Proposed	1,670	950	1,150	680	950
Proposed range fee	250	250	250	250	250

Proposed revenue and fee structure

Based on the preceding assumptions, Kerry produced a preliminary proposal for new memberships and fee structure (Table 7.18) to initiate discussions. Kerry saved the files and then prepared the following email:

> *Mark and Chris,*
> *The attached file provides the assumptions and fee structure proposal as a starting point for our upcoming meeting. Please let me know if you have questions or have other thoughts you would like me to include.*
> *Kerry*

The next morning, Kerry opened the following email from Chris:

> *Kerry,*
> *I think you are on the right track with the assumptions and proposals. Before we meet with Mark, please address the following additional questions and prepare a summary for our meeting.*
> *Chris*

Case Questions

1. State your assumptions and prepare a revenue forecast schedule by membership level assuming:

   - Current actual annual and weekday pass member levels remain constant. Use the current income statement to determine membership levels.
   - Proposed new membership levels sell out completely.
   - 50 percent of the members pay a range fee.

2.   Analyze the revenue forecast schedule you prepared:

- Assess the effectiveness of the proposal to increase revenues. Your assessment should include the likelihood of success based on the credibility of the assumptions.
- Based on both the revenue forecast and proposed revenue and fee structure, what else would you recommend that the BHGC try to improve revenues?
- What additional assumptions should they consider in their revenue forecasts?

3.   Prepare a pro forma income statement:

- State your assumptions.
- Assess the effectiveness of the revenue proposal on income.
- Make additional recommendations based on the pro forma income statement.

Case 7.2 Asia Motorworks (AMW): The Launch Decision

Sergio Canavati de la Torre

Platform production is a process innovation that allows firms to derive multiple products from a single core design, saving money on research and development and allowing many of their products to share as many parts and technologies as possible. Platform products enable economies of scale and scope by reducing the number of core designs needed for launching new products that a firm develops to satisfy the needs of different consumers. Platform products are based on a platform design composed of core components, which make up 80 percent of the costs, and peripheral components, which account for 20 percent of the costs. Platform products within a product family share the same core components, but are differentiated through customized peripheral components that address the specific needs of different consumers. For example, the Swedish heavy-duty truck manufacturer Scania AB produce a trailer truck and a bus, which share wheel, suspension, chassis, axles, and transmission, but are differentiated by a different body and a different engine. By using this process innovation, the Scania AB enjoyed a 40 percent reduction in research and development (R&D) expenses, a 10 percent reduction in manufacturing costs, and a 33 percent higher inventory turnover relative to the industry average (Kar, 2012).

Anirudh Bhuwalka, a 36-year-old MBA graduate from Babson, founded Asia MotorWorks (AMW) in India in 2002 and rolled out the first truck in 2005. According to Bhuwalka, he had no prior knowledge of the truck manufacturing industry and began operations in a garage in Nashik in Maharashtra. "The manufacturing facility came about much later. Our first trucks became available commercially in 2008," said Bhuwalka, who also explained that the factory construction was initiated in 2008 and was not ready until 2010. He financed the US$24 million initial investment with money from his family and the bank (Chakraborty, 2013).

Platform production reduced his startup investment by eliminating the need to build a manufacturing plant. "When we got into the industry, anyone putting up a truck plant was setting up an engine plant, a gear box plant, an axle plant; basically you had to put in a lot of capital, had a longer gestation period, and profits were based on building economies of scale," Bhuwalka recalled. "When we came, we created a new business model, where we partner with a gear box company, an engine company, and an axle company, and do the rest of the manufacturing. So you don't end up making a large investment, keep capex [capital expenditures] low and focus on the integration model, on distribution and aftermarket which is what this business is all about." AMW's revenues grew from US$20 million (1,125 trucks) in 2006 to US$60 million (9,000 trucks) in 2010 at an average rate of 60 percent per year (Mitra, 2011).

In 2012, AMW announced that it would launch a new division to manufacture luxury buses. "The luxury bus segment currently is of the size of about 3,000–3,500 units annually and it is growing. Looking at this demand, we are launching our 57-seater bus, which will be available by the middle of the year," Bhuwalka stated in January 2012 (The Hindu BusinessLine, 2012). Commercial Vehicle Design Solutions and TEAMPro UK and India forecast the cost of development of this new product line at US$1,221,338 (Commercial Vehicle Design Solutions, & TEAMPro UK and India, 2010).[1] They also estimated the size of the Indian Bus Market at US$488,535,570 and believed that AMW could capture 10 percent of this market after five years of operations. However, in 2013, AMW put the plans to launch the bus manufacturing division on hold because the firm had second thoughts about the viability of this new venture (Das, 2013). Bhuwalka said, "We are waiting for the right time to launch the vehicle... this segment is not a priority for us at the moment. We will launch the product as and when we see there is an opportunity."

Assess if the current market is the right one to launch the bus division.

Case Questions

1. AMW is a private company and did not disclose financial information. Using information about the industry average cost structure (Table 7.19), create financial projections for the bus manufacturing division for five years. Modify the industry averages to account for the fact that you will enjoy the same cost reductions that Scania does.

    a. Create an income statement for five years.

        i.   Assume a straight-line rate of amortization of 5 percent per year over a 20-year period.

Table 7.19 Truck and Bus Manufacturing Industry Cost Structure, 2011

Sales	100.00%
Cost of sales	54.26%
Gross profit	45.74%
Officers' compensation	4.44%
Salary, wages	18.27%
Rent	4.58%
Taxes	2.95%
Advertising	0.45%
Benefits, pension	0.24%
Customer service	0.78%
Bad debts	0.00%
Research & development	7.77%
Amortization & depreciation	0.00%
Interest earned	0.03%
Interest expense	0.96%
Other income	0.01%
Net profit	5.10%

      ii.   Assume that your sales growth rate will be 60 percent, exactly like AMW's.

   b.   How does platform production affect the bus division's gross margin?

   c.   How does platform production affect the bus division's operating margin?

2.   Estimate the new division's break-even sales.

3.   In 2012, during a period of sluggish demand, AMW searched for US$100 million to finance growth. "We are a growing company, and we are in the phase of growth capital. We are exploring various options, including selling stake to a PE [private equity] player. If we get a good value we may sell a minor stake, if not, we are open to raising debt as well," said Bhuwalka, who expressed interest in obtaining a combination of debt and equity financing (Thakkar, 2012).

   a.   Discuss three pros and cons of using equity versus debt financing.

   b.   Explain why the valuation during this period might be lower than Bhuwalka could expect.

   c.   Make an argument as to why the firm should be valued higher.

Note

1 As of October 31, 2014, 10 million Indian rupees was equivalent to US$162,845.19 according to http://coinmill.com/INR_USD.html and http://www.xe.com/currency converter/convert/?Amount=1&From=INR&To=USD.

Bibliography

Chakraborty, S. (2013, February 19). AMW Trucks makes a foray in the heavy vehicles manufacturing sector. *SME StepUp*. http://www.moneycontrol.com/sme-stepup/news/amw_trucks_makes_a_foray_in_the_heavy_vehicles_manufacturing_sector-827362.html (accessed 10/29/2014).

Commercial Vehicle Design Solutions, & TEAMPro UK and India. (2010, July 3). *NextGen Bus Coaches© for Asian Markets* www.teampro.org/Next_Gen_Bus_Coaches___AMW_TEAM.pps http://www.freepptdb.com/details-nextgen-bus-coaches169-for-asian-markets-327523.html (accessed 10/29/2014).

Das, S. (2013, April 23). Dull market conditions delay Asia Motor Works' luxury bus foray. *Business Standard Union Budget* http://www.business-standard.com/article/companies/dull-market-conditions-delay-asia-motor-works-luxury-bus-foray-113042300870_1.html (accessed 10/30/2014).

Erb, K. P. (2014, August 29). Credit Cards, The IRS, Form 1099-K and the $19,399 reporting hole. *Forbes* http://www.forbes.com/sites/kellyphillipserb/2014/08/29/credit-cards-the-irs-form-1099-k-and-the-19399-reporting-hole/ (accessed 10/14/2014).

Farrell, M. (2007, February 20). Saving on credit card processing fees. *Forbes* http://www.forbes.com/2007/02/20/visa-americanexpress-globalpayment-ent-fin-cx_mf_0220creditcard.html (accessed 10/14/2014).

Gorodesky, R., & Lange, K. Restaurant accounting: for profit's sake, inventory your food cost! *Restaurant Report* http://www.restaurantreport.com/features/ft_inventory.html (accessed 7/16/2014).

Internal Revenue Service. (2014). *Employment Taxes*. http://www.irs.gov/Businesses/Small-Businesses-&-Self-Employed/Employment-Taxes-2 (accessed 03/04/2014).

Kar, S. (2012, July 5). *Strategic Analysis of Platform Strategies of Major Heavy-Duty Truck Manufacturers*. Mountain View, CA: Frost & Sullivan Commercial Vehicle Research.

Mitra, K. (2011, May 29). Trucker with traction. *Business Today* http://businesstoday.intoday.in/story/anirudh-bhuwalka-asia-motorworks/1/15488.html (accessed 10/29/2014).

Stautberg, S., & Behrendt, T. (2012). *Selected Quotations That Inspire Us to Think Bigger, Live Better and Laugh Harder*. West Palm Beach, FL: Quotation Media.

Thakkar, K. (2012, April 13). Asia Motor Works plans to raise $100 million for expansion. *The Economic Times of India*. http://articles.economictimes.indiatimes.com/2012-04-13/news/31337570_1_expansion-asia-motor-works-plans (accessed 10/29/2014).

The Hindu BusinessLine. (2012, January 6). Asia Motor unveils 57-seater luxury bus. *The Hindu BusinessLine* http://www.thehindubusinessline.com/companies/asia-motor-unveils-57seater-luxury-bus/article2780538.ece (accessed 10/29/2014).

Module 5
Measuring Performance in the Long Term

8 Capital Budgeting and Costs of Capital

Don't tell me what you value, show me your budget, and I'll tell you what you value.

Joe Biden

In Chapter 7, we discussed pro forma financial statements. One of the important inputs is planned long-term investments. How do we decide what long-term investments should be made? In this chapter, we provide tools that enable entrepreneurs to answer this question, which is called the "capital budgeting decision." The amount of estimated long-term investments is referred to as the capital budget.

These decisions are called capital budgeting decisions because they involve committing significant funds for a long horizon. These investments range from acquiring fixed equipment and buildings to launching new products and entering new markets. Because these decisions impact a company's business strategies and operations for years to come, they warrant detailed analysis.

The tools we describe in this chapter are commonly used in practice. Each of these tools performs some form of cost-benefit analysis. The costs include direct operating costs, overhead, and costs of the allocated capital. It is important to consider the costs of capital because accounting profits do not take into account returns to investors. For a business to be successful in the long term, it must earn adequate returns for investors. The first section of this chapter covers the basic concepts of time value of money; the second section covers the calculation of costs of capital; and the third section covers capital budgeting methods.

Time Value of Money

An investment is worth undertaking if it creates additional value to the investor. For example, you have the opportunity to buy a house in a foreclosure for $80,000 and you estimate that it will cost $20,000 to fix it up to be marketable. You think you can sell the house for $115,000 when the remodeling is complete. Is this a valuable investment? At first glance, the purchase price plus remodeling puts the total costs at $100,000 ($80,000 + $20,000). If you are able to get $115,000, you will have a $15,000 ($115,000 − $100,000) profit or a profit margin of 15 percent (($15,000/$100,000) × 100 percent). Are we missing any factors in this calculation? Does it matter how long it takes for you to sell the house? Would your conclusion be different if you have to borrow some of the $80,000? What if you know that there will be three other properties going into foreclosure in the same neighborhood soon? Let us consider each of these factors in the context of time value of money.

From an accounting perspective, your profit from this investment is $15,000. But what is the value of this investment? The answer depends on your required return on your investment. To illustrate, assume that you can invest in a real estate mutual fund that has a similar risk to the property under consideration. You can earn 10 percent per year on this mutual fund. So if you have $100,000, your earnings in year one will be $10,000 ($100,000 × 0.10), and the ending value of your investment will be $110,000 ($100,000 × 1.10). If you leave this investment for another year, the earnings in the second year will be $11,000 ($110,000 × 0.10), and the ending value after two years will be $121,000 ($110,000 × 1.10). Notice that your earnings in year 2 is $11,000, not $10,000, because it is based on $110,000, not the original investment of $100,000. Another way to look at the earnings in year 2 is that you earn $10,000 on the original investment ($100,000 × 0.10) and $1,000 on the earnings from year 1 ($10,000 × 0.10), totaling $11,000 ($10,000 + $1,000). This concept is called compound interest. Now we can compare the value of the foreclosed property with this mutual fund. If it takes one year to remodel and sell the property, you will earn $15,000 in one year, higher earnings than the $10,000 on the mutual fund. If it takes two years to sell the property, you will earn $15,000 over two years, whereas the mutual fund will generate $21,000 ($10,000 + $11,000) over two years; the mutual fund is a better investment.

8.1 Computing Future Value

The process of computing future value is called compounding. The formula for computing future value is:

Future value = Present value × $(1 + r)t$

where r is the return per period and t is the number of time periods. For example, a real estate mutual fund provides an estimated return of 10 percent per year. An investor starts with $100,000. The future value of her investment will be:

After 1 year, Future value$_1$ = $100,000 $(1.10)^1$ = $110,000

After 2 year, Future value$_2$ = \$100,000 (1.10)^2 = \$121,000

After 3 year, Future value$_3$ = \$100,000 (1.10)^3 = \$133,100

The future value formula takes into account compounding, i.e. the investor's ability to earn interest on interest.

The simple fixer-upper investment illustrates several common themes in project analysis. The startup costs of a project are usually relatively straightforward to estimate. A fair amount of research is needed but the information is usually available. The size and timing of future cash flows, which include estimated revenues and production costs, are harder to predict. Figure 8.1 shows the cash flows of the foreclosure fixer-upper, assuming that it will take you one year to do the remodeling and another year to sell the property.

When considering an investment, we need to incorporate its required return when comparing inflows (benefits, revenues) against outflows (costs). A useful approach to summarize inflows, outflows, and required return is to compute the present value of all cash flows. The process of computing present value is called discounting. The interest rate used in the calculation is called the discount rate. When finance professionals refer to the value of an investment, they often mean the present value of its cash flows because that is the most common measure. We will discuss more business valuation methods in Chapter 9. Box 8.2 shows how to compute present value.

For the fixer-upper project, the estimated return on the real estate mutual fund (10 percent) is a good proxy for its required return because the fund is a viable alternative investment with similar risks. The present value of the initial purchase costs is \$80,000 because the cash flow occurs today. The present value of the remodeling costs is \$18,182 (\$20,000/1.10). Total cash outflows in present value are \$98,182. The present value of the future resale price is \$95,041 (\$115,000/1.10^2). Since the present value of its cash inflow is less than

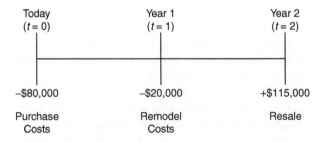

Figure 8.1 Timeline of Fixer-Upper Cash Flow

8.2 Computing Present Value

The process of computing present value is called discounting. The formula for computing present value is:

$$\text{Present value}_0 = \frac{\text{Future value}_t}{(1+r)^t}$$

where r is the return per period and t is the number of time periods.

For example, an investor desires to have $2,000,000 at the time of retirement. She finds a mutual fund that provides an estimated return of 8 percent per year. How much does she have to invest today to reach her retirement goal? The amount of the investment today is call the present value and we usually refer to today as $t = 0$.

If the investor plans to retire in 10 years, she needs to invest:

$$\text{Present value} = \frac{\$2,000,000}{(1.08)^{10}} = \$926,387$$

If she plans to retire in 20 years, she needs to invest:

$$\text{Present value} = \frac{\$2,000,000}{(1.08)^{20}} = \$429,096$$

If she plans to retire in 30 years, she needs to invest:

$$\text{Present value} = \frac{\$2,000,000}{(1.08)^{30}} = \$198,755$$

You can verify that the invested amount is sufficient given the estimated return. For example, the future value of $198,755 invested at 8 percent per year for 30 years is $2,000,003 ($198,755 × 1.08^{30}).

that of its cash outflows, this is not a valuable investment. Another way to look at this investment is that it takes an initial commitment of $80,000 today. The present value of the resale price net of remodeling cost is $76,859 ($95,041 − $18,182). We reach the same conclusion that this is not a valuable investment because after taking into account the required return of 10 percent, its net present value is less than the initial startup costs.

Now let us consider the question of borrowing part of the startup costs. Will the value of this project change if part of the investment is financed by debt? The classic finance textbook answer is, "The value will remain unchanged if we assume that there is no tax and no bankruptcy cost." Since both taxes and bankruptcy costs exist, the answer depends on how the risk of the business will be affected when debt is used. Chapter 3 introduces different forms of financing and general lending criteria and Chapter 7 discusses factors to consider and frameworks to use when making long-term financing decisions. We will assume that you adopt a conservative approach by borrowing 40 percent of the startup costs and will be able to make debt payments even in the worst-case scenario.[1] In other words, the risk of the project will not be greatly affected by the amount of borrowing. To keep this example simple, we assume you will pay interest only in the first year and repay the entire loan plus interest in the second year. The after-tax cost of borrowing is 4.20 percent per year. Recall that the purchase price is $80,000. This means that you will borrow $32,000 ($80,000 × 0.40) today (year 0). Interest on this loan is $1,344 ($32,000 × 0.042) per year. In year 2, you will repay the loan when you sell the property. Figure 8.2 shows the cash flows with borrowing.

The accounting profit is reduced by the interest expense and will be $12,312 ($15,000 − $1,344 − $1,344). But what about the present value of these cash flows? The initial cash flow is reduced by the loan amount to $48,000 ($80,000 − $32,000). The present value of year 1's remodeling and interest costs is $19,404 ($21,344/1.10). For year 2, the present value of the resale price less interest and loan repayment is $67,484 ($81,656/1.10²). The present value of the resale price net of all expenses, including interest, is $48,080 ($67,484 − $19,404). Since the initial startup cost is $48,000, the present value of future cash flow is greater, and this indicates a valuable investment. A key assumption in this example is that borrowing conservatively will not increase the risk of equity. If the risk of equity is increased, the required return will also increase. We will explore the relationship with risk of equity and required return further in the section on costs of capital.

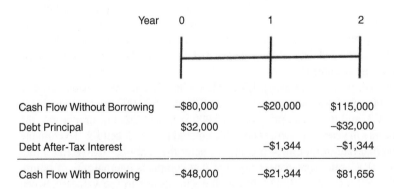

	Year 0	1	2
Cash Flow Without Borrowing	−$80,000	−$20,000	$115,000
Debt Principal	$32,000		−$32,000
Debt After-Tax Interest		−$1,344	−$1,344
Cash Flow With Borrowing	−$48,000	−$21,344	$81,656

Figure 8.2 Timeline of Fixer-Upper Cash Flows with Borrowing

Table 8.1 Cash Flows of Three Different Properties

Year	0	1	2	3
Cash flows of Property 1	−$80,000	−$20,000	$115,000	
Cash flows of Property 2	−$100,000	−$30,000	$145,000	
Cash flows of Property 3	−$65,000	−$10,000	−$10,000	$100,000

Now, consider the case where there may be other properties available. Table 8.1 shows the estimated cash flows of three properties that all have similar risks.

If we ignore the time value of money, each of the three properties generates $15,000 in profits. Since all these properties have similar risks, the estimated return on the real estate mutual fund (10 percent) is a good proxy for their required returns. With a 10 percent discount rate, the present value of the resale value less remodeling costs is $76,860 ($115,000/1.10^2 − $20,000/1.10) for property 1, $92,562 ($145,000/1.10^2 − $30,000/1.10) for property 2, and $57,776 ($100,000/1.10^3 − $10,000/1.10^2 − $10,000/1.10) for property 3. Notice that the value of all three properties is lower than their initial costs, and none of them is a valuable investment. Another approach to analyze these investments is to compute their annualized returns, called the internal rate of return (IRR). You will need a financial calculator or a spreadsheet for this calculation. The next section provides a brief introduction to using spreadsheets to compute future value, present value, and internal rate of return.

Using a Spreadsheet to Compute the Time Value of Money

We will use the cash flows of the three properties in Table 8.1 to illustrate how to compute the time value of money using a spreadsheet. Microsoft Excel© is a common spreadsheet software package. To perform calculations, create formulas using cell addresses that identify a cell by its column alphabet and row number. For example, the address of the cell in the upper left corner is A1 because it is located on column A, row 1. To its right is cell B1 (column B, row 1), and below it is cell A2 (column A, row 2). Figure 8.3 shows the cash flows entered into a spreadsheet and the formulas for computing the internal rate of return.

The cash flows for property 1 are entered in row 2 in the spreadsheet. The −$80,000 initial purchase price is in cell B2, the −$20,000 remodeling cost is in cell C2, and the resale price of $115,000 is in cell D2. For property 1, the sale occurs in year 2, so there is no value entered in year 3, cell E2. To compute the internal rate of return for property 1, enter the formula =IRR(B2:D2) into cell F2. IRR is the spreadsheet function that computes internal rate of return, and the cell reference, B2:D2, directs the spreadsheet to use values between cells B2 and D2, meaning cells B2, C2, and D2, in the calculation. It takes

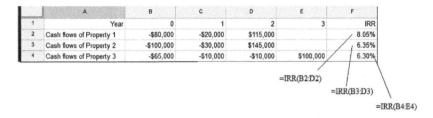

	A	B	C	D	E	F
1	Year	0	1	2	3	IRR
2	Cash flows of Property 1	-$80,000	-$20,000	$115,000		8.05%
3	Cash flows of Property 2	-$100,000	-$30,000	$145,000		6.35%
4	Cash flows of Property 3	-$65,000	-$10,000	-$10,000	$100,000	6.30%

=IRR(B2:D2)

=IRR(B3:D3)

=IRR(B4:E4)

Figure 8.3 Using a Spreadsheet to Compute the Internal Rate of Return

two years to remodel property 3, which is expected to be sold in year 3. Its cash flows are entered in row 4. The formula for computing its internal rate of return is =IRR(B4:E4) and is entered into cell F4. Figure 8.3 shows the results of the calculations. The internal rate of return is 8.05 percent for property 1, 6.35 percent for property 2, and 6.30 percent for property 3. Even though property 1 has the highest internal rate of return at 8.05 percent, it is still below the 10 percent an investor can earn on a real estate mutual fund. Therefore, these properties are inferior investments compared with the mutual fund.

A spreadsheet is also a useful tool for computing present values. Figure 8.4 illustrates two methods for calculating the present value of future cash flows for property 1. In the first method, the cash flows are entered in row 16 and the present values are computed in row 17. The present value for the remodeling cost in year 1 is $-$18,182$ ($-$20,000/1.1^1$). It is computed in cell C17 and the formula is =C16/(1+B13)^C15 where C16 contains the remodeling cash flow of $-$20,000$, B13 contains the required return of 10 percent, and C15 contains the year. The $\wedge$ sign tells the spreadsheet to treat the following value as an exponent.

The calculation for present value of the resale price is similar. In cell D17, the formula is =D16/(1+B13)^D15, which, when replaced with values, will look like this =$115,000/(1.10)^2$. The present value of future cash flows is the present value of resale price less the remodeling cost, $76,860 ($95,041 $-$ $18,182). The formula in cell B19 is =C17+D17. Notice that spreadsheet software does not round off decimal places when performing calculations, even if you change the format to display in whole dollars.

In the second method, we use spreadsheet function "NPV" to compute the present value of multiple cash flows in one formula. In cell B19, we enter the formula = NPV(B13, C16:D16), which instructs the software to use a discount rate in cell B13 (10 percent) to compute the present values of all cash flows between cells C16 through D16. Notice that the first cell contains the cash flow that occurs in year 1, the remodeling cost, not the initial purchase price. This is an assumption used in most spreadsheet software. If you use cash flow from year 0 as the first cell, the result will be wrong. Of course both methods return the same answer of $76,860. Now you can practice these

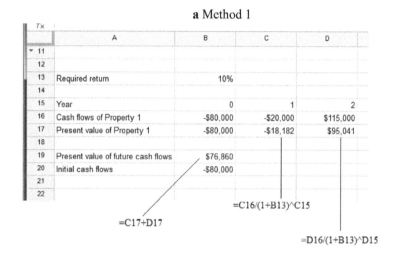

Figure 8.4 Using a Spreadsheet to Compute Present Values

spreadsheet skills. Try using them to compute the present values for cash flows of property 2 and property 3.

Costs of Capital

The costs of capital are the opportunity costs of funds to be invested in a new project. There are three general sources of funds: internal equity from the business or the entrepreneur, external equity from outside investors, and loans from banks or other lending agencies. Chapter 3 discusses different sources of financing. The costs of borrowing are interest rates charged by banks or lending agencies on new loans. It is important to use interest rates on new loans and not the firm's existing loans because interest rates fluctuate. In this chapter, we assume that an entrepreneur will secure the cheapest loans possible (see Chapter 3) and use the tools of financial planning from Chapter 6 when deciding how much to borrow to minimize the chances of bankruptcy. We will discuss in detail the differences between the cost of external equity from outside investors and the cost of internal equity from entrepreneurs in Chapter 10, which covers exit and harvest strategies. This chapter focuses on capital budgeting decisions that can be financed by internal funds generated by the business and entrepreneurs' personal wealth plus prudent borrowing. Estimating the cost of internal equity of a privately held business can be challenging and is often overlooked by entrepreneurs. The good news is that the basic finance principle of matching required return to the risk of an investment still applies. In this section, we will first discuss how to estimate the internal cost of equity for a private business and then the overall weighted average cost of capital that includes both debt and equity.

In the fixer-upper example, the expected return on a real estate mutual fund is a good proxy for the opportunity cost of the entrepreneur because the mutual fund is a realistic alternative with similar risk. The key to estimating the costs of capital is the risk of the investment. Therefore, it is important to get a deeper understanding of different types of risk. Business risk is affected by the cyclical nature of the product or service, competitiveness in the marketplace, and cost structure. An automobile manufacturer typically has very high business risk because auto sales are cyclical, owing to consumers' delaying new car purchases when the economy is poor. The auto market is very competitive, as evidenced by cash discounts and financing deals when sales are sluggish. The car manufacturing process requires a very high overhead. All these factors contribute to a high business risk. Financial risk depends on how much debt a firm uses in its capital structure. If a firm is financed 100 percent by equity, its financial risk will be zero. The total risk of internal equity incorporates both business risk and financial risk.

Entrepreneurs decide on the amount of debt they are willing to undertake and have direct control over the level of financial risk they want to take, but they have less discretion over the degree of business risk. For example, if an entrepreneur opens a restaurant, she can choose to use 100 percent equity and an overhead cost structure that can be supported by estimated sales, but she has no control over how much consumers will eat out due to changing economic conditions. An important contribution of the modern portfolio theory in finance is to provide a way to distinguish between systematic risks, which affect all businesses and are beyond the control of managers and entrepreneurs, and unsystematic risks. Unsystematic risks may or may not be within the control of managers but they are unique to each firm and can be eliminated for outside investors through diversification. For example, an entrepreneur might become seriously ill for a long time, and the business might fail as a result, since she has no control over her health. A well-diversified investor invests in many restaurants. If one of them fails, this will have only a small impact on his overall portfolio. In fact, the bad fortune of one restaurant might mean more business for another restaurant in his portfolio, and the outside investor might not be affected negatively at all. Traditional finance textbooks discuss return and risk from the perspective of a well-diversified outside investor and focus on systematic risk. Entrepreneurs and owners of privately held businesses often have a large portion of their personal wealth invested in the businesses and are not "well-diversified." When we estimate the costs of equity, we need to take into account all three factors: systematic risk, unsystematic risks, and financial risk. Since market prices of privately held businesses are not readily available, estimating the cost of equity for these firms usually involves several steps. The first step is to estimate the cost of equity, net of financial risk, for publicly traded firms in the same industry as a proxy for systematic risk. The second step adjusts for financial risk. The third step adjusts for reduced liquidity for a privately held business, and the last step adjusts for the degree of unsystematic risk when a firm represents a significant portion of an entrepreneur's wealth.

Estimating Cost of Unlevered Equity[2]

There are two common approaches to estimating the cost of equity for publicly traded firms. The first approach is based on dividend yield and assumes that dividends will grow at a constant rate forever.[3]

Cost of equity = Dividend yield + Dividend growth rate

$$\text{Cost of equity} = \frac{D_1}{P_0} + g$$

where D_1 is the expected dividend in year 1, P_0 is the stock price today (year 0), and g is the constant growth rate for dividend. This approach is called the dividend growth model or constant growth model. The constant growth rate of dividend in this model is also the capital gains yield. In other words, the price of the stock is expected to appreciate at the same rate as dividend growth. The main drawback of this approach is that it is only applicable to companies that pay dividends and increase dividends consistently. For companies that satisfy this assumption, the advantage of this method is that it is easy to apply. The 3M Company is a good example. Table 8.2 shows the quarterly dividends by 3M since 2003.

3M has consistently paid dividends since the 1970s and regularly increased dividends each year, by a larger amount in good years and a smaller amount in bad years. Table 8.2 shows that annual dividend growth rate for 3M ranged from 2 percent to 34.65 percent over the past 10 years, averaging 9.37 percent per year. We will use this average as a proxy for g, the constant dividend growth rate in the model. The most recent dividend was $0.855 per quarter, paid on August 20, 2014, and the stock price that day was $144.66, resulting in a dividend yield of 2.36 percent ((($0.855 × 4)/$144.66) × 100%).[4] The cost of equity for 3M is 11.73 percent (2.36% + 9.37%).

Table 8.2 Dividend Payment History of 3M

Year	Quarterly dividend	Annual growth rate
2003	0.3300	
2004	0.3600	9.09%
2005	0.4200	16.67%
2006	0.4600	9.52%
2007	0.4800	4.35%
2008	0.5000	4.17%
2009	0.5100	2.00%
2010	0.5250	2.94%
2011	0.5500	4.76%
2012	0.5900	7.27%
2013	0.6350	7.63%
2014	0.8550	34.65%

3M dividend data was obtained from http://finance.yahoo.com.

Some may argue that the 34.65 percent dividend growth rate in 2014 was an exception. A similar argument can be made for the low 2 percent growth rate in 2009. If we exclude the highest and the lowest dividend growth rate during this time period, the average would be 7.38 percent, approximately 2 percentage points lower than the full sample. The cost of equity for 3M using this truncated sample is 9.74 percent (2.36 percent + 7.38 percent). According to the dividend yield plus growth rate approach, the cost of equity for 3M ranged between 9.74 percent and 11.73 percent.

The second approach is based on asset pricing models. Much academic research in the past decades has been devoted to developing and studying the validity of these models.[5] Professors Markowitz, Miller, and Sharpe, pioneers of the capital asset pricing model (CAPM), were awarded the Nobel Prize in Economics in 1990 in recognition of their contributions and importance of the model. Some recent studies have raised doubts over the efficiency of the stock market, an important underlying assumption of the CAPM, while other studies argue that the CAPM is still a valid tool for estimating the cost of equity even if the market is not efficient.[6] The model is widely used by financial professionals in the investment industry and corporations for its simplicity and provides insight on the relationship between risk and return that can be easily understood by non-financial experts. The formula for the CAPM is:

Cost of equity of a
publicly traded firm, $r_{Equity} = r_{Risk\text{-}free} + \beta_{Equity} \times (r_{Market} - r_{Risk\text{-}free})$

which may be written as:

$$r_E = r_f + \beta_E (r_M - r_f)$$

where r_f is the risk-free rate, r_M is the expected return on the stock market, and β_E is the systematic risk of the firm's stock. Another name for β_E is beta. According to CAPM, β_E is the only relevant measure of risk for a well-diversified investor. It is a stock's relative fluctuation compared with the entire stock market. By definition, the risk-free rate has no risk; it does not fluctuate. If the market goes up by 10 percent, a stock with a beta of 2 will go up 20 percent and a stock with a beta of −0.8 will go down 8 percent. The market itself has a beta of 1. So any stock with a beta of 1 will move exactly in line with the market.

To use CAPM, we need proxies for the risk-free rate and stock market return because, in the real world, no investment is truly risk-free and no market includes all the assets in the world. We also need to estimate the firm's β_E. The average return on the S&P500 index is often used as a proxy for return on the stock market. Estimates for β_E of publicly traded firms are available on many finance websites, such as http://finance.yahoo.com.[7] For example, 3M had a beta of 1.2 in 2014. Choosing a proxy for the risk-free rate turns out to be less obvious than at first glance because there is no true risk-free investment in the real world. US Treasury debt is often used as a proxy for risk-free investment because of its extremely low default risk. However, interest rates on US Treasury bonds fluctuate over time. The challenge lies in deciding whether to use a 3-month Treasury bill or a 30-year Treasury bond or any other maturity. Recall that the cost of equity should reflect the opportunity cost for the entrepreneur if she does not invest in this particular project. We assume that a typical business venture will last around 10 years and use return on a 10-year US Treasury bond as a proxy for the risk-free rate. The rationale is that the entrepreneur is committing her money for the same amount of time. The yield to maturity for a 10-year US Treasury bond is around 2.5 percent in 2014. Unlike Treasury bonds, future return on the S&P500 index is unknown and we use the historical average as an estimate. The last hurdle is choosing the time period to compute this average. Return on the S&P500 index for the past 10 years averaged about 9.10 percent per year.[8] The cost of equity for 3M according to CAPM is:

$$r_E = 2.5\% + 1.2 \times (9.10\% - 2.5\%) = 10.42\%$$

The long-term average return for the S&P500 since 1928 is 11.50 percent. If we use the long-term averages as the proxy, the cost of equity is:

$$r_E = 2.5\% + 1.2 \times (11.50\% - 2.5\%) = 13.30\%$$

If our goal is to estimate the cost of equity for 3M, our job is almost done. The four values we computed with the two models are relatively similar, so we can use the average as a starting point. The base case cost of equity for 3M will be 11.30 percent ((9.74% + 11.73% + 10.42% + 13.30%)/4), and each estimate can be used as a possible scenario.

If our goal is to estimate the cost of equity for a privately held firm in the same industry as 3M, we have a few more adjustments to make. First, the financial risk of 3M is included in the cost of equity. One approach to remove financial risk from the cost of equity is by estimating unlevered beta. 3M has a long-term debt-to-equity ratio of 24.7 percent and a total debt-to-equity ratio of 91.7 percent in 2013. To remove 3M's financial risk from its beta we can use the following formula:

$$\text{Unlevered beta} = \frac{\text{Levered beta}}{1+(1-\text{Tax rate})\times\left(\dfrac{\text{Debt}}{\text{Equity}}\right)}$$

where levered beta is the estimated beta of a publicly traded firm using historic data or from financial websites, tax rate is the average tax rate, and debt/equity is the ratio of total debt to total equity. The total debt-to-equity ratio is a measure of financial risk, which is reduced by the tax rate because interest expense is tax deductible. The average tax rate for 3M in 2013 was 28 percent, so the unlevered beta of 3M using this formula is:

$$\text{Unlevered beta} = \frac{1.2}{1+(1-0.28)\times(0.917)} = 0.723$$

Applying the CAPM formula, the cost of unlevered equity for 3M is between 7.27 percent (2.5% + 0.723 × (9.10% − 2.5%)) and 9.01 percent (2.5% + 0.723 × (11.5% − 2.5%)). The cost of unlevered equity is lower than the cost of levered equity because financial risk is taken out. Estimating beta for an individual firm is associated with some econometric concerns that can be reduced by estimating beta for the entire industry instead of individual firms. Appendix 8.1 contains the values of unlevered beta for many industries. You can use these values to estimate unlevered cost of equity instead of estimating beta for individual firms and removing financial risk.[9]

If you use the constant dividend growth model to estimate the cost of equity, the adjustment for financial risk relies on ad hoc measures. We can use the difference between the firm's yield to maturity and a Treasury bond with the same maturity as a proxy for its financial risk. For example, the bonds of 3M have yield to maturity of 3.9 percent in 2014. Treasury bonds with similar maturity have a yield to maturity of 3.0 percent, suggesting that the default risk of 3M is relatively low. The financial risk adjustment will be 0.9 percent (3.9% − 3.0%). The unlevered cost of equity using these methods is between 8.84 percent (9.74% − 0.9 %) and 10.83 percent (11.73% − 0.9%). The average unlevered cost of equity for 3M is around 8.99 percent ((8.84% + 10.83% + 7.27% + 9.01%)/4). The unlevered cost of equity is the foundation for estimating cost of internal equity for a privately held firm. The most important principle is to start with the unlevered cost of equity for the industry of the proposed project. The next section discusses how to adjust this unlevered cost for a private firm's financial risk, reduced liquidity, and unsystematic risk to entrepreneurs.

Adjusting Unlevered Cost of Equity to Estimate Cost of Equity for Entrepreneurs

In this section, we will use Tasty Taco as an example to demonstrate how to adjust unlevered cost of equity to be used in capital budgeting analysis. We start with using CAPM and industry unlevered beta to compute the unlevered cost of equity for Tasty Taco. Recall that the formula for CAPM is:

$$r_{Equity} = r_{Risk\text{-}free} + \beta_{Equity} \times (r_{Market} - r_{Risk\text{-}free})$$

The unlevered beta for the restaurant, from Appendix 8.1 is 0.71. When we use unlevered beta in the calculation, the result is the unlevered cost of equity. If we use levered beta, we will get the levered cost of equity. The average return on the S&P500 index since 1928 is 11.5 percent and the 10-year Treasury bond yield is 2.5 percent. The unlevered cost of equity for Tasty Taco is:

$$r_{Tasty\ Taco\ Unlevered\ cost\ of\ equity} = 2.5\% + 0.71 \times (11.5\% - 2.5\%) = 8.89\%$$

The first adjustment is to incorporate the specific financial risk of the firm.[10] One way to compute the levered cost of equity is to add a financial risk premium to the unlevered cost of equity. The financial risk premium can be estimated using an ad hoc method based on the firm's cost of borrowing. It can also be estimated based on the difference between levered and unlevered beta. We compute levered beta using the formula:[11]

$$\text{Levered beta} = \text{Unlevered beta} \times \left\{ 1 + \left[1 - \text{Tax rate} \right] \times \left[\frac{\text{Debt}}{\text{Equity}} \right] \right\}$$

Recall that the unlevered beta for the restaurant industry is 0.71. The pro forma balance sheet in Chapter 7 projects the debt-to-equity ratio of Tasty Taco to be 0.2177 and the average tax rate from the pro forma income statement is 25%. Therefore, the levered beta for Tasty Taco is:

Levered beta
of Tasty Taco = $0.71 \times \{1 + [(1 - 0.25) \times 0.2177)]\} = 0.8259$

The formula for computing financial risk premium is:

Financial
risk premium = (Levered beta − Unlevered beta) × $(r_{Market} - r_{Risk\text{-}free})$

For Tasty Taco,

Financial risk premium = $(0.8259 - 0.71) \times (11.5\% - 2.5\%) = 1.04\%$

Adding the financial risk premium to the unlevered cost of equity results in the levered cost of equity:

$r_{\text{Levered cost of equity}} = r_{\text{Unlevered cost of equity}} +$ Financial risk premium

$r_{\text{Tasty Taco Levered cost of equity}} = 8.89\% + 1.04\% = 9.93\%$

8.3 Levered Cost of Equity

We can also compute the levered cost of equity for Tasty Taco using CAPM:

$r_{\text{Tasty Taco Levered cost of equity}} = 2.5\% + 0.8257 \times (11.50\% - 2.5\%) = 9.93\%$

The next adjustment is for illiquidity of privately held firms. Some financial analysts apply a 3–4 percent premium to small illiquid stocks. A recent study by Ibbotson et al. (2013) looked at liquidity premiums for large, small, value, and growth stocks. They estimated the overall average liquidity premium across all categories to be between 5 and 6 percent. For Tasty Taco we will add a 5 percent liquidity premium to its cost of equity:

$r_{\text{Tasty Taco Levered cost of equity with liquidity premium}} = 9.93\% + 5\% = 14.93\%$

Lastly, we adjust for the lack of diversification faced by the entrepreneur. Quite often, especially early in an entrepreneurial career, the business is a significant portion of an entrepreneur's wealth. The CAPM assumes that the investor is well-diversified and only incorporates systematic risk in its equation. The unsystematic risk is the portion of the firm's risk uncorrelated with the overall market. Appendix 8.1 also lists unsystematic risk adjustment factors by industry.[12] For restaurants, this factor is 2.3116. The unsystematic risk premium can be computed using the formula:

Unsystematic
risk premium = $\beta \times$ Unsystematic risk adjustment factor $\times (r_M - r_F)$

Unsystematic risk
premium of Tasty Taco = $0.8259 \times 2.3116 \times (11.5\% - 2.5\%) = 17.18\%$

The total cost of equity for Tasty Taco is:

$$r_{\text{Tasty Taco Levered cost of equity with liquidity premium and unsystematic risk premium}} = 14.93\% + 17.18\% = 32.11\%$$

In summary, there are four steps to computing cost of equity for an entrepreneur:

1. Start with the unlevered cost of equity for the industry.
2. Adjust for the firm's financial risk.
3. Adjust for liquidity premium.
4. Adjust for unsystematic risk.

$$r_{\text{Total cost of equity}} = r_{\text{Unlevered cost of equity}} + \text{Financial risk premium} + \text{Liquidity premium} + \text{Unsystematic risk premium}$$

For Tasty Taco,

$$r_{\text{Total cost of equity}} = 8.89\% + 1.04\% + 5.00\% + 17.18\% = 32.11\%$$

These steps help remind you to include all the factors when estimating the cost of equity. Remember that risk and cost of equity change over time, especially in changing economic conditions. If a firm uses debt or other forms of financing, their overall costs of capital will be different from the cost of equity. The next section looks at how to compute the weighted average cost of capital.

Weighted Average Cost of Capital

An important use of the weighted average cost of capital is for evaluating potential projects. Entrepreneurs want to identify projects that provide sufficient return to cover costs of operations and financing. Sources of financing include equity, debt and other forms, such as convertible bonds, preferred stocks, and accounts receivable factoring.[13] As the name suggests, we use a weighted average to incorporate the costs of all financing sources. Keep in mind two principles when computing this weighted average. First, use market value whenever possible to compute weights. Second, use after-tax return. Chapter 9 discusses valuation methods that can be used to estimate market values if they are not readily available. For startups and young firms, book values are usually relatively close to market values. Some financing costs, such as interest expense on debt, are tax deductible expenses. Their after-tax costs can be computed using the following formula:

After-tax return = Before-tax return × (1 − tax rate)

The weighted average approach can be applied to firms with any number of sources of financing. The following example assumes that the firm has two sources of financing, debt and equity. The weighted average cost of capital (WACC) captures the opportunity costs for both sources:

$$\text{WACC} = W_{\text{Equity}} \times r_{\text{Total cost of equity}} + W_{\text{Debt}} \times r_{\text{Debt}} \times (1 - \text{Tax rate})$$

where W_{Equity} is the weight of equity in the capital structure, W_{Debt} is the weight of debt in the capital structure, $r_{\text{Total cost of equity}}$ is the cost of equity, computed in the previous section, and r_{Debt} is the cost of new borrowing. It is important to use cost of new borrowing and not existing debt because the weighted average cost of capital should reflect the opportunity cost for new projects. The proposed capital structure for Tasty Taco from Chapter 7 includes $275,555 in equity and $60,000 in notes payable. The total firm value is $335,555 ($275,555 + $60,000).[14] Tasty Taco's capital structure has 82.12 percent in equity (($275,555/$335,555) × 100) and 17.88 percent in debt (($60,000/$335,555) × 100). Interest on notes payable for Tasty Taco is expected to be 6 percent and the average tax rate is estimated to be 25 percent. We have all the information needed to compute its weighted average cost of capital:

$$\text{WACC}_{\text{Tasty Taco}} = 0.8212 \times 32.11\% + 0.1788 \times 6\% \times (1 - 0.25) = 27.18\%$$

WACC is the appropriate required return because it takes into account the business risk, financial risk, and capital structure of the firm. If a business consistently earns this required return on its investments, it would satisfy its creditors and owners. The next section discusses capital budgeting methods for evaluating projects.

Capital Budgeting Methods

Capital budgeting methods help entrepreneurs identify projects that will add value to the business and avoid projects that reduce firm value. The usefulness of these methods depends critically on cash flow forecasts and their underlying assumptions, which are discussed in Chapter 6. For the purpose of capital budgeting, we want to focus on the project being evaluated, not cash flows for the entire firm. We accomplish this by applying the principle of incremental cash flow. We ask whether the amount of cash flow will be different if the project is undertaken or not. This seems a simple question at first glance but there are situations when the answer is not obvious.

An expense can be related to a project but is not incremental. One example is the cost of a market survey. The expense is related to the project and the results of the market survey are used in forecasting sales, but the cost of the survey does not change depending on whether the firm decides to undertake the project. This is an example of a sunk cost, which is not incremental. Another example is the impact on existing business when a new product is introduced. Sometimes the impact is positive and sometimes it is negative.

These cash flows will be different if the project is undertaken and so should be included. The main contribution of capital budgeting methods is in summarizing a large amount of financial data into a few key decision variables. A survey of chief financial officers (Graham & Harvey, 2002) reports that the most popular capital budgeting methods are internal rate of return, net present value, and payback period. In this section, we will discuss these three methods and profitability index, which is closely related to net present value.

Net Present Value Method

The net present value method, also called the discounted cash flow method, compares the difference between the initial investment and the present value of future cash flows. Future cash flows are defined as cash flows starting in period 1 and on. The decision variable under this method is the net present value:

Net present value = Present value of future cash flows − Initial investment

Net present value represents additional value created by the project. What do we mean by that? Remember that future cash flows are net of all operating costs, and the opportunity costs of invested capital are included in the discount rate. The net present value is not just profit or return on investment. It measures value creation. The decision rule is that a project should be accepted if its net present value is greater than or equal to zero. When the net present value is zero, the project generates sufficient cash flows to cover all operating costs and costs of capital. Investors, owners, and debt holders get their required returns. A firm can sustain its operation forever if all its projects have net present value of at least zero. In fact, in a perfect market, it is extremely rare to find projects with greater than zero net present values. If you find a project with large net present value, you need to ask where the value comes from and whether you have assessed risk properly. Proprietary technology and manufacturing methods and dominance in a market are common fundamental factors contributing to value creation. A mistake that entrepreneurs often make is to underestimate the risk of a project and, as a result, using a discount rate that is too low. For example, when a real estate developer wants to manage the apartments it built, it is entering a totally different industry. In Appendix 8.1, the unlevered beta for the real estate development industry is 0.85 and for the real estate operations and services industry is 0.94. If the discount rate is based on the existing development business, the capital budgeting analysis for expanding into apartment management will have underestimated the true risk of the project. Using a discount rate that is too low for the true risk of the project may result in a firm undertaking projects that should have been rejected and reduce the firm's value in the long run.

Chapters 6 and 7 discuss cash flow forecast and pro forma financial statements. For projects with known end dates, such as purchasing or replacing major equipment, it is possible to estimate all future cash flows. Many projects, such as opening a new location or starting a new product line, do not have known end dates. A common method of capturing future cash flows for open-ended projects is to use terminal value. The assumption of the terminal value method is that at some point in the future the project's cash flows will grow at a constant rate forever. This assumption may seem unrealistic, but forecasting the future is difficult and expecting accurate projection beyond 5 years is also unrealistic. The terminal value approach is a compromise between accuracy and feasibility. It starts with estimating cash flows for a project over the next 3 to 5 years and assumes that cash flows after that period will grow at a constant rate, often the long-term GDP growth rate or population growth rate. The formula for computing the terminal value is:

$$\text{Terminal value}_t = \text{Cash flow}_t \times (1 + g)/(r - g)$$

where t is the last year of the forecasting period, r is the required return and g is the long-term constant growth rate. Note that the term "Cash flow$_t \times (1 + g)$" results in cash flow in year $t + 1$. Therefore, another way to express the terminal value equation is to use cash flow in year $t + 1$:

$$\text{Terminal value}_t = \text{Cash flow}_{t+1} / (r - g)$$

We will use Tasty Taco as an example to illustrate evaluating a project with terminal value. Table 8.3 contains the summary of projected cash flows for Tasty Taco from Chapter 7. We add interest expense back to cash flows from operation to obtain total cash flows because the cost of debt is included in the weighted average cost of capital. If total cash flows are net of interest expenses, we would be double counting the cost of debt. An implicit assumption of using the WACC as the required return is that a firm will maintain its current capital structure and future projects will be financed by a similar mix of debt and equity. This assumption is usually correct for evaluating capital budgeting projects. If a firm is looking to change its capital structure radically, for example, by bringing in another equity partner, other approaches will be more appropriate. Chapter 9 on valuation and Chapter 10 on exit strategies will discuss other valuation methods.

The cash flow in the last year of the forecasting period is $95,094 in year 3. We will assume that the long-term growth rate is 3 percent. This assumption is based on the long-term average GDP growth rate in the USA from 1961–2013,

Table 8.3 Summary of Projected Cash Flows from Operations for Tasty Taco

Year	0	1	2	3
Net cash flow from operations		57,684	74,414	92,592
Add: Interest expense		3,407	2,968	2,502
Total cash flows from operations		61,091	77,382	95,094

Table 8.4 Projected Total Cash Flows for Tasty Taco

Year	0	1	2	3
Total cash flow from operations		61,091	77,382	95,094
Terminal value				405,073
Initial cash flow	−338,942			
Total cash flows	−338,942	61,091	77,382	500,167

which is 3.18 percent.[15] The WACC of Tasty Taco is 27.18 percent, which is used as the required return.

$$\text{Terminal value for Tasty Taco in year 3} = \frac{\$95,094 \times (1.03)}{(0.2718 - 0.03)} = \$405,073$$

The total startup cost for Tasty Taco is $338,924, from Chapter 7. Table 8.4 presents the cash flows used in computing the net present value for Tasty Taco. The first row contains total cash flow from operations, computed in Table 8.3. The second row contains the terminal value and the third row contains initial cash flows, which are the startup costs.

We need to compute the present value of total cash flows from years 1 through 3 with the WACC as the discount rate at 27.18 percent. We can use a spreadsheet, as described in the time value of money section earlier in this chapter. We can also use the present value formula as follows:

$$\begin{aligned}\text{Present value of total}\\ \text{future cash flow (years 1–3)} &= \frac{\$61,091}{1.2718} + \frac{\$77,382}{1.2718^2} + \frac{\$500,167}{1.2718^3}\\ &= \$339,017\end{aligned}$$

Therefore,

Net present value of Tasty Taco = $339,017 − $338,924 = $93

Recall that the decision rule for the net present value method is to accept projects with net present value greater than or equal to zero. Applying this rule, Tasty Taco is a valuable project and should be accepted. If all goes as expected, it will create $93 in extra value to the entrepreneur. As discussed in Chapter 7, the projected cash flows are our best estimates at this time and it is important to consider different scenarios. In addition to the best-case, worst-case, and most likely cash flows, we should include sensitivity analysis on the discount rate. Table 8.5 presents different scenarios and their resulting present values and net present values (NPVs) for Tasty Taco.

In this example, cash flow estimates have a greater impact on net present values than discount rates. When cash flows are 10 percent below the base case, NPV is negative at all three discount rates. Table 8.5 also illustrates that

Table 8.5 Net Present Value Scenario Analysis for Tasty Taco

	Total future cash flows at 10 percent over base case	Total future cash flows at 10 percent below base case
Present value at WACC as discount rate (27.18%)	$372,919	$305,116
Present value at 10% below WACC as discount rate (24.46%)	$394,321	$322,626
Present value at 10% over WACC as discount rate (29.90%)	$353,180	$288,966
NPV at WACC as discount rate (27.18%)	$33,995	−$33,809
NPV at 10% below WACC as discount rate (24.46%)	$55,396	−$16,298
NPV at 10% over WACC as discount rate (29.90%)	$14,256	−$49,959

NPV is higher at a lower discount rate. Therefore, if an entrepreneur underestimates the risk of a project and uses a discount rate lower than she should, she will overestimate the NPV of the project. The net present value method is considered the best method for evaluating capital budgeting projects. It takes into account the risk of the project explicitly, and considers the required return of all sources of capital and the time value of money. Its drawback is that it is not intuitive because it is not a profit or a return measure. It quantifies additional value created by the project.

Internal Rate of Return

The internal rate of return and net present value are the two most popular capital budgeting methods used by chief financial officers. The internal rate of return (IRR) measures the annualized return of an investment. The decision rule is to accept projects with IRRs greater than or equal to the required return used in the net present value method. For many projects, the required return is the WACC. Calculating the IRR involves using a financial calculator or a spreadsheet as described in the time value of money section.[16]

Even though the machine does all the calculations, there are a few quirks about IRR that are important to keep in mind. First, there might not be a solution or there might be multiple solutions if cash flows change signs multiple times; that is, if cash flow is negative in the beginning, becomes positive for a few years and drops to negative again. In these situations, be sure to use the NPV method in addition to computing IRR.

Second, for projects that do not have known end dates, it is technically impossible to compute IRR. A work-around is to estimate a future resale value. In the Tasty Taco example, we use the terminal value as the estimated future resale value. The IRR of the total cash flows in Table 8.4 is 27.19 percent, which is just slightly higher than the WACC at 27.18 percent, and the business should be undertaken. The assumption of the IRR method is that all future cash flows will be reinvested and earn the internal rate of return. Remember that WACC represents the returns investors can earn on investments with similar risk. This assumption is quite plausible for Tasty Taco because its IRR is very close to its WACC. For projects with very high IRR, the ability to earn returns significantly higher than other investments with similar risk is less likely.

Third, when you have to choose between mutually exclusive projects, the IRR and NPV methods may give contradicting recommendations. Projects are mutually exclusive when you can choose only one of the alternatives. This is a common capital budgeting decision for businesses and we will use two examples to illustrate.

One type of mutually exclusive choice involves equipment or a system for which only one is needed and having two does not make sense or would be redundant. An example is an accounting system. Another type is deciding whether to borrow and buy a piece of equipment or to lease it. Table 8.6 shows the estimated cash flows for a boutique soap maker. She can start the business with a large mold base machine or a small mold base machine. She must decide which action to take.

The large mold base costs more but can a handle larger volume while the small mold base costs less with smaller volume capacity. The required return depends on the total risk of the business and, while the large mold base carries slightly higher business risk, the difference is insignificant. We use 8 percent as the required return for both options. The NPV for the large mold base option is $7,871, and for the small mold base option is $7,010. Therefore, if we apply the NPV decision rule, we will choose the large mold base option. The IRR for the small mold base is 13.17 percent, higher than the IRR for the large mold

Table 8.6 Capital Budgeting Decision Example: Large Versus Small Mold Base Machines

Year	0	1	2	3
Large mold base cash flows	−95,000	36,500	39,550	44,300
Required return	8.00%			
NPV of using large mold base	$7,871			
IRR of using large mold base	12.38%			

Year	0	1	2	3
Small mold base cash flows	−72,500	29,000	31,050	32,800
Required return	8.00%			
NPV of using small mold base	$7,010			
IRR of using small mold base	13.17%			

base option at 12.38 percent. The IRR rule indicates that we should choose the small mold base option. The differences in NPV and IRR are relatively small in this example, and other factors might tilt the decision. The general rule of thumb is to rely on the NPV rule when there is a conflict with the IRR method.

In the second example, a business needs a data center for a 4-year government contract. It can purchase the equipment at $250,000 and finance the entire purchase with a 4-year term loan. Alternatively it can lease the equipment at $90,000 per year with payments due at the beginning of each year. The resale value of the equipment is estimated to be $85,000 before taxes at the end of year 4. The advantages of buying with a loan are tax deduction from depreciation and no cash outflow in year 0. Table 8.7 summarizes the net after-tax cash flows for both options, taking into account depreciation, interest expenses, loan principal repayments, lease payments, and taxes. Note that interest expenses and loan repayments are included in the cash flows in this example. This is because comparing leasing versus buying is a financing decision, not an investment decision. The required return in this case is the after-tax cost of borrowing, not the WACC because revenues and direct costs are not affected by the leasing versus buying alternative. In other words, the business risk of the firm is not relevant to this decision. The cost of borrowing is 6 percent and the firm's tax rate is 25 percent. The after-tax cost of borrowing is 4.5 percent $(6\% \times (1 - 0.25))$.

The cash flows for buying the equipment financed by a term loan change signs several times. In year 0 there is no cash flow because the entire purchase is financed by borrowing. The small positive cash flow in year 2 is largely a result of accelerated depreciation resulting in high tax write-offs. The large cash flow in year 4 is due to selling off the equipment at the end of the contract. The cash flows for the leasing option reflect the after-tax lease payment in year 0 and steady cash flows in years 1 through 3. In year 4, the lease payment has been paid in advance, resulting in a large cash inflow in that year. The IRR is

Table 8.7 Capital Budgeting Decision Example: Lease Versus Buy and Borrow

Year	0	1	2	3	4
Cash flows of borrowing and buying the equipment	0	−15,773	4,770	−23,971	44,752
Required return	4.50%				
Net present value	$5,796				
Internal rate of return	14.34%				

Year	0	1	2	3	4
Cash flows of leasing the equipment	−67,500	1,500	2,880	4,288	73,223
Required return	4.50%				
Net present value	$1,732				
Internal rate of return	5.20%				

not a reliable method for analyzing this decision because the cash flows for the buy option change sign several times. Applying the NPV rule, buying the equipment financed with a term loan is the better alternative.

Payback Period

Payback period remains a popular capital budgeting decision. It is usually used in conjunction with the NPV and the IRR methods. Table 8.8 uses the large and small mold base machine example to illustrate how to compute payback period. The startup cost of the large mold base is $95,000. Cash flow for year 1 is $36,500, resulting in a cumulative cash flow of −$58,500 ($36,500 − $95,000). In other words, the investment is still out by −$58,500 after one year. The cumulative cash flows show that the large mold base will take from 2 to 3 years to pay back its initial investment.[17]

In this example, the cumulative cash flows for the small mold base machine also show a payback period from 2 to 3 years. Unlike the NPV and IRR methods, there is no objective decision rule for the payback method. Entrepreneurs must decide how fast a project must pay back its initial investment to be acceptable. Many entrepreneurs have a gut feeling about what that time period is. The payback period may increase an entrepreneur's confidence in a project that is supported by NPV and IRR analysis. If a project has a positive NPV but an entrepreneur is concerned that the payback period is too long, this is a sign that more analysis is needed. There may be risk factors not included in the analysis that cause the entrepreneur's gut instinct to require a faster payback.

Profitability Index

The profitability index method is closely related to the net present value method. The profitability index is computed as:

$$\text{Profitability index} = \frac{\text{Present value of future cash flows}}{\text{Initial investment}}$$

Table 8.8 Payback Period Example

Year	0	1	2	3
Large mold base machine				
Net total cash flows	−95,000	36,500	39,550	44,300
Cumulative cash flows	−95,000	−58,500	−18,950	25,350
Small mold base machine				
Net total cash flows	−72,500	29,000	31,050	32,800
Cumulative cash flows	−72,500	−43,500	−12,450	20,350

The net present value measures the difference between the value of a project's cash flows and its initial investment, whereas the profitability index measures the ratio between the two. The decision rule is to accept a project if its profitability index is greater than or equal to 1. A profitability index of 1 implies that the project's present value of future cash flows is exactly equal to its initial investment. This is the same as a project with a net present value equal to zero. For Tasty Taco, the present value of its future cash flows is $339,017 and its initial investment is $338,924. It has a profitability index of 1.0003 and is a valuable investment because for every $1 invested, it creates $1.0003 in value. In other words, it has a value multiple of 1.0003.

In this chapter, we discussed the fundamental relationship between risk and return, the application of time value of money, costs of capital and capital budgeting methods. These decision tools enable entrepreneurs to evaluate projects and identify ones that will add value to their firms. The next chapter will build on these tools and discuss how to value entire businesses.

Appendix 8.1 Industry-Specific Values for Unlevered Beta and Unsystematic Risk Adjustment Factor

Table 8.9 Industry-Specific Values for Unlevered Beta and Unsystematic Risk Adjustment Factor

Industry	Number of firms in sample	Unlevered beta	Unsystematic risk adjustment factor for beta
Advertising	65	0.73	4.2660
Aerospace, defense	95	0.92	2.1175
Air transport	25	0.52	2.7867
Apparel	70	0.99	2.7381
Auto parts	75	1.23	1.8859
Beverages	47	1.24	3.5149
Beverages (alcoholic)	19	0.93	2.7359
Biotechnology	349	1.07	4.2222
Broadcasting	30	1.10	1.9887
Brokerage and investment banking	49	0.33	1.5462
Building materials	37	1.07	1.3430
Business and consumer services	179	0.75	2.2246
Chemical (specialty)	100	0.95	1.7817
Computer services	129	0.82	2.9972
Computer software	273	1.04	2.6655
Computers, peripherals	66	1.13	2.8819
Construction	18	0.77	2.4059
Educational services	40	1.04	3.3313
Electrical equipment	135	1.07	3.0638
Electronics	191	1.00	3.2237
Electronics (consumer and office)	26	1.08	2.6005
Engineering	56	1.13	1.5648
Entertainment	85	0.99	3.3646
Environmental and waste services	108	0.81	3.9113
Financial services	76	0.58	2.2173
Food processing	97	0.71	2.6459
Furniture, home furnishings	36	1.03	2.1108
Healthcare equipment	193	0.77	3.2200
Healthcare facilities	47	0.56	2.0639
Healthcare products	58	0.89	2.7051
Healthcare services	126	0.72	3.2714
Healthcare information and technology	125	0.92	3.6152
Heavy construction	46	1.22	1.2203
Homebuilding	32	1.23	1.2515
Hotel, gaming	89	0.90	2.5806
Household products	139	0.89	3.8576
Information services	71	0.81	1.7000
Internet software and services	330	1.05	4.4316
Machinery	141	0.96	1.6138

Table 8.9 Industry-Specific Values for Unlevered Beta and Unsystematic Risk Adjustment Factor (Continued)

Industry	Number of firms in sample	Unlevered beta	Unsystematic risk adjustment factor for beta
Metals and mining	134	0.90	3.8475
Office equipment and services	30	0.82	1.4741
Oil and gas distribution	80	0.55	1.8186
Oilfield services, equipment	163	1.17	1.9525
Packaging and container	24	0.73	1.0791
Paper, forest products	21	0.93	1.7822
Pharmaceuticals and drugs	138	1.03	3.2703
Publishing and newspapers	52	0.87	2.6891
Real estate (development)	22	0.85	2.8024
Real estate (operations and services)	47	0.94	4.0758
Recreation	70	1.11	2.8666
Restaurant	84	0.71	2.3116
Retail (automotive)	30	0.80	1.8263
Retail (distributors)	87	0.74	2.3800
Retail (general)	21	0.80	1.8299
Retail (groceries and food)	21	0.58	2.4285
Retail (Internet)	47	1.02	3.1829
Retail (special lines)	137	0.78	2.2239
Semiconductor	104	1.14	1.7847
Semiconductor equipment	51	1.21	1.9286
Shoes	14	0.81	2.0437
Telecommunication equipment	131	1.11	2.5700
Telecommunication services	82	0.63	3.4359
Trucking	28	0.77	1.6574
Total market	7766	0.64	2.5729

We thank Professor Aswath Damodaran for providing the unlevered industry beta data and industry correlation data. All data last updated as of January 5, 2014.

Case 8.1 The Local Café: New Project Analysis

Richard Borgman and Kirk Ramsay

Kirk Ramsay was a serial entrepreneur. Another way to characterize him was as a small businessman who enjoyed new challenges and new adventures. After earning his business degree at the state university, Kirk built several successful businesses. He designed and built homes, owned several rental properties, and ran a property management business, and continued to follow his musical passion by playing lead guitar in a successful local "cover" band. In the small city in New England where he lived, he saw a need for a local no-frills, good food, breakfast and lunch eatery located downtown, where the national chains did not locate. He had found his next potential project—which he planned to call "The Local Café." And he had found the empty storefront in which to put the restaurant. The landlord had urged Kirk to make his decision in a few days, because he claimed to have another interested party. To make the decision, Kirk would calculate NPV, IRR, and payback period.

The restaurant was part of a clearly defined life plan. His children were now grown; Kirk and his wife hoped to work about ten years more to solidify their retirement, and in ten years move to a warmer climate, hopefully fully retired or, if necessary, semi-retired. So if opened, Kirk expected to own and operate the restaurant for about 10 years. After establishing it as a successful business, he planned to sell the restaurant as part of his plan to move at least part of the year to a warmer climate.

The space Kirk had found was about 3,000 square feet, enough for a kitchen and ten tables. The monthly rent was $600, leased "triple net," meaning that the renter was responsible for all other costs, including utilities. He anticipated other building-related costs of $300/month for insurance and $500/month for utilities (water, sewer, gas, trash removal). He believed these costs would increase at least with inflation, which he assumed to be about 4 percent per year.

To prepare the space, which had not previously been a restaurant, Kirk anticipated the following costs: stove, $1,600; double fryer, $800; sinks, $700; preparation tables, $1,500; pots and pans, utensils, glasses, and dishes, $1,500; 10 tables and 40 chairs, $2,000 in total. The costs to renovate the space (plumbing, electric, carpentry, and signage) would be $10,000. All these costs were subject to depreciation. Kirk assumed a 5-year depreciable life and prepared a modified accelerated cost recovery system (MACRS) schedule (Table 8.10).

For the first year, Kirk assumed the following revenues. The average breakfast patron would spend about $7.50. He assumed that with a 40-person capacity, there would be about 30 people per sitting, and about two "turns" per day. The average lunch patron would spend about $11.50. There would be 30 people per sitting, and about three "turns" per day. The restaurant

Table 8.10 Modified Accelerated Cost Recovery System 5-Year Schedule

Year	Percentage
1	0.2
2	0.32
3	0.192
4	0.1152
5	0.1152
6	0.0576

would close in the early afternoon and would not serve dinner. The plan would be for the restaurant to be open 5 days a week (260 days per year).

To control costs, the restaurant would not have an extensive menu, serving standard breakfast fare (eggs and bacon and the like) and having rotating specials for lunch plus a standard menu. Kirk anticipated "consumables and perishables" costs to be about 60 percent of revenues. Other non-labor costs would be about 3 percent of revenues.

There would be three cooks working three overlapping 8 hour shifts, making $11 an hour. There would be two servers working two overlapping 8 hour shifts, making $4 per hour (plus tips). Finally, there would be a manager who normally operated a register as well, making $12 per hour for a daily 8 hour shift.

Over the following years, Kirk expected revenues to increase at least with inflation (as before, assumed to be about 4 percent per year). Costs would remain at the current percentage of revenues. Net working capital (NWC) was assumed to be 5 percent of revenues in the upcoming year (for example, NWC at $t = 1$ equals 5 percent of $t = 2$ revenues). The change in net working capital was calculated as NWC in the current year minus NWC in the previous year (thus change in NWC for $t = 1$ is NWC ($t = 1$) minus NWC ($t = 0$).

Kirk faced a 35 percent tax rate. He could borrow from a local bank at 9 percent. The loan would have five-year amortizing, monthly payments, and no prepayment penalty. The loan was secured by the equipment and, as was usual, required a personal guarantee by Ramsay. He estimated his cost of equity and financing weights using data from a sample of 84 publicly traded restaurant firms compiled by Answath Damodaran (http://pages.stern.nyu.edu/~adamodar/). These firms had an average unlevered beta (unlevered means the beta if there was no debt in their capital structure) of 0.69, an average debt-to-equity (D/E) ratio of 0.2757, and an average correlation with the market of 0.3053.

He knew that he could calculate a levered beta using the following simplified Hamada equation:

$$\beta_L = \beta_U \times \left[1 + (1-T) \times \frac{D}{E} \right]$$

Ramsay assumed that his mixture of debt and equity financing (D/E) would be close to the industry average.

Ramsay also realized that he was relatively undiversified in comparison with the stockholders of a large publicly traded firm. Damodaran suggested that an undiversified beta, called total beta, could be approximated by dividing the "market beta" (the firm's levered beta) by the correlation between the market and the individual restaurant firms.

The security market line equation from the capital asset pricing model, used to calculate the cost of equity, is:

$$r_E = r_{RF} + (MRP)\beta$$

where MRP is the market risk premium, γ_{RF} is the risk-free rate, and beta in this case is the total beta. He planned to calculate his project weighted average cost of capital (WACC) as,

$$WACC = w_e r_e + w_d r_d (1 - T)$$

where "w" are the weights of equity and debt, respectively, and "γ" refers to the costs of equity and debt, respectively. T is the tax rate.

In ten years, when Kirk expected to sell the restaurant to fund his retirement, he knew the value would depend on cash flow. To be conservative, he valued the sale in ten years as a no-growth perpetuity; that is, the firm would be worth the present value of a perpetual series of constant cash flows (based on $t = 10$ cash flow). Also, to be conservative, he assumed that the sale would be fully taxable.

Kirk wanted a payback within three years, assuming a risk-free rate of 3.04 percent and an equity risk premium of 5 percent.

Case Questions

1. Create ten years of forecast cash flows. It will be convenient to use spreadsheet software, such as Excel.
2. What is Ramsay's cost of capital to use in the analysis?
3. Calculate the expected sale price of the restaurant at the end of year 10 (that is, at $t = 10$).
4. Using all these answers, calculate the project's NPV, IRR, and payback period. Based on these calculations, should Ramsay go ahead with the project?
5. If you have created a spreadsheet to analyze the project, you should be able to create additional scenarios. What if revenues are not as good as Ramsay has forecast? What if costs are higher?
6. Are there any other issues you think are important? Considering the scenarios you have created, and any other issues you feel are important, what would you recommend Ramsay do?

Notes

1 In a real estate investment, 40 percent debt is considered conservative. Banks often loan up to 80% of a property's purchase price.

2 This section contains more advanced finance concepts. Appendix 8.1 contains unlevered costs of equity for many industries. Students can use values from Appendix 8.1 instead of estimating unlevered costs of equity.

3 This approach is also called the dividend growth model or the Gordon growth model.

4 Dividends and stock price data were obtained from http://finance.yahoo.com.

5 Examining the theoretical and econometric arguments about the exact form of the asset pricing models and the efficiency of the stock market is beyond the scope of this textbook. For a review article supporting asset pricing models, see Fama & French (2004). Lewellen et al. (2010) provide a skeptical appraisal of methodologies used in some prior studies.

6 The controversy over whether the stock market is efficient is reflected in the 2013 Nobel Prize in Economics, which was shared by Eugene Fama, the "father" of the efficient market hypothesis, Robert Shiller, a behavior financial economist whose works demonstrate inefficiency in the stock market, and Lars Hansen, an econometrician who pioneered methods for testing efficiency.

7 β_E can be estimated using regression methods. Most investment textbooks discuss methods for computing beta.

8 Treasury bill and S&P500 index averages were obtained from Professor Damodaran's website (http://pages.stern.nyu.edu/~adamodar/New_Home_Page/datafile/histretSP.html). He computed these results using treasury bond returns data from the Federal Reserve data in St. Louis.

9 We thank Professor Aswath Damodaran for generously sharing his estimates of unlevered beta and allowing us to reproduce them in Appendix 8.1 (www.damodaran.com, downloaded 9/28/2014).

10 This step is sometimes called relevering.

11 Notice that the levered beta formula is a rearrangement of the unlevered beta formula.

12 The unsystematic risk adjustment factor depends on the correlation between the industry stock return and the market return. The formula is: Unsystematic risk adjustment factor = (1/(Correlation with the market) − 1).

13 See Chapter 3 for a detailed discussion on different sources of financing.

14 The firm value does not equal total assets in Chapter 7 because wages payable is excluded from firm value. It is a very small percentage and is not a permanent component of the firm's capital structure.

15 http://data.worldbank.org/indicator/NY.GDP.MKTP.KD.ZG?page=6&order=wbapi_data_value_2009%20wbapi_data_value%20wbapi_data_value-first&sort=desc

16 Mathematically, IRR is defined as the discount rate that sets the net present value of a project to zero. Without a financial calculator or spreadsheet, calculating IRR is very difficult and relies on trial and error.

17 Some textbooks suggest computing the payback period with the assumption that cash flows occur evenly throughout the year. The payback period for the large mold base machine will then be 2 years + 18,950/44,300 years = 2.43 years. If such precision is needed, the payback period should be computed using monthly cash flow forecast instead of annual cash flows.

Bibliography

Amihud, Y. (2002). Illiquidity and stock returns: cross-section and time-series effects. *Journal of Financial Markets, 5,* 31–56.

Biden, J. (2007, June). In their own words: remarks by Senator Joe Biden. *The Philadelphia Jewish Voice, 24* http://www.pjvoice.com/v24/24302biden.aspx (accessed 3/9/2015).

Da, Z., Guo, R., & Jagannathan, R. (2012). CAPM for estimating the cost of equity capital: Interpreting the empirical evidence. *Journal of Financial Economics, 103,* 204–220.

Damodaran, A. *Annual Returns on Stock, T. Bonds and T. Bills: 1928–Current* http://pages.stern.nyu.edu/~adamodar/New_Home_Page/datafile/histretSP.html (accessed 9/27/2014).

Damodaran, A. *Damodaran Online* http://pages.stern.nyu.edu/~adamodar/ (accessed 9/28/2014).

Fama, E. F., & French, K. R. (2004). The capital asset pricing model: theory and evidence. *Journal of Economic Perspectives, 18*(3), 25–46.

Graham, J. & Harvey, C. (2002). How do CFOs make capital budgeting and capital structure decisions? *Journal of Applied Corporate Finance, 15*(1), 8–23.

Ibbotson, R., Chen, Z., Kim, D., & Hu, W. (2013). Liquidity as an investment style. *Financial Analyst Journal, 69*(3), 1–15.

Lewellen, J., Nagel, S., & Shanken, J. (2010). A skeptical appraisal of asset pricing tests. *Journal of Financial Economics, 96*(2), 175–194.

Stumpf, A., & Martinez, R. (2011). The SRR Restricted Stock Study. Washington, DC: Stout Risius Ross, Inc.

The World Bank. *GDP Growth (Annual %)* http://data.worldbank.org/indicator/NY.GDP.MKTP.KD.ZG?page=6&order=wbapi_data_value_2009%20wbapi_data_value%20wbapi_data_value-first&sort=desc (accessed 10/2/2014).

Yahoo. *Yahoo!Finance* http://finance.yahoo.com/ (accessed 9/21/2014)

9 Business Valuation

Whenever a man can get hold of numbers, they are invaluable...
Numbers are the masters of the weak, but the slaves of the strong.

Charles Babbage

All entrepreneurs find themselves confronting the problem of valuing a business sooner or later. They may want to acquire another business and need to know what price to offer the seller. They may need to buy out one of their partners. They may be the buyout target of another firm. They may be ready to seek equity from venture capitalists. In these situations, entrepreneurs should know how outsiders value their businesses so they can make informed decisions during negotiations. Sometimes lenders require business valuation as part of the loan application process. Valuation is also needed for succession and estate planning, a topic we will discuss in Chapter 10, along with exit and harvest strategies.

Most finance and accounting textbooks focus on publicly traded companies and do not address the unique challenges of valuing privately held businesses. In this chapter, we first discuss adjusting common financial statement items that are owner specific and will likely change with new ownership. Next, we address the impacts on valuation of under-diversification and illiquidity. Then we cover two valuation approaches: discounted cash flows and market multiples. We will approach valuation from the buyer's perspective throughout the discussion in this chapter. We also value the business as a going concern, i.e. we assume the business will continue to operate after transfer of ownership. Valuation, especially for privately held business, is an imprecise science. Entrepreneurs should use more than one valuation approach and sensitivity analysis to assure the most accurate valuation possible.

Income Adjustments

Even when financial statements are prepared in accordance with Generally Accepted Accounting Principles (GAAP), adjustments are often needed. For private businesses, especially those with a small number of owners organized as an LLC or partnership, expenses are often categorized to minimize tax and may not reflect the true costs of day-to-day operations. Interchanging salaries and dividends to minimize total taxes is a common strategy. There may also be expense items unique to the personal circumstance of the owners, e.g. health insurance coverage for part-time hourly employees who are family members. The first step in valuing a privately held business is to identify financial statement items that will be different if the business is acquired by an outsider and make appropriate adjustments. The incremental principle discussed in Chapter 8 applies equally well to making financial statement adjustments during business valuation. The second principle is sustainability. An owner may draw a salary that is below market rate to help the business succeed. A buyer, especially an investment buyer, should assume hiring all personnel at market wages. Other common subsidies include below-market rent and services provided for free by family members. Comparing common size financial statements and key ratios of the target firm with industry averages will highlight unusual items. The experience and expertise of the buyer is another important resource. This process of adjusting income is also called "earnings normalization." Adjustments are usually made to income from operation or EBITDA,[1] not net income, for the following reasons. First, business valuation should focus on the income-generating ability of the operations. Second, a buyer acquires the assets of the firm but usually does not assume existing liabilities. Third, other income and expenses are not part of regular business and are unlikely to repeat. Last, taxes and non-cash expenses will depend on the tax strategies of the new owners and will change after the purchase.

We will use Dimmons Fuel,[2] a family-owned propane distributor, to illustrate the business valuation process. Table 9.1 shows the income statement and owner's equity account for Dimmons for the past 4 years and projections for the current year.

The potential buyer, Koehler Propane, is a long time competitor of Dimmons from a nearby town. He notes that wages for officers, retirement plan contributions, and insurance premiums are unusually high. He estimates that he can reduce wages for officers by $100,000, retirement contributions by $10,000, and insurance by $8,000. If the acquisition is successful, the new company will buy in larger quantity and gain volume discounts on its cost of goods sold, saving between $27,000 and $42,000 per year. Our focus is on income from operations. The buyer does not expect other income, and expenses for Dimmons will continue at the current level. He plans to keep the same amount of cash after the acquisition, so interest income currently earned by Dimmons will cease. He does not plan to sell any assets from Dimmons, eliminating future gain or loss on sale of assets. Depreciation expense will be totally different after the acquisition. Table 9.2 shows adjustments to income from operations for Dimmons.

Assuming an average savings for cost of goods sold at $34,500 (($27,000 + $42,000)/2), adjustments to income from operations total $152,500. Projected

Table 9.1 Dimmons Fuel Income Statement and Owners' Equity: Fiscal Years Ending December 31

	Projected for this year	Actual Year −1	Actual Year −2	Actual Year −3	Actual Year −4
Net sales	$3,434,000	$3,676,000	$3,295,000	$3,118,000	$2,534,000
Cost of goods sold	$2,772,000	$3,050,000	$2,737,000	$2,608,000	$2,158,000
Gross profit	$662,000	$626,000	$558,000	$510,000	$376,000
Operating expenses					
Sales and marketing	$10,000	$19,000	$14,000	$14,000	$10,000
Insurance and legal	$77,000	$75,000	$62,000	$55,000	$49,000
Repairs and maintenance	$26,000	$26,000	$24,000	$22,000	$26,000
Office expenses	$10,000	$12,000	$12,000	$11,000	$12,000
Wages—officers	$259,000	$172,000	$195,000	$148,000	$113,000
Wages—others	$71,000	$71,000	$67,000	$65,000	$52,000
Payroll taxes	$22,000	$17,000	$17,000	$14,000	$13,000
Real estate taxes	$6,000	$5,000	$5,000	$5,000	$5,000
Retirement plan contribution	$49,000	$39,000	$43,000	$31,000	$24,000
Total operating expense	$530,000	$436,000	$439,000	$365,000	$304,000
Income from operations	$132,000	$190,000	$119,000	$145,000	$72,000
Other (income), expenses					
Interest income	($9,000)	($3,000)	($3,000)	($4,000)	($6,000)
Dividend income	$0	$0	$0	$0	$0
Gain on sale of assets	($22,000)	($29,000)	$0	$0	($13,000)
Depreciation expenses	$72,000	$40,000	$49,000	$56,000	$44,000
Total other (income), expenses	$41,000	$8,000	$46,000	$52,000	$25,000
Net income before taxes	$91,000	$182,000	$73,000	$93,000	$47,000
Provision for income tax	$0	$0	$0	$0	$0
Net income	$91,000	$182,000	$73,000	$93,000	$47,000
Retained earnings, beginning of year	$546,000	$412,000	$424,000	$369,000	$408,000
Distributions	($143,000)	($48,000)	($85,000)	($38,000)	($86,000)
Retained earnings, end of year	$494,000	$546,000	$412,000	$424,000	$369,000

Table 9.2 Dimmons Fuel Adjustments to Income from Operations

Adjustments to income from operations	Average	Low estimate	High estimate
Savings from reduction in officer's wages	$100,000	$100,000	$100,000
Savings from reduction in retirement contributions	$10,000	$10,000	$10,000
Savings from reduction in health insurance premiums	$8,000	$8,000	$8,000
Savings from reduction in COGS	$34,500	$27,000	$42,000
Total adjustments to income from operations	$152,500		

	Projected for this year	Average of past 4 years
Income from operations	$132,000	$131,500
Total adjustments to income from operations	$152,500	
Adjusted income from operations	$284,500	

income from operations for this year increases from $132,000 to $284,500 after the adjustments. We can also compute the average income from operations for the past four years, which turns out to be $131,500, very close to the projected income this year. The example of Dimmons Fuel shows an important reason for examining the financial statements carefully. The business has maintained steady growth and profitability for the past four years. This year, the owner is taking $87,000 more in wages, $95,000 more in distributions, and is selling the business. An observant buyer may suspect that the owner of Dimmons has financial needs for personal reasons and has been careful to increase his withdrawals without significantly reducing the business's income from its long-term average. This information is useful in negotiation.

Illiquidity Discount

The next adjustment is for illiquidity of privately held firms. Unlike shares of public companies, which are traded daily on organized exchanges, selling shares of private companies is much more difficult. Owners wishing to liquidate their holdings usually need the help of business brokers, and finding interested buyers takes time. There are two common approaches to adjust for illiquidity when valuing private business. Chapter 8 describes adding an illiquidity premium of 5–6 percent to the cost of equity, which is used as the discount rate in the discounted cash flow valuation method. Another approach is to apply an illiquidity discount directly to the estimated value.

Academic researchers study restricted stocks of publicly traded firms and pre- and post-initial public offerings to estimate the cost of illiquidity. Prior to 1980, the restriction period tended to be longer, over two years, and the illiquidity discount was estimated at around 35 percent. Studies covering the period between 1980 and 2000 estimated the discount to be between 20 percent and

22 percent. A recent study on data between 2005 and 2010 put the discount at 10.9 percent. The decline in estimated illiquidity discounts corresponds to changes in security rules governing these restrictions and increased trading activities in the private equity market. For example, the restricted trading period has been shortened from two years to six months. For entrepreneurs planning to stay with the business for five or more years, an illiquidity discount of 20–22 percent based on a longer holding period is more relevant. Damodaran (2006) recommends a base illiquidity discount of 25 percent for profitable firm with $10 million in revenues. He identifies five factors that affect illiquidity discounts:

- Liquidity of assets
- Firm size
- Profitability
- Cash flow generating capacity
- Percentage of firm for sale.

Illiquid assets, such as patents, small firm size, operating losses, low cash flow generating capacity, and the sale of a large percentage of a firm will increase the illiquidity discount. In general, the illiquidity discount is between 20 percent and 30 percent for privately held firms.

Valuation Methods

We will examine two approaches to valuation in this section: (1) discounted cash flow methods and (2) multiples or relative valuation methods. There is no perfect valuation method because assessing the value of a business involves many variables and uncertainties. We will discuss the pros and cons of each approach. Beware of models that are overly complex. Remember that the output of any valuation model is only an estimate, regardless of the number of input variables and equations. Pay attention to assumptions. The quality of an estimate is only as good as the quality of the assumptions. Going through the valuation process often requires entrepreneurs to make explicit assumptions about the future of their businesses. This exercise is beneficial as it helps entrepreneurs identify their biases and spot unexpected changes.

Discounted Cash Flow Methods

Discounted cash flow methods estimate the value of a business by computing the present value of expected future cash flows. This value is also referred to as the intrinsic value or the fundamental value because expected future cash flows are based on financial data and operations of the business. The discount rate is the required return consistent with the risk of the cash flows. The two common discounted cash flow methods are: (1) free cash flows to firm and (2) free cash flows to equity. The term "free cash flows" refers to cash flows net of all necessary reinvestments to maintain the long-term growth rate. Focusing on free cash flows is consistent with the sustainability principle.

The first approach is sometimes called enterprise valuation because it values the entire business assuming both debt and equity financing. It uses the weighted average cost of capital (WACC) as the discount rate when computing the present value of free cash flows to the firm. The second approach is referred to as equity valuation because it excludes debt financing in invested capital and uses the cost of equity as the discount rate when computing the present value of free cash flows to equity. The important principle is to match cash flows with discount rates, i.e. to use WACC when discounting free cash flows to firm and use cost of equity when discounting free cash flows to equity.

The mechanics of computing enterprise and equity valuations use the present value formulas and spreadsheet applications discussed in Chapter 8. Methods for estimating WACC and cost of equity are also discussed in Chapter 8. This chapter focuses on developing valuation assumptions and then applying these formulas. After adjusting operating income or EBITDA, the next step is to estimate after-tax cash flows by deducting taxes. The tax rate should be the buyer's expected marginal tax rate and is usually easy to obtain.

After-tax cash flows to firm = EBITDA × (1 − Marginal tax rate)

After-tax cash flows to equity = (EBITDA − Estimated interest expense) × (1 − Marginal tax rate)

To estimate future free cash flows we need assumptions about growth rates and reinvestment rates. We classify firms into two broad categories: (1) stable or constant growth and (2) transition or non-constant growth. Stable firms are currently growing at their long-term growth rate, whereas transition firms are currently in a high growth period and are expected to slow down to their long-term growth rate over a few years. Some firms may be in a transition phase of rapid decline due to competition in local markets but will stabilize to a long-term constant rate.

Stable Growth Discounted Cash Flows Model

Remember that we are valuing the business as a going concern. The stable growth discounted cash flow model assumes that a firm has attained its target long-term growth rate and will sustain this constant growth indefinitely. This model typically applies to established firms and is often used in business acquisition and succession planning. In Chapter 8, we recommended using the long-term GDP growth rate or population growth rate as the constant growth rate for computing terminal value. The same principle applies here. The industry or GDP growth rate should be the foundation for estimating target long-term growth rate. Some industries are in decline and long-term growth rate can be negative.

The Bureau of Labor Statistics (BLS, www.bls.gov) publishes projections on output and employment growth rates by industry every two years. For example, in 2012, BLS projected an annual growth rate of 2.9 percent for non-agricultural sectors for 2010–2012. The Bureau of Economic Analysis (BEA, www.bea.gov) is another government agency that provides industry statistics. Industry trade groups are also good resources for growth forecasts and average financial ratios. Similar to growth rate, return on assets (ROA) should be the long-term average and, unless there are good reasons, the industry average ROA should be used. Some good reasons for not using the industry average include proprietary technology or manufacturing process.

Long-term growth rate, return on assets, and reinvestment rate are closely connected. A firm can only grow with adequate reinvestment. Return on assets generates funds that can be used for reinvestment. The relationship of these three variables is expressed in this formula:

$$\text{Long-term reinvestment rate} = \frac{\text{Target long-term growth rate}}{\text{Return on assets}}$$

$$\text{Reinvestments (\$ amount)} = \text{After-tax cash flows} \times \text{Long-term reinvestment rate}$$

Next, we subtract reinvestments from after-tax cash flows to get free cash flows. For free cash flows to equity, we exclude the portion of reinvestments financed by debt. The formulas for computing free cash flows are:

$$\text{Free cash flows to firm (FCFF)} = \text{After-tax cash flows to firm} - \text{Reinvestments}$$

$$\text{Free cash flows to equity (FCFE)} = \text{After-tax cash flows to equity} - [\text{Reinvestments} \times (1 - \text{debt ratio})]$$

For firms with stable long-term growth rate, the formula for computing the present value of their future cash flows is the same as the terminal value formula in the last section.

$$\text{Enterprise value}_0\left(\text{Present value of FCFF}\right) = \frac{\text{FCFF}_0 \times \left(1 + \text{Growth rate}\right)}{\left(\text{WACC} - \text{Growth rate}\right)}$$

$$\text{Equity value}_0\left(\text{Present value of FCFE}\right) = \frac{\text{FCFE}_0 \times \left(1 + \text{Growth rate}\right)}{\left(\text{Cost of equity} - \text{Growth rate}\right)}$$

Like terminal value calculation, we can also express the formulas for enterprise and equity values using free cash flows in year 1:

$$\text{Enterprise value}_0\left(\text{Present value of FCFF}\right) = \frac{\text{FCFF}_1}{\left(\text{WACC} - \text{Growth rate}\right)}$$

$$\text{Equity value}_0\left(\text{Present value of FCFE}\right) = \frac{\text{FCFE}_1}{\left(\text{Cost of equity} - \text{Growth rate}\right)}$$

The one-year time difference between the present value today, year 0, and the first cash flow in year 1 is often a confusing concept. The easiest way to remember this time difference is to imagine buying a business today (year 0) and waiting one year before taking any distribution or dividend, cash flows in year 1. The last step is to adjust the values for illiquidity discount:

Enterprise value after illiquidity discount = Enterprise value ×
(1 − Illiquidity discount)

Equity value after illiquidity discount = Equity value × (1 − Illiquidity discount)

9.1 Stable Growth Discounted Cash Flow Model

$$\text{Long-term reinvestment rate} = \frac{\text{Target long-term growth rate}}{\text{Return on assets}}$$

$$\text{Reinvestments} = \text{After-tax cash flows} \times \text{Long-term reinvestment rate}$$

Enterprise value is computed as the present value of future free cash flows to firm (FCFF) discounted by the weighted average cost of capital (WACC). The formulas are:

$$\text{FCFF} = \text{After-tax cash flows to firm} - \text{Reinvestments}$$

$$\text{Enterprise value (Present value of FCFF)} = \frac{\text{FCFF} \times (1 + \text{Growth rate})}{(\text{WACC} - \text{Growth rate})}$$

$$\text{Enterprise value after illiquidity discount} = \text{Enterprise value} \times (1 - \text{illiquidity discount})$$

Equity value is computed as the present value of future free cash flows to equity (FCFE) discounted by the cost of equity. The formulas are:

$$\text{Free cash flows to quity (FCFE)} = \text{After-tax cash flows to equity} - \left[\text{Reinvestment} \times (1 - \text{Debt ratio}) \right]$$

$$\text{Equity value (Present value of FCFE)} = \frac{\text{FCFE} \times (1 + \text{Growth rate})}{(\text{Cost of equity} - \text{Growth rate})}$$

$$\text{Equity value after illiquidity discount} = \text{Equity value} \times + (1 - \text{illiquidity discount})$$

Table 9.3 Dimmons Fuel Valuation by Koehler Propane Stable Growth Discounted Cash Flow Method

Adjusted income from operations	$284,500
Marginal tax rate	35%
After-tax cash flows	$184,925
Return on assets (ROA)	19.56%
Target long-term growth rate	4.08%
Reinvestment rate	20.86%
Reinvestments	$38,573
Debt ratio	0%
Free cash flows to equity	$146,352
Cost of equity estimation	
Total beta (unlevered)	2.26
Estimate for long-term risk-free rate	4.39%
Estimate for equity risk premium	4.80%
Estimated cost of equity	15.24%
Equity value	$1,364,900
Illiquidity discount	30%
Equity value adjusted for illiquidity	$955,430

Table 9.3 shows the valuation of Dimmons Fuel by its potential buyer, Koehler Propane. Koehler Propane is a privately held family business organized as an LLC. It expects its marginal tax rate to be 35 percent, and currently does not use any debt. The fuel distribution industry is in a declining industry cycle characterized by high revenue volatility, high capital intensity, low concentration level, high competition, and medium barriers to entry and technology changes. Koehler has been a leader in the local market and has successfully acquired nearby competitors over the years. It assumes that the combined firm will achieve the industry projected growth rate of 4.08 percent and feels that this is a conservative estimate. It assumes that the return on asset will remain at 19.56 percent. The resulting reinvestment rate of 20.86 percent ((4.08%/19.56%) × 100) is consistent with the buyer's own experience.

The estimated after-tax cash flow for Dimmons is $184,925 ($284,500 × (1 − 0.35)). The annual reinvestments are $38,573 ($184,925 × 0.2086). Since Koehler does not have any debt and does not plan to use debt, the free cash flows to equity is $146,352 ($184,925 − $38,573). The cost of equity is estimated using the CAPM equation discussed in Chapter 8, 15.24% = 4.39% + 2.26 × 4.80%. The resulting equity value is $1,364,900 ($146,352 × (1.0408 /

(0.1524 − 0.0408)). With a 30 percent illiquidity discount, the net equity value after illiquidity discount is $955,430 ($1,364,900 × (1 − 0.3)). The enterprise value and equity value for Dimmons Fuel is the same because its purchaser, Koehler, does not use any debt. Recall that there are uncertainties regarding COGS savings, which ranges from $27,000 to $42,000. The valuation in Table 9.3 assumes that the average savings from reduction in COGS is $34,500 (($27,000 + $42,000)/2).

We now consider the best and worst cases. The net equity value in the worst case (COGS savings of $27,000) is $930,243 and in the best case (COGS savings of $42,000) is $980,617. In this example, a $15,000 ($42,000 − $27,000) difference in estimated cash flows in the first year translates into over $50,000 difference in valuation ($980,617 − $930,243 = $50,374).

Non-Constant Growth Discounted Cash Flows Model

Firms early in their life cycle, especially in the startup and expansion stages, typically experience a higher growth rate than the long-term stable rate. These firms are also prime candidates for external investors because they need additional capital to finance their rapid growth. The transition or non-constant growth discounted cash flows valuation model can capture the varying growth stages. This model also applies well to firms in industries just reaching maturity, where consolidation leads to rapid decline until a new long-term stable growth is achieved. There are generally four steps to this valuation approach:

1. Estimate free cash flows during the transition period.
2. Estimate long-term stable growth rate after the transition period.
3. Compute stable growth value.
4. Compute present value of transition period free cash flows and stable growth value.

The formulas used in these steps have been explained in Chapter 8 and in the stable growth discounted cash flows model section. We will apply the four-step framework to value Standing Desk, Inc. (SDI) as an example. SDI is a startup company that got its initial funding on a social crowdfunding site two years ago. Its products have been very successful and the company became profitable this year. Table 9.4 contains SDI's income statements.

The company has grown rapidly in the past two years. Sales revenues reached $853,500 in 2013, their first year of full operation, and are expected to increase 55% in 2014. More importantly, earnings before interest, taxes depreciation, and amortization (EBITDA) turned positive that year. The company has a promising prospect as it capitalizes on the popularity of healthy work habits. The Business and Institutional Furniture Manufacturers Association estimates industry sales to reach $12.1 billion in 2014, a 4.9 percent growth, and $13.3 billion in 2015, a 9.6 percent growth (Sanchez, 2014). The office furniture

Table 9.4 Standing Desk Inc. (SDI) Income Statement Fiscal Years Ending
December 31

	2014	2013	2012
Revenues	$1,325,000	$853,500	$449,600
Cogs	576,000	304,400	175,840
Wages and salaries	285,000	268,500	197,600
Employee benefits	25,650	24,165	17,784
Advertising	17,150	16,435	13,796
Rent	48,000	48,000	44,000
Utilities	21,600	21,600	12,600
Office administration	6,000	6,000	3,500
Total expenses	979,400	689,100	465,120
Earnings before interest, taxes, depreciation, and amortization (EBITDA)	$345,600	$164,400	−$15,520
Depreciation	25,000	83,000	58,000
Earnings before interest and taxes (EBIT)	320,600	81,400	−73,520
Interest	$0	$0	$0
Taxable income	320,600	81,400	−73,520
Taxes	$54,634	$1,182	$0
Net income	$265,966	$80,218	−$73,520

industry is cyclical, and sales fluctuates with business cycles. A University of
Iowa study (Jennings, 2012) estimates the long-term industry growth rate to be
around 3 percent. SDI is capturing a new niche market and the next couple of
years coincides with an above-average growth projection in the industry. It
expects EBITDA to grow at 45 percent over the next two years, but decrease
rapidly over the next three years, as it expects that competition will intensify.
After that, the company assumes that the growth rate will settle down to the
long-term industry average growth rate of 3 percent. The two owners of SDI
note that they have set their salaries at $50,000 each since the company's found-
ing to help the business succeed. Market salary for management at comparable
size firm is around $70,000 to $90,000 per person. Adjustment for the below-
market salaries of both owners totals $40,000 ($140,000 − $100,000) to
$80,000 ($180,000 − $100,000). Higher salaries will also increase benefits by
$2,000 to $5,000. Table 9.5 shows adjustments to EBITDA for SDI.

Total adjustments for salary and benefits range from $42,000 to $85,000,
averaging $63,500. The projected EBITDA for 2014 is $345,600. The adjusted
EBITDA for 2014 ranges from $303,600 to $260,600, with the expected
EBITDA at $282,100. SDI currently does not use debt and does not plan to
include long-term debt in its capital structure. For SDI, free cash flows to firm
(FCFF) and free cash flows to equity (FCFE) are the same. We will use the term
free cash flows in this example for simplicity. To estimate free cash flows we
also need return on assets. SDI expects return on assets to be 40 percent for the
next two years, 30 percent for the following two years, and 20 percent afterward.

Table 9.5 Standing Desk Inc. (SDI) Adjustments to EBITDA

	Average	Low estimate	High estimate
Current management salary	$100,000		
Market level management salary	$160,000	$140,000	$180,000
Increase in management salary	$60,000	$40,000	$80,000
Increase in associated benefits	$3,500	$2,000	$5,000
Total adjustments to EBITDA	$63,500	$42,000	$85,000
Projected EBITDA for 2014	$345,600		
	Expected	Best case	Worst case
Adjusted EBITDA projections for 2014	$282,100	$303,600	$260,600

Table 9.6 contains projections for free cash flows during the transition years. This is Step 1 of the non-constant discounted cash flows model.

In 2015, EBITDA is expected to reach $409,045 based on 2014 EBITDA and a 45 percent growth rate ($282,100 × 1.45). With a 35 percent average tax rate, the after-tax cash flows from operations is $265,879 ($409,045 × 0.65). The reinvestment rate in 2015 is 112.5 percent (0.45/0.40). In other words, in 2015, SDI is still actively investing for the growth of the firm, and additional capital from owners is needed. Reinvestments total $299,114 for 2015 ($265,879 × 1.125). Free cash flow to SDI in 2015 is −$33,235 ($265,879 − $299,114). The company is expected to start generating positive free cash flows in 2017.

Step 2 is to estimate long-term stable growth rate. For SDI, we decide to use the long-term industry average growth rate of 3 percent. In Step 3, we estimate the stable growth value using the constant growth discounted cash flow model from the last section. The long-term return on assets is 20 percent, resulting in a long-term reinvestment rate of 15 percent (0.03/0.2). Unlike the Dimmons Fuel example, the long-term reinvestment rate is different from prior years so

Table 9.6 Standing Desk Inc. (SDI) Free Cash Flows Forecast During Transition Years

	2015	2016	2017	2018	2019
Projected EBITDA growth rate	45%	45%	25%	20%	15%
Projected adjusted EBITDA	$409,045	$593,115	$741,394	$889,673	$1,023,124
Average tax rate	35%	35%	35%	35%	35%
After-tax cash flows from operations	$265,879	$385,525	$481,906	$578,287	$665,030
Return on assets (ROA)	40%	40%	30%	30%	20%
Reinvestment rate	112.50%	112.50%	83.33%	66.67%	75.00%
Reinvestments	$299,114	$433,716	$401,588	$385,525	$498,773
Free cash flows	−$33,235	−$48,191	$80,318	$192,762	$166,258

Unlevered beta	1.03
Estimated market return	11.5%
Risk-free rate	2.5%
Financial risk premium	0%
Unsystematic risk adjustment factor	2.1108
Liquidity premium	5%

Unlevered cost of equity: $r_{Equity} = r_{Risk-Free} + beta_{Equity} \times (r_{Market} - r_{Risk-Free})$
$$= 2.5\% + 1.03 \times (11.5\% - 2.5\%) = 11.77\%$$

Unsystematic risk premium $\quad$ = beta x unsystematic risk adjustment factor x $(r_M - r_F)$
$$= 2.1108 \times (11.5\% - 2.5\%) = 19.57\%$$

Total cost of equity $\quad\quad\quad\quad = r_{Unlevered\ Cost\ of\ Equity}$ + financial risk premium +
liquidity premium + unsystematic risk premium
$$= 11.77\% + 0\% + 5\% + 19.57\% = 36.34\%$$

Figure 9.1 Standing Desk Inc. (SDI) Cost of Equity Estimation

we have to estimate free cash flows in 2020 instead of extrapolating free cash flows from 2019 using the 3 percent long-term growth rate. The projected adjusted EBITDA in 2020 is $1,053,818 ($1,023,124 × 1.03 = the EBITDA in 2019 × (1 + Long-term growth rate)) and the after-tax cash flows from operations is $684,982 ($1,053,818 × 0.65). Long-term reinvestments are $102,747 ($684,982 × 0.15), and free cash flow in the first year after the transition period is estimated to be $582,235 ($684,982 − $102,747). To compute the stable growth value, we also need the cost of equity. Figure 9.1 and Table 9.7 show the calculation of cost of equity using the methods described in Chapter 8.

Table 9.7 Standing Desk Inc. (SDI) Estimated 2019 Value Using the Constant Growth Discounted Cash Flows Model

	Estimated value	Data source or calculations
Projected long-term stable EBITDA growth rate	3%	Industry long-term growth rate
Projected adjusted EBITDA in 2020	$1,053,818	= 2019 projected EBITDA × 1.03
Average tax rate	35%	From IRS
After-tax cash flows from operations in 2020	$684,982	= $1,053,818 × (1 − 0.35)
Return on assets (ROA)	20%	Assumption by analyst
Reinvestment rate	15%	= 0.03/0.20
Reinvestments in 2020	$102,747	= $684,982 × 0.15
Free cash flows in 2020	$582,235	= $684,982 − $102,747
Cost of equity	36.34%	From Table 9.7
Stable growth DCF value in 2019[1]	$1,746,356	= $582,235/(0.3634 − 0.03)

[1] We do not multiply $582,234 by 1.03 because this value is already free cash flows in 2020.

Since SDI does not use any debt in its capital structure, its financial risk premium is zero. From Appendix 8.1, the unlevered beta for the furniture industry is 1.03 and the unsystematic risk adjustment factor is 2.1108. We assume the market return to be 11.5 percent, the risk-free rate to be 2.5 percent and the liquidity premium to be 5 percent. The cost of equity for SDI is estimated to be 36.34 percent. Since this discount rate already includes a liquidity premium, we do not need to adjust the final value by an illiquidity discount. Table 9.8 presents the calculation of the estimated value for SDI in 2019 using the constant growth discounted cash flows model. Since we use estimated free cash flows from 2020, we use this version of the model:

Equity value$_0$ (Present value FCFE) = FCFE$_1$/(Cost of equity − growth rate)

The estimated enterprise stable growth value in 2019 is

$1,746,356 ($582,235/(0.3634 − 0.03)) = $1,746,356.

The last step is to compute the present value of all estimated future free cash flows, including the estimated future stable growth value. For SDI, free cash flows are estimated to be −$33,235, −$48,191, $80,318, $192,762 in 2015 through 2018.[3] In 2019, free cash flow is $166,258 and estimated future stable growth value is $1,746,356, totaling $1,912,614 in that year. We use cost of equity as the discount rate. Table 9.9 shows present value calculation using the present value formula from Chapter 8.

The value of SDI according to the non-constant growth discounted cash flows model is $443,162. Notice that the future stable growth value is a major

Table 9.8 Standing Desk Inc. (SDI) Non-Constant Growth Discounted Cash Flow Valuation

Year	2015	2016	2017	2018	2019
Free cash flows[1]	−$33,235	−$48,191	$80,318	$192,762	$1,912,614
Present value of free cash flows	−$24,377	−$25,925	$31,692	$55,786	$405,986
Calculations of present value of free cash flows	= −33235/ 1.3634^1	= 25926/ 1.3634^2	= 31693/ 1.3634^3	= 55791/ 1.3634^4	= 1912614/ 1.3634^5
Total present value of all free cash flows	$443,162				

Cash flows for 2015–2018 are from Table 9.6. Cash flow for 2019 = $166,258 + $1,746,356 (Cash flow for 2019 + Stable growth value).

portion of SDI's value today. This is common when valuing firms with high initial growth.

Enterprise and equity values estimated using discounted cash flows model are called intrinsic values because they are based on expected future cash flows and the discount rates used take into account risks specific to the firm and the entrepreneur. The next section considers valuation models that are based on relative market values of other firms. These models are used primarily by appraisers and by financial analysts as a robustness check for estimates from discounted cash flow models.

Multiples Valuation Methods

Multiples methods rely on current market values of comparable firms to estimate the value of a target firm. Choosing appropriate comparable firms is very important and can sometimes be challenging, especially for niche or innovative business. Comparable firms should be in the same industry and market segment, and have similar operating characteristics and ownership structure. Competitors in the same market are not always comparable firms. For example, when valuing a grocery delivery service, a large grocery chain that also provides delivery service is not a comparable firm even though it is a direct competitor. A limo company actually has more similar operating characteristics to a grocery delivery service, but they are in different industries and markets. Ownership structure affects market value because privately held firms have higher liquidity premium, and concentrated ownership often leads to a higher unsystematic risk premium. In this example, comparable firms are other small privately held grocery delivery services operating in cities with similar demographics.

Once these firms are identified, the next step is to obtain their multiples. A valuation multiple is a ratio of market value to a financial variable. For publicly traded firms, their stock prices are their market equity values. For private firms, market values are revealed when the businesses are sold. We will use the terms market value (MV) and price (P) interchangeably. For firms that use debt, equity values are affected by their capital structure. Enterprise market value or market value of invested capital reflects total firm value and is computed as market equity value + market debt value − cash. Cash is subtracted because it is not actively invested.

Another way to define enterprise market value is by looking at the asset side of the balance sheet. From this perspective, enterprise value is the sum of fixed assets and goodwill. Small business transactions are usually asset sales, not stock sales, and the transaction values represent enterprise market values. Multiples based on enterprise value are more useful than multiples based on equity value because they are not affected by the capital structure of the underlying firms. When using multiples based on equity values, the comparable firms must have a similar capital structure to the

Table 9.9 Computing Multiples Using Comparable Firms

	Shop4You	Stocked Fridge	Store on Wheels
Revenues	$395,000	$754,000	$620,000
Costs of revenue	323,900	640,900	496,000
EBITDA	71,100	113,100	124,000
Adjustments to EBITDA	−20,000	−14,500	18,900
Adjusted EBITDA	$51,100	$98,600	$142,900
Transaction date	5/15/2013	1/8/2013	10/25/2014
Market value	$765,000	$1,750,000	$2,280,000
MV-to-EBITDA ratio	14.97	17.75	15.96
Average MV-to-EBITDA ratio	16.23		

target firm, in addition to matching industry, market, operating, and ownership characteristics.

The denominator of a multiple is a financial variable, such as revenues, before-tax operating income (EBIT and EBITDA) or free cash flows. Common multiples include MV-to-EBITDA ratio, MV-to-free cash flows ratio and MV-to-sales ratio. Some industries may have multiples specific to their unique operating characteristics. The basic valuation principle is the same. The estimated value is the product of the multiple and the target firm's corresponding financial variable. For example, using the MV-to-EBITDA ratio,

Estimated value = MV-to-EBITDA ratio × Target firm's adjusted EBITDA

If detailed financial data of comparable firms are available, we can compute the multiples directly. Start with a financial variable that is a common benchmark for the industry, e.g. EBITDA, and make necessary adjustments, as described in the income adjustment section. The multiple is the market value divided by the financial variable, and the average is computed using all comparable firms. Table 9.10 shows an example of three comparable firms in the grocery delivery business, using EBITDA as the financial variable. The MV-to-EBITDA ratio for the first firm, Shop4You, is 14.97 ($765,000/$51,100). The average MV-to-EBITDA ratio is 16.23 ((14.97 + 17.75 + 15.96)/3). We can now use 16.23 as the MV-to-EBITDA multiple to estimate values for other small grocery delivery businesses. There are a few things to keep in mind when using this multiple. The transaction dates range from January 2013 to October 2014. If market conditions have changed significantly, the market value from January 2013 will be stale. There are only three firms in the comparable universe, which may not be representative of the overall market.

If financial data of comparable firms are not available, industry averages can be used as proxies. Investment banks, business data providers and industry associations publish industry analysis and aggregate financial data, including valuation multiples. Unfortunately, data from these sources can be expensive and many do not disclose how they compute the multiples. The biggest drawback of industry aggregate is that it may include many firms that are not comparable.

We will continue to use Dimmons Fuel to illustrate how to use the multiples methods. The first method is the EBITDA multiples method. The enterprise MV-to-EBITDA multiple for integrated oil and gas companies is estimated to be 6.53.[4] The adjusted EBITDA for Dimmons from Table 9.2 is $284,500. The firm's value according to the EBITDA multiple model is $1,857,785 ($284,500 × 6.53). Since Dimmons is a private company and the MV-to-EBITDA is based on publicly traded companies, we will apply an illiquidity discount of 30 percent. The final estimated value is $1,300,450 ($1,857,785 × 0.7). This estimate is likely to be high because unsystematic risk premium is not accounted for. The second method is based on annual gallons sold. This financial variable is unique to the propane and heating oil distribution industry, but is commonly used by business brokers and appraisers. According to the owner of Koehler, the multiple per annual gallons sold is $0.70. Dimmons sold 1,260,700 gallons last year. The value of Dimmons based on annual gallons sold is $882,490 (1,260,700 × $0.70). Since this multiple is based on comparable firms, no additional adjustment is needed.

The advantage of the multiples method is ease of calculation. The disadvantages include difficulty in controlling for differences in financial leverage, discretionary expenses, finding comparable firms, and inability to detect whether an entire market is over- or under-valued. Multiples valuation method is most commonly used by appraisal professionals and business brokers who have access to recent transaction values of private business sales and financial data of individual firms.

Some Final Words on Valuation

Business valuation is often more an art than a science. This chapter covers the techniques for calculating values based on quantitative data. Non-financial data can have an important impact on the final transaction value. Experience of the entrepreneur, special personal circumstances, and unique local market conditions should all be incorporated. Koehler Propane was the successful bidder for Dimmons. They offered a combination of cash and promissory notes totaling $650,000. Koehler was the lowest price bidder but won over the other competitors. One of them wanted to expand into this territory and their offer included a requirement for the owner of Dimmons to stay on the business for five years to build the program. Another bidder also offered a higher total price, but the terms were 50 percent cash and 50 percent in their stocks. Koehler knew Dimmons' motives for selling, which enabled him to win over other bidders at a lower price.

Case 9.1 Information Technology Experts of Maryland: What Price to Sell?

Susan White and Karen Hallows

The situation at the firm could not continue the way it was, and William Peace,[5] Chief Executive Officer of Information Technology Experts, Inc. of Maryland ITE), was considering his options. Founded ten years earlier by John Swenson, ITE provided an extensive menu of information technology services to its clients, including networking services, systems integration, custom back-up solutions, system administrator training, help desk setup and support, data security services, web design and hosting, building corporate intranets, data mining, and warehousing.

Five years ago, William and his business partner, Carl Boatwright, met John at a paint ball tournament. John's business was floundering, and William and Carl were ready for a new venture after the recent successful sale of their firm, Musicmedia.com. John brought William and Carl in as equal partners in ITE, a limited liability partnership (LLC), with William agreeing to turn the company around within a year to keep his share of the firm. William was the unofficial CEO for three years, becoming official CEO in 2012. Carl was the firm's chief technology officer, and John was the "rain-maker," bringing in new clients.

Shortly after he became a partner, William embarked on a program of acquisition of small information technology consulting firms, which increased the firm's revenues and client base significantly. Under William's leadership, revenues had increased by 27 percent per year over the preceding three years, growing from about $1.36 million to $2.79 million by 2013. About $1 million of the firm's $2.8 million in sales were contracted revenues, where the client had signed a formal contract outlining the term of service, the services to be provided, and the hourly rate. The remaining revenues came from clients without formal contracts, although many of these clients had been with the firm for years.

The acquisitions also increased the firm's debt, which created additional tension among the partners, who had been hard pressed to agree with one another for most of their mutual relationship. Carl refused to put up any personal capital or loan collateral, but was fine with John and William's receiving a one-time payment from the firm for providing all of the collateral requested by the bank. John's family home, valued at close to $1,000,000 at the peak of the housing boom in 2006 when the acquisition strategy began, served as his collateral, which made his wife increasingly unhappy since it had been in her family for generations. William put up financial assets as loan collateral.

William felt that the firm dynamics changed for the worse after ITE took on debt. He was frustrated because John became increasingly conservative—he was unwilling to make any decisions that would put his home at further risk.

"This is hampering the growth of the firm," William said. "We can't move forward or even successfully incorporate our new acquisitions without capital." After a frustrating two years, William was considering selling his one-third share of the company and exiting the business himself, or finding a buyer for the entire firm. Or, if the price was right, William thought he might buy out John and run the company the way he wanted with Carl's help.

"With the right financing and the right acquisitions, under ideal circumstances, ITE could achieve $6 million in sales in five years, and $14 million in 10 years, with a target 20 percent growth rate," William said. He realized that this was an ambitious goal, given that the industry was only growing at 2.4 percent. He estimated that ongoing capital expenditures would average 15–20 percent of sales to support this level of growth. William said that while some of the income statement and balance sheet accounts varied in recent years, he thought it was a fair approximation to use averages of the accounts as a percent of sales over the past three years. Overall, he thought that the past statements were reflective of the future. With an expectation of internal growth only and no additional acquisitions, ITE's capital needs were low. Growth would be much more modest, with sales growing at the rate of inflation and low maintenance capital expenditure equaling low depreciation expenses. William estimated that an appropriate cost of capital based on ITE's asset and financing risk level compared with similar firms was 17.75 percent.

William had found statistics about small companies that were in the same line of business as ITE. See Table 9.11 for comparable transaction information and Table 9.12 for selected ITE financial information. Now he had to find a way to set an asking price for ITE so he could decide whether to put the firm on the market, get himself out from under the frustrating burden of partnership, or buy out John's share of the firm.

Table 9.10 Recent Transactions in the Information Technology Services Industry (Source, Pratt's Stats)

Sales	*MVIC to net income*	*MVIC to sales*	*MVIC to gross profit*	*MVIC to EBIT*	*MVIC to book value of invested capital*
Under $1,000,000	4.974	6.009	6.493	29.943	16.437
$1,000,000–$5,000,000	2.700	4.023	11.423	10.721	37.419
$5,000,001–$20,000,000	4.080	3.301	6.017	138.583	5.131
$20,000,001–$50,000,000	1.790	0.490	1.343	7.395	1.073
$50,000,001–$100,000,000	Not available	1.982	6.778	22.460	11.841
Over $100,000,000	Not available	0.643	2.190	6.420	3.403
All companies	3.818	3.999	7.332	37.314	18.609

MVIC, market value of invested capital.

Table 9.11 ITE Financial Statement Information

Income Statement Information	2011	2012	2013
Total revenue	1,358,013	2,185,370	2,789,920
Cost of goods sold	322,862	379,726	591,497
Direct costs	226,525	439,816	685,430
Gross profit	808,626	1,365,828	1,512,993
Indirect costs	591,723	840,130	1,313,781
Operating income	216,903	525,698	199,212
Other expenses	54,606	62,220	137,779
Other income	10,750	3,792	736
Net income	173,047	467,270	62,169
Balance sheet information	*2011*	*2012*	*2013*
Assets			
Current assets	392,443	681,510	387,963
Computers, furniture, vehicles	91,502	137,613	151,604
Depreciation: computers, furniture, vehicles	(38,811)	(59,020)	(87,420)
Leasehold equipment	—	2,575	14,690
Goodwill on acquisitions	70,000	1,610,614	1,560,953
Other assets	3,668	1,711	1,205
Total assets	518,802	2,375,003	2,028,995
Liabilities			
Current liabilities	73,589	215,465	83,786
Bank loans	20,604	542,349	517,705
Partner loans	—	14,651	114,569
Non-owner notes	—	183,729	684,140
Total liabilities	94,193	956,195	1,400,201
Equity	424,610	1,418,809	628,794
Total liabilities and equity	518,802	2,375,003	2,028,995

Depreciation is part of indirect non-labor costs and was $159,752 in 2013.

Case Questions

1. If William were to sell either his share or find a buyer for the firm, how much would this be worth?
2. About $1,000,000 of revenues were from clients with formal contracts. How might this impact your valuation of ITE?

Case 9.2 Valuing REACH Health Inc.

Simon Medcalfe, William Hamilton, and David Hess

REACH Health, Inc. needed cash and David Hess (Chair of the Board and Founder) and Bill Hamilton (Chief Operating Officer and Founder) were going to raise funds from a venture capital firm. But what was the value of the company? If they under-valued their company they would leave funds on the table, if they overvalued the company they might not find investors.

Bill and David visited their accountant, Stephen Brown, in July 2008 to find out what REACH might be worth.

"There are many ways to value a company" said Stephen. "The two most popular are the discounted cash flow method and the multiples method. I will calculate both for you, but first I will need some information about REACH."

Bill responded, "Certainly Stephen. As you recall, REACH Health, Inc. was founded in early 2006 to provide telemedicine to rural Georgia. Telemedicine is the use of medical information exchanged from one site to another via electronic communications to improve a patient's clinical health status. From 2006 to 2008, we were able to sustain the company from current revenues and the initial small investment. However, in the fall of 2007, in the face of financial difficulties, we made a major corporate decision not take an angel investment of $250,000 and grow the company organically. But, as we feared, the cash flows proved inadequate to sustain and grow the company."

David continued, "At this point, we feel that it is time to consider a private equity investment in the company. We have been approached by a group that is willing to make a $2 million investment in the company. Before we bring this before the board of directors, we would like to have a firm valuation of REACH. This will help us make the most informed decision on how much of the company we are willing to distribute to the new investors, while minimizing the dilution of the current shareholders."

"Do you have a copy of your projected cash flows?" asked Stephen. Bill passed over a copy of the five-year projected cash flows (Table 9.13).

"Thanks," said Stephen. "I will use these and your financial statements to work up a valuation. I will assume that cash flows after 2013 will grow at 2 percent, the long run rate of inflation. I will also have to calculate the discount rate using the Black–Green build-up summation method. For the multiples method, I will need to find some companies that are similar to REACH that are publically traded and have financial statements available. Finally, I will also have to look into the marketability discount, since your firm's shares are not going to be publically traded. Let me do some research and I will call you in a week or so with an update."

Table 9.12 REACH Call, Inc. Financial Statements
a Projected Cash Flows

	2009	2010	2011	2012	2013
Gross sales	3,704,000	8,917,000	16,850,000	26,102,000	36,214,000
Cost of goods sold	842,000	1,857,000	2,560,000	3,631,000	4,357,000
Gross profit	2,862,000	7,060,000	14,290,000	22,471,000	31,857,000
Operating expenses	4,042,000	6,623,000	9,616,000	13,446,000	17,714,000
Operating income	(1,180,000)	437,000	4,674,000	9,025,000	14,143,000
Income tax	0	0	0	0	0
Net income	(1,180,000)	437,000	4,674,000	9,025,000	14,143,000
Provision for income taxes	(445,283)	164,906	1,763,774	3,405,660	5,336,981
Adjusted net income	(734,717)	272,094	2,910,226	5,619,340	8,806,019
Adjustments to calculate the cash flow to equity					
Depreciation and amortization	60,000	120,000	160,000	200,000	220,000
Decrease/(increase) in working capital needs	(321,000)	(823,000)	(819,000)	(1,314,000)	(1,255,000)
Capital expenditures	(240,000)	(240,000)	(240,000)	(240,000)	(240,000)
Cash flow to equity	(1,235,717)	(670,906)	2,011,226	4,265,340	7,531,019

b Income Statements, (2006–2008 (Annualized))

Revenue	2006	2007	2008 (annualized)
Gross sales	260,080	895,097	1,678,384
Cost of goods sold	104,924	217,264	405,398
Gross profit (loss)	155,156	677,833	1,272,986
Expenses			
Advertising	5,374	24,617	62,688
Bad debts	263	296	219
Bank charges			
Board expenses	0	861	1,135
Charitable contributions			
Commissions			
Contract labor			
Co-location fees	2,833	8,500	6,324
Depreciation and amortization	20,126	7,748	0
Dues and subscriptions	0	200	0
Employee benefit programs			
Entertainment and meals	21,488	32,361	18,245
Insurance	7,341	32,652	44,555
Interest	43	0	0
Internet	649	2,486	6,171
Legal and professional fees	11,130	59,387	16,129
Licenses and fees	11,272	28,964	1,122

Table 9.12 REACH Call, Inc. Financial Statements (Continued)

b Income Statements, (2006–2008 (Annualized))

Revenue	2006	2007	2008 (annualized)
Miscellaneous	(6,557)	5,287	1,050
Office expense			
Payroll taxes	11,581	24,010	36,639
Postage	366	552	484
Professional development	0	1,940	11,178
Public relations	0	0	32,462
Rent	0	1,400	6,057
Repairs and maintenance			
Software	0	8,054	0
Software consultants	92,607	90,736	162,804
Supplies	4,311	4,991	5,412
Telephone	1,453	3,427	6,751
Travel			
Utilities			
Vehicle expenses			
Wages	133,667	323,041	457,981
Total expenses	*317,947*	*661,510*	*877,406*
Net operating income	(162,791)	16,323	395,580
Other income			
Gain (loss) on sale of assets			
Interest income	0	174	491
Other income	50,000	50,000	0
Total other income	50,000	50,174	491
Income before tax	(112,791)	66,497	396,071
Income tax expense	0	593	0
Net income (loss)	(112,791)	65,904	396,071

c Balance Sheet

Assets	2006	2007	As of July 21, 2008
Current assets			
Cash	10,647	60,072	264,688
Investments	—	—	—
Inventories	—	—	—
Accounts receivable	—	—	—
Pre-paid expenses	—	—	—
Other	—	—	—
Total current assets	10,647	60,072	264,688

(Continued)

Table 9.12 REACH Call, Inc. Financial Statements (Continued)

c *Balance Sheet*

Assets	2006	2007	As of July 21, 2008
Fixed assets			
Property and equipment	20,126	27,673	27,993
Leasehold improvements	—	—	—
Equity and other investments	—	—	—
Less accumulated depreciation	(20,126)	(27,673)	(27,673)
Total fixed assets	—	—	320
Other assets:			
Intangible assets, net	5,800	5,600	5,600
Total other assets	5,800	5,600	5,600
Total assets	16,447	65,672	270,608
Liabilities and owners' equity			
Current liabilities			
Accounts payable	—	—	—
Accrued wages	—	—	—
Accrued compensation	—	—	—
Accrued expenses	22,826	5,751	(12,595)
Income taxes payable	—	—	—
Unearned revenue	—	—	—
Other (credit cards payable)	412	—	—
Total current liabilities	23,238	5,751	(12,595)
Long-term liabilities			
Mortgage payable	—	—	—
Total long-term liabilities	—	—	—
Owners' equity			
Common stock	106,000	106,000	110,085
Retained earnings	(112,791)	(46,079)	173,118
Total owners' equity	(6,791)	59,921	283,203
Total liabilities and owners' equity	16,447	65,672	270,608

One week later

The phone in Bill's office rang.

"Hi Bill, it's Stephen Brown. I have an update on your valuation. For the discount rate, the current yield on 20 year Treasury bonds is 4.69 percent, so I will use that as the risk-free rate. Morningstar estimates that the current equity risk premium is 7.10 percent and the micro-capitalization equity size premium for capitalizations below $505 million is 3.65 percent. I think your company-specific risk premium is 12 percent, based on my subjective analysis of various internal and external factors affecting the company, such as management ability and industry conditions. Moreover, a summary of academic peer-reviewed

Table 9.13 Comparable Firms to REACH

	Virtual Radiological	*NightHawk Radiology*
Sales	93,280,000	166,752,000
EBITDA	17,576,000	24,824,000
Market value of invested capital (MVIC)	255,014,704	386,698,137

journals suggests that the marketability discount is 30 percent. Finally, I have also found two other firms that are in web-based telemedicine and have no other significant lines of business. I think they would be good comparable firms to REACH. I have sent you an email with some of their pertinent financials" (Table 9.14).

"Why don't you and David come to my office tomorrow morning at 9am and I will tell you what your company is worth" said Stephen.

Bill and David were excited. What was the value of their company?

Case Questions

1. Calculate the discount rate using the Black–Green build-up summation method.
2. Calculate the value of REACH Health, Inc. using the discounted cash flow method.
3. Calculate the value of REACH Health, Inc. using the multiples method.
4. What is the value of REACH Health, Inc.?

Notes

1 EBITDA is earnings before interests, taxes, depreciation and amortization. (See Chapter 4 for a review of financial statements and accounting terms.)
2 Financial data for Dimmons Fuel are drawn from Lam & Luther (2012).
3 From Table 9.7.
4 Value multiples by sector (http://pages.stern.nyu.edu/~adamodar/).
5 The names of the owners and of the company have been changed to protect the privacy of the principals.

Bibliography

Babbage, C. (1864). *Passages From the Life of a Philosopher*, London: Longman, Green, Longman, Roberts, & Green.

Damodaran, A. Data: current. *Damodaran Online* http://pages.stern.nyu.edu/~adamodar/ (accessed 11/8/2014).

Damodaran, A. (2006) *Damodaran on Valuation*, 2nd edition, Hoboken, NJ: Wiley.

Ibbotson, R., Chen, Z., Kim, D., & Hu, W. (2013). Liquidity as an investment style. *Financial Analyst Journal, 69*(3), 1–15.

Jennings, R. (2012, April 13). Office furniture mfg. (US based). *Henry Fund Research*. Iowa City, IA: The University of Iowa School of Management.

Lam, M. & Luther, R. (2012). The offer price. *The CASE Journal, 8*(2), 75–89.

Ransome, J. P., & Satchit, V. (2009, July 1). Valuation discounts for estate and gift taxes. *Journal of Accountancy* http://www.journalofaccountancy.com/Issues/2009/Jul/20091463.htm (accessed 10/21/2014).

Sanchez, Mark. (2014, September 14). Updated forecast tempers outlook for office furniture industry. *MiBiz* http://mibiz.com/item/21819-updated-forecast-tempers-outlook-for-office-furniture-industry (accessed 10/31/2014).

United States Department of Commerce Bureau of Economic Analysis. *US Economic Accounts* www.bea.gov (accessed 11/2/2014).

United States Department of Labor. *Bureau of Labor Statistics* www.bls.gov (accessed 11/2/2014).

Module 6
Exit Strategies

10 Exit and Harvest

> Not everything that can be counted counts, and not everything that counts
> can be counted.
> William Bruce Cameron

Creating a popular product or service is the dream of entrepreneurs. Ironically, success brings changes that sometimes lead to an entrepreneur's deciding to leave the business, often to start something new again. Entrepreneurs are creators, founders, makers. Markus Persson, founder of Mojang and creator of the popular game Minecraft, wrote a letter to fans after the sale of the company to Microsoft for $2.5 billion. Persson, known as Notch to his fans, is candid about his reasons for the sale.

> [I] started to realize I didn't have the connection to my fans I thought I had. I've become a symbol. I don't want to be a symbol, responsible for something huge that I don't understand, that I don't want to work on, that keeps coming back to me. […] I'm aware this goes against a lot of what I've said in public. I have no good response to that. I'm also aware a lot of you were using me as a symbol of some perceived struggle. I'm not. I'm a person, and I'm right there struggling with you.
>
> I love you. All of you. Thank you for turning Minecraft into what it has become, but there are too many of you, and I can't be responsible for something this big. In one sense, it belongs to Microsoft now. In a much bigger sense, it's belonged to all of you for a long time, and that will never change.
>
> It's not about the money. It's about my sanity.
>
> (Persson, 2014)

Needing substantial capital to take a business to the next stage is another reason to seek external equity. Finally, changes in an entrepreneur's personal life may necessitate diversifying her wealth to beyond her company. Exit and harvest strategies include going public and private sale of the business. The most important question for the entrepreneur is how much of the business she is selling in the transaction. The first section in this chapter explains pre- and post-money valuation. The next section covers financing rounds and deal terms, followed by going public and succession planning.

Pre-Money and Post-Money Valuation

The first step in exit, harvest and succession planning is to estimate the value of the business. If an entrepreneur is selling the entire company, the valuation techniques discussed in Chapter 9 will suffice. For partial sale and when raising equity from venture capitalists and angel investors, it is important to distinguish between pre-money and post-money valuation. The central issue is the amount of control and share of future earnings an entrepreneur must give up in exchange for the cash she receives today.

When entrepreneurs sell part of their businesses to fund growth the amount of new cash is not negotiable because raising less than the required amount will prevent the company from achieving its next milestone. The key item to be negotiated is the number of shares or percentage of ownership provided to the new investors. Once the percentage of ownership is agreed upon, the number of shares needed can be computed as:

$$\text{Number of new shares} = \frac{\text{Percentage post-money ownership} \times \text{Existing number of shares}}{\left(1 - \text{Percentage post-money ownership}\right)}$$

The market value of the firm per share is:

$$\text{Market value per share} = \frac{\text{New cash raised}}{\text{Number of new shares}}$$

Post-money valuation is the value of the company after the sale of new shares. It includes both the entrepreneur's stake and cash from new investors:

$$\text{Post-money valuation} = \text{Market value per share} \times \text{Total number of shares after transaction}$$
$$\text{Pre-money valuation} = \text{Post-money valuation} - \text{New cash raised}$$

We will use Standing Desk Inc. (SDI) as an example to illustrate pre- and post-money valuation. Table 10.1 shows the pre-money ownership structure, called the capitalization (caps) table, of SDI. The company currently has 50,000 shares outstanding. Janet Stuart, founder of the company, owns 40,000 shares (80 percent). Stephen Jones, head of development, was given 10,000 shares (20 percent) when he joined the company and contributed "sweat equity" during the company's embryonic stage. SDI has developed three prototypes, which receive very positive feedback from focus groups.

The company is ready to start manufacturing on a commercial scale and needs $750,000 to start up production. They are in negotiation with a venture capital firm, Golden Beech Associates (GBA), who want 60 percent ownership in the investment. Box 10.1 and Table 10.2 shows the post-money and pre-money calculations and the new ownership structure.

Table 10.1 Standing Desk Inc. (SDI) Pre-Money Ownership Structure (Capitalization Table)

Stockholders	Date of issue	Number of shares	Percentage ownership
Janet Stuart	1/1/2015	40,000	80%
Stephen Jones	3/1/2015	10,000	20%
Total		50,000	100%

10.1 Standing Desk Inc. (SDI) Pre-Money and Post-Money Valuation and Ownership Structure (Golden Beech Associates' First Offer Requesting 60 Percent Ownership)

- Current number of shares outstanding: 50,000
- Amount of new cash needed: $750,000
- Golden Beech Associates (GBA) requests 60 percent ownership post-money
- Number of new shares for GBA = $(0.6 \times 50,000)/(1 - 0.6) = 75,000$ shares
- Market value per share = $750,000/75,000 = $10 per share
- Total number of shares post-money = 50,000 + 75,000 = 125,000
- Post-money valuation = $10 × 125,000 = $1,250,000
- Pre-money valuation = $1,250,000 − $750,000 = $500,000.

Table 10.2 Standing Desk Inc. (SDI) Post-Money Capitalization Table (Golden Beech Associates' First Offer Requesting 60 Percent Ownership)

Stockholders	Date of issue	Number of shares	Percentage ownership
Janet Stuart	1/1/2015	40,000	32.00%
Stephen Jones	3/1/2015	10,000	8.00%
Golden Beech Associates (GBA)	To be determined	75,000	60.00%
Total		125,000	100.00%

If GBA get 60 percent ownership after the transaction, they will have 75,000 shares of new stock. The market value for SDI will be $10 per share ($750,000/75,000 shares). The company will have 125,000 shares outstanding (50,000 + 75,000), and the post-money valuation will be $1,250,000 ($10 × 125,000 shares). The pre-money valuation will be $500,000 ($1,250,000 − $750,000). GBA will become the majority shareholder with 75,000 shares (60 percent). Janet still owns 40,000 shares, which now only represents 32 percent ownership. Stephen's 10,000 shares translate into 8 percent ownership. As stated earlier, SDI needs $750,000, so that amount is not up for negotiation. If Janet and Stephen are able to negotiate with GBA to lower the number of new shares from 75,000 to 50,000, they will give up a smaller percentage of the firm and increase both SDI's pre-money and post-money valuation. Box 10.2 and Table 10.3 show the calculation if they can negotiate with GBA to accept 50 percent ownership (50,000 shares) for $750,000.

By negotiating down the number of shares or percentage of ownership to the outside investor, an entrepreneur increases both the post-money and

---

10.2 Standing Desk Inc. (SDI) Pre-Money and Post-Money Valuation and Ownership Structure (Negotiate Down to 50 Percent Ownership)

- Current number of shares outstanding: 50,000
- Amount of new cash needed: $750,000
- Golden Beech Associates (GBA) accepts 50 percent ownership post-money
- Number of new shares for GBA = (0.5 × 50,000)/(1 − 0.5) = 50,000 shares
- Market value per share = $750,000/50,000 = $15 per share
- Total number of shares post-money = 50,000 + 50,000 = 100,000
- Post-money valuation = $15 × 100,000 = $1,500,000
- Pre-money valuation = $1,500,000 − $750,000 = $750,000.

Table 10.3 Standing Desk Inc. (SDI) Post-Money Capitalization Table (Negotiate Down to 50 Percent Ownership)

Stockholders	Date of issue	Number of shares	Percentage ownership
Janet Stuart	1/1/2015	40,000	40.00%
Stephen Jones	3/1/2015	10,000	10.00%
Golden Beech Associates (GBA)	To be determined	50,000	50.00%
Total		100,000	100.00%

pre-money valuation of her firm. In the case of SDI, the post-money valuation increases from $1,250,000 to $1,500,000 and the pre-money valuation increases from $500,000 to $750,000. Notice that the increase in value, $250,000, is retained entirely by the original owners.

It is important to know what and how you can negotiate before you approach outside investors. If the entrepreneur of an established company wants to exit the business completely, the best option is to find a business broker who specializes in the industry and can identify strategic buyers. Strategic buyers are either competitors or companies in a related industry who are interested in entering the market, acquiring proprietary technology, or gaining economies of scale. Strategic buyers are often willing to pay a premium price for these options. Conversely, financial buyers are primarily interested in earning returns on their investment and not in managing the company. While some strategic buyers are interested in keeping the current management team, financial buyers almost always require founders to stay on with the company. Financial buyers are great for entrepreneurs who are seeking external capital for growth. Private equity firms, angel investors, and venture capital firms are examples of financial buyers. Chapter 3 discusses different sources of capital and their characteristics. Angel investors are typical early investors, followed by venture capitalists. Private equity firms tend to prefer established companies, and some specialize in turning around distressed companies. This chapter focuses on negotiating deals when raising funds from these sources, particularly angel investors and venture capitalists. Negotiations are often challenging for entrepreneurs of startups because of the high degree of uncertainty. The next section discusses strategies used by entrepreneurs and outside investors when constructing deals.

Financing Rounds and Deal Terms

The first hurdle in seeking funding with angel investors and venture capitalists is understanding their lingo. Here are some headlines:

> NatureBox unwraps a $2M *seed round* [emphasis added] for healthy snack delivery
>
> (Carney, 2012)

> bus and train ticket aggregator Wanderu raises $5.6M *series A* [emphasis added]
>
> (Perez, 2014)

A seed round is the first time that significant capital is raised for a business. It includes money from friends, family and angel investors. Funds from the seed round are usually earmarked for turning a concept into a real business, including expanding the management team and setting and achieving concrete milestones in preparation for the next round of financing. A series A round is usually the first round of funding from venture capital firms. These firms operate more like institutions compared with the personal relationship that angel investors often have with entrepreneurs. Subsequent rounds are labeled series B, series C, etc.

Each time an entrepreneur raises funds from an outside investor is called a "round" of investment. Labeling the rounds is important because each round is associated with a new market value for the business. Early investors share the gain with the entrepreneur if the market value increases in the next round. If the market value decreases in the next round, called a down round, early investors will be concerned that their ownership could be diluted. They may put in a stipulation in the deal to protect their interests in the event of a down round. Entrepreneurs may be able to negotiate a better deal at the current round by agreeing to such stipulations. Details such as these are listed on the term sheet during negotiations. The National Venture Capital Association provides a set of legal document templates related to financing, including a term sheet, on their website.[1] Term sheets are complex legally binding documents, and you should have a qualified attorney review them before committing to a deal.

The minimum information on a typical term sheet includes the amount of the investment, the percentage ownership calculation, and anti-dilution provisions. Anti-dilution provisions are also called "ratchet provisions." We will use the example of SDI to illustrate the possible consequences of an up round, a down round without anti-dilution, and a down round with anti-dilution. Recall that GBA had invested $750,000 for 50 percent equity ownership in SDI, valuing it at $15 per share ($1,500,000 in total) during the seed round. Now the company has reached its next stage of development and will need an additional $2,000,000 to start manufacturing, distributing, and marketing its products. They identify a venture capital firm, Peartree Partners, that is interested in funding SDI in a series A round.

An Up Round

Box 10.3 and Table 10.4 show an up round scenario in which Peartree Partners requests 50 percent ownership for the $2,000,000 investment, implying that they value SDI at $4,000,000 ($2,000,000/0.5) after the series A round financing. Peartree Partners will receive 100,000 new shares. The new market value per share for SDI is $20, $5 higher than the value at seed round.

Since this is an up round, both the original entrepreneurs and GBA gain. The new total number of shares, as shown in Table 10.4 is 200,000, and the post series A round valuation is $4,000,000. The equity value of GBA is

10.3 Standing Desk Inc. (SDI) Series A Round (Up Round Scenario)

- Shares owned by original entrepreneurs: 50,000
- Shares currently owned by GBA: 50,000
- Total existing shares = 50,000 + 50,000 = 100,000
- Amount of new cash needed: $2,000,000
- Peartree Partners requests 50 percent ownership post series A round financing
- Number of new shares for Peartree Partners = $(0.5 \times 100,000)/(1 - 0.5)$ = 100,000
- Market value per share at series A round = $2,000,000/100,000 = $20 per share
- Total number of shares after series A round = 50,000 + 50,000 + 100,000 = 200,000
- Post series A round valuation = $20 × 200,000 = $4,000,000.

$1,000,000 (0.25 × $4,000,000), a gain of $250,000 over their original investment of $750,000. It is not surprising that when things go well all parties are happy. Now let us look at the scenario of a down round.

A Down Round

The amount of cash needed remains at $2,000,000 but in this scenario Peartree Partners requests two-thirds ownership (66.67 percent) of the firm. This implies that Peartree values SDI at $3,000,000 ($2,000,000/0.6667) after the series A round financing. Box 10.4 and Table 10.5 show the calculations for this down round scenario, assuming that GBA did not include any anti-dilution provision in the seed round.

To achieve two-thirds ownership (66.67 percent), Peartree Partners will be issued 200,000 new shares. The new market value at this round is $10 per

Table 10.4 Standing Desk Inc. (SDI) Post Series A Round Capitalization Table (Up Round Scenario)

	Date of issue	Number of shares	Percentage ownership
Janet Stuart	1/1/2015	40,000	20.00%
Stephen Jones	3/1/2015	10,000	5.00%
Golden Beech Associates (GBA)	6/1/2015	50,000	25.00%
Peartree Partners	To be determined	100,000	50.00%
Total		200,000	100.00%

10.4 Standing Desk Inc. (SDI) Series A Round (Down Round Scenario With No Anti-Dilution Provision)

- Shares owned by original entrepreneurs: 50,000
- Shares currently owned by GBA: 50,000
- Total existing shares = 50,000 + 50,000 = 100,000
- Amount of new cash needed: $2,000,000
- Peartree Partners requests 2/3 ownership (66.67 percent) post series A round financing
- Number of new shares for Peartree Partners = 0.6667 × 100,000 / (1 − 0.6667) = 200,000
- Market value per share at series A round = $2,000,000/200,000 = $10 per share
- Total number of shares after series A round = 50,000 + 50,000 + 200,000 = 300,000
- Post series A round valuation = $10 × 300,000 = $3,000,000.

Table 10.5 Standing Desk Inc. (SDI) Post Series A Round Capitalization Table (Down Round With No Anti-Dilution Provision)

	Date of issue	Number of shares	Percentage ownership
Janet Stuart	1/1/2015	40,000	13.33%
Stephen Jones	3/1/2015	10,000	3.33%
Golden Beech Associates (GBA)	6/1/2015	50,000	16.67%
Peartree Partners	To be determined	200,000	66.67%
Total		300,000	100.00%

share ($2,000,000/200,000). The new total number of shares is 300,000 and GBA's ownership decreases to 16.67 percent. The new equity value of GBA is $500,000 (0.1667 × $3,000,000), a loss of $250,000 from its original investment of $750,000. Janet and Stephen, the entrepreneurs, experience the same amount of loss because the ownership structure after the seed round was 50/50. Together they lost $500,000 in equity value. When there is no anti-dilution provision, the original entrepreneurs and existing investors share the loss proportionally.

Remember that in the original negotiation, GBA had wanted more ownership percentage for their $750,000 investment. Anti-dilution provision is often used in negotiation to get better terms in early rounds. Assume that Janet and Stephen agree to a full anti-dilution provision with no minimum price in order to get GBA to accept 50 percent equity at the seed round. Anti-dilution provision has no impact in an up round but shifts losses to entrepreneurs in a down round by issuing addition shares to existing investors.

Box 10.5 and Table 10.6 show the same down round scenario with full anti-dilution provision. Peartree Partners is still providing $2,000,000 for

---

10.5 Standing Desk Inc. (SDI) Series A Round (Down Round Scenario With Anti-Dilution Provision and No Minimum Price)

- Shares owned by original entrepreneurs (Jane and Stephen): 50,000
- Shares currently owned by GBA: 50,000
- Amount of new cash needed: $2,000,000
- Peartree Partners requests 2/3 ownership (66.67 percent) post series A round financing
- Post series A round valuation = $3,000,000
- Post series A round equity for Peartree Partners = $2,000,000
- Post series A round equity for GBA with full anti-dilution provision = $750,000
- Post series A round equity for Janet and Stephen = $3,000,000 – $2,000,000 – $750,000 = $250,000
- Diluted market value per share at series A round = $250,000/ 50,000 = $5 per share
- Number of shares issued to new investor, Peartree Partners = $2,000,000/$5 = 400,000 shares
- Number of total shares for GBA = $750,000/$5 = 150,000
- Number of new shares issued to GBA = 150,000 – 50,000 = 100,000
- Total number of shares after series A round = 50,000 + 50,000 + 100,000 + 400,000 = 600,000.

Table 10.6 Standing Desk Inc. (SDI) Post Series A Round Capitalization Table (Down Round with Anti-Dilution Provision and No Minimum Price)

	Date of issue	Number of shares	Percentage ownership
Janet Stuart	1/1/2015	40,000	6.67%
Stephen Jones	3/1/2015	10,000	1.67%
	6/1/2015	50,000	8.33%
Golden Beech Associates (GBA)	To be determined	100,000	16.67%
Peartree Partners	To be determined	400,000	66.67%
Total		600,000	100.00%

66.67 percent ownership in the firm and the new market value at series A round remains $3,000,000. However, the anti-dilution provision from the seed round is triggered in a down round, and additional new shares will be issued to GBA along with new shares to Peartree Partners. Since the provision is for full anti-dilution, GBA will receive sufficient new shares so that its new equity position in the firm will remain $750,000, no loss from its original investment. The entrepreneurs will bear all the decrease in value in this case because there is no minimum floor price. The residual equity value to the entrepreneurs is $250,000 ($3,000,000 − $2,000,000 − $750,000), resulting in a diluted price of $5 per share ($250,000/50,000 shares). To maintain its 66.67 percent ownership, Peartree Partners requires 400,000 shares for its investment ($2,000,000/$5).

Notice the dramatic decrease in ownership percentages of the entrepreneurs. The post series A round valuation is $3,000,000, the same as without the anti-dilution. This is because the market value of the entire firm depends on its expected future cash flows. The anti-dilution provision only affects how the firm is divided up among existing investors and entrepreneurs, not the aggregate value of the firm. Since GBA is promised $750,000 in equity under the provision, they should have 150,000 shares ($750,000/$5) after the series A round, implying that 100,000 new shares will be issued to them. With the additional shares, GBA owns 25 percent of the firm with $750,000 in equity and no loss from its original investment. The new combined equity value of Janet and Stephen is $250,000 ($5 × 50,000 shares), a loss of $500,000 from their seed round equity of $750,000. Tables 10.5 and 10.6 represent two extreme scenarios; no anti-dilution, where losses are shared equally between entrepreneurs and existing investors, and a full anti-dilution provision, where losses are born only by entrepreneurs. In many negotiations, a minimum price is included in the anti-dilution provision so that existing investors share some of the losses, though not proportionally.

Box 10.6 and Table 10.7 show the scenario when GBA agrees to a minimum floor price of $8 per share. With this minimum floor price, any decrease in market value up to $8 will be shouldered entirely by the entrepreneurs, but an additional drop in value beyond $8 will be shared by the existing investor, GBA.

The post series A round valuation remains at $3,000,000. Since the fully diluted price would be $5, which is less than the minimum floor price of $8, GBA will bear part of the loss. This is reflected in the total number of shares owned by GBA. Based on GBA's original investment of $750,000, they are entitled to a maximum of 93,750 shares ($750,000/$8) given the minimum floor price of $8. They currently own 50,000 shares so 43,750 new shares will be issued to them at the same time as shares are issued to Peartree Partners. The amount of new cash needed remains $2,000,000 and Peartree Partners still want 66.67 percent of the business for their investment. This now translates into 287,500 shares to Peartree Partners, resulting in a new market value

10.6 Standing Desk Inc. (SDI) Series A Round (Down Round Scenario With Anti-Dilution Provision and Minimum Price)

- Shares owned by original entrepreneurs (Jane and Stephen): 50,000
- Shares currently owned by GBA: 50,000
- Amount of new cash needed: $2,000,000
- Peartree Partners requests 2/3 ownership (66.67 percent) post series A round financing
- Post series A round valuation = $3,000,000
- Minimum floor price to GBA = $8
- Maximum total shares to GBA = $750,000/$8 = 93,750
- New shares to GBA = 93,750 − 50,000 = 43,750
- Shares of existing shareholders including new shares to GBA = 50,000 + 50,000 + 43,750 = 143,750
- Number of shares issued to new investor, Peartree Partners = (0.6667 × 143,750)/(1 − 0.6667) = 287,500 shares
- New market value per share at series A round with minimum price = $2,000,000/287,500 = $6.96 per share
- Total number of shares after series A round = 50,000 + 93,750 + 287,500 = 431,250.

of $6.96 per share ($2,000,000/287,500). Notice that the percentage ownership of Janet and Stephen does not drop as much in this scenario. The new equity value of GBA is $652,500 ($6.96 × 93,750 shares), a loss of $97,500 from their original investment of $750,000. The new equity value of Janet and Stephen combined is $348,000, a loss of $402,000 from their old equity of $750,000. The combined loss is, of course, still approximately $500,000.

The three scenarios in Tables 10.5, 10.6, and 10.7 demonstrate how provisions in the term sheet affect ownership structure and potential gains and losses during a down round. There are a few important reminders. Post round

Table 10.7 Standing Desk Inc. (SDI) Post Series A Round Capitalization Table (Down Round with Anti-Dilution Provision and $8 Minimum Price to GBA)

	Date of issue	Number of shares	Percentage ownership
Janet Stuart	1/1/2015	40,000	9.28%
Stephen Jones	3/1/2015	10,000	2.32%
	6/1/2015	50,000	11.59%
Golden Beech Associates (GBA)	To be determined	43,750	10.15%
Peartree Partners	To be determined	287,500	66.67%
Total		431,250	100.00%

market value is determined by the new investor, who provides the new cash needed and specifies the percentage of the firm required. In our example, Peartree Partners invests $2,000,000 for two-thirds (66.67 percent) ownership of the firm in all three down round scenarios, establishing the market value of $3,000,000 ($2,000,000/0.6667). Provisions from the previous round affect how gains or losses are shared between entrepreneurs and existing investors through additional new shares. The example in Tables 10.7 demonstrates how a minimum floor price prevents entrepreneurs from shouldering all the losses. Be cautious if the deal involves convertible debt or convertible preferred stocks. The convertible features have characteristics similar to anti-dilution provisions in a down round. Always work out the worst- and best-case scenarios, assuming that all convertible features and provisions are triggered so that you will not be surprised by the outcome. When working with venture capitalists and lawyers during negotiation, entrepreneurs should keep in mind the big picture, which is the percentage ownership they are giving up under all possible provisions.

The term sheet includes other important clauses. Pre-emptive rights allow entrepreneurs and existing investors first right of refusal when new shares are issued. There should be a detailed description of how dissolution or liquidation will be handled and how remaining cash will be distributed should the company fail. Some deals have a "go along" provision that requires all stockholders to sell their shares or take the firm public if the board of directors and majority shareholders agree to the sale or to going public. Raising money from venture capital firms can be stressful but is often necessary for the company to reach its next stage. Venture capital firms also require seats on the board and many will only invest if they can become majority shareholders. Many VC firms invest in companies with intent to take them public, the topic of the next section. Before seeking funds from VC firms, entrepreneurs must consider carefully how important independence and control are to them.

Going Public

When a company sells its shares to the public for the first time, it undertakes its initial public offering (IPO). This is a giant step for a company. Once the company becomes public, its stocks will be listed on stock exchanges, such as NASDAQ and the New York Stock Exchange, and the company will be subject to public financial reporting requirements and regulated by the Securities and Exchange Commission (SEC). Venture capital firms often play a key role, both in providing funds to take the company to the stage ready for IPO and in mentoring entrepreneurs through the process. VC partners sit on the board of directors, which must approve the decision to go public. VC firms have experience in working and negotiating with investment banking firms that will act as underwriters. The process of going public is time consuming and stressful. This section will focus on the advantages and disadvantages of being a public company and some reasons for going public.

The advantages of being a public company include easy access to capital markets to raise money for future growth, liquidity for outstanding shares, lower cost of capital, and increased prestige and visibility. The cost of capital will decrease because of reduced illiquidity premium and unsystematic risk premium. Increased prestige and visibility may also help sales and employee recruitment. Entrepreneurs can diversify their wealth without selling the entire company. The disadvantages include compliance with SEC regulations and pressure by financial analysts. SEC regulations require quarterly and annual filing of audited financial statements. In addition, the regulation on fair disclosure requires that if a company shares material information with non-insiders, it must disclose that information to the public. Under the insider trading rule, it is illegal for public company officers and directors and other insiders to profit from trading based on insider information. These insiders must file stock transactions related to the company with the SEC. The intent of these SEC regulations is information disclosure and equal access for all investors. Navigating these rules is not easy, and the penalties can be severe. One well-known insider trading case relates to Martha Stewart, famous TV host, designer, and entrepreneur, who served a five-month prison sentence for her violations. In addition to complying with SEC regulations, the pressure on management to meet earnings estimates by financial analysts is strong. Increased visibility also puts entrepreneurs in the spotlight, and their personal lives may come under public scrutiny.[2]

10.7 Advantages and Disadvantages of Being a Public Company

Advantages of Being a Public Company

- Access to capital for future growth
- Increased liquidity for shareholders
- Lower cost of capital
- Diversification opportunity for entrepreneurs
- Increased prestige and visibility.

Disadvantages of Being a Public Company

- SEC regulations on financial reporting and public disclosure
- Scrutiny by financial analysts
- Pressure to meet investor and analyst expectation
- Increased public scrutiny
- Distraction from running the company.

The decision to go public should be considered before seeking VC funding. According to the National Venture Capital Association, VC firms typically realize returns on their investment when the companies they invest in go public or are merged or purchased by another company. Once you accept VC funding, the focus becomes growing the company and preparing for the IPO or acquisition over the next five to ten years. Although the optimal time for going public is when the advantages outweigh the disadvantages of being a public company, the decision of eventually becoming a public company is often made when an entrepreneur seeks VC funding. Some good reasons for wanting to be a public company include an entrepreneur's desire for a large company and a business model that operates on economies of scale. Becoming a public company is particularly important if an entrepreneur plans a growth strategy based on mergers and acquisitions. Shares of public companies are liquid with established market value and are viewed much more favorably than private equity when used to acquire another company. Conversely, if you want your company to stay personal, going public or selling to a financial investor is not a good option. The next section discusses succession planning so entrepreneurs can keep their business in the family.

Succession Planning in Family-Owned Businesses

Another means of exit and harvest that is dedicated to family-owned businesses entails succession planning. Succession planning in general describes a means of assuring that the right people are on hand to fill positions as they open. However, succession planning in a family business ensures, by concentrating on succession at the top, that the business will continue whether or not the founder is at the helm.

Family-owned businesses face unique challenges when it comes to long-term sustainability. The biggest challenge has to do with acceptance of mortality on the part of the founder and the founder's children. Giving up responsibility for running the business can be a traumatic process for the founder, who has worked hard to conceptualize, launch, run the business through the early days, and enjoy its successes after years of effort. The pain of letting go can be mitigated in part, however, if the entrepreneur makes plans for sustaining the business before a major transition is necessary.

Items to Include in Succession Planning

We have already discussed some of the elements involved in relinquishing partial control over the business to outside investors. These issues are relevant in relinquishing control in a family business as well. The additional items to consider in a family-owned business are:

- Which of the children (if there are more than one) will take the reins?
- How can all the children benefit fairly?

- What will the financial impact be in estate-planning terms?
- How can the founder feel confident of his or her ongoing legacy?

Who Should Take Over?

Succession is one of the most challenging of activities undertaken by the small business owner or the management of a larger business. The selection of one's successor is difficult not only because of the self-examination that is required, but also because there are likely to be multiple internal contenders for the position as well as external potential candidates. Determining the relevant parameters and establishing a rubric for the "ideal" candidate demands focus, clarity of goals, and a trusting environment. The exercise in Appendix 10.1 provides the opportunity to practice the process of selecting a successor in preparation for future internal change process.

Fair and Equal Are Not Always the Same

Consider that your parents have built a successful business over time. You have been working summers in that business since you were 15 years old, and you intend to work full-time alongside your folks upon graduation. In fact, your parents are counting on your help and participation. Your older brother is a cop and is on the fast track to becoming a detective. Your younger sister is planning a career in music, as a violinist for an orchestra. She takes advanced lessons year-round and shows particular skills in music. The bottom line is that you are the only one of the three children who has any interest in the business.

If your parents were to treat you all equally, you would each have an equal share in the business for the future. But is that fair? Both your siblings have career interests far from the business world, while you are studying business in college, working in the business continuously, and will be there for your parents upon your graduation.

What would be the fair way for your parents to make sure that all their children are taken care of, that each of you has a share in the proceeds of their life work? This is the puzzle that business owners are faced with when thinking about their children and the future.

Estate Planning and Financial Impact

In the USA, failing a formal will, upon the death of the business owner, the estate is handled differently depending on the state in which the business exists. If the business is a sole proprietorship (with or without rights of survivorship), the business and its assets may have to go through the process of probate before ownership can be formalized. As you can imagine, this sometimes lengthy legal process can take a tremendous toll on the viability of the business during the time of transition. Therefore, a will is essential to protect the sustainability of the business.

Some of the issues involved in estate planning include wealth transfer from company to family, from one generation to the next and subsequent generations, funding retirement, organizing personal and marital assets for future needs, and the distribution of property after death. The general goals of such a plan are to determine how the stock and assets of the business will be owned, how they will be managed, and how to minimize taxes and legal concerns.

Factors that complicate these decisions are family and non-family partnerships, and other shareholders, such as external investors or board members. Estate and gift taxes can be onerous, and the heirs need financial liquidity to pay these taxes. In addition, the day-to-day management of the business must be covered, along with the executive leadership that will keep the business on its strategic trajectory.

Some of these challenges can be addressed through gifts, trusts, the establishment of family partnerships, stock redemption plans, selling part of the company, establishing an employee stock ownership plan, launching an IPO, obtaining additional third-party investors, or selling non-voting stock.

There are no easy answers to the conundrum of estate planning, but there are many options to consider. This is an area where it is best to seek out a specialized advisor to help address the key issues by identifying three things:

- The family's priorities
- The owner's needs for retirement
- What is best for the company.

Assuring Your Legacy

Assuring your legacy for the future requires establishing a set of shared values today. Shared values transcend generational differences and provide the foundation for a permanent organizational mission. Shared values endure over time and provide guidance for action, no matter who sits in the leader's chair. Shared values help the organization make decisions and adapt to change by providing a solid foundation for behavior.

Waiting until retirement to formalize core values is a major error that can cost you a lifetime's effort. As you begin your business, even as early as the pre-conception discussions, you need to commit to a set of value statements, such as a corporate creed, a mission statement, a vision statement, human resource policies, customer service policies, and similar items, that will serve as a roadmap for your organizational behavior. As your business grows, celebrate activities that underline these values and make them part of your organizational story.

In this way, your business can become as associated with your core values as is Walmart with low cost, Ben & Jerry with environmental sustainability, Apple with innovation, or Nordstrom with customer service.

Contemplating how you will exit the company you founded is not easy but the payoff is well worth the effort. Just as writing your own obituary is a popular assignment given by life coaches to help individuals figure out how they want to live their lives, evaluating different exit strategies helps entrepreneurs set the course for their businesses. Do you want to build an empire? Do you want to keep pushing the next innovation frontier? Do you want to leave a legacy? Do you want to become a celebrity? Or are you happier tinkering in the workshop or experimenting in the kitchen?

Appendix 10.1 Exercise for Selecting a Successor[3]

The purpose of this exercise is to provide practice in determining organizational succession.

Instructions:

1. Read the story, *CLEANCO at the Crossroads*.
2. Using the "successor qualities" worksheet, fill it out for the six names listed above the columns. You will have to make some assumptions based on the brief descriptions of the players in the CLEANCO story.
3. Using the personal qualities in column A of the worksheet, weight them from 1 to 20 in terms of importance for the selection of a successor.
4. Using the totals at the bottom of the form, select the "best" candidate for Marge's job. Then, take into account the preferred weighting of each personal quality in column A and determine if there is any change in the final outcome.
5. These weightings may be discussed with the entire class or with your own study group.

CLEANCO at the Crossroads

You are Marge Owens, owner of CLEANCO, a manufacturer of heavy-duty soap and industrial cleaning supplies. CLEANCO was founded 37 years ago by you and your husband, and currently employs 300 workers at two sites, half a mile apart. Site A (the older location) has 200 employees and Site B (opened four years ago) has 100 employees. Your husband died three years ago (one year after opening Site B) and you, at the age of 72, are ready to retire. "Hand over the reins, let someone else have the worries and the work—it's Florida for me," you are fond of saying. After a lifetime of putting the customer first, it is finally your turn.

You have been handling the marketing, sales, customer service, and product development areas since the beginning. Your husband, Henry, had handled finance and administration. When Henry died, your son-in-law, Dan (41 years old) took over those responsibilities. He had 12 years' experience as an accounting manager at Procter & Gamble, and earned his MBA while working there. His current title at CLEANCO is Vice President—Finance.

Steve, the Operations Manager, has been with the company for nine years, and currently has two assistants reporting to him. These assistants started at CLEANCO as line workers, and are the latest in a series of laborers that Steve has taken under his wing. At present, each one monitors operations at one of the facilities. Although he is not a relative, Steve has been like a son to you, especially since Henry's death.

You have three children. Your son, Jack, is 43 years old. He is a math teacher at a local high school. He worked at CLEANCO in the factory throughout high school and college, but decided to pursue teaching over joining the family business. He is married to Sharon, also a teacher. They live, with their two children, in a small house in the Valley. Your older daughter, Betty (Dan's wife), is 41 years old. She has an MBA and is the Director of Data Processing at a Fortune 1000 company. Your youngest, Eleanor, is 36 years old and also has an MBA. She is currently Vice President—Administration. Eleanor has been with CLEANCO for 11 years and works 25 hours per week in order to be at home as much as possible with her three children under the age of 10. She devotes many hours each week to working with underprivileged youth and high school dropouts in a literacy program. Her husband Arthur (43 years old) is a jeweler with a successful business in a nearby upscale town.

Retirement is more and more on your mind, but who should be the successor? Who can handle the responsibility? The diverse activities? The time required to do the job? You want the business to continue to thrive, at least because it currently supports two of your children and your own household. You have earned a rest and you don't want to have to spend the next dozen years managing a transition team.

Successor Qualities Worksheet

Complete Table 10.8. On a scale of 1 (lowest) to 5 (highest), rate each candidate for successor on the following qualities. Then total each column to rank the candidates. Some of the qualities may be more important than others to you; circle those qualities and weight them more heavily in the final comparison. The maximum possible score is 100 on the 5-point scale.

Table 10.8 Successor Qualities Worksheet

	Personal quality	Dan	Steve	Jack	Betty	Eleanor	Arthur
1	Knowledge of the business (or ability to learn)						
2	Honesty						
3	Ability						
4	Energy and alertness						
5	Enthusiasm						
6	Good health						
7	Degree of perseverance						
8	Stability and maturity						
9	Aggressiveness						
10	Thoroughness and respect for detail						
11	Problem-solving ability						
12	Resourcefulness, creativity						
13	Ability to plan and organize						
14	Talent for developing others						

(*Continued*)

Table 10.8 Successor Qualities Worksheet (Continued)

	Personal quality	Dan	Steve	Jack	Betty	Eleanor	Arthur
15	Personality of a starter and a finisher						
16	Consonance with the owner's philosophy						
17	Commitment						
18	Desire, passion						
19	Ability to inspire others						
20	General willingness to learn						
Total							

Case 10.1 Harvesting Tom Seely Furniture: An Owner's Decisions

Caroline Glackin

Tom Seely had a life-changing decision facing him. Should he sell his company to 29-year old Gat Caperton? If so, what did he want out of the transaction? At 75 years of age, Seely was active and in no hurry to retire from the business that he had built for 40 years. Although he was considering selling, he did not actually have the business listed for sale. His step-daughter and step-grandson were not going to take over the business, and he was not ready to stop working entirely.

Seely started out as an antiques dealer in the Eastern Panhandle of West Virginia, specializing in Early American furniture, and ended up creating and growing a well-respected furniture manufacturing company with 130 employees. During the intervening 40 years, much had changed. As Seely's antiques business grew, he began to broaden his distribution beyond the local area. This meant traveling far and wide to find and sell products. Ultimately, he recognized that he could not meet the market demand for his Early American antiques and saw an opportunity. Seely began small-scale creation of antique reproductions, hand-crafted from solid wood, primarily from the Appalachian Mountains. As demand grew, so did Tom Seely Furniture. He made a comfortable living for himself and his family, as well providing employment for local people.

One day Seely was told that Gat Caperton was on the telephone. He took the call, thinking that the caller was the West Virginia Governor. To his surprise, it was the governor's son, calling at the elder Caperton's suggestion. Governor Caperton had toured Tom Seely Furniture, knew that his son wanted to acquire a small manufacturing firm, and remembered that Seely used West Virginia goods. At the time, young Caperton was working in mergers and acquisitions for Sam Zell and completing his MBA in Chicago.

Caperton scheduled a factory tour and at the conclusion of the visit asked whether selling Tom Seely Furniture appealed to Seely. Seely was interested, but he was clear that he would not sell to just anyone. It was critical that the business stay in the local community and be operated in a manner that he preferred. Caperton agreed.

Seely shared his financial information with the prospective buyer and asked for an offer. Caperton recognized that the company's growing sales, numerous customers, and differentiated product had merit. Plus, he identified an opportunity to apply lean manufacturing methods and strengthen Tom Seely Furniture's profits. Caperton offered to pay approximately six times EBTIDA, which equaled the company's book value. He invested 5 percent of his own money, 5 percent from outside investors, and brought in 10 percent of the purchase price from a bank loan. The bank loan was secured by the assets of the company. Seely had to take back a promissory note secured with the stock of the company and subordinated to the bank loan for the remaining 80 percent of the price. The note from Caperton was for 5 years at 6 percent interest with 1/3 balloon payments at the end of years 3, 4 and 5.

Seely had devoted most of his adult life to the business and was concerned both about the employees and about maintaining his own lifestyle. He wanted to continue working for the company and agreed with Caperton to add a five-year employment contract with decreasing responsibilities. He also required paid health insurance, someone taking out his trash weekly, and other life-style accommodations. Caperton promised to relocate from Chicago to the community and run the company in a way that would "make Tom proud."

Case Questions

1. Was the offer fair? How do you know?
2. What was the debt-to-equity ratio? How does that compare with the industry?
3. What non-monetary aspects were significant for Seely? Why?
4. What factors, if any, did Seely need to know and understand with respect to Gat Caperton? Why?
5. What, if any, other factors should Seely have considered?
6. Would you have agreed to the deal? Why or why not? If not, what would you accept?

Case 10.2 Exit Strategy: The Sale of Hotmail

Richard H. Borgman

Sabeer Bhatia, along with his partner Jack Smith, had founded a firm they called JavaSoft in January 1996. Less than two years later, in December 1997, Bhatia was about to become very wealthy. His shares in the young firm they started, now called Hotmail, were worth over $113 million. This payoff from the developme nt of their idea—free web-based email—was the culmi-nation of a rapid period of growth funded by venture capital (VC) investments and helped along in other ways by these venture capitalists.

Young rapidly growing firms often received financing from VC firms—professionally managed private equity firms that specialized in financing young firms. This was a risky endeavor—most young firms did not "make it." Only a few became very successful. Thus venture capital firms diversified and invested in a number of firms—usually 10 to 15 in any fund. The funds were financed by equity investments by so-called "sophisticated" investors, essentially wealthy individuals or moderately large institutions.

VC firms made finite-life investments. That is, they invested with an expectation of exiting their investments within five to ten years. A highly desired exit was a successful IPO (initial public offering). At the IPO, shares in the firm became available to the general public and the VC investors sold their shares, almost always at a significant gain. The original venture capital investors in Apple paid 9 cents a share; they did very well when Apple went public at $22 a little less than two years later. But that was not the only successful exit. A sale to another firm could also be a very lucrative outcome. When Facebook bought WhatsApp in 2014 for $19 billion, the early investors in WhatsApp made a great return.

The original idea for JavaSoft was a product that allowed users to manipulate sophisticated databases over the web. Later the firm developed the idea of free web-based email. The firm was a pioneer in the free product–advertising revenue model so popular on the Internet.

When the firm was started, the two founders owned 4 million shares each. Another 2,490,272 shares were set aside for an employee pool. Typically for a young technology firm, compensation to employees was primarily by equity shares and stock options.

The first stage (VC investments typically were made in stages) of venture capital investing occurred on February 9, 1996. A valuation of a firm was implied by the investment and number of shares received. In this case, the VC firm Draper Fisher Jurvetson (DFJ) offered $300,000 for 30% of the firm, implying a firm valuation of $1 million. But investors from Asia were offering an implied $2.5 million valuation. DFJ counter-offered a $2 million valuation ($300,000 for 1,867,704 shares), which was ultimately accepted. DFJ was preferred because of the expertise they could add. Note that DFJ included an interesting provision: the father of one of the founders had to invest $15,000 at the same valuation. As was typical, DFJ received preferred stock. The founders were left with 32 percent of the firm each.

In the spring of 1996 the firm's name was changed to HoTMaiL (after the HTML programming code); a bit later it was changed to Hotmail. The free email product went live in the summer of 1997.

The second stage of VC investments occurred in August 1996. DFJ invested an additional $750,000 for an implied firm valuation of $7.5 million. The third stage of VC investing occurred in October 1996. Another VC firm, Menlo Investors, invested $1.5 million. Although the firm valuation continued to increase, there was still no significant revenue and certainly no profits. But Hotmail needed money to add employees, launch products, and build infrastructure.

Finally, the fourth stage occurred in early 1997. Together, Menlo Investors and DFJ invested another $3 million at $1.25 per share. At this point there were 10,490,272 common and 3,426,607 preferred shares outstanding (total 13,916,879 shares). At $1.25 per share, the firm was valued at $17.4 million.

On December 31, 1997, just less than two years after the firm was founded, Hotmail was sold to Microsoft for an estimated $395 million. Microsoft was

Table 10.9 Venture Capital Financing and Exit: Hotmail

Round	Date	Investment	Per share	Implied firm value
Stage 1	February 1996	$315,000	16 cents	$2 million
Stage 2	August 1996	$750,000	52.2 cents	$7.5 million
Stage 3	October 1996	$1,500,000	$1.00	$15.4 million
Stage 4	March 1997	$3,000,000	$1.25	$17.4 million
Exit	December 1997		$28.38	$395 million

countering a move from Yahoo the previous October. Yahoo had bought Four 11 Corporation, which owned Hotmail's biggest competitor RocketMail, for $95–100 million. Hotmail still did not have any profits, but it did have 9.5 million subscribers and was the 14th most visited site on the web at the time. It also was outperforming the market leader, AOL, in speed and dependability. Bhatia, who had served as president and CEO of Hotmail, had successfully guided his young firm's investors to a very successful exit (see Table 10.9 for a summation of the investment stages for Hotmail).

Case Questions

1. Why do young rapidly growing firms like Hotmail seek funding from VC firms, rather than a bank or from the owners' savings?
2. Why did the founders of JavaSoft accept the original investment from DFJ rather than the investment from the Asian investors that implied a higher firm value?
3. Why might DFJ have included the provision that one of the founder's fathers must also invest $15,000?
4. What is the advantage of funding a young firm like Hotmail in stages rather than all at once?
5. Why did Microsoft buy Hotmail?

Notes

1 For example, see National Venture Capital Association (www.nvca.org) and Y Combinator (www.ycombinator.com).
2 For example, Larcket et al. (2013) have studied the impact of CEO divorce on shareholder value.
3 This exercise has been adapted from Vega (2004).

Bibliography

Cameron, W. B. (1963). *Informal Sociology: A Casual Introduction to Sociological Thinking*. New York, NY: Random House.

Carney, M. (2012, December 11). NatureBox unwraps a $2M seed round for healthy snack delivery. *pandodaily* http://pando.com/2012/12/11/naturebox-unwraps-a-2m-seed-round-for-healthy-snack-delivery/ (accessed 11/16/2014).

Denton, N. (1998, January 2). Microsoft to buy free e-mail provider, *Financial Times*, p. 10.

Holloway, C., & Mukherjee, P. (1999). Hotmail Corporation, Case No E64. Stanford, CA: Graduate School of Business, Stanford University.

Hong, F. (1998, January 1). Microsoft buys Hotmail, free e-mail provider. *San Francisco Examiner*, p. D.15.

Larcker, D., McCall, A., & Tayan, B. (2013, October 1). Separation Anxiety: The Impact of CEO Divorce on Shareholders. *Stanford Closer Look Series – CGRP36*. Stanford, CA: Rock Center for Corporate Governance, Stanford University.

Licken, E. (1997, October 27). Hotmail—land of the free, *Irish Times*, p. 10

Microsoft. (1999, February 8). MSN Hotmail: From zero to 30 million members in 30 months. *Microsoft News Center* http://news.microsoft.com/1999/02/08/msn-hotmail-from-zero-to-30-million-members-in-30-months/ (accessed 03/05/2015).

Montgomery, A. L. (2001). Applying quantitative marketing techniques to the Internet, *Interfaces*, *31*(1), 90–108.

O'Day, M. (2011, July 5). Hotmail still new and cool—even after 15 years. *The Official Microsoft Blog* http://blogs.technet.com/b/microsoft_blog/archive/2011/07/05/hotmail-still-new-and-cool-even-after-15-years.aspx (accessed 03/05/2015).

Perez, S. (2014, November 6) Just in time for the car-less generation, bus and train ticket aggregator Wanderu raises $5.6M series A. *Techcrunch.com* http://techcrunch.com/2014/11/06/just-in-time-for-the-car-less-generation-bus-and-train-ticket-aggregator-wanderu-raises-5-6m-series-a/ (accessed 11/16/2014).

Persson, M. (2014, September 15). I'm leaving Mojang. *notch.net* http://notch.net/2014/09/im-leaving-mojang/ (accessed 11/9/2014).

Roberts, M. J., & Mahesh, S. M. (1999). *Hotmail*. Technical report, Harvard University, Cambridge, MA. Case 899-185, Harvard Business School Publishing.

Shi, G., & McBride, S. (2014, February 19). Facebook to buy WhatsApp for $19 billion. *Reuters* available at http://www.reuters.com/article/2014/02/19/us-whatsapp-facebook-idUSBREA1I26B20140219 (accessed 03/05/2015).

Suster, M. (2011, January 14) What are good examples of good startup term sheets? *Quora* http://www.quora.com/What-are-examples-of-good-startup-term-sheets (accessed 11/20/2014).

Vega, G. (2004). Assessing Successor Qualities. In M. Silberman (Ed.) *2004 Team and Organization Development Sourcebook* (pp. 53–57). New York, NY: McGraw Hill.

Wilson, D. L. (1998, January 1). Microsoft Buys Hotmail, *San Jose Mercury News (California)*.

Wingfield, N. (1998, January 2). Microsoft to buy E-mail startup in stock deal, *Wall Street Journal*.

Module 7

A Winning Approach

11 How to Win Business Plan Competitions

If we are true to plan, our statures touch the skies.

Emily Dickinson

Why Bother with Competitions?

A recent visit to bizplancompetitions.com uncovered the following information, among other valuable hints: On April 3, 2014, there were 110 international business plan competitions with $24,243,254 in prize money available. All 50 US states had competitions scheduled, as did numerous international locations ranging from Ireland to Qatar.

There is a competition for every kind of business interest and prizes or awards at every level. Interested in technology? Raising prize bulls? Providing nanny services? Baking monster cupcakes? There is a competition designed for you. And the money is serious. The top prize awarded at the 2014 Rice Business Plan Competition, the largest of its kind, was $641,600, with an astounding number of other prizes offered at a wide variety of levels, totaling more than $1 million.

Business plans, even for small businesses, can be big business.

Competitions and Judging

Business plan competitions are sponsored by a wide variety of organizations, ranging from state governments through academic institutions. Each competition has a unique focus and its own specific evaluation processes. The more traditional competitions require submission of a full business plan, then proceed through a set of stages designed to eliminate all but the most complete, fundable, and credible plans. Each judging stage becomes increasingly rigorous until only a limited number of plans remain. These finalists then compete head-to-head, often publicly, for the prize, which is awarded by a team of judges selected for their business acumen and general respect within the economic community.

But not all competitions are created equal. Some competitions require creative entries, such as video pitches, for the first cut. This approach puts the more traditional business founder at a disadvantage, but it plays to the strengths of today's young entrepreneurs. Or, the competition may limit submissions to pre-launch ventures, ventures in operation for a specific period of time, businesses that focus on a social mission, or on non-profit undertakings. There are faith-based competitions, competitions designed for students, for women, for various minority groups, for retired people, and for just about any specific group you can imagine.

Many competitions offer an initial workshop to potential participants to clarify requirements and expectations prior to the competition launch. It is always wise to attend such workshops, as you will pick up pointers to make your proposal more appealing. In addition, when these workshops are offered, they are often designed to provide guidance for the initial elimination process, comprising most frequently a concept paper or full description of the proposed business. A limited number of plans is selected to continue further, and only those entrepreneurs are invited to submit a complete business plan.

Judging of the intermediate and final rounds is just as diverse. Juried competitions have judging panels comprised of some combination of business professionals, entrepreneurs, and investors. In some cases, the judges' names are not released to the public or to the competitors, and the names of the entrepreneurs are also redacted in a double blind review process (until the final presentation). Most often, however, the role of judge is a prestigious one and the judges themselves want the publicity that goes along with the role. Voting, based on structured and publicized criteria, is generally a matter of a simple majority of judges' votes, but occasionally there are more inventive methods of determining competition winners.

Online voting has been introduced now that technological advances have made this process straightforward. A credible example of this kind of judging was conducted in 2013 by the Department of Energy. More than 300 college teams submitted business plans for the National Clean Energy competition, which had two first prizes: the money prize for the winner as selected by the panel of judges, and for the winner as selected by the popular vote—"likes" on a Facebook page. The electronic popular vote was monitored carefully to identify the prohibited use of bot or other electronic automatic voting approaches. The contestants went through a staged set of smaller competitions and regional competitions; finally, the last six were invited to Washington, DC to make their formal pitches and be voted on by the judges and the public.

Juried voting is designed to simulate presentation in front of angel investors or venture capitalists and often focuses most specifically on the potential ROI of the plan as determined by the judges. For this reason, good preparation for a business plan competition includes a careful evaluation of who will be judging it.

Elements of a Business Plan

The purpose of this chapter is not to teach you how to write a business plan; there are ample opportunities and resources for you to learn that. This chapter will help you structure your plan and presentation to position yourself to win.[1]

The Executive Summary

Your plan will be designed cafeteria-style: you put on your tray only what you like. But just as a meal comprised primarily of chocolate pudding is not nourishing, neither is a business plan functional if it only reflects operations (or any one element). You need a selection from each of the elements or groups: financials, marketing, management, and operations, especially as your plan will be judged on the whole picture of your business, rather than just one element.

Financials

Although the financials rarely appear as the first section of a business plan, we must acknowledge one truism—if the numbers don't work, the business will fail.

Making the numbers work will have different meanings according to your specific situation. At a minimum, a business plan needs to provide a balance sheet, a break-even analysis, a cash flow statement, and a 3-year income projection. An established firm in business for three or more years may also include a 3-year income statement, copies of tax returns, a profit and loss statement, a history of financial reports, and selected ratios. Other, more specialized reports may be included if they satisfy specialized needs.

Operations

This is the core of your plan. It tells the reader what you do and how you do it. Whether you provide a service, a product, or some combination of the two, this element needs to embody all the passion and excitement you can muster. If you're not a "true believer," you will find it very difficult to interest others.

"Musts" for this section are a full and complete description of the product or service, full product design information, a production plan, and the location both of the facility and of the sales areas. Results of studies of industry trends, information about production systems and goals (for example, quality assurance (QA) indicators), lists of suppliers, and the overall strategy specifying your competitive advantage may also appear.

Marketing

The best product in the world still has to be sold. Your marketing plan can make or break you—research, analysis, and access to markets will protect your product or service while you establish your sales beachhead.

Regardless of the stage of development your business is in, you will want to be sure you include three key sections in your marketing plan—an analysis of the competition, a description of the target market, and a general marketing strategy (the way you intend to position your product). You may include within these sections information about specific promotions, pricing, the rationale for the timing of your market entry, distribution channels, and an indication of your sales areas. Some of you will also want to provide sales forecasts and related budgets, if these do not appear in your financials.

Management

Sometimes this part of the business plan is called the organizational plan, but no matter what you call it, it is the first place investors or funding institutions will look. This is where you must establish your business's credibility if you expect to attract any outside support, debt or equity funding, or entice new talent to join your team.

An overall description of your business, an explanation of your basic management structure, a portrait of key management personnel, an indication of general staffing policies or needs, and an organization chart are critical components of this section. You will want to name the members of your advisory board, to provide additional support for the strength and stability of your management team. For the same reason, you will include other advisors (such as attorney, CPA, consultants, etc.) and their credentials in this section as part of your support organization. Mission and organizational goals and objectives play a prominent role in this section, and should be written in plain English. In fact, avoiding jargon as much as possible will make your plan more attractive to the reader, judges, and potential supporters.

Here is where you describe the organization's legal structure, its administrative procedures, licenses required and obtained, and specific record-keeping processes that add value or differentiate your business from the one next door. A third level of description would relate to international operations, anticipated effects of use of the competition proceeds, or other unique management or administrative issues that need to be disclosed.

Ethics

Traditionally, ethics has not had its own section in business plans, at least not in *initial* plans for businesses. However, many companies recognize that, if they do not formally articulate their ethics, the danger of inadvertent lapses increases. Nearly all industries and professional societies maintain a code of ethics, geared to the specific needs of the group in question. An extensive list of these can be found at the Online Codes of Ethics Project (http://ethics.iit.edu/ecodes/), compiled in 1999 by the Center for the Study of Ethics in the Professions at Illinois Institute of Technology.

Your ethics plan should include a process for performing regular ethical audits as well as a formal code of ethics and, if the nature of your business warrants it, a set of procedures to ensure the ethical conduct of employees at all levels. The US Department of Commerce has established a set of five areas of concern that a business is likely to want to address. These include:

1. Provision of a safe and healthy workplace.
2. Fair employment practices, including avoidance of child and forced labor and avoidance of discrimination based on race, gender, national origin or religious beliefs; and respect for the right of association and the right to organize and bargain collectively.
3. Responsible environmental protection and environmental practices.
4. Compliance with US and local laws promoting good business practices, including laws prohibiting illicit payments and ensuring fair competition.
5. Maintenance, through leadership at all levels, of a corporate culture that respects free expression consistent with legitimate business concerns, and does not condone political coercion in the workplace; that encourages good corporate citizenship and makes a positive contribution to the communities in which the company operates; and where ethical conduct is recognized, valued and exemplified by all employees.

Supporting Documentation

Attach copies of any documents that will enhance the way your company presents itself to others. This consists of personal resumes of key personnel, the owner's financial statement (for a startup), copies of relevant leases, licenses, contracts, letters of reference, pre-production orders, and any credit reports that support your funding application. You may also wish to supply location studies, various financial or operational projections, demographic reports as appropriate, job descriptions, a list of capital assets if it does not appear in your financials, or any other material that will suggest your stability, engender confidence in your future, or provide appropriate disclosure.

The Order of the Plan

All plans contain certain critical elements. These elements play a more or less significant role, according to the specific use of the plan. How you label the sections of your plan is totally irrelevant, as long as you are careful to include the appropriate pieces necessary for a coherent presentation. You should assemble your plan in a way that makes sense to you and that serves your needs, while still being clear and understandable to your reader. An executive summary focusing on the reason you have written the plan will guide the reader through your design. If your purpose is to win a competition, here is where you present your initial "case."

Presenting the Plan

Your plan may be excellent, clear, well thought-out, and skillfully written. However, if you cannot present it credibly, your efforts will be for naught. Each competition has its own set of presentation rules and guidelines; what follows is meant to provide general assistance for two kinds of pitches: the elevator pitch and the funding pitch. For more extensive information about this topic, we recommend downloading Caroline Cummings' e-book, *How to Pitch and Get Funded*. It's worth the read.

The Elevator Pitch

The elevator pitch is shorthand for the amount of information you can convey during a short elevator ride—one to two minutes, tops. It is geared to be concise and engaging, to make you and your business or value proposition appealing and memorable, and to encourage exchange of business cards or the scheduling of an appointment.

Putting together an elevator pitch is not difficult, but it does require the ability to cut straight to the core of your message, avoiding all filler language and padding. There are four components to an elevator pitch: introduction, value proposition, question, and close. Each of these elements needs to convey a sense of urgency and enthusiasm to the listener, resulting in action (such as a question or a comment) on the listener's part. To put together a strong elevator pitch, the following steps may be helpful:

- Make sure you know what you want to convey before you begin to speak. "Hi, how 'ya doing? My name is John" is not a strong opening statement. A much better beginning would be, "Hi, my name is John. I provide a service that may increase your customer retention by a significant amount."
- State your value proposition clearly to spark interest in the listener. "My company has figured out a way to shorten delivery time by 30 percent over Fedex's delivery schedule, getting your product to your customer even faster."
- Ask a question so that the listener commits to the conversation. For example, "How long does it normally take you to ship your product from Chicago to Tampa?"
- Conclude with a strong close. With your business card in your hand, "I'd like to make an appointment to talk about how my company can save you money and time and impress your customers with speedy service."

Most business plan competitions will only use the elevator pitch as a brief introduction to the full business plan presentation or funding pitch, but it always pays to have an elevator pitch at the tip of your tongue for those fortuitous meetings in the lunch line, waiting for your car at the parking garage, at a trade show or convention, or even actually in the elevator.

The Funding Pitch

This is the real deal. You are asking people to give you money for your project. Keep in mind throughout the funding pitch, "People first." Investors give, lend, or make available money to people, not projects. Your first job is to make absolutely certain that YOU are a credible investment. You do this in several ways:

- Look the part. Dress the part. Act the part. If you are seeking big bucks or competing against formidable opponents for a piece of a limited pie, you don't want to lose on simple appearances. This means, unless you are proposing launching a baseball team, no baseball caps. No casual clothes unless they make sense in the context of your business proposal. We are not suggesting the navy blue suit and white shirt combination you learned about in Careers 101, but establishing credibility starts with the visual. Clean, neat, professional attire (remember to polish your shoes) goes a long way toward looking trustworthy and investment-worthy.

- Don't run off at the mouth; keep it short and sweet. There will be plenty of time for you to expand upon your ideas when answering the (often pointed) questions asked by the judging panel. At first pitch, think in terms of sound bites, tweets, pithy and interesting statements. You will sound more confident and present a self-assured picture that engenders trust rather than a dithering, frantic, all-over-the-place picture of a disorganized individual at the helm of a business. Even if you are brilliant, people do not want to get tangled up with disorganization.

- Tell a story that engages the listeners' imagination. Most people would prefer to hear about an experience than a theory, an application than a concept, a practice than a principle. Tell how you came up with your big idea or how the big idea has worked for you or others. Tell your story in an attention-grabbing way. In other words, be interesting!

- Know your facts and your numbers. Commit it all to memory—this is not the time to scrabble through your notes to find a key number or a proposed rollout date. Know your material cold.

- Share the credit with your team. No one will fund the Lone Ranger.

- Be sure you know what you are asking for before you ask. Of course, you are negotiable and interested in hearing proposals from investors. But you need to be confident of your own proposal and able to back it up when asked. And you will be asked… What do you need the money for? How will you use it? What is the payback time frame? How will I get my money out? What are your long-term goals? Where do you see the business in two years? Five years?

Advice from the Experts

Advice about designing winning business plans is ubiquitous. A quick Internet search returned 33 million hits, with advice ranging from brilliant to just plain silly (and obvious). We have compiled some of the most credible advice by speaking to competition judges and winners, and by sifting through the vast web-based collection of suggestions. We have tried very hard not to offer conflicting advice, but it is clear that not all experts are in agreement with one another.

What Consultants Recommend

Tom Leach, Certified Business Counselor at the Maine SBDC and Professor of Marketing at University of New England, has some specific advice to offer pre-business plan competition. Tom has been advising businesses for more than 20 years in Maine, and his experience suggests that startups have their most pressing problems in two areas: identifying their competitive niche and obtaining funding.

The very first step pre-business planning is to perform a complete market analysis. How big is the market and how is it segmented? Why is the market in pain? How is your solution dramatically better than existing alternatives? What is your value proposition? How are you going to sell your product? How will you find customers? Often, new business owners will underestimate the three levels of competition. It is important to remember these three levels:

1. *Direct competition* There is always a whole lot of direct competition for your business. There is always somebody close by who is doing a similar thing.
2. *Indirect competition* If it is difficult to identify the direct competition, it is often easy to determine the indirect competition. For example, a hookah parlor, which seems a unique business, may have indirect competition in the various nightlife alternatives available in every town.
3. *Demands on discretionary money* There is a lot of competition for discretionary funds, so if you are creating a business that depends on discretionary expenditures, your competition will include every sort of amusement there is, from shopping to movies to athletics.

The second step in the pre-plan is to identify sources of funding at levels 1 and 2. Level 1 funding may include seed grants, competitions, government grants, and other "free" money. Often grants may require matching funds by the entrepreneur. However, these are rarely sufficient to meet the needs of a business as it grows. Personal savings and loans from family and friends are very often the source of early-stage financing.

Angels may invest or loan funds if they can believe in the business idea. This could happen early on or later in the development of the business. Another possible source of funding is from business suppliers for short-term credit. Level 2 funding may include investments or loans from angels. Other sources could include banks and community development financial institutions and many of these loans, if they qualify, may be partially guaranteed by the SBA to SBA-approved financial institutions. Venture capitalists are interested in firms that demonstrate the potential for significant growth over the next year or two. They would also be interested in understanding milestones to be achieved as benchmarks of success. As a firm grows, it may need additional funding for ramping up for new levels of development. Level 3 financing could come from VCs, additional loans from banks or community-based financial institutions, private investors, etc. Some firms that have shown dramatic growth may investigate an initial public offering (IPO). For early-stage financing, winning a business plan competition might make the angels and VCs sit up and take notice and may create a welcoming atmosphere for you in larger funding circles.

Most new entrepreneurs excel at visioning and often have a credible experience base. What they tend to lack is a solid understanding of management operations and the costs of doing business. If you do your homework, you are far more likely to succeed.

What the Judges Say

K. Brewer Doran, dean of the Bertolon School of Business at Salem State University, has been a judge in business plan competitions for a dozen or more years, often as the only woman on the panel. She maintains some strong opinions about what works and what doesn't work in these competitions. The elements that you cannot do without are:

- Really good financials. This means that the numbers are defensible, they include a clear description of the assumptions that support them, and they have been looked over by a professional, such as the local SBDC, for reasonableness.
- A good elevator pitch that matches the hook to the business and the audience's goals (more about this later).
- An executive summary that matches the pitch. Although this last bullet may seem redundant, in reality many entrepreneurs forget that internal consistency in their planning and funding pitch is key to obtaining the funds they are seeking.
- A strong advisory board that fills in the blanks in your own skill set. Many new entrepreneurs overestimate their own experience and learn, sometimes too late, that an advisor with deeper background could have helped them to avoid pitfalls.

When in competition mode, preparation for the presentation can be as important as the plan itself. Judges will base their decision in great part on how well you are able to sell your proposal, and they are more willing to overlook poorly conceived financials than an unenthusiastic or disjointed presentation. So, practice, practice, practice. Practice alone in your room. Test the technology in the presentation room. Practice before a friendly audience before you face the real thing. The presentation of the business plan is a good indicator to the panel of referees of what you are willing to do to make your business succeed… If you are not willing to do a real, professional sales job against the competition, your credibility in terms of the potential success of your business is in question. And that comes back, once again, to matching.

Matching your hook, your vision, and the goals of the judging panel is not always a simple task. Dean Doran tells a funny story about one business proposal for an organic farm. The entrepreneurs were credible, and so was their business plan. They wanted to establish an organic farm north of Boston. Their presentation was well designed and their enthusiasm carried the day until the judges looked at the financials and sat back, horrified. The organic farm, on which the entrepreneurs were going to raise vegetables and animals, such as goats and chickens, encompassed an area of one acre. One acre in total. Their financials showed that they could get a return of $2,000.

Not surprisingly, the VCs in the room were not interested. Also not surprisingly, the judges whose focus was economic development were not interested. How did the entrepreneurs go so far wrong? First of all, their vision was small, far too small for the goals of the competition. Had they proposed a micro-farm model that could be replicated throughout the region, coincidentally resulting in significantly higher financial returns, they might have had more success. Had they run their presentation past a friendly, but critical audience, they might have learned early on that they had to think a bit bigger. Had they checked their financials with professionals, either their accountant consultants or the local SBDC, they would have been made aware of how much they underestimated the potential of their business because of the limited scale they presented.

Your advisors will help you—do not be afraid to consult them before you step in a mess.

Hint: Anticipate the questions you are likely to be asked and prepare some slides that answer those questions to whip out if you need them. You will impress the judges!

What the Popular Press Says

These highlight some tips presented in the credible business press. For more information, a selection of useful websites is provided in the bibliography.

- Write a *succinct overview* that includes your business idea, why your business is necessary or needed in the marketplace, how much profit it is likely to make, and why you are the right person to implement the plan.
- *Research, research, research.* You need to know more about your business, its industry, and your place in the industry than the judges know.
- *Be selective* about the contest or competition you enter. A big-money contest will attract more competitors and lower the odds of your winning, while a more modest competition may put you in close touch with local or regional funding sources and experts who are interested in facilitating your success.
- *Prepare* an engaging and interesting presentation.
- Practice your pitch. Then practice it some more.
- *Get feedback* before you present.
- *Focus on customer needs and wants* rather than developing a solution in search of problem.
- *Anticipate questions* (and plan the answers for them). There is very little more embarrassing than being unable to answer a question about your own business proposal in public.
- *Read the instructions.* If you do not take the time to read instructions about submission requirements and related information carefully, you are unlikely to convince a judge or a funder of your reliability or organizational skills.
- Create a *dependable advisory board and a strong team*, one that you can go to for solid advice and guidance.
- *Don't marry your plan*—it is more important to make connections and build relationships with judges and participants than it is to be "right" or convinced of the perfection of your own ideas.
- *Look at the plans that have won* your chosen competition in the past. They will give you an idea of how to present your own plan.
- *Be prepared for things to go wrong.* They almost always do, and your ability to manage problems says a great deal for your ability to handle business challenges.

Our Advice for You

Try it. You have nothing to lose and everything to gain. Good luck!

Note

1 This section is taken from Vega (2001).

Bibliography

Borgefalk, G. (2013, May 29). 5 tips to win business plan competitions. *Student competitions.com* http://studentcompetitions.com/posts/5-tips-to-win-business-plan-competitions--3 (accessed 04/03/2014).

BPC Discover Compete Win http://www.bizplancompetitions.com/ (accessed 04/03/2014).

Brown, H. (2010, June 18) How to write a winning business plan. *Forbes* http://www.forbes.com/2010/06/18/great-business-ideas-venture-capital-funding-forbes-woman-entrepreneurs-business-plan.html (accessed 04/03/2014).

Center for the Study of Ethics in the Professions at Illinois Institute of Technology. *CSEP: Codes Repository* http://ethics.iit.edu/ecodes/ (accessed 02/28/2015).

Cummings, C. *How to Pitch and Get Funded* http://www.bplans.com/members/downloads/how-to-pitch-and-get-funded/ (accessed 05/27/2014).

Danigelis, A. (2015, December 15). How to win a business-plan competition. *Inc.* http://www.inc.com/guides/2010/12/how-to-win-a-business-plan-competition.html (accessed 04/03/2014).

Dickinson, E., & Johnson, T. H. (editor). (1960). No 1176, stanza 1 (c. 1870) *The Complete Poems of Emily Dickinson*. Boston, MA: Little, Brown & Co.

Energy.gov. *National Clean Energy Business Plan Competition* http://www.energy.gov/science-innovation/innovation/commercialization/national-clean-energy-business-plan-competition (accessed 05/19/2014).

Goodman, M. (2013, January 16). Crash course in business plan competitions *Entrepreneur* http://www.entrepreneur.com/article/225023 (accessed 04/03/2014).

Hill, R., & The Mind Tools Team. Crafting an elevator pitch. *MindTools* http://www.mindtools.com/pages/article/elevator-pitch.htm (accessed 05/27/2014).

Illinois Institute of Technology. *CSEP: Codes Repository* http://ethics.iit.edu/ecodes (accessed 03/05/2015).

Pagliarini, R. How to write an elevator speech. *Business know-how* http://www.businessknowhow.com/money/elevator.htm (accessed 05/27/2014).

Peters, D. (2013, August 27). 6 tips for perfecting your elevator pitch. *Entrepreneur* http://www.entrepreneur.com/article/228070 (accessed 05/27/2014).

VanderMey, A., & Rapp, N. (2013, April 12). How to win a business plan competition. *Fortune* http://fortune.com/2013/04/12/how-to-win-a-business-plan-competition/ (accessed 04/03/2014).

Vega, G. (2001). *A Passion for Planning* (pp. 10–13). Lanham, MD: University Press of America.

Glossary

504 loan program   Provides long-term, fixed-rate financing for businesses acquiring new facilities or purchasing equipment to update existing locations.

Accounts payable   Money owed for a good or service purchased on credit. Accounts payable are a current liability for a company and are expected to be paid within a short amount of time, often 10, 30, or 90 days.

Accounts receivable   Money owed to a business by customers who have bought goods or services on credit. Accounts receivable are current assets that turn into cash as customers pay their bills.

Accrual accounting   Matches revenues to expenses (the matching principle) at the time that the transaction occurs rather than when payment is made (or received).

ACH   Automated clearing house.

Amortization   Amortization is the gradual repayment of a debt over a period of time, such as monthly payments on a mortgage loan or credit card balance.

Angel investor   An investor who provides financial assistance in the earlier stages of a business and is willing to remain a minority owner while acting as mentor to the entrepreneur.

Asset-backed loan   Secured by real assets, such as mortgages, equipment loans, and inventory loans.

Assets   Resources owned by the firm so it can operate and generate revenues.

Balance sheet   A summary of the financial status of an organization, including assets, liabilities, and owner's equity.

Bankruptcy   Occurs when a business defaults as the result of a failure to make interest or principal payments on a loan.

Business plan   A presentation that includes the basic necessary elements of your proposal—financials, marketing, management, and operations—beginning with an executive summary that touches upon all of these.

Capital account   Record of contributions to partnerships.

Capital expenditures   Amount used during a particular period to acquire or improve long-term assets such as property, plant, or equipment.

Capitalization   The sum of a corporation's stock, long-term debt, and retained earnings.

CAPM   Capital asset pricing model.

Cash accounting method   Records revenues when cash is received and expenses when bills are paid.

Cash budget   Computes cash balance based on estimated future cash inflows and outflows.

Cash cycle (cash conversion cycle)   The time between paying your suppliers and receiving cash from your customers. Expresses the length of time in days it takes a company to convert resources into cash.

Cash flow   The pattern of income and expenditures, as of a company or person, and the resulting availability of cash.

Cash ledger   Details all cash receipts and disbursements, transaction by transaction.

Cash on hand   Change funds kept in registers for cashiers and small purchases.

CDC   Certified development company.

Chart of accounts   A list of all accounts in a business.

C-level   High-ranking executive roles in an organization, the "C" standing for "chief".

COGS   Cost of goods sold.

Collateral   Assets pledged as security for a loan.

Common size   Standardized income statements and balance sheets that present financial data as percentages instead of total dollar amounts.

Common stock account   Par value of stock issued by a corporation.

Compound interest   Interest earned on previously earned interest in addition to the interest generated by the principal amount.

Corporation   A body that is granted a charter recognizing it as a separate legal entity having its own rights, privileges, and liabilities distinct from those of its members.

CPA   Certified public accountant.

Crowdfunding   The practice of funding a project or venture raising many small amounts of money from a large amount of people, typically via the Internet.

Current assets   Short-term assets that are expected to be used up and converted into cash within one year, such as inventory and accounts receivable financing.

Current liabilities   A company's debts or obligations due within one year.

Debt   Money borrowed by one party from another.

Depreciation   A method of allocating the cost of a tangible asset over the course of its usable lifetime.

Diversify   To acquire a variety of assets that do not tend to change in value at the same time. To diversify a securities portfolio is to purchase different types of securities in different companies in unrelated industries.

Due diligence Thorough investigation of a business prior to signing a contract.

EBITDA Earnings before interest, taxes, depreciation, and amortization. Shows whether the business is generating enough revenues to cover overhead.

Elevator pitch Information about your company that can be conveyed orally in one or two minutes, about the length of an elevator ride.

Entrepreneur A person who organizes, operates, and assumes the risk for a business venture.

Equity Funds provided to the business by the sale of stock.

External equity Equity provided by an outside investor.

Factoring Receiving cash in exchange for future revenues or payment of accounts receivable.

Fair disclosure (or regulation fair disclosure) All publicly traded companies must disclose information to all investors at the same time.

FASB Financial Accounting Standards Board, a non-profit organization designated by the SEC to develop and update accounting standards (GAAP).

FICA Federal Insurance Contributions Act tax.

FIFO First-in-first-out. Assumes that the oldest inventory will be used up first so that ending inventory reflects most recent purchase costs.

Financial leverage ratio Measure of a firm's long-term financial risk. Determines a firm's ability to support its loan obligations beyond the current year.

FINRA Financial Intermediary Regulatory Authority.

Fixed-rate A traditional approach to determining the finance charge payable on an extension of credit. A predetermined and certain rate of interest is applied to the principal throughout the term of the loan.

GAAP Generally Accepted Accounting Principles, a framework to which companies must adhere when selling shares to the public.

GDP Gross domestic product.

Gross working capital Current assets, include inventory, accounts receivable, prepaid expenses, and cash.

Illiquid Describes an asset that is difficult to sell because of its expense, lack of interested buyers, or some other reason. Examples of illiquid assets include real estate, stocks with low trading volume, or collectibles.

Income statement Also known as a profit and loss statement, a summary of a company's profit or loss during any given period of time, such as a month, three months, or one year. The income statement records all revenues for a business during this given period, as well as the operating expenses for the business.

Interest payments Payments that cover the interest collected on a loan's principal amount.

Internal equity Equity provided by the entrepreneur.

Internal rate of return (IRR)   Measures the annualized return of an investment.

Inventory valuation   Determines costs associated with inventory.

Investment policy   The type of investment a small business investment company is willing to make (e.g., loans, equity or debt with equity features).

IPO   Initial public offering. The first sale of stock by a private company to the public.

IRS   Internal Revenue Service.

JOBS Act   Jumpstart Our Business Startups Act, 2012.

Liability   An obligation or debt reported on the balance sheet.

LIBOR   London Inter-bank Offered Rate. The benchmark rate that the world's leading banks charge each other for short-term loans.

LIFO   Last-in-first-out. Assumes that newest inventory will be used first, so that ending inventory reflects the oldest purchase cost.

Liquidity ratio   Provides information about a firm's ability to meet its current liabilities.

Loan Guaranty Program   The most basic and most popular of the SBA's loan programs. Its name comes from section 7(a) of the Small Business Act, which authorizes the agency to provide business loans to American small businesses.

Long-term assets   Assets that are not expected to be used up or converted to cash in the near future, including fixed assets such as equipment and buildings and intangible assets, e.g. goodwill, trademarks, and patents.

Long-term liabilities   Liabilities with a term greater than one year. In both investing and personal finance, a long-term liability is often a loan with a long payback period. Examples include a 30-year mortgage or a 10-year Treasury note.

Microloan program   Provides loans up to $50,000 to very small businesses through intermediary, non-profit, community-based lending organizations.

MACRS   Modified accelerated cost recovery system.

Mutual fund   An investment company that uses its capital to invest in diversified securities of other companies.

Net fixed assets   The book value of fixed assets after accumulated depreciation expenses are deducted.

Net intangible assets   The book value of intangible assets after accumulated amortization expenses.

Net revenues or net sales   The amount of revenue with all allowances and reserves subtracted.

Non-operating revenues and expenses   Interest expense on loans directly related to the business and interest revenue that a business earns on its bank accounts and security holdings, and associated expenses.

Non-recourse factoring   The financing company assumes responsibility for collecting payments from the business customers and purchases the business's invoices so that if the business defaults, it does not have to repay the financing company.

Operating expenses   Expenses incurred in carrying out the daily operations of a business, but not directly associated with production.

P & L statement   Profit and loss statement, also known as an income statement.

P2P lending   Peer-to-peer lending companies, which match small businesses directly with investors.

Par value   The stated or face value of stock.

Pass-through   A business structure that reduces the effects of double taxation by allocating income among the members of the corporation and allowing them to be taxed at the individual rate only.

Periodic inventory system   Inventory is updated periodically based on a set schedule, perhaps weekly, quarterly, or annually.

Perpetual inventory system   Inventory quantities are increased when goods arrive from suppliers or a customer returns merchandise and are reduced when goods are sold.

Petty cash   Designated money for small expenditures, recorded in batches rather than as part of the formal accounting systems.

Pitch   A short sales summary of a business designed to present a value proposition and encourage questions.

Pro forma statements   Used by potential investors to assess a firm's value and ability to generate future returns.

Profitability ratios   Assess the profitability of the business's operation and are based on items from the income statement.

R&D (research and development) expenses   An operating expense that covers a trial and error process meant to improve or develop a product.

Ratchet provision   An anti-dilution provision that applies the lowest sales price as the adjusted option price for existing shareholders.

Recourse factoring   The financing company purchases accounts receivable from the business, but the business is responsible for buying back any bad accounts receivable resulting from non-payment by customers.

ROA   Return on assets. Measures the amount of profit generated per dollar of assets.

ROE   Return on equity. Measures the amount of profit generated per dollar of total equity.

ROI   Return on investment.

SBA   Small Business Association.

SEC   Securities and Exchange Commission.

SG&A (selling, general, and administrative) expenses   Selling expenses typically include advertising, promotional events or sales materials, while general and administrative expenses include rent, utilities, office supplies, and managerial salaries.

Small business loan   Loans provided to small businesses for various purposes by a lender. These loans may have less restrictive requirements, enabling the small business to secure the funds. A small business loan might provide other incentives for the borrower, which could minimize expenses for the business.

Stipulation   A condition of an agreement or contract.

Supplier   A company that provides goods or services to another company.

SWOT analysis   A structured planning method used to evaluate the strengths, weaknesses, opportunities, and threats involved in a project or business venture.

Systematic risk   Events impacting a business that are within the control of the entrepreneur, and therefore more easily foreseen.

Term sheet   A document that outlines the terms and conditions of a business agreement.

Terminal value   The assumption that, at a certain point, a business's cash flows will grow at a consistent amount forever.

Turnover ratios   Reveal the efficiency of a firm's operation by examining the data in the income statement and balance sheet.

Unsystematic risk   Events impacting a business that are outside the control of the entrepreneur, making them more difficult to foresee

Usury   Making unethical or immoral monetary loans that unfairly enrich the lender.

Variable rate   Interest rates that are tied to changes in the financial market.

VC   Venture capital.

Vendor   Seller or supplier.

WACC   Weighted average cost of capital.

Working capital   Indicates whether a company has enough short-term assets to cover its short-term debt.

Index

Page numbers in *italics* refer to figures. Page numbers in **bold** refer to tables.